ONLINE
BUSINESS
COMPUTER
APPLICATIONS

ONLINE
BUSINESS
COMPUTER
APPLICATIONS

Alan L. Eliason
University of Oregon

SCIENCE RESEARCH ASSOCIATES, INC.
Chicago, Henley-on-Thames, Sydney, Toronto

A Subsidiary of IBM

Acquisition Editor	*Terry Baransy*
Project Editor	*Judith Fillmore*
Copy Editor	*Joy Dickinson*
Compositor	*Allservice Phototypesetting Co.*
Illustrator	*Patrick Long*
Text Designer	*Carol Harris*
Cover Designer	*Edith Ge*

ACKNOWLEDGEMENTS

Figures 1-2, 1-4, 1-5, 1-8, 8-8, 8-23, 9-3, 9-13: *Hewlett-Packard Company*; Figure 1-10: *Northern Telecom Systems Corporation*; Figure 1-11: *Diebold Incorporated*; Figures 1-12, 5-15, 5-16: *Courtesy of NCR Corporation*; Figure 1-13: *International Entry Systems, Inc.*; Figures 2-7, 3-5, 8-3, 8-14, 8-15, 8-16, 8-17, 8-18, 8-19, 8-20, 9-4, 9-14, 9-15, 10-13, 10-14, 12-7, 12-17, 12-21, 13-20, 14-16, 15-8, 15-9, 15-10, 15-11, 15-13, 15-14, 15-15: *Courtesy of International Business Machines Corporation*; Figure 3-3: *NEC Information Systems Inc.*; Figure 3-4: *Copyright 1978—Blackman Marketing Group, Inc., Box 18746, San Antonio, TX 78218*; Figures 3-14, 3-15, 12-5: *Burroughs Corporation*; Figures 5-18, 5-19: *Emporium, Inc.*; Figure 6-1: *Eugene Hospital and Clinic*; Figure 6-4: *Published by permission of NEBS Computer Forms, Townsend, MA 01469*; Figures 6-14, 12-18: *PBS Computing*; Figure 7-2: © *Digital Equipment Corporation 1982, all rights reserved*; Figure 7-5: *Apple Computer Inc.*; Figures 7-20, 10-5, 10-6, 11-17, 12-4: *MCBA (Mini-Computer Business Applications, Inc.) copyright © 1975, 1976, 1977, 1978, 1979, 1980, 1981, 1982 by Mini-Computer® Business Applications, Inc. MCBA is a registered trademark of Mini-Computer Business Applications, Inc., 2441 Honolulu Avenue, Montrose, California 91020*; Figures 8-11, 13-19: *Computer Pictures Corporation*; Figures 9-5, 10-4: *North Coast Electric Company*; Figures 9-6, 11-7: *McCormack and Dodge Corporation*; Figure 9-20: *Weber Marking Systems*; Figures 10-17, 10-18: *Moore Business Forms, Inc.*; Figure 11-16: *Computype, Inc.*; Figure 12-2: *Kronos, Inc.*; Figure 12-8: *Software AG of North America, Inc.*; Figures: 13-2, 13-4, 13-7, 13-18, 14-4, 14-5: *Global Software, Inc.*

Library of Congress Cataloging in Publication Data

Eliason, Alan L.
  Online business computer applications.

  Includes index.
  1. Business—Data processing. I. Title.
HF5548.2.E427 1983   658'.054   82-16743
ISBN 0-574-21405-4

Preface

This book explores the design characteristics of the most common types of online business computer applications. Written for a large audience, it should interest students of business or students of computer and information science. It will be useful in the study of management information systems, business data processing, accounting, systems science, or systems analysis and design. Besides the university and college audience, the book should appeal to practicing computer programmers, systems analysts, accountants, and business managers. They will find it to be a valuable reference, especially when faced with the challenge of beginning to develop an online design. Its practical rather than theoretical approach should be especially attractive to them.

The text follows a two-section format and is divided into five main parts. The first section, Part I, introduces the student to concepts important to online systems. Chapter 1, for example, examines the business computing environment and compares batch and online processing. Chapter 2 continues this introduction by describing the common properties of online business computer applications, and Chapter 3, even more applied in its orientation, describes the main features of online systems design.

The second section of the text, Parts II–V, describes features specific to the design of twelve online business computer applications. The initial three-chapter part, entitled "Receivables Applications," examines the ways in which customer invoices, cash receipts, and accounts receivable are processed by computer. The next three-chapter part, "Materials-Control Applications," deals with the computer processing of customer orders, inventory receipts, and purchase orders. It explains how computer technology can assist in the management of finished goods inventory. Part IV, "Payables Applications," describes the online processing associated with the payment of suppliers and employees. The last three-chapter set, Part V, examines "Financial and Marketing Applications"—the use of the computer to analyze cost, revenue, budget, profit, sales, and market information.

The twelve application chapters in Parts II–V are all organized similarly. Following a brief introduction, a section entitled "Preliminary Overview of Processing" introduces the majority of the terms important to the chapter; it explains the makeup of computer files and describes the main inputs to and outputs, or products, that follow from processing. The next section then describes the more detailed features of applications processing: it examines the computer programs important to the application; it explains the interactive and the batch features of processing. Third, most chapters include a section entitled "Processing Controls." These sections underscore the importance of control in applications processing. Each chapter concludes with a brief section entitled "Management Implications," which explores the impact of the application on the internal workings of a business organization.

An important feature of the book is that materials described early on are used in subsequent chapters. For example, the product master file introduced in the discussion of customer invoicing (Chapter 4) is featured again in the chapters on the materials-control, the payables, and the financial and marketing applications.

Another important feature is that the book attempts to communicate in clear terms how online designs are developed. All designs presented in the book, for example, feature program- and file-processing menus; they require users of an application to signify what specific step in processing is to be executed. This menu-driven, step-by-step approach helps to clarify the component parts of each online business computer application.

Still other important features include a wide range of visual-aid materials, end-of-chapter reviews, lists of key words, review questions and exercises, and short case studies. The visual-aid materials were either selected or designed to provide a better comprehension of terms, concepts, and application designs. End-of-chapter materials were developed to simplify the review process and to provide practice in systems design. The four case studies attempt to tie together materials from several chapters. Although not long, these materials provide more complicated systems design problems.

This book was developed as a sequel to *Business Computer Systems and Applications* (second edition), 1979, also published by Science Research Associates. The earlier book describes the design characteristics of batch applications, whereas this one is limited to online, interactive applications. An interesting and valuable exercise is to have students compare the online designs presented here with the batch designs prepared for the other book. In this way it becomes possible to gain a better appreciation of possible design variations.

I wish to thank the many companies and people who helped me in preparing this book. I am indebted to a number of companies who supplied me with computer display and graphics materials, preprinted forms, and computer-printed reports. Second, I am indebted to the corporate and college and university reviewers of the book. Their extremely thorough reviews led me to clarify several areas in the text. Third, I must compliment the people assigned to my project by Science Research Associates. They were personable, talented, and professional in every way.

I must thank several individuals. I would like to thank people in and around the Eugene area, especially Mike Antonelli of IBM, Ted Wierman of Hewlett-Packard, and Ki-Won Rhew of Pacific Information Processors. I wish to thank the individual members of the review team: Terry E. Berryman of Davenport College, Marilyn Bohl of IBM, William D. Burrows of Florida Junior College, William R. Cornette of Southwest Missouri State University, Robert Frolich of Digital Equipment Corporation, and Carolyn M. Johnson of Mitre Corporation.

Special appreciation must be given to Joy Dickinson, who copyedited the manuscript, and to Judith Fillmore, the development editor. These two people were able to find and fix the awkward passages in the manuscript and to make the book much more readable. They kept the book on schedule, which, at times, was more than difficult. Special thanks must also be given to Terry Baransy, the senior editor. Terry offered the encouragement to keep on going, especially on those days when it was so hard to write.

I thank my wife, Jane, and our two boys, Edward and Brian, for their encouragement. At times it is difficult for our boys to understand why their dad spends so much time on the word processor. I thank them for their patience.

Alan L. Eliason

Contents

ONLINE
BUSINESS
COMPUTER
APPLICATIONS

PART

I

INTRODUCTION

In the past ten years, most business firms have begun a changeover from batch to interactive methods of data processing. Interactive processing offers two important advantages: first, business transactions can be processed one at a time, as they occur, and, second, the person using the computer can communicate directly with it. This second advantage, known as being *online* to the computer, permits the user to command the attention of the computer. He or she is able to direct the computer to process instructions entered into processing, to retrieve and display information immediately, and to modify directly information stored on computer files.

This introductory three-chapter section provides a brief review of the purpose, scope, and makeup of online business computer applications. In a review, the attention given to any one topic is necessarily limited. The intent was to examine three broad subject areas as they relate to the more general development and design of online computer applications. We set out to examine the following questions:

- Why do most business firms process the majority of their transactions by computer and why are online capabilities important to this process?
- How are business computer applications related to one another and why do they feature both interactive and batch methods of data processing?
- Which tasks must be undertaken by computer specialists in preparing written specifications for an online business computer application?

1

Beginning Concepts

Most large business firms currently process the majority of their routine business transactions by computer. The greater efficiency of the computer, compared to human processing, has been a principal factor in the movement to automate clerical, managerial, and administrative activities. Business firms are often introduced to computing once they decide to automate everyday financial and accounting activities, such as payroll, invoicing, and accounts payable. After these applications have become operational, more complex materials-control and management-information-systems applications are automated.

One result of this continuing developmental process is that business firms become increasingly dependent on computer applications and systems. Another result is that business firms treat the computer as a machine that is capable of doing a substantial amount of work. Besides the processing of large numbers of everyday business transactions, computers are used to prepare a wide variety of managerial reports and summaries and to store large quantities of business information. Finally, some firms believe that the end result is to use the computer in perfecting decision-support systems. These systems assist managers directly in making complex business decisions.

This evolutionary process of designing increasingly wide-ranging and complex computer applications has been caused by many factors. In part, increased computer usage is a result of more economical and sophisticated computer *hardware* (the physical and functional properties of computing equipment) and computer *software* (the logical instructions that tell the computer what to do). As this book demonstrates, one of the most significant changes in hardware and software in recent years has been the development of easy-to-use *online computing systems*. The hardware and software designed for these systems permit human beings to communicate directly with the central processing unit (CPU) of the computer and the CPU to communicate directly with human beings.

Besides sophisticated hardware and software, the involvement of larger numbers of skilled people has contributed to ever-increasing systems complexity.
Currently, many more people understand how computers work and how computer software can be effectively applied than were knowledgeable about these
matters ten years ago. These same people acknowledge that the potential of
computing is great and that the applications and systems developed thus far
represent only the very beginning. They contend that the future will undoubtedly reveal more foolproof types of automated business systems. Certainly, the
systems will be much more advanced than those described in this book. It
should be pointed out, however, that more advanced systems do not mean increased business complexity. On the contrary, future systems designers will
develop systems that simplify the internal workings of the administrative process. These future systems will add greater clarity to the types of information
needed by management for planning and control and for decision making.

The prospect of reduced business complexity is consistent with the applications described in this book. As you will come to appreciate, online business
computer applications help to simplify and clarify the tasks associated with
obtaining, improving, and using business information.

1-1 BUSINESS COMPUTER APPLICATIONS

Before we examine specific features of an online computing application, it is
important to understand what is meant by a business computer application. We
begin with a definition, followed by an example.

A *business computer application* describes the way in which a computer is
used to process a particular type of business transaction and to prepare specific
types of management information. Each application consists of one or more
computer programs (coded instructions that tell the computer how to process data).

To help you remember this concept, imagine that you are assigned the task of
processing the company payroll. You might begin by defining the major processing tasks to be done by the computer. Next, you or someone else might
write computer programs that tell the computer how to perform these tasks.
These programs might be called "employee payroll computer programs." Last,
you would need to explain the payroll-processing procedures you developed so
that others might understand. This explanation might be entitled "the employee
payroll computer application." It would explain how the computer will be used
to process employee time cards in order to produce employee paychecks, maintain employee records, and provide information to document payments made
to employees.

Two functions of a business computer application are paperwork processing
and management-information processing. *Paperwork processing* consists of
using the computer to process different types of paperwork associated with business transactions—the agreements made between a business and its employees,

stockholders, customers, vendors, and so on. Customer orders, shipping papers, and customer billing statements are three types of paperwork that must be processed. Each of these documents is printed to verify the taking of a specific action and to record the details of that action. *Management-information processing* involves using the computer to provide detailed and summary information required by managers. A report of aged accounts receivable lists the names of customers slow in making payments—a type of management report that can be created by computer processing. A collections summary report, which shows what percentage of customers are slow in making payments, is another example of management information.

Generally, both paperwork processing and management-information processing are built into an online business computer application. The paperwork-processing part of the application deals with checking each business transaction for correctness, adding additional, supporting information to each transaction where necessary, listing each processed transaction, and producing business documents (such as paychecks and invoices). The management-information-processing part of the application stores, compares, and summarizes information needed by managers. A detailed employee listing might be required, for example. The listing might show the names of all employees who have been paid for more than a hundred hours of overtime.

1-2 THE COMPUTER PROCESSING ENVIRONMENT

Various computer hardware components and types of software are combined in processing online business computer applications. The computer hardware must be capable both of processing data and of communicating the results of processing to and from remote locations. Different types of computer software instruct the computer how to process data, how to transmit data to remote locations, and how to store data awaiting transmission or processing.

Computer Hardware

Figure 1-1 illustrates a simplified computer-processing environment to show five processing functions: input, output, data transmission, central processing, and data storage (external).

Input consists of reading and transmitting data to the computer. Before data processing can begin, data must be read by an input device and transformed into machine-readable form. Punched-card readers, punched-tape readers, and computer terminals are among the variety of input devices designed to perform this processing function. As we will see, computer terminals are of particular importance in the design of online computer applications.

Output consists of transmitting and distributing data processed by the computer. Output is the reverse of input. It involves the translation of machine-

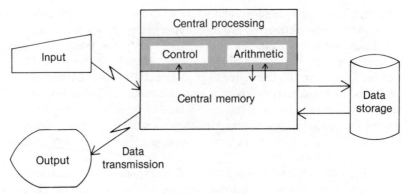

Figure 1-1 Simplified computer processing environment

readable data to a form that can be easily understood by human beings. Processed results can be printed or displayed on an output device. As with input devices, a variety of output devices are commercially available. The most common one, the line printer, produces both formal business documents and formal and informal business reports. Computer terminals are becoming more and more popular as output devices. Terminals permit output to be either printed, line by line, or displayed on a screen for review by the user.

Data transmission entails the flow of data to and from the central processing unit (CPU). The hardware used in this part of processing might be viewed as a switching station: data flowing into processing must not interfere with data leaving processing. The hardware units designed to regulate data transmission include front-end processors and network processors. They coordinate and control slow-speed input/output data transmission and high-speed central-processing data transmission.

Central processing performs numerical calculations, stores data internally, and integrates the activities of input, output, data storage, and data transmission. The CPU is made up of the central processor and central memory (internal storage). The *central processor* performs calculations and controls the various parts of the computer system. The *central memory* stores data waiting to be processed, data being processed, data that have been processed, and, finally, computer program instructions used to tell the computer how to process data.

Data storage (external) stores data in machine-readable form in a location external to the CPU. From this location, data are read from storage in processing or written to storage following processing. The capability to store data separately from the CPU permits input data to be combined with previously stored data, then entered into processing. Likewise, not all processed results need be printed or displayed: portions of processed results, or all of them, can be written to data-storage devices. Much like input and output units, data-storage devices can take several forms. The two most popular are magnetic-disk and magnetic-tape storage devices. We will discuss only these two types in this book.

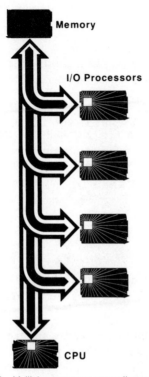

Figure 1-2 Multiple processor computing environment

Figure 1-2, a modified processing environment, shows the effects of combining input/output (I/O) processors with a single central processor. Input/output processors regulate high-speed and low-speed data transfers between the central memory and *peripheral computing equipment*—input, output, and data-storage devices. In some systems, each I/O processor has full access to memory, as does the central processor. Communications between processors and memory use a common communications bus. By having separate processors regulate I/O traffic, the central processor is free to concentrate on its main job of computation. In addition, I/O processors permit the computer to work on several tasks simultaneously. The central processor can work on one job while it waits for the transfer of data to be completed for a second job.

Computer Software

Figure 1-3, a second simplified processing environment, highlights the main types of software used by an online computer system. These types include operating systems software, data communications software, data base management software, and application program software.

Operating systems software allocates, schedules, and assigns computer resources to specific jobs submitted for processing. Computer memory and pe-

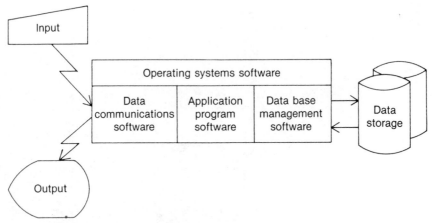

Figure 1-3   Types of computer software

ripheral computing equipment, for example, are assigned to each job. Following the completion of a job, the operating system assigns its computing resources to other jobs.

Data communications software controls the transmission of messages back and forth from the computer, between a single CPU and a large number of slow-speed I/O devices. It is required, first, to *multiplex* the data—to intermix messages from several I/O devices to create what appears to be simultaneous data communications—and, second, to *regulate* the data by keeping track of each message being transmitted, so that each retains its identity.

Data base management software (DBMS) handles the organizing, cataloging, locating, storing, and retrieving of data in a data base. In a data base setting, software is designed to integrate a collection or large "pool" of data. Through integration, duplication of stored data can be avoided; data can be extracted from the data base and used by more than one business computer application.

Application program software instructs the CPU how to process data. This type of software, unlike the other types, is typically prepared by computer programmers employed by the business firm that is doing the computing. (The other three types of software are written by the computer vendor or by a soft-ware-development firm.) Application program software is designed to perform specific sets of paperwork-processing and management-information-processing tasks. It is usually written in a symbolic-language code, or *source code,* such as COBOL or BASIC. Another type of software, a *compiler program,* translates the source code into *object code,* which is machine readable.

Computer Systems

Figure 1-4 shows a commercial computer system. This particular system, like all digital computer systems, consists of hardware and software. The hardware

Figure 1-4 Commercial computer system

includes a typewriter-like keyboard, a video display screen, a magnetic-disk storage unit, and a CPU. All equipment is *online;* that is, all input, output, and data-storage devices are connected and controlled by the CPU. The software, the invisible part of a computer system, unfortunately cannot be illustrated; here it consists of an operating system, data communications software, data base management software, compiler programs, and application programs.

Figure 1-5, the schematic version of Figure 1-4, shows how a single computer is able to distribute processing in order to disperse the processing power of the machine to geographically separated locations. Up to five remotely located I/O terminals can be added to this computer system. These terminals, in turn, permit up to five users to access the computer, using different (or similar) sets of processing instructions, which are transmitted directly to the CPU. Likewise, processed results are transmitted back to the user as video displays or printed results.

Maximum HP 250 system configuration

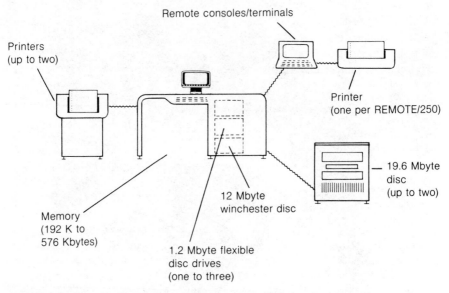

Figure 1-5 Schematic diagram of a commercial computer system

The commercial computer system illustrated in Figures 1-4 and 1-5 is a small business computer, often referred to as a *minicomputer.* Whereas it can accept input from five terminals, medium- and large-scale computer systems can be accessed by hundreds of computer terminals or several of these smaller computers. Back at the other end of the spectrum are a variety of computers that are smaller than minicomputers. These *microcomputers* are assembled using a single integrated circuit board. Because they typically accept input from a single computer terminal and are purchased for individual use, they are often called "personal computers."

1-3 METHODS OF PROCESSING

The ability to connect large numbers of remote computer terminals, online, to a single CPU has led to different methods of processing. One of these methods, *real-time processing,* enables the CPU to respond extremely quickly to a request to transmit and process data. The high speed of response, measured in milliseconds, is the crucial element in real-time processing: in military defense environments, for example, response must be immediate, and in many business environments, response must be fast enough to resolve the decision facing the end user (the individual who needs the information processed by the computer). Two popular real-time processing applications, airline-reservation and stock-market-inquiry systems, well illustrate the advantages of this method. With each, computer terminals are used to transmit short messages that inquire about the status of an event—the availability of an airplane seat or the price of a stock. Very fast response, indicating processing of the inquiry and communication of the processed result, enables the end user to make a decision based on the latest information. The decision might be to reserve a seat on an airplane or to purchase a hundred shares of stock at the listed price.

Online systems are also associated with another method of processing known as *time sharing*. In this method, a small amount of time is allocated for processing each of several jobs submitted simultaneously; the CPU works on one job for a brief period, or "time slice," which is defined in terms of milliseconds. If a job is not completed during the time slice allocated to it, it is placed at the end of a job queue to await further attention by the CPU. This method of processing makes it possible for several end users to share the available processing time of a single CPU. Although fast response is still a requirement, it need not be as instantaneous as in a real-time environment. A one- to three-second response is generally adequate. Response time, however, is not the most important distinction between real time and time sharing. Rather, with real time, a job is worked on by the computer until it is completed. Only then can the computer turn its attention to another job.

Besides real-time processing and time sharing, three other important methods are used in data processing. The first, *batch processing,* preceded the development of online systems. Batch processing requires that data be initially grouped (as a batch) before it is processed serially. The batch might be a group of customer orders or a set of employee time cards. Following the preparation of a batch, it is read into processing by an input device. Each transaction in the batch is processed in serial order. For example, data relating to the first customer order in a batch are processed first, followed by data relating to the second, and so on, until the data relating to the last customer order have been processed.

In contrast, in the second method, *transaction processing,* a single transaction (such as a single customer order) is processed as it is received by the CPU. This technique avoids the need to initially group transactions, but it can only be used with computer terminals that are connected online to the CPU. In this way the terminals are available to feed individual transactions into processing one at a time.

The third method, *interactive processing,* should be viewed as a modified version of transaction processing. This method is "interactive" because it permits users to enter into a conversation with the computer in order to process single business transactions, using computer terminals to send and receive messages. Following the terminal entry and transmission of a message, the computer processes the message, displays the results on the terminal, and typically asks for a response. One response sequence might be:

ARE THE RESULTS ACCURATE?
ENTER Y OR N

By entering a Y (for yes), the terminal operator informs the computer that the results are accurate and that it is safe to continue processing. Entering an N (no) leads to a different computer response. For example, the computer might respond with the message

DO YOU WISH TO TERMINATE PROCESSING? Y OR N

or,

DO YOU WISH TO BACK UP TO IDENTIFY THE ERROR? Y OR N

The capability to communicate directly with the computer explains in large part why interactive methods of processing have become so popular. Human beings find it easier to work with a computer if they can monitor the steps in processing. This step-by-step procedure permits them to go from one transaction to another with greater assurance that the actions taken by the computer are correct. Human beings also find it more enjoyable to be able to command the computer to take a particular action. They feel that they are able to control the machine, rather than the reverse.

1-4 INTERACTIVE VERSUS BATCH PROCESSING

The majority of online computer systems are multifunctional: they support multiple methods of processing and can effect these different methods simultaneously. In many larger-scale processing environments, for example, interactive processing occurs while batch processing is also taking place. In other processing environments, interactive processing occurs during normal business hours; batch processing is restricted to before and after normal business hours.

This mixing of processing methods is advantageous because interactive and batch processing are each especially suited to certain kinds of activities. Interactive methods, where transactions are processed one at a time, are especially suited for

- entering and transmitting small amounts of data to the computer;
- visually reviewing data to ensure that processing is correct;
- making adjustments to a small number of business records stored on computer files;
- making inquiries to determine what data are stored on computer files; and
- displaying different combinations of data before deciding which data are to be printed.

Interactive methods are not always superior, however. Batch methods are better for

- printing listings or registers of large numbers of business transactions;
- printing sets of formal business documents, such as paychecks;

• printing business summary listings and reports; and
• backing up computer files to ensure that processing could be continued if a file were lost or destroyed.

More Efficient Use of the Computer

A dilemma associated with a strictly batch approach to processing is that it makes efficient use of the computer, but often leads to inefficient use of human beings. As an example, consider the steps required in creating an approved-purchase-order file when batch processing is used. (See Figure 1-6 to help you understand this work flow.)

Step 1   Prepare data-entry forms for keypunching (transfer by hand information from purchase orders, to be keypunched to special forms).

Step 2   Keypunch and verify purchase order information recorded on data-entry forms.

Step 3   Load the batch of punched and verified cards into the card reader connected online to the computer.

Step 4   By computer, read and edit each transaction (each card or set of cards) in the batch. Read all edited transactions to a computer file. If no errors are found, the file becomes the approved-input-transactions file. However, if an error is found, print the error on a purchase-order edit report. Discontinue processing after all transactions have been edited.

Step 5   Correct the errors printed on the purchase-order edit report. Repeat Steps 1 through 5 until no errors are found.

Step 6   Sort the approved-input-transaction computer file by vendor number. The sort must place all transactions in a desired sequence, such as vendor 10026, 10027, 10043, 10078.

Step 7   Update the sequenced file by adding vendor name and address to each transaction in the file. If an update cannot be completed because of an incorrect or missing vendor number, list the transaction-in-error on a missing-vendor report. Place all correctly updated transactions on an approved-purchase-order computer file. Place all transactions-in-error on a second file, the disapproved-purchase-order computer file.

Steps 8–12   Correct transactions-in-error (this procedure is not shown in Figure 1-6).

We hope this example demonstrates that with batch methods processing is efficient as long as data are error free. When errors are encountered, however, processing becomes long and involved. Moreover, what may not be evident is that several people must work together to monitor batch processing activities. People in purchasing, for example, are responsible for preparing data-entry forms for purchase orders and for reviewing purchase-order edit reports and

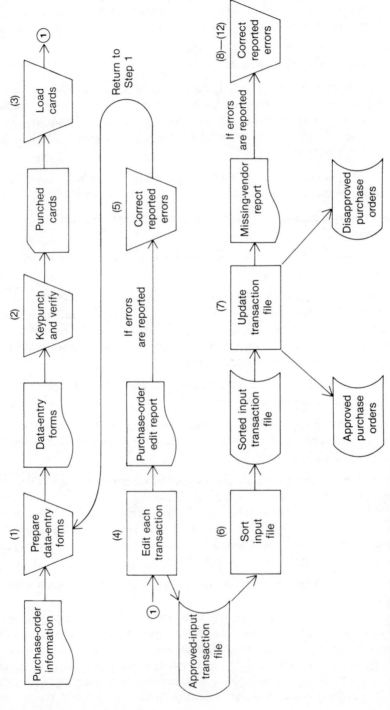

Figure 1-6 Work steps in a batch processing environment

missing-vendor reports. People in data processing are responsible for preparing keypunched cards, scheduling computer processing, running computer programs in the correct order, loading computer files, maintaining computer programs, and distributing the results of processing.

The problem of managing large amounts of paperwork is also associated with batch processing. Consider the following cycle in resolving errors appearing on an edit report.

1. Each time an error is discovered in processing, it is printed on an *edit report* that is distributed to an administrative office for review. When the report is received, administrative personnel are required to identify the cause of each error and to make corrections.

2. Corrected errors are recorded on data-entry forms that are routed to data processing for keypunching.

3. The data-entry forms are used to produce a new batch of punched cards. Once the cards have been processed by the computer, they must be temporarily stored.

4. Errors discovered in processing are printed on a second edit report that, again, must be reviewed by people in an administrative office. Thus, the edit cycle continues until all editing errors have been resolved.

5. Errors discovered in attempting to update the file are printed on a missing-vendor report that must also be reviewed by people in an administrative office. And, once more, the cause of an error must be found and recorded on data-entry forms—which leads to a repeat of the update cycle.

More Efficient Use of People

Interactive processing makes better use of people, but less efficient use of the computer. Administrative personnel key data directly into processing and also revise data directly. In an interactive environment, the steps associated with the processing of purchase orders are as follows. (See Figure 1-7 to help you understand this processing environment.)

Step 1 Key data directly into processing using a computer terminal. (Data-entry forms are not needed if the spaces showing where data are to be keyed appear on the screen of the terminal.)

Step 2 Edit each transaction by computer. If an error is found, the computer will print the error and, where possible, the reason for the error, on the screen of the terminal. The computer will ask the terminal operator to enter the correct data. If the error is not corrected, the transaction-in-error is not permitted to be entered into processing (added to the approved-purchase-order transaction file).

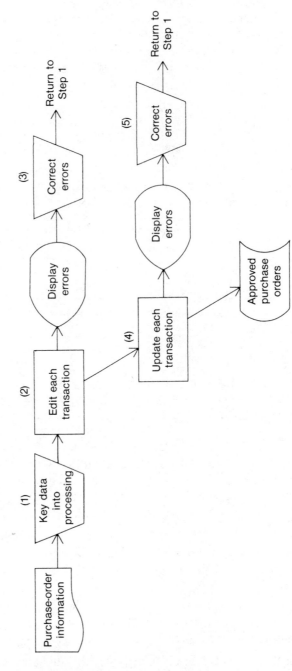

Figure 1-7 Work steps in an interactive processing environment

Step 3 Correct the error shown on the screen of the terminal and process again.

Step 4 Update each transaction by computer immediately following the edit of the transaction. Write the approved transaction to an approved-purchase-order computer file.

Step 5 Correct any update error shown on the screen of the terminal. For example, if a transaction cannot be correctly processed because of an incorrect vendor number, the computer will inform the operator of this problem and ask that the correct vendor number be entered. If the correct number is not entered, the transaction-in-error is not written to a computer file. Instead, the computer blocks the transaction from further processing.

Advantages and Disadvantages

A comparison of the interactive design with the batch design should make it clear why interactive methods are favored. The advantages of interactive processing are several.

- Interactive methods make it easier to integrate the work performed by administrative and operational groups in an organization with the work performed by data processing groups. For example, an interactive application permits members of the purchasing staff to prepare and enter data directly into processing, to review keyed input data for errors, and to make changes when instructed to by the computer.

- Interactive methods simplify the paperwork needed to support processing. Not only are punched cards eliminated, but edit and missing-record reports, (such as missing-vendor reports) are also no longer needed. In addition, direct retrieval of data stored on computer files eliminates the looking up of account information printed on lengthy file listings.

- Interactive methods eliminate special error files such as the disapproved-purchase-order file. This streamlining is accomplished by "trapping" errors before they are entered into processing. For example, if a vendor number is found to be in error, the error must be corrected before the transaction can be successfully written to a computer file.

- Interactive methods reduce the number of job steps required in a processing run. Combining an edit with an update program, for instance, eliminates one job step. Eliminating a sort program saves another job step. Eliminating the distribution and routing of reports to and from administrative offices saves several other steps.

- Interactive methods are often easier to understand. With batch processing, it is difficult to explain to others how input data are processed after the data leave an administrative office. With interactive methods, this situation changes. It now becomes possible for a terminal operator to demonstrate how input data are processed by the computer.

Along with these considerable advantages, several disadvantages are associated with interactive methods of processing.

- Interactive methods tend to be more expensive. They require the purchase or lease of communications equipment, including computer terminals; I/O processors; and direct-access computer files.

- Interactive computer programs tend to be more difficult to write than batch application programs. Besides recording how data are to be processed by the CPU, interactive programs must include conversational instructions— a dialogue that serves to transmit messages to and from the computer to the user.

- Interactive methods require that the computer be always ready to handle incoming data. Since transactions are processed one at a time, rather than as a batch, CPU time is used less efficiently.

- Interactive methods of processing are slow. Terminal operators must process each transaction separately, which can present a major problem when hundreds of transactions must be processed within a short time period. In severe cases, it may be necessary to substitute batch for interactive methods even though interactive methods are superior.

1-5 DATA BASE MANAGEMENT

The collection and organization of logically related sets of business information stored on computer files constitutes the *data base* of a business. The management of this data base is one of the most important functions of online business computer applications. As a concept, data base management consists of programmed procedures for establishing, updating, and backing up information stored on computer files. These procedures permit business firms to keep track of all stored data; they facilitate the retrieval and display of important business records.

With online operating systems, data base management software and application programs are integrated so that data stored on computer files can be inspected and, where necessary, altered prior to processing. Consider, once again, the processing of purchase orders.

First, assume that there is a problem with Account 10023 and, as a consequence, that it must be inspected. In a batch processing environment, a listing showing the contents of the account would have to be examined to discover what information was stored. An interactive processing environment, by contrast, permits the direct examination of the account. Following the keying of the account number into processing, the computer retrieves the account and displays it directly on the computer terminal screen.

Next, assume that Account 10023 cannot be found. Suppose that a data-input error has established Account 10032 instead. In a batch environment, this type of error might be difficult to find and would take several hours to correct:

1. A listing of the contents of the file would be printed and inspected. This review would indicate that Account 10023 did not exist.

2. A search would have to be undertaken. This search might begin by requesting that another listing be prepared, sequencing all accounts by alphabetic name.

3. An error correction would be necessary once the second listing revealed that Account 10023 was improperly assigned. A change form would be filled out and sent to data entry for keypunching.

4. Punched cards would be processed to provide the change instructions needed to create Account 10023 and to delete Account 10032.

Now, compare those steps to the steps required in an interactive environment:

1. An online account-inquiry procedure tells the terminal operator that Account 10023 does not exist.

2. The terminal operator begins to search for the name of the vendor, using a *search routine*. For example, most online operating systems feature interactive search capabilities that permit a terminal operator to locate any string of characters existing in a computer file. Suppose the string of characters is FEERSON SUPPLY. Using the search capability, the operator would find the name FEERSON SUPPLY stored under Account 10032.

3. The terminal operator would add the correct account and delete the incorrect account. In this instance, most interactive, online operating systems also contain interactive *search-and-replace* capabilities. These features permit the operator to search the data base for an account and, once found, to rename the account.

Capabilities such as search, and search and replace, greatly simplify the writing of application programs and the revising of data stored on computer files. Although estimates vary, the availability of commonly needed precoded routines can lead to a two- to fivefold increase in programmer productivity. Savings in user time are even greater. These savings result from easy-to-follow methods of retrieving, examining, and modifying data stored within the data base.

1-6 ONLINE DATA COMMUNICATIONS

The ways in which data are transmitted to and from the computer are also of primary importance in designing online business computer applications. The term *data communications* implies both telecommunications and the use of remote computer terminals. The transmission of data as signals—generally by conventional wire or cable—is one type of *telecommunications.* With telecommunications equipment it becomes possible to send messages from several remote locations to a single receiver—a single CPU. These messages can be as short as a single bit (a 0 or 1) or can consist of several thousand characters. Remote computer terminals function as sending-and-receiving stations in a telecommunications network. When the terminals are designed both to send and receive data, two-way communications takes place: the user is able to transmit data to the computer and to receive processed instructions and output in return. Because the user is thus able to converse directly with the CPU, he or she is said to be online (on a direct line) to the computer.

The data communication devices that are sold commercially comprise six classes of computer terminals: keyboard/printer terminals, display terminals, remote job-entry terminals, banking terminals, point-of-sale terminals, and data-collection terminals.

Keyboard/Printer Terminals

Keyboard/printer terminals are hard-copy terminal devices that act as small-scale printers. Smaller keyboard/printer terminals look much like typewriters, whereas larger units look like stand-alone computer printers (see Figure 1-8). With these units, an alphanumeric keyboard is used to key data into processing; output, known as *hard copy,* is printed character by character. A built-in acoustic coupler permits the connection of the terminal to a standard circuit, such as

Figure 1-8 Keyboard/printer terminal

a telephone circuit. In this way the terminal can be remotely connected to a computer.

Display Terminals

Display terminals feature visual review of data as *soft copy* (see Figure 1-9). These devices use an alphanumeric keyboard; however, keyed input, computer instructions, and processed results are displayed on a screen instead of printed as hard copy. Display terminals consist of several types: data-entry terminals, multipurpose display terminals, intelligent display terminals, and computer graphics terminals.

Data-entry terminals are limited-use devices, generally restricted to entering and displaying the details associated with business transactions. These terminals are used in place of keypunch machines. Instead of keying data on cards, data-entry terminals permit data to be keyed directly to processing or to magnetic-disk storage, as in key-to-disk processing.

Multipurpose display terminals are similar to data-entry terminals, but are used for a variety of purposes including entering and displaying transaction input; entering, reviewing, and testing computer programs; and retrieving and displaying data stored on computer files. Some multipurpose terminals, known as page readers, allow the user to display, page by page, the contents of a large document stored on computer files.

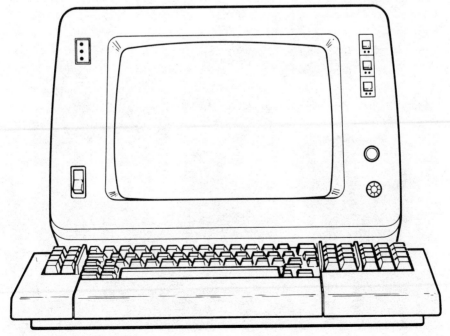

Figure 1-9 Display terminal

Intelligent display terminals are small-scale computers that can effect limited-scale data processing as well as data communications. They are often designed to operate independently from the computer to which they are connected. Besides being used to transmit and receive data, these units are able to test input data for correctness and to store small amounts of data. As such, they take away some of the duties normally performed by the CPU and thus free the CPU to perform other functions.

Computer graphics terminals are used to prepare and display two- and three-dimensional line drawings as well as charts and tables. With these units, end users are able to analyze data, picture by picture. Since many individuals prefer to work with pictures rather than tables and lists of data, computer graphics terminals are becoming increasingly more popular. Leading authorities predict that color graphics will become the preferred way of presenting many types of business information.

Remote Job-Entry Terminals

Remote job-entry (RJE) terminals are typically minicomputers that are linked to a larger CPU. There are two types of RJE terminals: *remote batch terminals,* which limit processing to punched-card data entry, data storage, and printed output, and *remote interactive terminals,* which support both interactive and batch methods of processing (see Figure 1-10). Besides sending indi-

Figure 1-10 Remote job-entry system

vidual instructions to the CPU for processing, interactive processing is used to enter data into processing, transaction by transaction, until an entire batch is assembled. It can then be transmitted in batch form to a larger CPU.

Banking Terminals

Banking terminals consist of automated tellers and teller-controlled devices. Automated tellers accept as input an identification number, printed on a plastic card, and a numeric password, which must be keyed into processing (see Figure 1-11). If the terminal finds both numbers acceptable, it will permit and process a number of banking transactions, including the withdrawal of cash from a customer's account. Teller-controlled terminals are limited-use keyboard/printer terminals that allow the teller to determine, and when required to revise, a customer's account balance.

Figure 1-11   Bank terminal

Figure 1-12 Point-of-sale (POS) terminal

Point-of-Sale Terminals

Point-of-sale (POS) terminals look much like cash registers; however, they accept, transmit, and receive data as well as holding cash (see Figure 1-12). These terminals can be used in several ways: besides registering cash, they keep track of sales and inventory data. Operators are required to key in product or line-item numbers, quantity-sold totals, and dollar totals (or to enter this data with an optical scanning device). This information is transmitted to a larger computer in order to revise in-store inventory counts and dollar amounts and to summarize daily sales totals. Since POS terminals capture sales data at the time of sale, these data need not be entered separately by data-entry staff.

Data-Collection Terminals

Data-collection terminals typically provide for the entry and transmission of limited amounts of data, such as the count of inventory available for sale, or an employee's identification number and the number of a work station. Data-collection terminals feature one-way data communications: they send messages from the user to the CPU. Accordingly, some data-collection terminals are called badge readers. They are limited-use terminals, designed only to read a plastic badge, much like an automatic teller. Other data-collection terminals are limited-use data-entry terminals (see Figure 1-13).

Figure 1-13 Data-collection terminal

REVIEW OF IMPORTANT IDEAS

Most large business firms process the majority of their business transactions by computer. Online computing systems simplify this process. They permit human beings to communicate directly with the central processing unit (CPU).

A business computer application describes the way in which the computer is used to process business transactions and to prepare management information. The processing of business transactions, known as paperwork processing, documents the details of business dealings. The processing of business information, known as management-information processing, provides information to managers for purposes of decision making.

A computer system consists of hardware and software. Hardware is the mechanical aspect of the computer and is designed to accomplish the functions of input, output, data transmission, central processing, and data storage. Software is the logical aspect of the computer. Different types of software are required to make the computer operate, to transmit and store data, and to run user-prepared computer programs.

The different methods of processing include real time, time sharing, batch, transaction, and interactive. Of these, batch and interactive methods are of greatest importance in the design of online business computer applications. With batch processing, data must be initially grouped before it can be processed. With interactive processing, transactions are processed one at a time;

the user is able to enter into a conversation with the computer. This ability to communicate directly helps to explain the popularity of online systems.

Interactive processing also provides for more efficient use of human beings; batch processing, on the other hand, makes for more efficient use of the computer. The main advantages of interactive processing include better integration of computing and administrative activities, reduced paperwork processing, better methods of trapping data-entry errors, reduced processing job steps, and better user understanding of how processing works.

With online systems, operating systems software, data base management software, and application programs are integrated. This integration provides processing capabilities such as the direct examination of an account stored on file. Following the keying of the account number, the computer retrieves and displays account information.

Both one- and two-way communication are required by online computer systems. With one-way communication, the user is able to send, but not receive messages (or vice versa). With two-way communication, the user is able to transmit messages to the computer and to receive computer output. The six classes of computer terminal devices that support online data communications are keyboard/printer terminals, display terminals, remote job-entry terminals, banking terminals, point-of-sale terminals, and data-collection terminals.

KEY WORDS

Hardware	Real-time processing
Software	Time sharing
Online computing system	Batch processing
Business computer application	Transaction processing
Computer programs	Interactive processing
Paperwork processing	Data base
Management-information processing	Data communications
Central processing unit (CPU)	Telecommunications
Source code	Hard copy
Object code	Soft copy
Minicomputer	Remote job entry (RJE)
Microcomputer	Point of sale (POS)

REVIEW QUESTIONS

1. Explain the difference between paperwork processing and management-information processing.

2. Name the five processing functions associated with computer hardware.

3. What types of computer software are used in an online computer system?

4. How is a computer able to distribute processing?

5. Explain the difference between batch processing and transaction processing. Between batch processing and interactive processing.

6. What tasks are interactive methods of processing especially suited for? What tasks are batch methods especially suited for?

7. What are the advantages of interactive methods of processing? Of batch methods of processing?

8. What is an automated search routine?

9. Name the six classes of computer terminals.

10. How does a keyboard/printer terminal differ from a display terminal?

11. What is the difference between remote batch and remote interactive processing?

12. Why is point-of-sale (POS) processing important?

EXERCISES

1. Visit a local store in your area that uses POS equipment. Report back on how the five processing functions (input, output, data transmission, central processing, and data storage) are accomplished in this environment.

2. Even though interactive methods of processing lead to more efficient use of people, a number of business firms continue to use only batch methods of processing. Give several reasons to explain why this occurs.

3. Why is it important for business firms to reduce the number of job steps in an administrative process? Does computing always lead to fewer job steps? Explain.

4. A review of the six classes of computer terminals indicates that there are a number of ways in which telecommunications can take place in organizations. What factors would be important in deciding which types of terminals are best?

2

Properties of Online Applications

Before we consider specific types of online business computer applications, a review of their general properties will be useful. We begin by examining four such properties.

- Business computer applications are related to one another. Output from one application provides input to another application; a linking of applications results. This linking serves to integrate various administrative and operational *information systems* and activities in a business.

- Business computer applications consist of common input, processing, output, and control operations. Besides these operations, common types of computer files and computer programs are used in applications processing.

- Business computer applications can be designed to follow a batch, an interactive, or a combined interactive/batch method of processing. Typically, interactive methods are used to enter and to process data stored on computer files. Batch methods are used to print business documents, listings, and standard management reports.

- Business computer applications are relatively easy to understand provided that a uniform method of systems documentation is adopted. Documentation includes an overview of the flow of information through a system and a detailing of the contents of computer files that are important to the system.

Even though the properties of business computer applications and systems are similar, most business firms find their description difficult. What tends to be missing is a systematic method that depicts, in a simplified way, what online applications are designed to accomplish. Those who begin the task of providing such descriptions quickly discover that most systems documentation is highly technical, if it exists at all. Many business firms tend to document only the programming features of the design. Little attention is usually given to the logical features, or to the relationships between applications.

This chapter considers ways in which business computer applications are interrelated and how they might be documented. We begin with a look at business information systems and cycles. Later on we will examine systems documentation and systems flowcharting.

2-1 BUSINESS INFORMATION SYSTEMS AND CYCLES

A *business system* consists of a series of procedures for processing business transactions and for providing a written record of processing. Within a business, four main information systems can be identified: the revenue system, the expenditure system, the conversion system, and the cash-management system.

The revenue system processes financial transactions associated with the sale and delivery of goods and services. It includes the processing steps needed by a business to exchange its goods or services with customers for cash.

The expenditure system processes financial transactions associated with the acquisition of and payment for property, labor, and goods and services. The reverse of the revenue system, it includes the processing steps needed by a business to exchange its cash with vendors for goods and services.

The conversion system processes material, labor, and financial transactions associated with production (the transformation of raw materials into finished goods). This information system includes the processing steps that account for the acquisition, use, and movement of resources (property, material, labor, and dollars).

The cash-management system processes financial transactions associated with the management of capital funds. This information system includes the processing steps used to determine the cash requirements of a business for internal purposes and for repayment of funds to creditors and investors.

Business information systems can be broken down into transaction-processing and management-information-processing cycles. Business computer applications, in turn, are designed for each cycle in order to transform information into a more usable form and to comply with the terms and conditions of business agreements. Figure 2-1 illustrates a revenue-collection information-processing cycle. As shown by this data-flow diagram, the cycle begins with the notification that goods have been shipped to a customer. The document known as the *packing slip* provides these shipping details. It records the name of the customer and the quantity of merchandise shipped (the quantity-shipped total) to the customer.

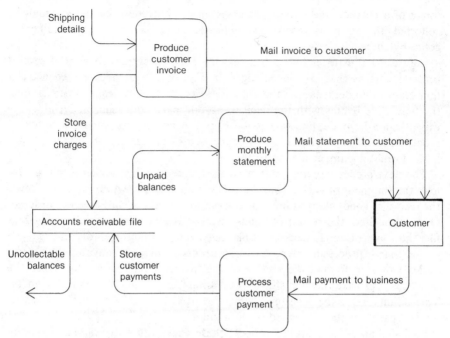

Figure 2-1   Revenue-collection data-flow diagram

Processing begins following the receipt of the packing slip. As Figure 2-1 shows, three business processing steps use some of the information recorded on the packing slip (shipping details), together with other information, to speed the collection of revenue to a business. These steps—produce customer invoice, produce monthly statement, and process customer payment—can each be automated, which, in turn, leads to the development of three business computer applications:

The customer-invoice computer application transforms quantity-shipped totals into customer charges, prints the customer invoice, and prepares summary data for the accounts receivable computer application. The computer-printed invoice is mailed to the customer.

The cash-receipts computer application processes payment information received from customers. The products of processing are a bank deposit slip (not shown) and summary data for the accounts receivable computer application.

The accounts receivable computer application compares outstanding invoice charges with incoming customer cash receipts and attempts to reduce to zero all customer receivable accounts. When an account fails to reduce to zero and when charges are older than a specified cutoff point, such as thirty days, a monthly statement is prepared and mailed to the customer, notifying the customer of a balance due. Finally, in cases in which account balances cannot be collected, the accounts receivable application must write off outstanding account balances.

Figure 2-1 illustrates that a business information system consists of several processing steps that are linked together. Figure 2-2 provides a second data-flow diagram to demonstrate the linking of expenditure cycles. In this example, the first cycle begins with the decision to purchase additional material. Once this decision is made, one processing step is necessary to prepare a purchase requisition; another is required to prepare a purchase order. The purchase order is the formal document mailed to the vendor.

The next processing step, match goods ordered against goods received, follows the shipment of goods from the vendor to a business. As Figure 2-2 shows, the record of goods shipped must be compared with the record of goods ordered. Once reconciled, the record of goods received is placed in a pending payables file; the count of goods received is placed in the product inventory file.

The fourth processing step, verify accuracy of invoice, activates the second cycle. This step follows the receipt of the invoice from the vendor. Once the invoice is approved, the next step in processing is preparing the vendor payment. This action follows the decision of which invoices to pay; the product of processing is a payment that is mailed to the vendor.

Four computer applications support these expenditure cycles. They are the purchasing computer application, the receiving computer application, the inventory computer application, and the accounts payable computer application.

The purchasing computer application processes the data necessary to prepare a purchase order. This formal business document is mailed to the vendor.

The receiving computer application compares the quantity received from the vendor with the quantity ordered. This application is activated following the actual receipt of the merchandise. Included in the shipment from the vendor is a packing slip, which serves as input to processing.

The inventory computer application does two things: it shows what items need to be added to inventory, and it records the quantity of merchandise that is added to inventory. In the latter case, the application must be designed to revise inventory records to show a new on-hand quantity.

The accounts payable computer application determines if the vendor invoice charge is consistent with the quantity ordered and the quantity received. In addition, it keeps track of when the invoice must be paid; it produces the voucher check to be mailed to the vendor.

Processing cycles, such as the revenue-collection cycle and the expediture-processing cycles, are similar in design; however, the reasons for their implementation differ. Revenue cycles, for example, speed the processing of invoices and statements to customers, thus helping to minimize the average accounts receivable collection period and to reduce receivable write-offs. Expenditure cycles, in contrast, determine whether vendor charges are legitimate and which

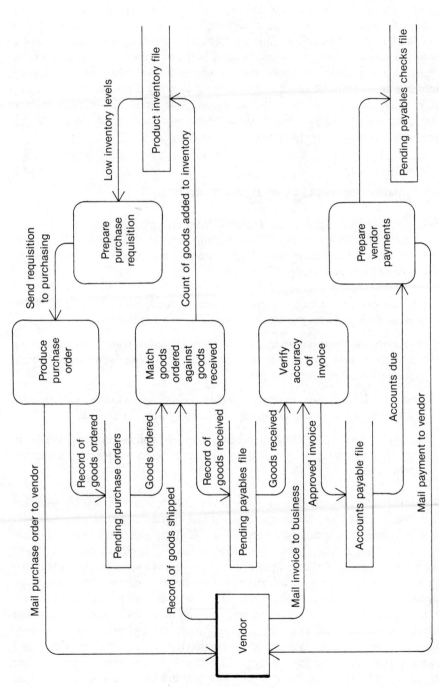

Figure 2-2 Expenditure-processing data-flow diagram

vendor to pay, in what amount, and when. These cycles help to ensure correct payment of vendor invoices and to preserve the use of internal cash.

Besides differing in purpose, processing cycles differ in their frequency of use. With revenue cycles, customer-invoice and cash-receipts computer applications are scheduled more frequently than is the accounts receivable computer application. Generally, customer invoices and cash receipts are processed daily; accounts receivable are processed weekly or monthly. Expenditure cycles also differ in processing frequency: the purchasing and receiving computer applications are scheduled daily, whereas the accounts payable computer application is generally scheduled weekly or twice each month.

2-2 COMMON BUSINESS COMPUTER APPLICATIONS

Business computer applications, unlike business information systems and cycles, are designed to automate specific information-processing activities. Each application is designed to accomplish a limited set of processing tasks. Most applications, for example, are designed to prepare:

- formal business documents, to be used in conducting the affairs of the business (paychecks, purchase orders, financial statements);

- summary information, to describe facts important to transaction processing (such as current and year-to-date amounts paid to each employee individually and paid to all employees);

- summary information, to analyze business conditions (such as payroll costs by department as a percentage of total departmental costs); and

- computer files, to be used in printing formal business documents and in preparing summary information, as well as for reference by other computer applications.

Approximately twenty-five business computer applications can be classified as belonging to either the revenue, expenditure, conversion, or cash-management information systems (see Figure 2-3). Collectively, these twenty-five applications would automate the information-processing cycles common to almost any business. Many of these applications are designed to process business transactions, such as employee paychecks and customer invoices. These might be called *transaction-based applications*. Other applications are designed to provide important types of management information. The sales-analysis and market-analysis applications, for example, assist management in the development of sound business strategies by identifying the types of products and markets most profitable and the types of products and markets expected to be the most profitable. These are more appropriately called *management-based applications*.

Revenue-Related Business Computer Applications

1. Order entry
2. Customer invoicing
3. Cash receipts
4. Accounts receivable
5. Sales analysis
6. Customer and product analysis
7. Market analysis

Expenditure-Related Business Computer Applications

1. Employee payroll
2. Accounts payable
3. Check reconciliation
4. Fixed assets
5. Purchasing
6. Receiving
7. Personnel
8. Cash disbursements

Conversion-Related Business Computer Applications

1. Product inventory
2. Work in process
3. Labor distribution
4. Job costing
5. Property accounting

Cash-Management-Related Business Computer Applications

1. General ledger
2. Budget planning and control
3. Profit planning and control
4. Cash management
5. Portfolio management

Figure 2-3   Twenty-five business computer applications

2-3 SIX TYPES OF COMPUTER FILES

A primary purpose of business computer applications is to create, improve, and use files of business information. Computer files store logically related sets of business information. If these sets are accurate, complete, and easy to gain access to, a business has at its disposal both detailed and summary information that is important for business record keeping and for management decision making.

Computer files store business records. A *record* is made up of a set of facts, known as *data elements,* that are logically related. Each record describes an event, an object, or a person. For example, a record describing your background might begin with your Social Security number (the first data element), your name (the second data element), and your home address (the third data element). Each of these facts is important in identifying and describing you as a person.

When data elements are written to computer files, the storage areas they occupy are physically defined as *fields*. Thus, facts are expressed logically as data elements, but are stored physically in data fields. This difference in terms often confuses people new to data processing. Since our concern in this book is with the logical design of online business computer applications, we will use the term *data elements* more frequently.

Business firms must create and maintain several types of business records. Almost all firms create and maintain employee records, vendor records, customer records, and product records. Firms must also create and maintain records of their receivables, payables, assets, and liabilities. In each case, a computer file can be used to store these types of records. Within each file there is one record for each event, object, or person. The collection of a firm's files makes up the data base of the organization.

Six types of computer files are used in the design of online business computer applications. Each type stores business records; however, as the following discussion makes clear, each is created and maintained for a different purpose.

The Transaction File

A transaction file contains records that describe the details of business dealings, such as information used in printing a customer invoice or information used in printing an employee paycheck. Most transaction files are created online for a specific processing run. When the run has been completed, there is little need to retain the file: at that point the information to be retained has been stored elsewhere. Thus, a transaction file contains temporary business records. It is saved long enough to provide a backup to processing—to permit rerunning steps in processing, if necessary. Then the storage space required by the file can be released.

The Master File

A master file contains records that describe the details of an event, object, or person. Unlike a transaction file, a master file contains relatively permanent records. A product master file, for example, contains records that describe the products carried in inventory by a business. These records change only if a product is dropped from inventory, a product is added to inventory, or the information describing a product carried in inventory needs to be modified. During a processing run, information stored on a master file can be updated (or otherwise modified), or extracted and transferred to a transaction file. Figure 2-4 shows the advantage gained by the transfer of information from one file to another. Because information can be transferred, each logical record in the invoice transaction file need contain only ten data elements. Three elements, number 6 (the customer account number), number 7 (the first product number) and number 9 (the second product number) are *data-extraction keys*. These

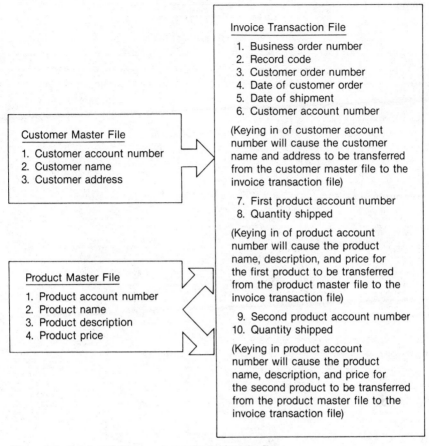

Figure 2-4 Relationship between transaction and master files

keys permit records stored on master files to be matched with records stored on transaction files. Following a match, information is extracted and transferred—either from the master file to the transaction file or from the transaction file to the master file. As Figure 2-5 shows, the matching of customer numbers leads to the transfer of the customer name and address from the customer master file to the invoice transaction file. Likewise, for each product shipped, a match of product account numbers leads to the transfer of the product name, product description, and product price from the product master file to the invoice transaction file.

The Summary File

A summary file contains condensed versions of transaction- or master-file data. Summary files are used in preparing management summary reports and in linking together computer applications. They are products of processing, since they are created by a processing run. Figure 2-6 shows the relationship between

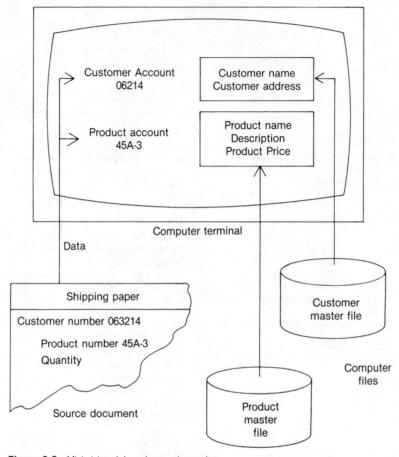

Figure 2-5 Minimizing data-entry requirements

a transaction file and a summary file. When the invoice summary file in Figure 2-6 is created, only seven out of the twenty-three data elements contained in the invoice transaction file would be saved. Even so, this considerably smaller file enables a business to summarize the financial totals associated with preparing invoices. The file is now suitable as input to accounts receivable and sales-analysis processing.

The Suspense File

A suspense file contains records in error. Because online business computer applications block or trap errors before they can be entered into processing, suspense files can often be omitted from an online design. There are, however, some exceptions. Suspense files are normally used to store keyed data that, for some reason, have been blocked from entry into processing. As an example,

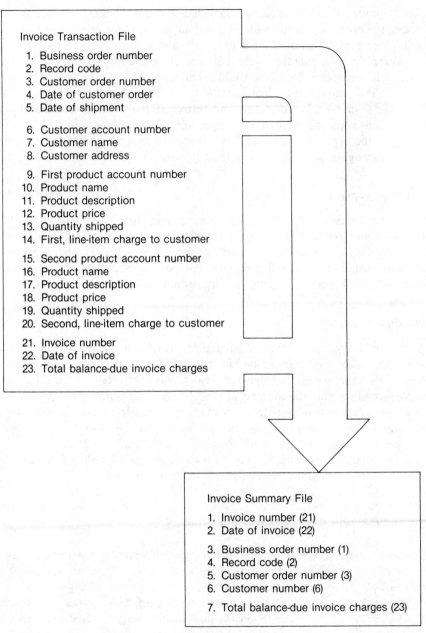

Figure 2-6 Relationship between transaction and summary files

suppose that in keying data for a customer shipment, a data-entry operator notices that although the first twenty product numbers have been accepted by the computer, the twenty-first number is rejected as incorrect. Two alternatives then exist. The operator could stop processing and disallow the data for the first twenty products entered successfully; when the questionable number is corrected, the operator would resubmit the data for all other product numbers as well. (This duplication of effort is obviously undesirable, however.) In the second alternative, the operator could halt processing and transfer the transaction-in-error to a suspense file. This would avoid rekeying the data. Once the problem with the transaction is identified, the transaction-in-error could be removed from the suspense file, corrected, and tested. If the tests are successful, the transaction would be entered into processing. If the tests indicated another problem, the type of error would be identified, and the transaction-in-error would once again be transferred to the suspense file.

The Backup File

A backup file is a copy of a transaction, master, summary, or suspense file. Copies of files are made for security reasons. If a file is destroyed or tampered with, the copy of the file can be used to restore processing. File-backup procedures are required by all online business computer applications. They protect a business against natural disasters and from human failings.

The Change File

A change file is a special type of backup file. It contains all adjustments made online to master- and transaction-file records. Most change files store two versions of the same record: one showing the contents of the record before a change and a second showing the contents after a change. This *before-after recording* is done for security reasons. If the legitimacy of a change to a file is questioned, for example, the contents of the change file can be listed to determine what changes were made and who made the change. Before-after recording also has a backup purpose: the change file can be used as an input file should it be necessary to restore changes made to a master or transaction file.

2-4 SEVEN TYPES OF COMPUTER PROGRAMS

Besides six types of computer files, seven types of computer programs are used in the design of online business computer applications. These are the edit, update, display, register, action-document, summary, and change-report programs. Understanding these programs together with the six types of computer files will greatly help you to follow the flowcharting notation used in describing online business computer applications.

The Edit Program

Almost all online business computer applications begin with either an edit program or, as we will see later, a combined edit and update program. An edit program tests for errors in data submitted for processing. It is written to ensure proper input of data to the computer and to block or trap input errors by performing two types of tests: computer-controlled edit tests and human-controlled edit tests.

Computer-controlled edit tests consist of individual record-checking and file-balancing procedures. Because records in an online environment are entered into processing transaction by transaction, records must be checked individually. Each data element keyed into processing is subjected to one or more edit tests. These tests can include mixed-mode tests, limit tests, reasonableness-of-data tests, consistency tests, and check-digit tests. When a test identifies an error or a possible error, the terminal operator is notified. Suppose, for example, that an operator erroneously keys in Account 65032 instead of 60532. A check-digit test would trap this transposition error. The computer might respond by telling the terminal operator to rekey the number.

Human-controlled edit tests are designed to require the terminal operator to visually review and verify the correctness of keyed data. This type of test also takes a wide variety of forms. For example, the computer might produce the following display:

```
ACCOUNT NUMBER : 354778
    THE NEW BUILDING ADDRESS FOR MARTIN J. JOHNSON IS

    JOHNSON'S BUILDING SUPPLY
    2555 BROWN AVENUE
    SAN CRUSES, CA 94302

    IS THIS BUILDING ADDRESS CORRECT (Y OR N)?
```

This display requires the operator to visually verify the new building address. If the address is incorrect, the operator would enter the letter N. The computer would respond by telling the operator the steps to follow to modify the address.

A *file-balance procedure* is an important part of an edit program. This procedure creates and maintains control records to be placed at the beginning of a computer file. The records store beginning and ending balances of record counts and amounts, as well as the number of changes to these counts and amounts. The interpretation of these control records is accomplished by simple equations. For example, one file-balance equation used in an online payroll computer application keeps track of the number of employees on file:

> Number of old employees + Employee additions −
> Employee deletions = Number of new employees

Here four record counts are required: the number of old employees, the number of additions, the number of deletions, and the number of new employees. Each time the employee master file is changed, the four records counts are changed to document the effects of processing.

The Update Program

An update program either creates or modifies one or more files of business records. In online systems, transaction files are generally created, and master files are modified. Creating a record to be stored on a transaction file is a multistep process. First, some data must be keyed into processing to form part of the record. Second, some data are extracted from one or more master files and transferred to enlarge the contents of the transaction-file record. Third, some data are computed directly and stored. If, as an example, the computer calculates the line-item charge for merchandise shipped to a customer in the customer-invoice computer application, the calculation, which is computed directly, is based on the quantity ordered, which is keyed into processing, times the unit price of the item, which is extracted from the product master file and transferred into processing.

The modifying of master-file records involves the revising of variable data elements either prior to or during transaction processing. Changing the address of a customer prior to processing exemplifies the first way of modifying master-file records. Adding current data (the current sales total) to a historical sales total (the year-to-date sales total) during transaction processing exemplifies the second way. This type of modification involves the transfer of data from a transaction file to a master file.

In data base processing, a single update program may consult, revise, and transfer data from several files. Besides creating one or more transaction files, the program may extract data from several master files and modify data stored on several other master or summary files. Typically, one set of file-balance control records must be developed for each file affected by processing. This procedure helps to ensure that processing is correct. It also provides a means of control by establishing a formal *audit trail*—a method of tracing output back to original source documents.

The Display Program

A display program extracts records or portions of records from computer files for display on a video display terminal. It may also print information shown on the display screen, following the terminal operator command to "print the display." Unlike update programs, which modify file records, display programs permit records to be examined, but not changed.

Display programs are generally written to limit access to portions of a record, so that information judged as sensitive cannot be displayed or can be displayed but not changed. Fields that cannot be displayed are known as *restricted fields*. Fields that can be displayed but not changed are known as *protected fields*. An employee's salary, for example, is usually considered sensitive information. In designing a display of an employee's record, a firm might restrict the salary and limit display information to less sensitive facts such as name, address, home telephone, business telephone extension, department, and job title.

Display programs are used to directly retrieve records from transaction, master, and summary files. This processing capability clearly separates online from batch methods of processing. Online displays enable search activities to be performed by the person needing information. With batch methods, in contrast, the search must be delegated to a data processing technician.

The Register Program

A register program provides a printed listing of information entered into processing and stored on a transaction, master, summary, or backup file. These listings serve a number of important uses. They can be inspected to determine if actions taken by the computer were correct. They permit information to be looked up when it cannot be displayed. They represent the permanent record of processing. If a question arises concerning the details of a transaction, for example, the transaction-file register can be examined to find out the contents of the record in question.

An alternative to printing a register on computer paper is to initially write the register listing to a magnetic-tape file and to input this file to computer output microfilm (COM) processing. A product of COM is *microfiche*: a card-sized film on which photographic images of information are placed. Microfiche processing is less costly than printing registers on paper and storing these bulky documents for long periods. A single four-by-six-inch microfiche card, for instance, costs 15 cents and can store up to 270 pages of printed material. The equivalent cost for paper is approximately 90 cents.

The Action-Document Program

An action-document program produces formal business documents such as payroll checks, customer invoices, and vendor voucher-checks—materials that require action by parties external to data processing. Most transaction-processing computer applications contain an action-document program. Their preparation is often a major reason for developing an application.

The Summary Program

A summary program extracts information from transaction files in order to create summary files and print summary displays and reports. These programs often feature management-information processing rather than transaction processing. Some business firms even use summary programs to create a management-information data base for use in online color graphics applications. A requirement of these systems is that the data base be limited to only essential information.

The Change-Report Program

A change-report program is a special type of register program that provides a listing of information stored on a change file. A change-report listing is commonly referred to as an *is/was report*. It might show, for example, the contents of records stored on a master file after a change (the "is" condition) and the contents of records before the change (the "was" condition).

2-5 SYSTEMS DOCUMENTATION

To be understood and used successfully, online business computer applications must be properly documented. *Systems documentation* provides a detailed description of what a system will accomplish. It typically includes a statement of purpose, systems organization charts, systems flowcharts, processing menus, and computer program descriptions. Collectively, these materials provide a clear picture of the logical properties of an application.

A statement of purpose clarifies the reasons for developing the computer application. It includes an explanation of why the application was designed and what results should follow its implementation.

Systems organization charts show the functions performed by the computer programs written for a business computer application.

Systems flowcharts illustrate the movement of data through the various processing stages in a business computer application. Standard flowcharting symbols are used to depict the component parts of processing and their functions relative to other parts of processing.

Processing menus describe the processing selections that can be made from a computer terminal. Program-processing menus show which computer programs can be brought into processing. File-processing menus show how computer file records can be modified.

Computer program descriptions provide a nontechnical description of what each computer program is designed to accomplish and of the inputs, outputs, and controls important to processing.

In addition to the logical properties of an application, systems documentation must include a detailed, technical description of processing. These materials are prepared as part of online systems design (see Chapter 3). They include printed report layouts, video-screen report layouts, video-screen input layouts, file-coding structures, data-element dictionary specifications, computer program specifications, and processing-control specifications.

Printed report layouts describe the registers, action-documents, summary reports, and change reports that are to be printed by a business computer application. Each report produced in processing must be documented. Report layout sheets show how the design will be fitted to common stock paper or to special-order custom business forms.

Video-screen report layouts include report and message formats to be transmitted as displays during processing. Each display must be documented. Video-screen layout sheets show how the design is fitted to the display screen.

Video-screen input layouts consist of data-entry instructions to be followed in transmitting data from the video terminal into processing. Instructions must be prepared for each type of input to be processed. Video-screen input layout sheets show how data will be keyed into processing.

File-coding structures explain the various numeric, alphabetic, and alphanumeric codes used in processing. Coding worksheets explain the meaning of each digit or character of a code.

Data-element dictionary specifications include the name, field type, field length, and purpose of each data element in a computer file. Record format-analysis sheets define all data elements to be contained in a record.

Computer program specifications provide a detailed discussion of each computer program to show the way in which coded instructions are to be organized. Special attention is given to explaining programmed decision rules. Other specifications such as program run times and memory requirements must also be stated.

Processing-control specifications clarify how each step in processing is to be controlled. Computer- and human-controlled tests must be described. The equations used in file-balance procedures must be explained.

2-6 SYSTEMS FLOWCHARTING

Because systems flowcharts are used extensively throughout this book, it is essential to understand their purpose, the symbols used in their design, and the guidelines to be followed in their actual construction. Once systems flowcharts are understood, it becomes possible to visualize the movement of data through the various processing stages of an online application. These flowcharts attempt to show only major stages in processing, unlike computer program flowcharts, and are specifically developed to show the main inputs to processing, outputs from processing, and computer programs written for processing.

Flowchart Symbols

The standard symbols used in designing systems flowcharts are available on specially prepared flowcharting templates. One such template—there are several different types—features twenty-three standard symbols (see Figure 2-7). These twenty-three are more than adequate to describe the features of online computer applications. In fact, to describe the important features of the applications developed for this text, only eight are needed: the punched-card symbol, the manual-input symbol, the document symbol, the display symbol, the communication-link symbol, the online-storage symbol, the magnetic-tape symbol, and the process symbol.

Punched Card

This symbol indicates either a punched card or a set of punched cards. It usually shows card input to processing. Because online computer applications

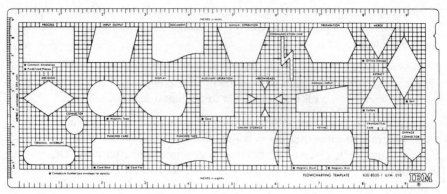

Figure 2-7   Template of flowchart symbols

feature direct terminal input, this symbol will be used infrequently. For the most part, terminal input has replaced punched-card input.

Manual Input

In most online environments, input to processing is entered directly from a terminal keyboard. This direct entry of data is indicated by the manual-input symbol.

Document

The document symbol represents either source documents or computer-printed material. *Source documents*—those that have been prepared prior to processing—include customer orders received in the mail, purchase requisitions, and employee-change forms. Information is extracted from these documents and entered into processing. *Computer-printed documents* consist of listings and reports, such as registers and summary reports, and of formal business action documents such as employee paychecks, customer invoices, and purchase orders. These documents are produced by the computer.

Display

The display symbol indicates that data are to be displayed on a video screen. Like the punched-card symbol, the display symbol can represent either a single screen (a single display page) or multiple screens (several display pages). Most online applications require the terminal operator to use several display screens to enter or retrieve data to and from processing.

Communication Link

The communication-link symbol represents the transmission of data to the computer from remote locations. It is used together with the manual-input symbol to show the transmission of data to the computer, or together with the display symbol to illustrate the transmission of data from the computer.

Online Storage

The online-storage symbol represents a computer file that can be read from or written to directly. In an online processing environment, online file storage generally means direct-access magnetic-disk storage. Disk-storage devices permit individual records to be read directly into processing, examined, adjusted, and written back to the disk, where they are stored sequentially. Thus, records can be adjusted, one at a time, and refiled in sequential order.

Magnetic-Tape Storage

The symbol for magnetic-tape storage can also represent online storage. Compared with magnetic disks, however, tape cannot be used efficiently either to access or to insert individual records in a file. In online computer applications, magnetic-tape storage is mainly used for backing up computer files.

Process

The most prominent symbol in a systems flowchart for an online business computer application is the process symbol. It represents a computer program and shows the point at which information is brought into and altered by processing. In a systems flowchart, only one process symbol is used to show the different processing steps in any one computer program. Only a single symbol is required, for example, for a combined edit and update program, even though the program does several things: checking keyed input data for errors, enlarging the input transaction file, displaying messages to the terminal operator, and maintaining file-balance equations. Computer program flowcharts, not systems flowcharts, are used if the details of a computer program are to be illustrated.

Flowchart Layout

Besides using standard symbols, it is important to follow a set of guidelines for describing the sequence of events illustrated by systems flowcharts. The more standard the layout, the more information the chart will convey. The following five guidelines were used in designing the flowcharts that appear in the following chapters.

1. A systems flowchart should be simple enough to be placed on one 8½-by-11-inch page.

2. The flow of information in the chart should move from the top of the page to the bottom. Edit, update, display, register, action-document, summary and change-report computer programs should be placed in sequence whenever possible.

3. Inputs to processing, including computer files, should appear on the left side of the main flow of processing. A single arrow from a computer file to a computer program shows that information is read into processing. A double arrow indicates that information is both read from and written to a computer file.

4. Outputs from processing should appear on the right side of the main flow of processing. Note two exceptions, however: if a file of records is created by processing, this output file can be placed at the bottom of the computer program symbol; and if a file of records is updated by processing, this input/output file should be placed to the left of the computer program symbol. As before, a double arrow indicates that both input and output are possible.

5. Titles should be given to each symbol placed on the flowchart. For computer programs, the title for the process symbol should consist of a verb followed by one or two adjectives followed by an object—for example, "print customer credit report."

Figures 2-8 and 2-9 illustrate the layouts of two different processing designs. The flowchart in Figure 2-8 shows the steps required in the batch processing of purchase-order requisitions, up to the point of creating an approved-purchase-order transaction file. The steps required in processing were described in Chapter 1, pp. 13-14. The systems flowchart now clarifies the relationships between the three required programs: the edit purchase-order requisitions program, the

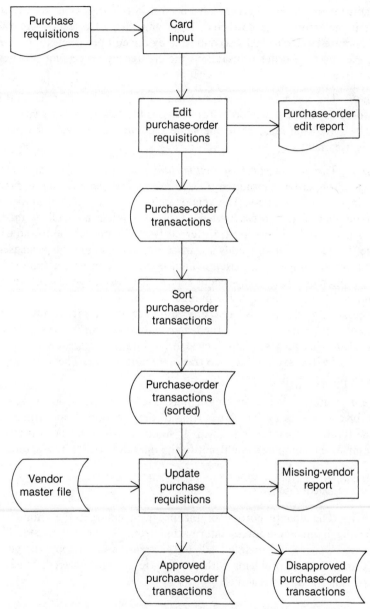

Figure 2-8 Batch processing of purchase-order requisitions

sort purchase-order transactions program, and the update purchase requisitions program. Each computer program is designed to work as follows:

Step 1. The *edit purchase-order requisitions program* accepts a serially read batch of punched-card transactions. As each transaction is brought into processing, it is edited by the edit purchase-order requisitions program for correctness; if an error is found, the transaction-in-error is printed on a purchase-order edit report. After all errors have been printed, processing is discontinued to permit the errors to be corrected. Following this, all corrected transactions are resubmitted and checked a second time by the edit program. If no errors are found, the purchase-order transactions file created by processing is believed to be error free.

Step 2. The *sort purchase-order transactions program* arranges all transactions stored on the purchase-order transactions file sequentially by vendor number. (The sorted file must be in the same sequence as the vendor master file, which is used next.)

Step 3. The *update purchase requisitions program* enla:ges the contents of sorted purchase-order transactions file. In processing, the update program must first match vendor numbers. The vendor master file is searched until the first vendor number in the transaction file is found. When a match is made, the vendor's name and address are transferred from the master file to the transaction file. A successful match adds a transaction to the approved-purchase-order output transaction file. If a match cannot be made, however, a transaction-in-error is printed on the missing-vendor report. The transaction is also suspended by being written to a disapproved-purchase-order suspense file.

Figure 2-9 flowcharts this same procedure for an interactive processing environment. Only one program, the *enter purchase requisitions program,* is now needed. This program edits keyed transactions and creates an approved-purchase-order transaction file, one transaction at a time. The steps important to processing are as follows:

Step 1. Information describing a purchase-order requisition is keyed and edited for correctness by the edit portion of the program. If an error is identified, the terminal operator is notified. If some data had not been transmitted, for example, the computer might notify the operator with a message reading:

THE QUANTITY TO BE ORDERED WAS NOT INDICATED.
WHAT QUANTITY IS DESIRED?

Step 2. The update portion of the program enlarges the transaction by transferring name-and-address information from the vendor master file into processing. A successful update leads to the creation of an approved-purchase-order transaction. If problems with the update are encountered, the terminal operator is notified. For instance:

VENDOR ACCOUNT 10023 CANNOT BE FOUND.
DO YOU WISH TO SUBMIT A NEW VENDOR NUMBER? (Y OR N)

Comparing batch processing and interactive processing gives the impression that since fewer programs are required in an interactive environment, it will be more machine efficient. This is a false impression: actually, the interactive edit and update of each transaction takes considerably more computer time than is

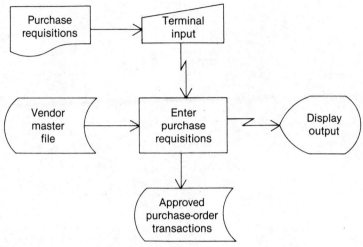

Figure 2-9 Online processing of purchase-order requisitions

used to read and process all transactions as a batch. The clearest advantage of the interactive approach is that transactions are more carefully edited by human beings prior to their storage as "approved." This careful human inspection is needed both to save time and to ensure accuracy in data processing. Both factors are vital in processing business information.

Another comparison of batch processing to interactive processing reveals that in an online environment, both types of processing are used, but in different ways. Typically, interactive methods are used to create or update a file; batch methods are required to produce various types of listings and reports, such as a listing of the contents of computer files. Printing a master list of vendors, for example, is accomplished by the batch program entitled "print vendor register." As the flowchart in Figure 2-10 shows, this report can be produced directly, since the records of the file are arranged in the correct sequence. In a second example, we see that a slightly different processing arrangement is needed to

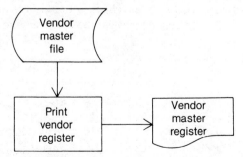

Figure 2-10 Printing the vendor master register

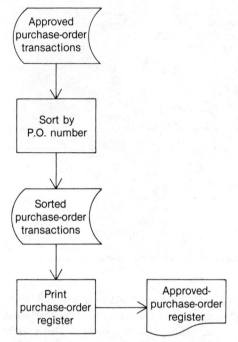

Figure 2-11 Printing the approved-purchase-order register

show how the approved-purchase-order register is prepared (see Figure 2-11). Before the register can be printed, the approved-purchase-order transactions file is sorted by purchase order number to arrange all transactions in serial order. After the sort, a second batch program, appropriately entitled "print purchase-order register," produces the final document.

Finally, Figure 2-12 features another interactive processing procedure to show the relationship between a master and a change file. In this instance, new vendor information must be added to the vendor master file. As the double arrow in the flowchart indicates, the vendor master file is updated by processing. At the same time, any change to the master file is written to the vendor change file. This action backs up all changes (additions, modifications, deletions) to the master file. These changes can be reviewed once a batch program is activated to print the contents of the change file. All master-file changes would be printed on a vendor change report.

REVIEW OF IMPORTANT IDEAS

Business computer applications are characterized by four general properties: they are related to one another; they consist of input, processing, output, and control operations; they are designed to permit batch and interactive methods of processing; and they are relatively easy to understand, provided that systems documentation is logical and complete.

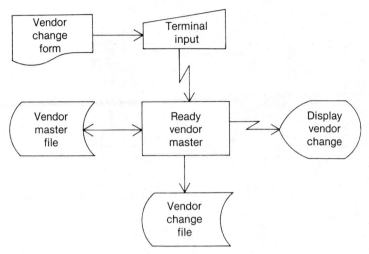

Figure 2-12 Updating the vendor master file

Four business information systems are common to most business firms: the revenue system, the expenditure system, the conversion system, and the cash-management system. Each of these information systems can be broken down into information-processing cycles. Each cycle consists of several business computer applications.

Approximately twenty-five business computer applications can be classified as belonging to one of the four main business information systems. These applications are designed to automate specific information-processing activities.

Six types of computer files are common to the design of business computer applications: the transaction file, the master file, the summary file, the suspense file, the backup file, and the change file. Each file stores business records; each is created and maintained for a specific purpose.

Seven types of computer programs are common to business computer applications: the edit program, the update program, the display program, the register program, the action-document program, the summary program, and the change-report program. Edit, update, and display programs are generally used in interactive processing; register, action-document, summary, and change-report programs are used in batch processing.

Systems documentation is required to describe and illustrate the systems overview and technical parts of a computer application. Systems organization charts, systems flowcharts, program-processing menus, and file-processing menus are used extensively in providing a systems overview. More technical documentation describes input and output requirements and explains how processing is accomplished.

Systems flowcharts are of special importance in preparing a systems overview. These diagrams chart the flow of data through the various stages in a business computer application.

KEY WORDS

Information systems	Before-after recording
Business system	Edit program
Processing cycles	File-balance procedure
Business computer applications	Update program
Transaction-based applications	Audit trail
Management-based applications	Display program
Record	Register program
Data element	Microfiche
Fields	Action-document program
Transaction file	Summary program
Master file	Change-report program
Summary file	Is/was report
Suspense file	Systems documentation
Backup file	Systems flowchart
Change file	Source document

REVIEW QUESTIONS

1. Name the four main business information systems.

2. Explain the following statement: A business information system consists of several processing cycles that are linked together.

3. What is accomplished by the revenue-collection cycle?

4. How do business computer applications differ from information-processing cycles? How do they differ from business information systems?

5. Why are computer files important to a business?

6. What is the difference between a transaction file and a master file? Between a summary file and a suspense file? Between a backup file and a change file?

7. What is the difference between a computer-controlled and a human-controlled edit test?

8. What does an update program do?

9. What is the difference between a register program and a change-report program?

10. What types of information are contained in the logical overview portion of systems documentation? In the technical portion of systems documentation?

11. Why are systems flowcharts important in describing online business computer applications?

12. Explain why online processing requires some type of direct-access storage.

EXERCISES

1. Individuals as well as business firms require information systems. Discuss the information system you require in
   (a) handling your personal income;
   (b) managing your personal expenses.

2. Suppose a computer application is designed to process and store personal check information. The design includes a check-register master file and a personal-check transaction file. Data entered into processing for each check consists of a record code (type of record), the check number, date of check, check description, and amount of check. Deposit information would also be entered into processing. The checking account balance would always be calculated and kept by the computer.
   (a) Using the symbols described in this chapter, design an online systems flowchart to show how this personal checking application works.
   (b) After your design is completed, answer the following questions:
       (i) Why is a record code required?
       (ii) What information would be contained in master file records?
       (iii) When are edit procedures required in processing?
       (iv) What changes are made to the master file when it is updated?
       (v) How must your design in part (a) be modified to permit checks to be shown as written, returned, and reconciled (checked off as being correctly processed)?

3. Why should systems documentation include a logical description of processing? Give several reasons.

3

Online Systems Design

Once a logical overview of processing has been developed, fully documented, and approved by management, it must be translated into a detailed technical description. This process is *systems design*. The work associated with design is assigned to an individual known as a *systems designer*. It is the designer's job to develop the logical overview of processing and to translate it into a fully operational computer application. Viewed in a broader perspective, the systems designer builds business computer systems.

In preparing a systems design, the designer must include written specifications for five areas: systems inputs, computer files, systems outputs, computer programs, and processing controls. Completion of these areas leads to the development and documentation of the technical features of processing: video-screen input and report layouts, computer-printed report layouts, file-coding structures, data-element definitions, and specifications both for computer programs and processing controls. In short, systems design defines the way in which a business application is to be processed by the computer.

Systems design also encompasses the technical and human factors of processing and seeks to make them clear and accessible. *Technical factors* include a variety of items: the sets of instructions to be translated into code, the types of data to be stored on computer files, the data to be keyed in or retrieved from computer files, and the equations to bring about control in processing. *Human factors* deal with the use of the completed computer application. They stress details important to the design from the user's perspective, such as the display of error messages and user-assist instructions.

3-1 DESIGNING SYSTEMS INPUT

A major advantage of online business computer applications is the capability to edit and visually review the input of data into processing from remote locations. Unfortunately, providing this capability is not as easy as it may appear. In design, the systems designer must determine what data must be entered into processing, how these data are to be physically entered, and what checks are necessary to determine whether data have been entered correctly.

Data-Element Requirements

In deciding what data must be entered into processing, the systems designer reviews the list of required data elements and separates those to be keyed directly to processing from those to be stored on computer files in advance of processing. Storing data on master files means that data can be transferred rather than keyed.

The documentation describing data to be keyed typically includes the name of the field; whether the field is numeric, alphabetic, or alphanumeric; the number of characters in the field; the source of the data; and other comments important to the data element. *Input-analysis forms* record these descriptions (see Figure 3-1). These forms, combined with copies of all source documents, show the specific pieces of information to be keyed directly to processing.

The documentation describing data to be stored on computer files is similar to the documentation for data entered directly. *Record-analysis forms* describe each logical data element, its field name, its description (numeric, alphabetic, or alphanumeric), the source of the data, the number of characters in the field, and the data-storage format. These forms, combined with copies of all source documents, show how computer files are to be developed for use in processing.

SYSTEM DOCUMENTATION			
NAME OF APPLICATION Customer Invoice	DATE October 15, 19XX	PAGE 1 OF 2	
PROGRAMMER/ANALYST B. Thompson	TYPE OF ANALYSIS Input Analysis		

Field	Description	No. of Characters	Source	Comments
Order Number	Numeric	7	Packing Slip	4 bytes
Record Code	Numeric	1	Packing Slip	1 byte
Customer Number	Numeric	5	Packing Slip	3 bytes
Date of Order	Numeric	6	Packing Slip	4 bytes
Date of Shipment	Numeric	6	Packing Slip	4 bytes
Product Number	Numeric	5	Packing Slip	3 bytes
Quantity Shipped	Numeric	5	Packing Slip	3 bytes

Figure 3-1 Input-analysis form

SYSTEM DOCUMENTATION			
NAME OF APPLICATION Customer Invoice		DATE October 15, 19XX	PAGE 2 OF 2
PROGRAMMER/ANALYST B. Thompson		TYPE OF ANALYSIS Customer Master Record Format Analysis	

Field	Description	No. of Characters	Source	Comments
Customer Number	Numeric	5	New Customer Form	3 bytes
Customer Name	Alphabetic	30	New Customer Form	Last, First, M.I.
Bill-to Address:				
Street	Alphanumeric	18	New Customer Form	
City	Alphabetic	8	New Customer Form	
State	Alphabetic	2	New Customer Form	
Zip	Numeric	5	New Customer Form	3 bytes

Figure 3-2   Record format analysis form

Data-Entry Procedures

Data-entry procedures must be designed following the determination of requirements for data elements. These procedures show how data will be entered into
processing, edited by the computer and transmitted back to the terminal for
review, and corrected by the terminal operator and transmitted to the computer
for further editing and visual review.

An important data-entry rule is to require the terminal operator to key into
processing as little as possible, using the computer to interpret and fill in as
much as possible. The objective is to reduce the number of *keystrokes*—the
number of times a terminal operator must strike the keys of a keyboard. One
method of reducing the number of keystrokes is to require numeric codes. Assume, for example, that a five-digit code is used to identify company employees.
If the number 92189 is interpreted in processing as the employee record for
Barbara J. Wilson (seventeen characters, including spaces), twelve keystrokes
are saved. It is thus understandable that one design solution for improving the
efficiency of data entry is to make input data numeric. This technique permits
the data-entry operator to use the *numeric pad* placed to the right of a terminal
keyboard (see Figure 3-3). The numeric pad contains ten number keys plus a
period key and four or more arithmetic operator keys (addition key, subtraction
key, and so forth).

The numeric pad can be used for reasons other than the entry of numerical
data into processing. Some video display terminals permit the ten to sixteen
keys contained on the pad to be used directly as commands. Hitting an upper-
right key marked CLERK, for instance, tells the computer that the "clerk
number" is to be entered next into processing. Hitting a lower-left key marked
VOID tells the computer to cancel the data transmitted for a transaction.

Light pens and optical character readers are also used to enter data into

Figure 3-3 Terminal keyboard with numeric pad

processing. A *light pen* is a small pencil-like instrument that is used to activate positions on the face of a video display screen. Most pens are designed to pick, move, and construct lines or to point to a specific set of X and Y coordinates. A *hand-held optical scanner* is similar to a light pen. It features a light-sensitive cell that permits it to optically "read" characters. The cell distinguishes between patterns of black and white, and the scanner is able to match these patterns against character-recognition circuits.

Video display screens for data entry should be designed with operator efficiency in mind. Many key-entry design procedures begin with the layout of easy-to-use processing menus and processing commands. These menus are typically defined early on as part of the logical description of processing. A *processing menu*, as the name suggests, defines the different parts of processing that can be selected by a terminal operator. A *program-processing menu* shows the computer programs available to be run. For example, such a menu for a membership-accounts-receivable application might read as follows:

    1. ENTER CHARGES/CREDITS
    2. ENTER MEMBER PAYMENTS
    3. CHANGE MEMBER ACCOUNTS
    4. ENTER ACCOUNT ADJUSTMENTS
    5. DISPLAY MEMBER ACCOUNTS
    6. DISPLAY FILE-BALANCE TOTALS
   (7) EXIT

This menu would be followed by a *prompt*, such as ENTER PROGRAM NUMBER, which serves as a signal to the operator to select from the menu and to enter a command. Entering the number 3, for example, commands the computer to execute the programmed instructions designed to CHANGE MEMBER ACCOUNTS. A *command* in this usage means a special type of instruction. It is a single, direct order from the user. It thus features a direct mode of processing in which an instruction is entered and executed without delay.

Video-display layout sheets help in designing screen displays. As Figure 3-4 shows, a layout sheet sizes and arranges information to be displayed. Screen displays must be designed with care, because of their small size. Small-screen terminals, for instance, restrict a design to 16 lines and 64 characters per line,

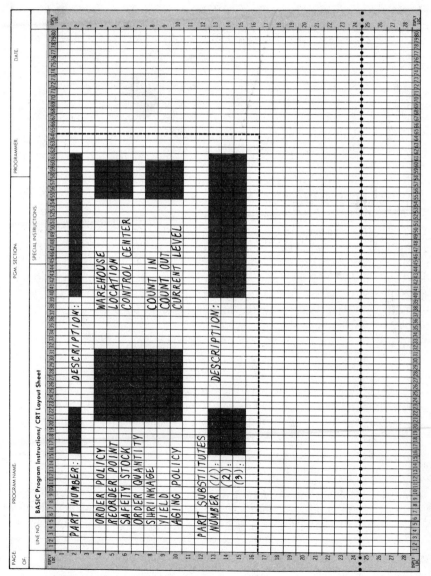

Figure 3-4 Video display layout sheet

or a total of 1,024 characters. Larger screens, such as 24 lines and 80 characters per line, restrict an input design to 1,920 characters. If additional lines are required beyond the screen maximums, multiple screens, or "pages," become necessary. A *page* is a display formatted to fit the screen of a video display terminal. In designing data-entry procedures, systems analysts often use several pages to enter data into processing. As you will observe in later chapters, some pages contain program-processing menus, others contain file and self-help menus, and still others display business forms to be completed by the terminal operator.

Specific design techniques are advised to highlight data-entry requirements and to identify problems in processing. These include prompts by the computer to check keyed information, blinking lights to show accounts to be inspected, soft sounds to indicate when an error has been made, and reverse video (shaded areas on a terminal screen) to emphasize what data to enter.

3-2 DESIGNING COMPUTER FILES

Although a major reason for creating online business computer applications is the capability to edit and visually review the entry of data into processing, it is the computer files rather than the data-entry procedures that represent the most sizable investment in business computer applications. Computer files are dominant in information processing. As we discussed in Chapter 2, business firms use computer files to store information required for both business record keeping and management decision making.

Like data entry, computer files are designed according to certain basic rules, some of which are simply good common sense. For instance:

- Do not place data in a computer file unless file maintenance is easy. As an example, suppose someone in a business decides that it is important to know the age of an employee. In this situation, a record should contain "date of birth" rather than "age of employee," since "date of birth" can be used to calculate an employee's age. Moreover, "age of employee" must be revised yearly and thus is difficult to maintain.

- Do not place data in a computer file unless the cost of storage space can be justified. Continuing with the "age of employee" example, we should raise the following questions: How much will it cost to maintain "date of birth" in the file? How will "age of employee" information be used by a business?

- Do not place data in a computer file unless the accuracy of the stored information can be checked periodically by people able to detect errors. For example, placing the name of an employee's beneficiary in a file is often worthless unless the employee is periodically asked to review the name.

Besides these commonsense rules, several file design guidelines aid the systems designer.

- *Account codes* should be used to sequence business accounts and identify events, objects, and persons. Each customer of a business should be assigned a unique account code, for example, as should each product carried in inventory by the business.

- *Record codes* should be used to distinguish between different types of financial transactions such as credits, debits, and adjustments. Properly designed record codes simplify the process by which dollar amounts are added to or subtracted from business accounts.

- *Sort keys* should be grouped and placed in a common location in a record. These keys permit a file to be sequenced in an order different from the account-code sequence. Placing them in a common location simplifies the design of sort procedures.

- Data elements in a record should be arranged by *common characteristic*. Each customer's name should be followed by his or her address, for example; it would be confusing if instead the customer's name were followed by the salesperson's name, which was then followed by the customer's address.

- File records should be divided into *header* and *trailing sections*. The header section should contain the relatively permanent elements of a record, such as the customer's name. The trailing section should contain variable elements whose values change as a result of processing. "Year-to-date product sales," for example, would be revised each time a product is sold to a customer.

- *Change* or *addition records* should be kept separate from transaction records. Change or addition records update the header section or adjust the trailing section of a record. In contrast, transaction records, as discussed in Chapter 2, are enlarged during processing—by transferring information from computer files or by entering information directly.

- Records should be blocked to save file space and to improve the efficiency of processing. *Blocking* is the grouping of logical records to form a single physical record (the record read into or written from central memory). The *blocking factor* specifies the number of logical records placed within a physical record.

Figure 3-5 provides record layouts for the fields specified by the input analysis form and the record format analysis form in Figures 3-1 and 3-2. These layouts help to clarify how design rules are applied in practice. The top half of Figure 3-5 shows that the invoice transaction file contains an order number

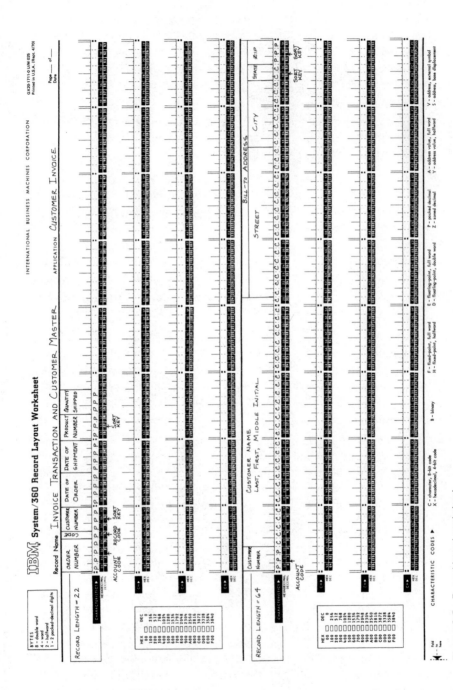

Figure 3-5 Record layout worksheet

code, a record code (to indicate a credit or debit), the customer number, date of order, date of shipment, product number, and quantity shipped. The customer and product numbers are used as sort keys. The length of the record is 22 characters (00 to 21).

The bottom half of Figure 3-5 shows the customer master file record. It too contains an account code (customer number) as well as two sort keys (state and zip code). The fields on this record are arranged by common characteristic so that the customer's name is followed by the customer's bill-to address. As the figure shows, the master record contains only a header section. However, if a variable field such as "year-to-date customer sales" were added to the record, a trailing section would exist.

File Organization

After file records have been designed, the systems designer must determine how the various files containing these records are to be organized. Usually the designer will choose one of the two main types of file organization: *direct* organization, which gives immediate access to records stored on external storage devices, or *sequential* organization, which stores records in a file in sequence, generally in numeric order. Magnetic disk and drum storage devices permit direct file organization; magnetic tape, disk, and drum storage devices permit sequential storage of data.

Direct-access storage is common in online systems. This type of storage permits input data to be entered directly into processing and output data to be retrieved directly. Online computer systems contain a number of features that simplify this movement of data in and out of processing, as well as simplifying the management of file storage space. For example, most online systems include software to automatically handle the searching and movement of data, the reading and writing of data from direct-access files, and the allocating of space in memory. In addition, file-management software permits records to be entered directly into processing, while storing each record in a desired, sequential order. This combining of direct with sequential file organization is known as *indexed-sequential file organization.* With indexed-sequential online capabilities, individual records can be added, changed, or deleted from a file, directly. Or, all records contained on the file can be printed in sequence, such as by customer order number, when all records follow a customer-order-number sequence, or by product number, when all records follow a product-number sequence.

Direct-access files are used in conjunction with data base management software to add even greater flexibility to file processing. As Figure 3-6 shows, a data base approach to processing updates several files concurrently. In this example, an invoice record is enlarged by transferring information from customer and product master files, both of which are direct-access disk files. After the transfer is made, the enlarged record is added to the invoice transaction file. The updating of the salesperson master file is another result of processing. In

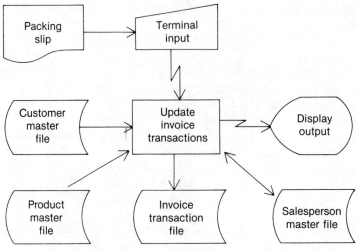

Figure 3-6   Data base approach to processing

this instance, the customer master file indicates the number of the salesperson assigned to the customer's account. This information, combined with the dollar amount of the sale, is used to automatically update the salesperson master file.

The updating of several files concurrently requires that some files be organized to permit direct access to stored records. However, it does not mean that all files must be organized in this way. In the last example, the adding of a record to the invoice transaction file suggests that this file can be organized sequentially.

File-Updating Procedures

After determining what types of data are to be stored on computer files and how files are to be organized, the systems designer must prepare file-updating procedures. These are similar to data-entry procedures. They feature easy-to-use file-processing menus, combined with sets of processing commands. A *file-processing menu* is much like a program-processing menu, except that it shows what actions can be taken to change the contents of a direct-access file. The following menu, for example, was developed to modify a membership master file.

```
1. INSERT NEW MEMBER ACCOUNT
2. MOVE TO A MEMBER ACCOUNT
3. MOVE TO NEXT MEMBER ACCOUNT
4. CHANGE MEMBER ACCOUNT
5. DELETE MEMBER ACCOUNT
(6) RETURN TO MAIN PROCESSING MENU
```

This menu would be displayed and followed by a prompt, such as ENTER SELECTION HERE. If the operator responds by entering a 2, this selection would command the computer to locate a specific member account on the membership master file. To begin this process, the computer would require the operator to key-in the member's account code. Following this, the computer would locate and display the member's account.

Besides file-processing procedures, the systems analyst must design *file-backup procedures,* which make it possible to restore processing in case of a total or partial systems failure. As Figure 3-7 shows, three different processing runs are associated with backing up a master file. The first run updates the membership master file and creates a change file. The second run creates a tape backup copy and a change listing that shows the contents of master-file records before and after they were modified. Finally, the third run creates a tape backup copy and a master-file register that lists all records stored on the master file. Moreover, the tape backup copy of the master file together with the tape backup of the change file permits a fourth processing run to be scheduled. The fourth run—the run to restore processing—permits another membership master direct-access file to be built, tested, and modified as needed.

3-3 DESIGNING SYSTEMS OUTPUTS

Systems outputs, like systems inputs, must be designed to permit visual review of processed results. With outputs, several questions must be answered:

- What types of information will be needed by the end users of a system?
- How should information be presented? How should it be distributed?
- Will specialized forms of output, such as computer-output microfilm or audio response, be required?
- Is any information sensitive? Who should receive sensitive information? How will access to sensitive information be controlled?

Historically, the design of systems outputs has meant the design of printed business listings, documents, and reports. Even today, printed information is the most widely used and accepted form of computer output. However, video-display terminal output is being used with ever-greater frequency. The advantage of a display over hard copy is that information can be retrieved from computer files, inspected, manipulated, and then discarded or saved, depending on the importance of the display. In some information retrieval systems, such as a customer-shipping-inquiry system, an inquiry is made to determine if a customer's shipment has been made. Once the answer to the inquiry has been displayed, the information is discarded. In other retrieval systems, such as a hotel-motel reservation system, an inquiry is made to determine the availability of a room. If a room is available, it can be assigned to a customer, and the information associated with the reservation (customer name, room number, and

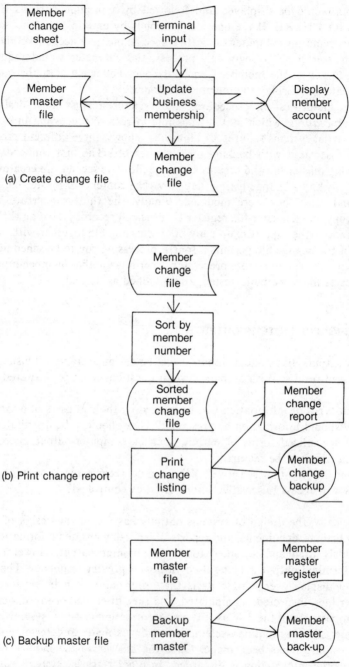

Figure 3-7 File-backup processing procedures

room rate) can be saved. Some reservation systems allow the terminal operator to command the computer to transmit information to a computer printer stationed nearby. The printer provides the customer with written confirmation of his or her reservation.

Classification of Output

In defining output requirements, computer-printed and computer-displayed reporting requirements must be kept separate. Three primary classifications for computer-printed information are detail listings, action documents, and summary reports.

Detail listings provide a complete, printed, historical record of all transactions that are generated by processing. A payroll register is one example of a detail listing. It shows all the detail used in preparing employee paychecks.

Action documents are formal business materials, such as paychecks, customer invoices, and packing slips, that require the persons receiving the information to do something—to take some action.

Summary reports show consolidated totals. These reports reduce the information contained in a detail report by highlighting important features, such as exceptions, or by showing portions of the transaction detail, such as subtotals and totals.

Figure 3-8 illustrates a "report-with-subtotals" summary report. For this report, transaction details are summarized by sets of activities and by different groups. The activities shown are those associated with the different departments (or groups) of a legal firm. Activity totals are added to show departmental or group totals. When the group totals are added, they equal the "company totals" printed at the bottom of the form. This particular report can be interpreted in several ways. For example, civil rather than criminal litigation accounts for the greater level of billable dollar totals.

Besides computer-printed output classifications, there are different classes of computer-displayed information. Two of these are fixed-form and free-form displays.

Fixed-form displays are permanent parts of a processing design. They are used when hard copy is not required and when managers prefer visual rather than printed results. Figure 3-9 illustrates three display pages to show how the computer-printed "summary report with subtotals" report would be displayed. The pages were prepared for a small video display screen of 16 lines and 64 characters per line. The first and second displays provide the user with two summary pages, showing month-to-date and year-to-date billable totals. The third display screen shows the first of six more detailed pages. These pages provide a more detailed breakdown of departmental billable totals. The user is able to move from one page to another by pressing the "return key" located alongside the terminal keyboard.

Run Date: XX/XX/XX   Billing Analysis

Group Business Analysis Summary

---------------- Activity ----------------		---- Month-To-Date ---		----- Year-To-Date ----	
No.	Description	Amt-Billed	%-Total	Amt-Billed	%-Total
10	Civil Litigation				
10-1	Matrimonial	$26,544	27%	$178,264	29%
10-2	Contracts	8,554	09	48,324	08
10-3	Bankruptcies	12,102	13	68,612	11
10-4	Arbitration	4,600	05	28,900	05
	Total Civil Litigation	$51,800	54%	$324,100	53%
20	Real Estate				
20-1	Commercial	$ 3,250	03%	$ 23,000	04%
20-2	Residential	1,230	01	7,440	01
	Total Real Estate	$ 4,480	04%	$ 30,440	05%
30	Criminal Litigation				
30-1	Felonies	$ 9,560	10%	$ 52,335	09%
30-2	Juvenile	3,210	03	24,635	04
30-3	Mental Commitment	530	01	2,260	00
	Total Criminal Litigation	$13,300	14%	$ 79,230	13%
40	Estates				
40-1	Estate Planning	$10,496	11%	$ 67,976	11%
40-2	Estate Administration	13,560	14	87,352	14
	Total Estates	$24,056	25%	$155,328	25%
50	Corporate				
50-1	Contracts	$ 895	01%	$ 6,872	01%
50-2	Bankruptcies	2,143	02	14,858	03
	Total Corporate	$ 3,038	03%	$ 21,730	04%
	Company Totals	$96,674	100%	$610,828	100%

Figure 3-8 Summary report with subtotals

Free-form displays are variable parts of a processing design. These ad hoc displays are designed by the user rather than by a systems designer. The user retrieves and manipulates information, visually reviewing the results on the screen. With a free-form display option, for example, the user might perform different types of billing analyses. Consider the following output instructions:

WOULD YOU LIKE TO PERFORM A BILLING ANALYSIS? (Y OR N) Y
WHAT TYPE OF BILLING ANALYSIS?

    A. BY DEPARTMENT
    B. BY ATTORNEY
    C. BY CLIENT
    D. EXIT

```
RUN DATE:  XX/XX/XX                    BILLING ANALYSIS

GROUP BUSINESS ANALYSIS SUMMARY
------------- ACTIVITY -------------    ----- MONTH-TO-DATE -----
 NO.           DESCRIPTION            AMT-BILLED    %-TOTAL

  10        CIVIL LITIGATION          $51,800        54%
  20        REAL ESTATE                 4,480        04
  30        CRIMINAL LITIGATION        13,300        14
  40        ESTATES                    24,056        25
  50        CORPORATE                   3,038        03

            COMPANY TOTALS            $96,674        100%

PRESS RETURN TO CONTINUE
```

(a) Summary display page 1

```
RUN DATE:  XX/XX/XX                    BILLING ANALYSIS

GROUP BUSINESS ANALYSIS SUMMARY
------------- ACTIVITY -------------    -------YEAR-TO-DATE-------
 NO.           DESCRIPTION            AMT-BILLED    %-TOTAL

  10        CIVIL LITIGATION          $324,100       53%
  20        REAL ESTATE                30,440        05
  30        CRIMINAL LITIGATION        79,230        13
  40        ESTATES                   155,328        25
  50        CORPORATE                  21,730        04

            COMPANY TOTALS           $610,828        100%

PRESS RETURN TO CONTINUE
```

(b) Summary display page 2

```
RUN DATE:  XX/XX/XX                    BILLING ANALYSIS

ITEM BUSINESS ANALYSIS SUMMARY
----------------- ACTIVITY -----------------    ----- MONTH-TO-DATE -----
 NO.           DESCRIPTION            AMT-BILLED    %-TOTAL

  10        CIVIL LITIGATION

  10-1      MATRIMONIAL               $26,544        27%
  10-2      CONTRACTS                   8,554        09
  10-3      BANKRUPTCIES               12,102        13
  10-4      ARBITRATION                 4,600        05

            TOTAL CIVIL LITIGATION    $51,800        54%

PRESS RETURN TO CONTINUE
```

(c) Detail display page 1

Figure 3-9 Summary report display pages

```
ENTER SELECTION HERE:   A

WHICH ACTIVITIES ARE TO BE DISPLAYED?

     A.  GROUP HEADINGS ONLY
     B.  ALL ACTIVITIES
     C.  SELECTED ACTIVITIES
     D.  EXIT

ENTER SELECTION HERE:   C

WHAT TYPE OF OUTPUT IS DESIRED?

     A.  TABULAR
     B.  GRAPHIC
     C.  EXIT

ENTER SELECTION HERE:   B
```

As this interactive dialogue suggests, each user response tells the computer what to do next. When the user enters a "C" for SELECTED ACTIVITIES, the computer brings into processing a list of activities and requests the end user to make his or her selections from the list. Likewise, when selection B, GRAPHIC, is indicated, the computer would display the existing types of graphic manipulation. The user might be required to specify whether a pie chart, a bar chart, or a distribution curve is desired. Following this, the computer would require the user to set output specifications.

Output Procedures

Like data-entry procedures, systems outputs are designed by using special layout sheets. For computer-printed output, *printer-spacing charts* illustrate the layout of a printed listing, document, or report. The chart indicates the print positions for each item to be printed and the various document headings. It also shows how a carriage-control paper tape should be designed when printing continous forms. This information is placed on the carriage-control section of the printer-spacing chart.

Most computer-printed output can be produced directly from a transaction or summary file, provided that the sequence of the file is suitable. When this is not the case, however, the file must be sorted to sequence the records in a desired order. This sorted file is often called a *print file*—it is used to print a desired report; it is organized in the same sequence as the sequence shown on the report.

Because a print-processing run can require several hours to complete, print procedures must feature provisions to guard against delays and *reruns* (the rerunning of an entire processing run). One such provision is the ability to *restart* printing from the point at which an error occurred, instead of beginning the processing run again. This provision saves several hours of computer time and helps to minimize the investment in computer printing. Besides restart, another provision is to establish *checkpoints* in processing. Checkpoints are points at which printed subtotals are to be reviewed to determine if they are normal. If the review is acceptable, processing is continued.

In designing video display output, systems designers also use layout forms and employ restart provisions. Video-display-output layout sheets are the same as video-display-input layout sheets (see Figure 3-4). They show the amount of information that can be displayed. Restart provisions are generally built into each set of output processing instructions. Or, they may consist of one or more special processing commands. For example, each set of processing instructions generally contains either the commands EXIT or RETURN TO MAIN MENU. Either choice restarts processing. Likewise, most output procedures provide for some emergency command sequence. The pressing of the control key, CTRL, and uppercase "C" simultaneously, for example, is a common "panic command." This command terminates processing and leads the terminal operator back to a beginning point.

Besides restart and emergency procedures, output procedures are designed to limit access to processing. These restrictions are accomplished with user account codes and passwords. To receive output, the user is required to log on, following a step-wise procedure. First, he or she is required to key in an *account code*—a numeric code that has been previously assigned. This code is checked against a master-account-code file to verify that the user's code is legitimate. Second, the user is required to key in a *password*—an alphanumeric or alphabetic code. This second code is checked against a password master file. If the password does not agree with the password on file and assigned to the account code, the user is prohibited from gaining access to the computer.

3-4 DESIGNING COMPUTER PROGRAMS

Prior to the design of the processing runs for an online business computer application, the systems analyst must identify the types of computer programs that are required by the interactive and by the batch portions of processing, and the functional parts or *modules* of each computer program. As stated in Chapter 2, seven types of computer programs are placed in various combinations in the construction of a business computer application. Three of these seven are used primarily for interactive processing; four of the seven are used for batch processing. Edit and update programs, for example, are typically designed for the interactive portion of processing; display programs are used exclusively in interactive processing. Register, action-document, summary, and change-report programs represent different types of computer-print programs that are used in the batch portion of processing.

Systems Organization Chart

A systems organization chart shows the types of computer programs written for a business computer application, the function of each in relation to processing, and whether a program is to be written for the interactive or the batch portion of processing. As Figure 3-10 shows, a systems organization chart consists of three levels. Level 0 indicates whether processing is interactive or batch. Level 1 shows different processing functions, such as "build transaction file," "update master file," or "display accounts," for the interactive portion of processing, and "print file registers," "print action documents," "print summary reports," or "print change reports," for the batch portion of processing. Level 2 provides the names of the computer programs designed for the application. The interactive portion consists of four programs, beginning with "edit/update billing transactions"; the batch portion consists of five programs, beginning with "print billing register."

Program-Processing Menu

The design of the program-processing menu is based on the completed systems organization chart. It shows how a specific computer program is selected and executed. Using the chart in Figure 3-10, a systems designer would prepare the following menu:

```
    I.1   EDIT/UPDATE BILLING TRANSACTIONS
    I.2   UPDATE MEMBER MASTER
    I.3   DISPLAY MEMBER ACCOUNTS
    I.4   DISPLAY CONTROL ACCOUNTS

    B.1   PRINT BILLING REGISTER
    B.2   PRINT MEMBER MASTER REGISTER
    B.3   PRINT MEMBER STATEMENTS
    B.4   PRINT MEMBER RECEIVABLES SUMMARY
    B.5   PRINT MEMBER CHANGE REPORT
    (6)   EXIT

    ENTER SELECTION HERE.
```

Processing menus such as this will be used throughout the following chapters. The "I" and "B" notations indicate interactive and batch processing, respectively. They help make clear which parts of a business computer application are processed transaction by transaction and which parts require transactions to be grouped prior to processing.

Program Structure Charts

The final component of program design is the creation of program structure charts. These charts show the modules to be designed, coded, and documented for each computer program. Figure 3-11 illustrates a simplified program struc-

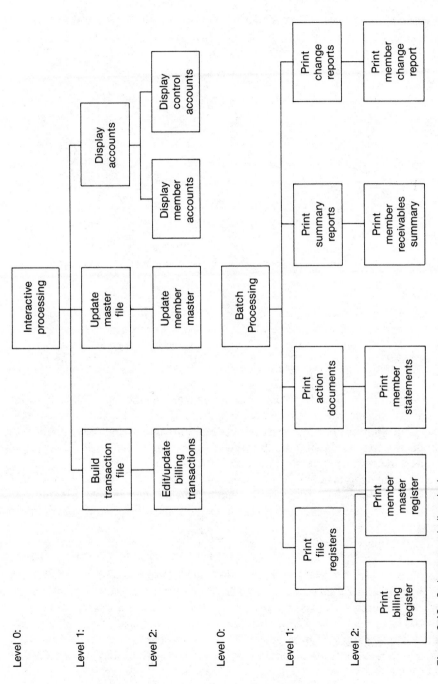

Figure 3-10 Systems organization chart

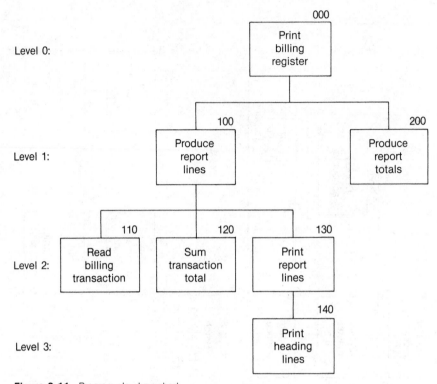

Figure 3-11 Program structure chart

ture chart for Program B.1, "print billing register." At the top level, level 0, one module represents the entire computer program. Level 1, the next level, divides the print program into two parts, one to produce report lines and another to produce report totals after the printing of all report lines. Level 2 breaks the produce-report-lines module into three finer modules: "read billing transaction," "sum transaction total for calculating cumulative billing totals," and "print report lines." Finally, level 3 contains only a single module. Module 140, "print heading lines," shows that report headings must be printed in addition to report lines.

A structure chart, such as the one in Figure 3-11, is called a *visual table of contents* (VTOC). It is sometimes also called a *hierarchy chart*. Regardless of how it is named, its development, together with a systems organization chart, is advised when designing an online business computer application. Such an approach features a two-stage *top-down design*. The system organization chart divides a computer application into processing functions, which in turn are divided into computer programs. The program structure chart divides each computer program into major functional modules, which in turn are divided into subordinate modules.

3-5 DESIGNING PROCESSING CONTROLS

A difficult, yet most important phase of systems design is the preparation of processing control requirements. Adequate controls must be established for a variety of reasons:

- To verify that all data have been processed
- To block or trap faulty data from entry into processing
- To be able to reconstruct information if computer files are destroyed
- To prohibit tampering with information by unauthorized individuals
- To prevent employee fraud, embezzlement, and theft

With online systems, the need for controls in processing is especially critical. Since data input, processing, and output are oftentimes directed by individuals at remote locations, control techniques must ensure that all records (and only the intended records) are processed and that only authorized people are able to gain access to processing.

In designing a set of processing controls, a systems designer must include provisions for four types: source-document controls, input (transmission) controls, programmed controls, and output controls. In addition, online systems require both group and transaction control procedures. *Group control procedures* verify that counts and amounts in a batch of records are in balance. *Transaction control procedures* verify that each transaction is accurate and complete. Where possible, these controls also test to ensure that counts and amounts internal to the transaction are in balance.

Source-Document Controls

Source-document controls typically involve the matching of counts and amounts recorded on source documents to counts and amounts entered into processing. If a match cannot be made, it is possible to trace the error back to the original document. Both group and transaction control procedures help verify that counts and amounts are correct. An example helps to clarify the differences between the two. Assume that the five invoice totals shown in Figure 3-12 are to be entered into processing. Next assume that prior to entering these invoice totals, the *batch-balance total* (the group total) is entered. By keying in the batch balance first, the computer is able to sum the individual invoice amounts and to compare this summed total to the batch-balance total. In effect, the computer is able to "balance back" to the batch-balance total.

Batch balances work well with groups of transactions, but what happens when only a single transaction is entered into processing? Another illustration helps to answer this question. Assume that the five invoice totals in Figure 3-12 are replaced by the quantity ordered by a customer for five line items on a single invoice and that the batch balance is replaced by the total quantity

```
                        INVOICE TOTALS

              INVOICE                 INVOICE
              NUMBER                  AMOUNT

                 1                   $500.62
                 2                    630.00
                 3                     50.00 CR
                 4                    420.00
                 5                     60.53


                   BATCH BALANCE TOTALS

              TOTAL                   TOTAL
              BATCH                   BATCH
              COUNT                   AMOUNT

                 5                  $1,561.15
```

Figure 3-12   Batch balance control

ordered, a *transaction-balance total* (see Figure 3-13). In this instance, the terminal operator would key in the total quantity ordered, followed by the quantity ordered for each line item. Unless the computer is able to balance back to the total quantity ordered, the line-item totals will be in error.

Input Controls

Input controls include procedures to ensure that data transmission is accurate and complete. Most input controls are built into the computer system, as integral parts of computer terminals and of data communications software. Pressing the terminal key marked RETURN, for example, tells the computer that a message has ended.

Additional input controls are usually designed for such purposes as protecting against unauthorized access to the computer. As was discussed earlier, user account codes and passwords are common methods of attempting to stop unauthorized access to processing. Unless both the account code and the password agree with an on-file code and password, access to processing is prohibited.

Checking data transmission is another form of input control. Online computer systems keep a journal tape (or disk) of all transactions entered into processing from remote locations. Should problems in processing or transmission be detected, this procedure—known as *journaling*—permits recovery of transmission, from the file copy. Online cash registers similarly feature small cassette tapes to record daily sales transactions. After the cash register has been closed for the day, the tape is sent to the company's internal audit group, where it is used to isolate the reasons for any differences that appear in the daily cash audit.

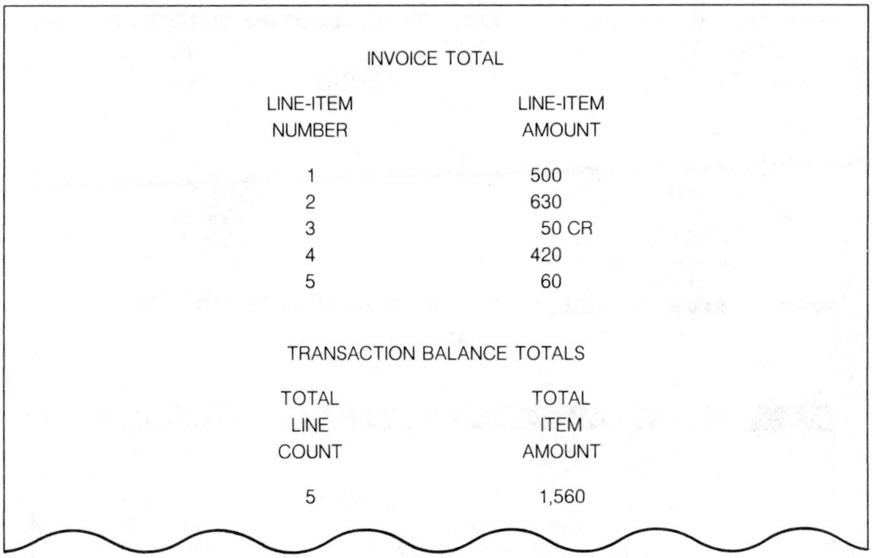

```
                        INVOICE TOTAL

          LINE-ITEM                    LINE-ITEM
          NUMBER                       AMOUNT

              1                           500
              2                           630
              3                            50 CR
              4                           420
              5                            60


                TRANSACTION BALANCE TOTALS

          TOTAL                         TOTAL
          LINE                          ITEM
          COUNT                         AMOUNT

              5                         1,560
```

Figure 3-13 Transaction balance control

Programmed Controls

Programmed controls are procedures written into computer programs. Some programmed controls block or trap data-in-error from entering processing. These controls are generally written into edit and update programs, where tests such as mixed-mode tests, limit tests, and check-digit tests are conducted on data transmitted as input. For example, a mixed-mode test might check for alphabetic characters in a numeric field. Likewise, a range test might compare the value of a field to determine if it falls below a predetermined minimum level. Finally, a check-digit test might verify that the digits of a customer number have been entered into processing correctly. Other programmed controls verify that control totals balance. Batch- and transaction-balance tests are among these types of controls. Finally, programmed controls maintain file-balance procedures that store beginning and ending balances of record counts and amounts. As such, they enable the parties responsible for controlling a business computer application to keep track of all additions, deletions, and adjustments to business records.

Output Controls

Output controls are designed to prevent unauthorized access to computer output. They also ensure that output transmission is accurate and complete. Once again, typical output control techniques employ user account codes and passwords. A special type of output control uses printed registers and voided action documents. An example helps to clarify the importance of these printed materials.

Figure 3-14 Safety II check

Consider for the moment that you are designing a computer system to process personal checks. After all outstanding bills are entered, your design permits you to decide which bills to pay. Before writing checks for these bills, however, you find it necessary to produce a check register. The register shows the beginning check balance, the name of the person or company and the check amount for each check to be written, and the ending check balance. Following the printing of the register, you will review it.

After review, you print the checks. The first step in printing produces a voided check showing your beginning check balance. The word *void* would be clearly printed across the face of the check. Then personal checks are printed. After the last check is printed a second voided check is produced. This check shows the ending check balance, the number of checks written, and the total dollar amount for which checks were written. These totals, together with the beginning check balance, are compared with the check register. Before any personal checks are endorsed and mailed, the counts and financial amounts must be in balance.

Finally, still another type of output control involves the use of output materials that contain special properties. For example, Figure 3-14 shows a check that cannot be safely photocopied. If a person does attempt to take a picture of

THE FACE OF THIS DOCUMENT HAS A COLORED BACKGROUND – NOT A WHITE BACKGROUND

JOYNER MANUFACTURING CO.   No. 083520
123 MAIN STREET
ANYWHERE, U.S.A. 12345

PAY EXACTLY 738 60 CTS

| PAY TO THE ORDER OF | DATE | DISCOUNT | $ 738.60 | AMOUNT |

Quantity Purchasing Co.
5748 East Street
Somewhere, U.S.A. 54321

NOT VALID

THE BACK OF THIS DOCUMENT CONTAINS AN ARTIFICIAL WATERMARK – HOLD AT AN ANGLE TO VIEW

⑈083520⑈ ⑆123456780⑆ 52⑈347⑈64⑈

FIRST NATIONAL BANK • ANYWHERE, U.S.A.

PLEASE DETACH BEFORE DEPOSITING

083520

MEMO	INVOICE DATE	INV. NO.	REFERENCE	INV. AMT.	DEDUCTIONS	BALANCE
	9/10/82	65218	N14 bolts	$738.60		

JOYNER MANUFACTURING CO.
123 MAIN STREET
ANYWHERE, U.S.A. 12345

Figure 3-15 Photocopy of Safety II check

the check, the word COPY becomes visible (see Figure 3-15). Special output materials such as these discourage attempts by employees to embezzle funds from a company.

REVIEW OF IMPORTANT IDEAS

Several tasks are undertaken by a systems designer in preparing written specifications for an online business computer application. Designing systems input, for instance, requires that the designer first determine which data elements are required in processing. Following this, the designer must decide which data must be keyed into processing, which data are to be stored on computer files, and which data are to be computed. An important objective in designing input procedures is to minimize the number of keystrokes. This is done by designing data-entry video display screens with operator efficiency in mind and by using special data-input instruments, such as light pens and hand-held optical scanners.

Designing computer files is based on the knowledge of what data are to be stored. In design, several rules and guidelines should be followed. The designer should not attempt to place in a computer file data that cannot be easily revised, justified, or reviewed. The designer must use care in record layout. He or she must determine how each file is to be organized and develop efficient file-processing menus and file-backup procedures.

Designing systems output requires that the designer deal with computer-printed and computer-displayed materials. Computer-printed information includes detail listings, action documents, and summary reports. These are developed using printer-spacing charts. Computer-displayed information includes fixed- and free-form displays. These designs are placed on video-display layout sheets.

Designing computer programs requires that the designer specify the interactive and batch features of the design. Following this, the systems organization chart is developed to show the types of computer programs to be written and their functions relative to the overall design. Another requirement of the designer is to show the computer program modules to be designed, coded, and documented. Program structure charts illustrate the hierarchy of program modules within a computer program.

Designing processing controls requires an appreciation of what numeric checks are needed to verify the accuracy of processed data and to prevent unauthorized use of computer systems. Source-document and programmed procedures are most effective in determining whether processed data are accurate and complete. Input and output control procedures are used extensively to prevent unauthorized use of computer systems.

KEY WORDS

Systems design
Systems designer
Input-analysis form
Program-processing menu
Command
Video display page
Account code
Record code
Sort key
Header section
Trailing section
Change or addition record
Direct file organization
Sequential file organization
Indexed-sequential file organization

File-processing menu
File-backup procedures
Fixed-form display
Free-form display
Printer spacing chart
Print file
Restart
Account number
Password
Systems organization chart
Visual table of contents (VTOC)
Top-down design
Batch-balance total
Journaling

REVIEW QUESTIONS

1. What is systems design?

2. Name the five areas of systems design.

3. How does an input-analysis form differ from a record-analysis form?

4. Explain why the following statement is true: An important objective of systems design is to reduce the number of keystrokes.

5. Video displays often consist of several pages. Why?

6. What three commonsense rules should be followed in the design of computer files?

7. What is the difference between direct-access and sequential file organization?

8. How does a program-processing menu differ from a file-processing menu?

9. Why are file-backup procedures needed?

10. Name the three classes of computer-printed output.

11. What is the difference between a fixed-form and a free-form video display?

12. With online systems, output procedures are designed to control access to the computer. Explain how this is done.

13. What information is placed on a systems organization chart?

14. What is a VTOC and how is it used?

15. Why must different types of processing controls be designed?

16. Name the four types of processing controls.

17. Why is journaling important?

EXERCISES

1. For each of the following, indicate what systems design feature is overlooked.

    (a) A business discovers that a change can be made to a customer's billing account online, but once added, it cannot be corrected or adjusted. This situation has contributed to large suspense files. For example, if an incorrect charge is added to a customer's account, the account must be transferred from a customer master file to a suspended records file. To correct this problem, a batch processing run is required. This run restores the account to its original amount.

    (b)   Cash receipts transmitted from a remote processing station to a central office look suspicious. Normally, cash sales should be higher than the totals indicated. Unfortunately, there is no way to determine if someone is stealing from the company.

    (c)   The instructions for a video-display program-processing menu have tended to cause problems. If the terminal operator makes an incorrect selection, several additional pages must be reviewed before the computer program finally returns to the menu a second time.

2.   Suppose a systems designer agrees in principle with the need for comprehensive systems documentation—covering all areas of systems design—but admits: "Actually, we document very little. We just don't have the time." Explain why this situation is tolerated? Give several reasons.

3.   Systems designs are often criticized because too much emphasis is given to technical factors and too little emphasis is given to human factors. What is your reaction to this criticism? How might designers give more emphasis to human factors?

PART

RECEIVABLES APPLICATIONS

Most business firms carry their customers "on account." When a sale is made, credit is extended to a customer, and the dollar amount of the credit is added to the customer's account. This practice of extending credit requires careful management. A business cannot permit its outstanding receivables (customer account balances) to reach levels that place the firm in a "cash poor" position. Instead, a business must constantly work to reduce its receivables to a level consistent with the terms and conditions specified by its credit arrangements.

In Part II, the first of four sets of three computer applications, we will examine the processing of accounts receivable information and will see demonstrated the advantages of online processing. Perhaps the greatest value of online designs is that they shorten the time required to bill customers and to match customer payments and outstanding account balances. Moreover, these applications improve the accuracy of receivables processing, standardize the processing of account collections, reduce clerical and administrative costs, and permit transactions to be processed where they occur, at the time of sale.

Customer Invoicing

An *invoice* is a billing statement. It is used to inform customers of the charges for goods and services supplied to them, and to specify when payment is due. Whenever a business extends credit to a customer, an invoice must be prepared. The invoice documents the date of the sale, the name and address of the customer, the charges for the merchandise, and the terms and condition of payment. If these charges are not paid within the period specified by the invoice, a second billing statement, the *monthly statement,* is prepared. This second statement reminds a customer that an invoice is outstanding. Whereas an invoice provides a complete description of the charges of each item shipped to a customer, a monthly statement provides only a summary of outstanding invoice charges.

An invoice is not required when a company receives cash for merchandise at the time of the sale, or when it accepts a bank or company credit card instead of cash payment. When cash is received, a sales receipt is usually prepared. Handing the receipt to the customer completes a cash sales transaction. When a credit card is accepted, a *sales draft* (a draw on an established line of personal credit) is prepared. In this instance, the customer is not expected to make payment on the sales draft. Instead, he or she is to wait until a monthly statement is sent. Credit card monthly statements do list in summary form all outstanding charges. These cards are used almost exclusively in retailing, however; they are not common to wholesaling or to manufacturing. There invoices are used. This distinction should help to clarify why customer invoicing is so important to many large business firms.

This first application chapter describes the features of an online customer-invoice application that has been developed for a wholesaler, or business that sells merchandise to a large number of retail establishments. (An online sales-draft computer application is discussed in the next chapter.) Businesses develop customer-invoice applications for a variety of reasons other than to produce a printed record of processing and formal invoice documents. This application can shorten the time between the shipment of goods to customers and the mailing of invoices, reduce the costs of customer billing, cut the number of billing errors, improve processing controls, determine sales patterns, and create files for determining which customers and products are the most profitable to a business.

An online design also permits checks and balances to be built into the interactive parts of processing. Besides reducing the number of billing errors, these checks and balances block input data-in-error from entering processing. Finally, an online design typically avoids the problems of transporting billing information to and from a company data center. With distributed processing, for example, data are keyed, inspected, and corrected directly from customer order-processing and billing centers.

4-1 PRELIMINARY OVERVIEW OF PROCESSING

Understanding the main flow of processing is critical in the study of an online customer-invoice business computer application. As Figure 4-1 shows, the main flow consists of six steps:

1. *Ready customer file* to ensure that all customer accounts stored in the customer master file are correct.

2. *Ready product file* to ensure that all product accounts stored in the product master file are correct.

3. *Enter invoice transactions* to record what items are shipped to a customer (or were returned by the customer) and to calculate customer charges (or credits).

4. *Print daily register* to document the contents of the invoice transaction file.

5. *Prepare customer statements* to produce customer invoices (or credit memos).

6. *Prepare summary reports* to provide a summary of charges (or credits) that are to be added to the invoice accounts receivable (A/R) summary file.

Inputs to Processing

The main inputs to the customer-invoicing computer application are shipping documents and customer return slips. *Shipping documents* consist of either a packing slip and a bill of lading or a document that combines these two forms. A *packing slip* shows which items were packed for shipment, as well as business and customer order information. Five main types of information are provided by the packing slip:

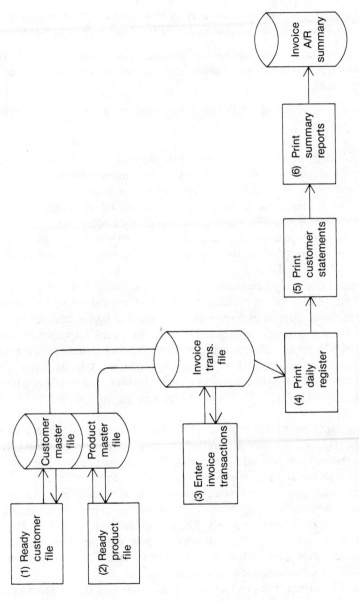

Figure 4-1 Six steps in preparing customer invoices

- *Business order information* documents the business order number (the number assigned by the business to a customer order).

- *Customer order information* indentifies the customer number, customer purchase order (P.O.) number, and date of the purchase order.

- *Packing information* identifies each product number, the quantity ordered, shipped, back-ordered, or canceled, and the date of the shipment.

- *Customer information* shows the customer name and address, customer credit terms, and the salesperson and distributor assigned to a customer's account.

- *Product information* identifies each product by name and describes each product.

A *bill of lading* shows how the goods were shipped and the charges for shipment and insurance. This document may also summarize the contents of shipment by indicating the number of boxes, parcels, or bags.

Figure 4-2 illustrates a combined packing slip and bill of lading. The original copy of this form is sent with the shipping papers that accompany the shipment; a second copy is packed with the shipment. The company also retains a copy to serve as a main source of input to customer-invoice processing and as a record of goods packed and shipped.

Customer return slips resemble packing slips, except that they record the return of merchandise from customers or show differences between the quantity reported as being shipped and the quantity indicated by the customer as being received. Customer return slips generally provide coded responses to describe the reasons why merchandise is being returned. These reasons are often limited to a fixed set of responses, such as wrong color, incorrect size, defective item, or incorrect count. If a business plans to conduct further studies of the causes for customer returns, this is the point in processing to capture the relevant information.

Another input to invoice processing consists of information stored on computer files. This information is required in calculating invoice charges. It also simplifies the entry of data into processing. The *customer master file,* for example, contains information on every customer that conducts business with a company. In processing customer invoices, the file is used to transfer into processing information such as customer name and address, customer credit terms, and salesperson and distributor numbers. The automated transfer follows the input of the *primary record key:* the customer account number. The advantage of such a transfer should be evident: it is easier to transfer information from a file than to key the information into processing.

A second input file, the *product master file,* contains information on every product sold by a business. This file transfers into processing information such as product name, description, and product price and discount information. The automated transfer follows the entry of a second record key: the product number.

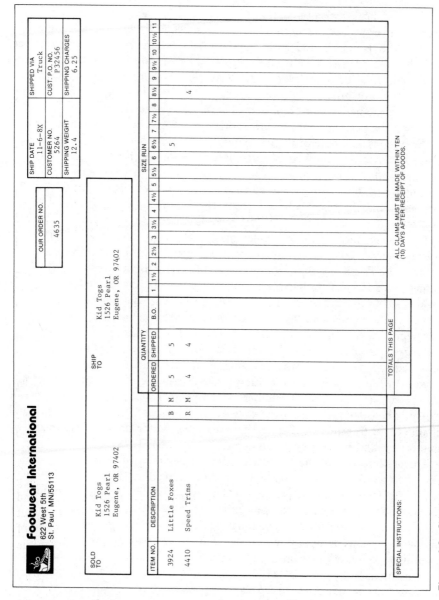

Figure 4-2 Shipping document

Before beginning to develop the computer programs required by a computer application, the systems designer must carefully define the types of data to be keyed into processing, the types of data to be transferred into processing from computer files, and the types of data to be computed. Figure 4-3 illustrates the relationships between data sets that are important to customer invoicing. Keyed information begins with the entry of "business order information": the business order number and the record code. The *business order number* is assigned by the business, is unique, and documents the fact that an order has been received and filled. The record code is vital to processing. It indicates whether a charge or a credit is to be processed. Next, customer order information and packing information are brought into processing. Customer order information begins with the customer account number, which is the key to the customer's records stored on the customer master file. Other customer order information consists of the number and date of the customer's purchase order. Packing information consists of one or more sets of information, as determined by the number of products ordered. Data elements to be keyed include the product number, the breakdown of the quantity ordered versus the quantity shipped, the date of the shipment, and the cost of the shipment. Similar to the customer number, the product number is the key to product records stored on the product master file.

The organization of the customer master file begins with the customer account number, followed by three record segments. The first, the customer name-and-address segment, contains identifiers for both sold-to and ship-to names and addresses. In business, goods are often shipped to one location; bills are mailed to another location. The second segment contains customer credit terms: credit limit code, last revision of the customer's credit, and terms of payment. Under terms of payment, one subcode separates retail accounts from commercial accounts. Typically, retail accounts are expected to make payment on receipt of the invoice, whereas commercial accounts are expected to make payment within 30 days. Last, a salesperson/distributor record segment permits salesperson and distributor numbers to be printed on an invoice or a credit memo. These numbers are *secondary keys*. They permit invoice charges and credits to be transferred to sales summary files, where data are organized by salesperson and by distributor numbers.

The organization of the product master file begins with the product number and two record segments. The first—product name and description—identifies the product by name and provides a description of the product. The unit of measure (dozen, pound), and the size run (size S, M, L; 34, 36, 38, etc.) are generally needed to fully describe the product. The second segment, pricing and discount, contains product price, cost, and quantity-discount information. If the quantity discount is based on a percentage of the unit price, the breakpoint and the percentage are stored in the file. For example, the notation 3% 1000 would indicate that the unit price is reduced by 3 percent for orders equal to or greater than a thousand units. If the quantity discount is not based on a straight percentage of the unit price, the volume levels at which price breaks are to take place and the product prices at these levels must be stored on file.

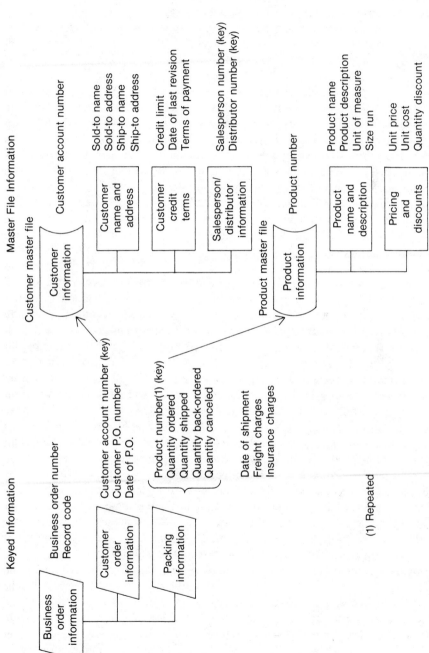

Figure 4-3 Relationships between invoice data sets

Storing retrievable information in the customer and product master files reduces data-entry activity considerably. For all new customer and product accounts, however, the complete record must be keyed to processing prior to the entry of invoice details. Special input forms are thus required for adding new accounts to master files.

Outputs from Processing

Three types of output follow from processing: transaction documents (customer invoices and credit memos), processing summaries, and an invoice accounts receivable (A/R) summary file. Figure 4-4 illustrates a typical customer invoice. It contains information previously recorded on shipping papers and shows how line-item invoice charges are calculated. A number of business firms use the invoice to show differences between the quantity ordered by the customer and the quantity that was actually shipped. This difference is explained by the terms "back order" and "cancel." *Back order* (B.O.) means that another shipment will follow, once sufficient stock is available. *Cancel* means that a second shipment will not follow; if additional merchandise is required, the customer is expected to reorder.

Any discounts or penalty charges included in the *terms of sale* are printed on the invoice. If a *cash discount* is permitted, the invoice will provide terms such as "2% 10, net 30," or "3% 20, net 31." The percentage indicates the amount discounted if the invoice is paid within the first time period specified (i.e., 10 or 20 days). If payment is not received during this time, full payment is due by the end of the second time period specified (30 or 31 days). The invoice may also specify a *service charge*—a cash penalty to be added to all past-due accounts. Most business firms provide a grace period of 60 days or more before adding a service charge amount to a customer's account. Practices vary, however; some companies add a charge whenever an invoice is past due by more than 30 days.

Like many other business documents, the invoice is a two-part form. The upper portion serves as the *customer copy:* it documents the charges and is retained by the customer. The lower portion is the *customer remittance slip.* The customer is requested to detach and return it together with his or her cash payment. Another design alternative is to send the customer two copies of the invoice. The first copy is kept by the customer for his or her records; the second is the return copy (the remittance slip). Duplicate forms have become more common with the introduction of carbonless business forms.

Figure 4-5 illustrates a *customer credit memo.* This document informs the customer that a credit has been applied to offset outstanding invoices charges. It is similar in design to the customer invoice with the following exceptions: the credit memo number and date are printed, and neither shipping information nor terms of sale are printed, since this information is not pertinent.

There are several reasons for crediting a customer's account. If an error is made in a customer's bill, for example, it is often necessary to issue a business credit. Or, if the customer finds shipped merchandise to be unacceptable and

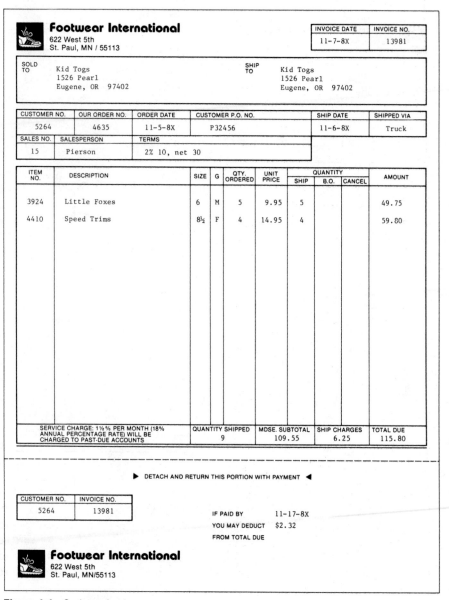

Footwear International
622 West 5th
St. Paul, MN / 55113

INVOICE DATE	INVOICE NO.
11-7-8X	13981

SOLD TO
Kid Togs
1526 Pearl
Eugene, OR 97402

SHIP TO
Kid Togs
1526 Pearl
Eugene, OR 97402

CUSTOMER NO.	OUR ORDER NO.	ORDER DATE	CUSTOMER P.O. NO.	SHIP DATE	SHIPPED VIA
5264	4635	11-5-8X	P32456	11-6-8X	Truck

SALES NO.	SALESPERSON	TERMS
15	Pierson	2% 10, net 30

ITEM NO.	DESCRIPTION	SIZE	G	QTY. ORDERED	UNIT PRICE	QUANTITY SHIP	QUANTITY B.O.	QUANTITY CANCEL	AMOUNT
3924	Little Foxes	6	M	5	9.95	5			49.75
4410	Speed Trims	8½	F	4	14.95	4			59.80

SERVICE CHARGE: 1½% PER MONTH (18% ANNUAL PERCENTAGE RATE) WILL BE CHARGED TO PAST-DUE ACCOUNTS

QUANTITY SHIPPED	MDSE. SUBTOTAL	SHIP CHARGES	TOTAL DUE
9	109.55	6.25	115.80

▶ DETACH AND RETURN THIS PORTION WITH PAYMENT ◀

CUSTOMER NO.	INVOICE NO.
5264	13981

IF PAID BY   11-17-8X
YOU MAY DEDUCT $2.32
FROM TOTAL DUE

Footwear International
622 West 5th
St. Paul, MN/55113

Figure 4-4 Customer invoice

returns it, a customer credit will be requested. Finally, when a "request for credit slip" is enclosed with merchandise being returned, the number of the request is generally entered into processing. This number serves the same purpose as the customer purchase order number: it permits a customer to locate a document, should the details appearing on it be questioned.

Footwear International
622 West 5th
St. Paul, MN / 55113

CREDIT DATE	CREDIT NO.
11-25-8X	6714

SOLD TO		SHIP TO	Kid Togs 1526 Pearl Eugene, OR 97402

CUSTOMER NO.	OUR ORDER NO.	CUSTOMER C/R NO.		INVOICE DATE	INVOICE NO.
5264	4635	CR1526		11-7-8X	13981

SALES NO.	SALESPERSON	CUST. DEBIT MEMO NO.	
15	Pierson	4635CR	

ITEM NO.	DESCRIPTION	SIZE	G	QTY. CREDITED	UNIT PRICE	AMOUNT
3924	Little Foxes	6	M	2	9.95	19.90

	QUANTITY CREDITED	TOTAL CREDIT
	2	19.90

CREDIT MEMO

Figure 4-5   Customer credit memo

Outputs other than customer invoices and credit memos can include a variety of processing lists and summaries. One of these, an *invoice register,* lists all invoice and credit transactions. Another output, an *invoice A/R summary,* is a condensed version of the invoice register. It shows the invoice charges to be added or the customer credits to be subtracted from a customer's account during A/R processing. Still other possible listings and summaries include a report of back orders or of canceled orders, or a summary of invoices and credits processed by a particular computer terminal workstation.

The final type of output, the *invoice A/R summary file,* contains the condensed version of the records created during processing and stored on the invoice transaction file. This file is retained for accounts receivable processing. Its contents are usually printed on the invoice A/R summary.

4-2 INVOICE PROCESSING

Figure 4-6 illustrates the systems organization of the customer-invoice computer application. As the chart shows, the interactive portion of the application consists of three processing functions that comprise five computer programs. The first function, "build transaction file," enters invoice and credit details into processing. As the title indicates, this file is built transaction by transaction. The second function, "update master files," adds, deletes, and revises records stored on the customer and product master files. In this instance, data can be read to, revised, or deleted from computer files. The third function, "display accounts," completes the interactive part of processing; it permits individuals to retrieve (but not update) records stored on the customer and product master files.

The batch portion of the customer-invoice application is made up of four processing functions and eight computer programs. All batch programs print processed results. The function "print file registers," for example, consists of the three print programs needed to show the contents of the invoice transaction file, the customer master file, and the product master file. The remaining functions, "print transaction documents," "print processing summaries," and "print file change reports," lead to the printing of customer invoices and credit memos, two processing summaries, and two file-change reports. Because two master files are required by this application, two file-change reports must be prepared: one shows additions, deletions, or revisions to customer master records; the other to product master records.

The systems organization chart in Figure 4-6 represents a minimal processing design. The batch function entitled "print processing summaries" could be expanded, for example, to produce a list of canceled orders or a report showing daily sales by distributor. In this particular function, the summaries needed vary considerably, depending on the need for information specific to the managers of a certain business.

The invoice-processing program menu follows from the systems organization chart. Figure 4-7 shows that the menu is limited to the five interactive computer programs and eight batch computer programs. The computer terminal operator activates processing by selecting one of these programs. As you will see, however, the selection of programs is not random. Initially, interactive programs are used to ready master files. After this is done, Program I.1, "enter invoice transactions," is selected to key invoice details into processing.

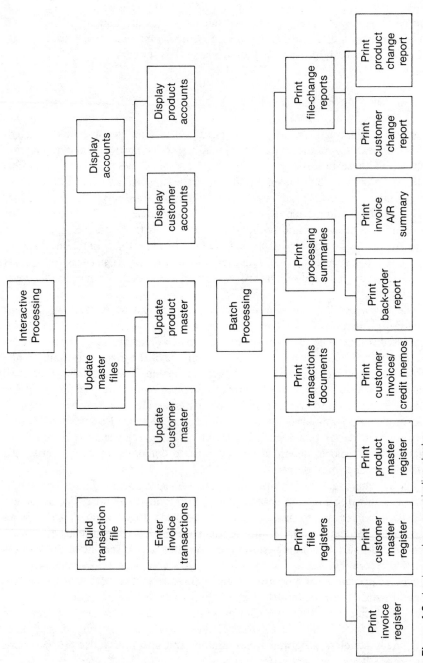

Figure 4-6 Invoice systems organization chart

```
I.1   ENTER (EDIT/UPDATE) INVOICE TRANSACTIONS
I.2   UPDATE CUSTOMER MASTER
I.3   UPDATE PRODUCT MASTER
I.4   DISPLAY CUSTOMER ACCOUNTS
I.5   DISPLAY PRODUCT ACCOUNTS

B.1   PRINT INVOICE REGISTER
B.2   PRINT CUSTOMER MASTER REGISTER
B.3   PRINT PRODUCT MASTER REGISTER
B.4   PRINT CUSTOMER INVOICES
B.5   PRINT BACK-ORDER REPORT
B.6   PRINT INVOICE A/R SUMMARY
B.7   PRINT CUSTOMER CHANGE REPORT
B.8   PRINT PRODUCT CHANGE REPORT
(9)   EXIT
```

Figure 4-7   Invoice-processing program menu

The Enter Invoice Transactions Program

The flowchart in Figure 4-8 shows the main steps associated with the daily processing of invoice charges and credit transactions. Inputs to processing are shipping documents and customer return slips. Once activated, the program performs a variety of processing functions: it edits keyed data, it transfers data from the customer and product master files, it calculates line-item invoice charges and the total invoice charge, and it adds the completed transaction to the invoice transaction file.

Program processing is designed around an input display, such as the split-screen display shown in Figure 4-9. This display design permits business order data and customer order data to be keyed to the top half of the screen and computer messages to be shown on the lower half. With a split-screen format, conversation between the user and the computer works as follows. After the customer account number is keyed and transmitted, the computer retrieves the name-and-address segment of the customer master record and displays it on the lower half of the screen. The computer then asks:

IS THIS INFORMATION CORRECT?

If the answer is yes, the customer's name and address are added to the transaction record.

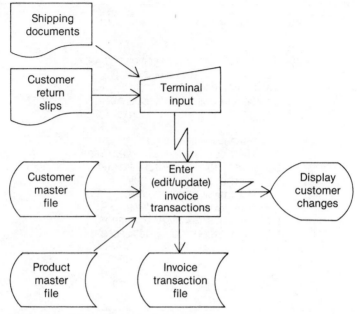

Figure 4-8 Building the invoice transaction file

After business order and customer order information have been successfully edited, another split-screen design is used to display packing information (see Figure 4-10). The upper half displays packing order information as it is entered to processing, line item by line item; the lower half (not illustrated) displays data for visual verification, noting the total quantity shipped, the date of the shipment, and insurance and freight charges.

As Figure 4-10 shows, the initial step in processing packing-slip information is to enter the product number, followed by the quantity ordered, shipped, back ordered, and canceled. Entering the product number first enables the computer to retrieve the product record stored on the product master file and to transfer into processing the record segments for product name and description and product price. After the line-item charge has been calculated and added to the invoice transaction, the computer generally responds by asking:

DO YOU WISH TO ADD ANOTHER LINE ITEM?

If the answer is yes, the cursor moves to the next line. This sequence continues even if the number of line items exceeds the ten lines initially shown on the screen; for the eleventh item, the program supplies a new display screen containing lines 11 through 20, and so on. If the answer is no, however, the cursor moves the lower half of the display, signaling that the quantity-shipped total is to be keyed into processing.

```
BUSINESS ORDER NO.:       XXXXXXX
RECORD CODE (1 OR 2):     X

CUSTOMER ACCOUNT NO:      XXXXXXX
CUSTOMER P.O. NO:         XXXXXXXXXXXXXXXXXXXXX
DATE OF P.O. (MMDDYY):    XXXXXX


--------------------------------------------------------------------------------
THE SOLD-TO NAME AND ADDRESS OF THE CUSTOMER IS:

    XXXXXXXXXXXXXXXXXXXXXXXXXXXXXXXXXXXXXXXXXX
    XXXXXXXXXXXXXXXXXXXXXXXXXXXXXXXXXXXXXXXXXX
    XXXXXXXXXXXXXXXXXXXXXXXXXXXXXXXXXXXXXXXXXX
    XXXXXXXXXXXXXXXXXXXXXXXXXXXXXXXXXXXXXXXXXX

IS THIS INFORMATION CORRECT?
```

Figure 4-9 Display for business order information and customer order information

Control totals are checked line item by line item to ensure that data entry is correct. For each line item, the following condition must be true:

$$\text{Quantity ordered} = \text{Quantity shipped} + \text{Quantity back-ordered} + \text{Quantity canceled}$$

Unless this condition is met, an error message will be displayed. For example:

QUANTITY TOTALS ARE NOT IN BALANCE

A second control total is based on the quantity-shipped total keyed. This control equation is:

$$\text{Total quantity shipped} = (\text{Quantity shipped, line 1}) + (\text{Quantity shipped, line 2}) + \ldots + (\text{Quantity shipped, last line})$$

If this condition is not met, the computer will respond with a message, such as:

QUANTITY SHIPPED TOTAL NOT IN BALANCE

Once all line items have been entered into processing and all control totals have been approved, the program computes the total invoice charge and transfers the completed invoice transaction record to the *invoice transaction file*. After the transfer, the computer returns to await input of another business

LINE	PRODUCT NO.	ORDERED	SHIPPED	B.O.	CANCELED
1	XXXXXXXX	XXXXXXX	XXXXXXX	XXXXXXX	XXXXXXX
2	XXXXXXXX	XXXXXXX	XXXXXXX	XXXXXXX	XXXXXXX
3					
4					
5					
6					
7					
8					
9					
10					

TOTAL QUANTITY SHIPPED: XXXXXXXXXX
DATE OF SHIPMENT (MMDDYY):   XXXXXX
INSURANCE CHARGES: XXXXXX
FREIGHT CHARGES: XXXXXX

Figure 4-10   Display for packing information

order number. This number is keyed to the business and customer order display (see Figure 4-9).

The process of entering packing-slip information continues throughout the business day or until the decision is reached to process the invoice transaction file. At this point, the file is "closed," and batch programs are called into processing.

The Print Invoice Register Program

The first batch program called into processing prints the invoice register—the list of invoice and credit transactions contained in the invoice transaction file. Because this file is not arranged in any particular order, it is necessary to sort the file prior to printing. The sort separates invoices from credit memos and sequences each set by invoice number (see Figure 4-11).

Figure 4-12 illustrates a small section of an invoice register. The upper portion of each invoice entry identifies the customer order and information important to the shipment: customer number, customer order number, invoice number (business order number), ship date, and so forth. The lower portion of each entry lists the line-item entries to be printed on the invoice, the extended line-item price, and the total invoice charge. At the bottom are invoice control totals: quantity ordered, shipped, back-ordered, and canceled. These totals must

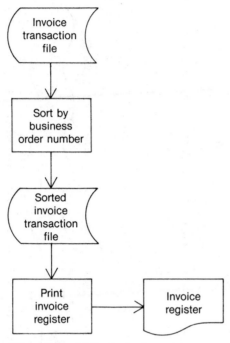

Figure 4-11 Printing the invoice register

balance to the quantity totals entered into processing. The program also computes the invoice gross dollar total, cash discount dollar total, and invoice net dollar total. These totals establish the dollar controls for the next two batch computer programs.

The Print Customer Invoices Program

Another batch program produces custom-formated customer invoices and credit memos, similar in design to those previously illustrated (see Figures 4-4 and 4-5). Processing is scheduled after the invoice register has been visually inspected and approved. As you might imagine, the running time of this statements program is determined by the number of statements, the number of line items per statement, and the speed of the computer printer. Typically, several hours are needed to complete printing; so the program should contain a restart provision. With restart, control subtotals are maintained for groups of printed statements. These subtotals permit printing to be restarted at a point prior to the occurrence of an error (the most recent subtotal).

Besides restart, the program must contain a provision for computing control totals to ensure that invoice and credit memo dollar counts and amounts are in balance. The usual operating procedure is to print the computed invoice count

Invoice No.	Cust No.	Cust Sold To/Ship To Name and Address	State	Zip	Sales/Dist No.	Cust P.O./Date of P.O.
11532	44831	International Supply S and P Stores 5160 SW Ferris 3rd and Oak	Seattle Burian	WA 98166 WA 98164	064 014	Z03489 05-13-8X

No	Line Code	Ord	Ship	B/O	Canc	Price	Disc	Ext Price	Prod $	Tax $	Fht $	Ins $	Gross $	C.D. $	Net $
1	37813	10	10			4.50		45.00							
2	42164	5	5			8.30		41.50							
3	52132	120	120			5.95	.45	660.00							
4	33117	25	25			8.20	.06	203.50	950.00	0.00	45.00	0.00	995.00	29.85	965.15

11538	39662	Home Stores, Inc. —Same as Above— 166703 Adams	Kent Burian	WA 98172 WA 98164	064 014	1362 05-14-8X

No	Line Code	Ord	Ship	B/O	Canc	Price	Disc	Ext Price	Prod $	Tax $	Fht $	Ins $	Gross $	C.D. $	Net $
1	22661	15	15			9.85		147.75							
2	44132	12	12												
3	55419	5	5			39.00	1.55	187.25	335.00	0.00	25.00	5.00	365.00	7.30	357.70

	Ord	Ship	B/O	Canc				Prod $	Tax $	Fht $	Ins $	Gross $	C.D. $	Net $
Totals	546	492	36	18				3973.50	76.55	256.50	33.00	4339.55	111.14	4228.41

Total Invoices Processed   5
Total Credit Memos Processed   0
   Total Count   5

Figure 4-12 Invoice register

and dollar amount on a blank invoice, following the printing of the last invoice, and to print the computed credit count and dollar amount on a blank credit memo, following the printing of the last credit memo. If these counts and amounts differ from those printed on the invoice register, the program must be rerun, but without producing custom forms. The purpose of the rerun is to list, by invoice number, running invoice gross and net dollar totals. This listing is compared with the invoice register in order to determine the point at which discrepancies in processing occurred.

The Print Back-Order Report Program

The back-order report is designed to list customer orders that could not be filled because of temporarily insufficient stock. Besides showing the customer account number and name, the report should include the number and date of the customer purchase order, and the number and quantity of each product reported as a back order. This information greatly assists the order-processing staff: for example, it enables them to write or call people whose orders are more than 30 days old to determine if these customers still want the ordered merchandise. The back-order listing also helps the purchasing staff to identify where product demand is greater than expected or where product shipments from vendors are slower than expected. To provide this information in a useful form, the back-order report should ideally be printed in product-number sequence instead of in customer-account-number or invoice-number sequence. This means an additional processing step: the computer must be instructed to create a separate back-order file during the printing of the invoice register. Once readied, the additional file is sorted prior to beginning the back-order program.

Besides listing back orders, back-order reports are used to show different types of summary sales statistics, which are usually prepared according to the following common formulas:

$$\text{Average invoice dollar total} = \frac{\text{Invoice gross dollar total}}{\text{Number of invoices}}$$

$$\text{Average invoice line-item dollar total} = \frac{\text{Invoice gross dollar total}}{\text{Number of invoice line items}}$$

$$\text{Percentage of back-orders} = \frac{\text{Number of line items back-ordered}}{\text{Number of invoice line items}}$$

$$\text{Percentage of canceled orders} = \frac{\text{Number of line items canceled}}{\text{Number of invoice line items}}$$

By themselves, these summary statistics may not be very meaningful. When examined over the longer term, however, they usually show some interesting trends. In Chapter 15 we will examine sales analysis in more detail.

The Print Invoice A/R Summary Program

Still another batch program is required to produce an *invoice A/R summary file* and to list the information placed on the file. This particular summary file is used to integrate the customer-invoice computer application with the accounts receivable computer application. It enables a business to post customer charges and credits to customer accounts.

The invoice A/R summary produced by processing usually separates product charges from nonproduct charges, determines total allowable cash discounts, and calculates dollar control totals. Figure 4-13 illustrates an abbreviated invoice A/R summary. This listing separates product charges from sales tax charges, freight charges, and insurance charges. It shows the maximum cash discount allowed if customers take advantage of the terms printed on the invoices. Finally, the invoice gross dollar total, cash discount dollar total, and invoice net dollar total are printed once again. These figures form one set of input-control totals for the accounts receivable computer application.

Invoice Transaction File

The combining of data keyed into processing with data transferred from computer files defines in large part the contents of the invoice transaction file. As the listing of file contents in Figure 4-14 shows, only a few data elements must be added to complete the transaction record. These elements are:

- An *invoice number* must be assigned to the record. This is true unless the business order number is defined as the invoice number. Using the same number actually simplifies paperwork processing, because it permits the

---

Invoice A/R Sales Summary   Date   15-May-8X

Invoice	Product $	Tax $	Freight $	Ins $	Invoice Gross $	Cash Discount	Invoice Net $
11532	950.00	0.00	45.00	0.00	995.00	29.85	965.15
11538	335.00	0.00	25.00	5.00	365.00	7.30	357.70
11539	436.50	21.83	57.00	15.00	530.33	10.61	519.72
11542	1340.00	0.00	87.00	13.00	1440.00	43.20	1396.80
11546	912.00	54.72	42.50	0.00	1009.22	20.18	989.04
Totals	3973.50	76.55	256.50	33.00	4339.55	111.14	4228.41

Total Invoices Processed   5
Total Credit Memos Processed   0
Total Count   5

Figure 4-13 Invoice A/R summary

Invoice Transaction File

Invoice number (Business order number)
Record code
Date of invoice
Customer account number

(Entering account number transfers
customer information from the customer
master file to the invoice transaction file)

> Customer sold-to name
> Customer sold-to address
> Customer ship-to name
> Customer ship-to address
> Terms of payment
> Salesperson number
> Distributor number

Customer purchase order number
Date of purchase order

Product number (1)

(Entering the product number transfers
product information from the product
master file to the invoice transaction file)

> Product name
> Product description
> Unit of measure
> Size run
> Unit price

Quantity ordered
Quantity shipped
Quantity back ordered
Quantity canceled

Line item extension (price times quality)

Product number (2)

> Product name
> Product description
> Unit of measure
> Size run
> Unit price

Quantity ordered
Quantity shipped
Quantity back ordered
Quantity canceled

Line item extension (price times quality)

Date of shipment
Total product charge
Sales tax
Freight charge
Insurance charge
Cash discount

Total invoice charge

Customer Master File

Customer account number
Customer sold-to name
Customer sold-to address
Customer ship-to name
Customer ship-to address
Terms of payment
Salesperson number
Distributor number

Product Master File

Product number
Product name
Product description
Unit of measure
Size run
Unit price
Unit cost

Figure 4-14 Invoice transaction file

invoice to be quickly matched against shipping documents if the customer questions a charge.

- The *invoice date* must be assigned to the record. In this instance, the date is usually obtained from the computer operating system.

- The *line-item extensions* and the *total invoice charge* must be calculated and added to the record. Line-item extensions result from multiplying the unit price of the product times the quantity shipped. The total invoice charge is the sum of the line-item extensions plus the charge for insurance and freight.

- *Sales tax* might also need to be calculated and added to the record. If so, it is a percentage of the total invoice charge.

Once completed, the invoice transaction record consists of a header and a trailing portion. The *header portion,* the fixed part of the record, consists of business order information and customer information. The *trailing portion,* the variable part of the record, is made up of product information that must be appended to the record for each product ordered. Thus, the transaction record will be much shorter for the customer ordering one product from stock compared with the customer ordering twenty products.

Because invoice records vary in length, the invoice transaction file is typically a sequential file rather than an indexed-sequential file. The problem with a sequential file is that it must generally be sorted into a desired sequence before it can be used. In addition, once a record is stored on a sequential file, it is difficult to modify.

Invoice Summary File

The other file created by processing is the invoice A/R summary file (see Figure 4-15). Produced by the "print invoice A/R summary" program, this file is created primarily for the accounts receivable computer application. Since accounts receivable only summarizes outstanding invoice charges, the information placed in the summary file is limited to invoice-identification information and the total invoice charge.

The invoice summary file may contain data elements other than those shown in Figure 4-15 and may be used in applications other than accounts receivable. After salesperson numbers are added to the file, for example, the summary file can be used to analyze customer sales by salesperson. A sort of the file by salesperson number permits a company to determine the sales dollar totals attributed to each member of the sales force. Similarly, the summary file can be used to analyze sales by distributor, provided the distributor number is added to the summary file. A sort by distributor number determines the sales dollar totals by distributor. Although creating a sequential file poses severe design problems in some computer applications, this is not the case with the invoice transaction file. If invoices are printed by invoice number sequence rather than customer

---

Invoice A/R Summary File

Customer account number
Invoice or credit number
Record code
Date of invoice or credit
    Product charge
    Sales tax
    Freight charge
    Insurance charge
    Cash discount
Total invoice or credit charge

Figure 4-15 Invoice A/R summary file

number sequence (see Figure 4-14), there is no need to sort the sequential file prior to the scheduling of invoice printing.

4-3 INVOICE MASTER-FILE PROCESSING

Adjustments to customer and product master files are generally completed before invoice processing. This practice not only permits file records to be corrected and verified prior to entering customer-invoice details, but also allows the different tasks associated with file updating to be distributed so that persons who are the most familiar with the types of changes needed can be responsible for making them. Thus, the customer order department can be made responsible for spotting new customer orders and changes to customer names and addresses—information that is generally supplied by customers when they call in an order, or by salespersons assigned to customers' accounts. Likewise, merchandising departments can be responsible for approving product price changes and discounts. These departments are best able to determine if product prices and discount schedules are competitive.

The flowcharts in Figures 4-16, 4-17, and 4-18 show the processing steps required to update and to backup the customer and product master files. Interactive processing leads to the updating of these two master files; display procedures describe the way in which the terminal operator is to alter master-file records. Besides updating the file and displaying the results of processing, each update program produces a change file. The customer and product change files store the before-and-after effects of processing.

Batch processing is required to backup master files. As Figure 4-18 illustrates, two batch programs are associated with each interactive file-update program. These programs print the contents of the master files and the contents of the change files. The programs to "print customer master register" and "print product master register," for example, are designed for the invoicing application to list the contents of the customer and product master files; the programs to "print customer change report" and "print product change report" are designed to list the contents of the customer and the product change files.

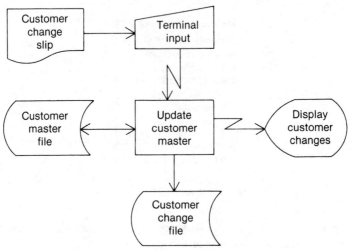

Figure 4-16 Updating customer records

The Update Customer Master Program

The program to update the customer master file must be designed to add, change, or delete records stored on the file. After the operator calls the program into processing, using the main processing menu, a secondary, file-processing menu is activated. Figure 4-19 shows a typical processing menu for a customer master file. This secondary menu permits the operator to add a record to the file, to change a record currently on file, and to delete a record from the file. It makes it possible to move to the next customer record in the file, to only display a record, and to exit from the program and return to the main program menu.

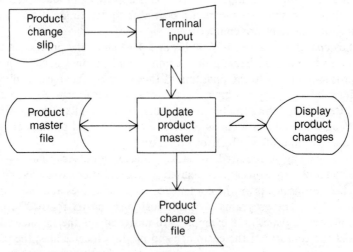

Figure 4-17 Updating product records

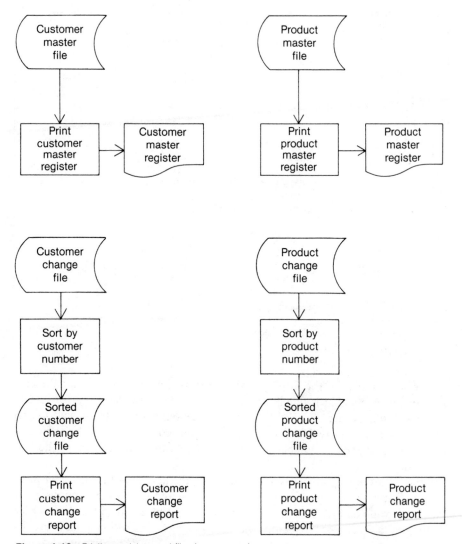

Figure 4-18 Printing registers and file-change reports

Figure 4-20 illustrates the first page of a *two-page display* designed for adding a customer account to the customer master file. To begin processing, the terminal operator assigns a seven-digit customer account number. Following input, the cursor jumps to the sold-to name line on the screen; the computer waits for the customer's sold-to name to be keyed and transmitted. Data entry continues until the attention line is reached. This final line is reserved for entering a person's name, if one has been specified on the customer order. If no name is indicated, the line is left blank.

```
                         FILE COMMANDS

                  1.  ADD CUSTOMER ACCOUNT
                  2.  CHANGE CUSTOMER ACCOUNT
                  3.  DELETE CUSTOMER ACCOUNT
                  4.  MOVE TO NEXT CUSTOMER ACCOUNT
                  5.  DISPLAY CUSTOMER ACCOUNT
                  6.  RETURN TO MAIN MENU
```

Figure 4-19   Processing menu for a customer master file

The second page of the display is the same as the first, except that the customer account number is filled in by the computer and the headings for sold-to name and address are changed to ship-to name and address. If the sold-to and ship-to information are identical, a special input code, such as SA (same address), informs the computer to skip this page and to return control to the file-processing menu.

Other types of display pages associated with the update of the customer master file deal with entering customer credit terms, and salesperson and distributor information on file. Customer credit terms must be assigned before an order is filled by a business. Frequently the credit department will contact a credit-rating service, such as Dun and Bradstreet, for a composite credit appraisal and estimation of the customer's financial strength. In most cases, customers will have been successfully screened by salespersons. Thus, verifying customer credit information is often routine. When a customer's credit is suspect, however, a business may decide to refuse to sell merchandise to the customer or to require cash payment before a shipment is made. Selling on a cash-only basis means that a cash code must be added to the credit segment of the customer record. Finally, it is common to adjust credit terms periodically. If a customer is slow in making payments, credit terms are often adjusted to be less liberal. Very slow-paying customers are often placed on a cash-only basis.

Compared with customer credit terms, salesperson and distributor information is easier to add to the customer master file, provided one salesperson and

```
┌─────────────────────────────────────────────────────────────────────────┐
│                                                                           │
│                                                                           │
│     CUSTOMER ACCOUNT NUMBER:     XXXXXXX                                   │
│                                                                           │
│     CUSTOMER NAME AND ADDRESS:                                            │
│                                                                           │
│        SOLD-TO NAME:     XXXXXXXXXXXXXXXXXXXXXXXXXXXXXXXXXXXXXXXXX         │
│                                                                           │
│        SOLD-TO ADDRESS:                                                   │
│                                                                           │
│        STREET ADDRESS    XXXXXXXXXXXXXXXXXXXXXXXXXXXXXXXXXXXXXXXXX         │
│        CITY              XXXXXXXXXXXXXXXXXXX                              │
│        STATE             XX                                               │
│        POSTAL CODE       XXXXX                                            │
│                                                                           │
│        ATTENTION:        XXXXXXXXXXXXXXXXXXXXXXXXXXXXXXXXXXXXXXXXX         │
│                                                                           │
│                                                                           │
│                                                                           │
└─────────────────────────────────────────────────────────────────────────┘
```

Figure 4-20 Name-and-address display for customer master file

distributor, and not several, are assigned to a customer's account. When one salesperson and distributor are assigned, for example, code numbers are added to the customer master file. In processing, the computer is instructed either to add these numbers to the invoice or, using the numbers, to look up the names of the salesperson and the distributor from a table and then add these names to the invoice. When more than one salesperson and distributor are assigned to an account, processing becomes more complicated: multiple salesperson- and distributor-code numbers must be appended to customer records. In addition, the salesperson and distributor number for each customer order must be keyed into processing and edited. Editing, in this case, consists of matching a keyed number against the same number stored on file. If a match cannot be made, the error is displayed. The operator must then either enter a different number or change one of the code numbers stored on the customer file.

The Update Product Master Program

The program to update the product master file is similar in design to the update customer master program. It too must be able to add, change, and remove records from a file. It should permit the terminal operator to move to the next product record, to display a record, and to exit and return to the main processing menu.

Figure 4-21 illustrates a typical product display, with spaces provided for the

PRODUCT NUMBER: XXXXXX

PRODUCT NAME: XXXXXXXXXXXXXXXXXXXXXXXXXXXXXXXXXXXXXXXXX
DESCRIPTION: XXXXXXXXXXXXXXXXXXXXXXXXXXXXXXXXXXXXXXXXX
SIZE RUN: XXXXXXXXXXXXXXXXXXXXXXXXXXXXXXXXXXXXXXXXX

PRICE EFFECTIVE 1-10-8X

PRODUCT PRICE	PRODUCT COST	PRICE BREAK
$9.95	$7.75	1–999
$9.45	7.35	1000–2999
$8.95	6.95	3000–

Figure 4-21   Display for product master file

product number, product name and description identifiers, and product pricing and discount information. In adding a record to the product master file, the terminal operator is required to key in product information line by line. After filling in the product number, the operator enters the name of the product and its description. Following this, the program moves the cursor so that the price, cost, and price break for the first product can be keyed and transmitted. After the first price line, the computer responds with:

DO YOU WISH TO ENTER ANOTHER PRICE?

If the answer is yes, the computer waits for additional pricing information. If the answer is no, control is returned to the main processing menu.

A different set of processing instructions is required to change a record stored on file. Initially, the terminal operator would be required to state what type of change is required: product number change, product name and description change, or pricing and discount change. After the operator responds, the update program branches to a specific set of conversational instructions. Suppose, for example, that the second of the three product prices shown in Figure 4-21 is to be changed from $9.45 to $9.49. In processing this change, the operator would indicate that a pricing and discount change was to be made. Following this, the computer would respond with the message:

DO YOU WISH TO CHANGE THE FIRST PRODUCT PRICE?

Since the answer to this question is no, the computer would ask next:

THE SECOND PRODUCT PRICE?

A "yes" response to this question moves the cursor to the second price line. After the revised price has been entered and transmitted, the computer would ask next:

THE THIRD PRODUCT PRICE?

At this point, either a "no" response or a special command would be entered by the terminal operator. The special command informs the computer to exit and return control to the main processing menu. A "no" leads to the following message:

THE FOURTH PRODUCT PRICE?

This option permits a new price and discount category to be added to the product record.

Deleting a record from the file is the easiest change to make. One processing possibility is to branch to the delete-record section of the update program and to enter the product number to be deleted. Once the number is transmitted, the computer automatically removes the record from the file. Another, less dangerous processing possibility is to branch to the delete-record section, to enter the product number to be deleted from the file, and to display the record. If the display shows that the name of the product is the same as the product to be deleted, the record is flagged. A *flag* leaves the record in the file, but prohibits its use in invoicing. Finally, once the product change register has been approved, the product is deleted from the file.

Master-File Backup and Reporting

After all changes have been made to the customer and product master files, file-backup procedures must be scheduled. Although operating practices differ, file backup usually occurs during the late evening or early morning hours. A common practice is to produce a daily magnetic-tape file copy of all master files stored on magnetic disks and to print weekly master-file registers. For this application, a *customer register* and a *product register* are required (see Figure 4-18). These registers show what information is contained on the customer and product master files. An alternative to printing the registers on computer stock paper is to use the tape file copies as input to create microfiche. As a storage medium, microfiche not only are less costly but also are often easier to work with than lengthy printed listings.

In addition to registers, two change reports must be produced (see Figure 4-18). The *customer change report* shows all new customer accounts, all updates to customer accounts, and all customer accounts removed from the file as a result of file updating. Likewise, the *product change report* shows all new product accounts, all updates to product accounts, and all product accounts removed from the file or flagged to be removed from the file. Both change reports are printed daily. This practice permits all file changes to be visually reviewed and approved. If the review indicates an improper update, new change instructions must be keyed into processing.

Master-File Display Programs

The last two programs that utilize data stored in master files are the programs to display customer accounts and display product accounts. Both are designed to allow users to examine (but not alter) information stored on master files. Each is written to answer ad hoc questions. The display customer accounts program, for example, generally answers questions such as, "What is the name of the salesperson assigned to the S and P Stores account?" A search of the customer file reveals that the salesperson assigned to this account is 064; a lookup procedure then finds and displays the name of the salesperson. The display program might be used to answer the question, "Are the ship-to and sold-to addresses the same for the S and P Stores?" A search of the account indicates that they are not the same.

The product display program can be written to answer ad hoc questions; however, its main purpose is the display of product pricing and discount information. Assume that a customer calls to find out the price and price breaks for a product. In times past, the only way to find this information was to look through a business catalog for the product number. If this search required several minutes, the customer was placed on hold. The other alternative was to take the customer's name and to call back with the pricing information. In contrast, when the product master file is online, the keying in of the product number locates pricing information in seconds. If the product master file is current, an online approach means that response to customer inquiries can be close to immediate.

4-4 PROCESSING CONTROLS

The design of processing controls for the customer-invoicing computer application is relatively straightforward, provided that the differences between transaction and batch controls are understood. Remember that before an invoice is added to the invoice transaction file, the quantity ordered must be the same as the sum of the quantity shipped, back-ordered, or canceled. Checking this information illustrates a *transaction control procedure:* it verifies that each transaction keyed into processing is accurate. Remember, too, that once the batch processing of invoices begins, batch controls are used. The invoice register program (see Figure 4-12), for example, provides for three types of batch-balance controls: counts of invoice and credit memos processed, quantity totals, and invoice dollar totals. When transactions are combined, the quantity-total balance consists of equating the total quantity ordered to the total quantities shipped, back-ordered, and canceled. The batch balance of invoice dollar totals is slightly different. In this instance, the equations are

$$\text{Total invoice charge (gross dollar amount)} =$$
$$\text{Product dollars} + \text{Tax dollars} + \text{Freight dollars} + \text{Insurance dollars}$$

$$\text{Total invoice receipts (net dollar amount)} =$$
$$\text{Total invoice charge (gross dollar amount)} - \text{Cash discount}$$

These dollar amounts are carried forward in processing. They ensure that customer invoices and credit memos are printed for the correct dollar amounts and that the correct dollar amounts have been transferred to the invoice A/R summary file. Carried one step further, these same dollar totals become the file-balance control totals for the invoice A/R summary file.

It should be emphasized that the design of dollar control totals requires care. Typically, all dollar control totals will be used later on in processing other types of business information. The tax dollar total, for example, is required in filing state and federal tax returns. Freight and insurance dollar totals must be accounted for and are shown separately on the corporate chart of accounts. The cash discount total shows the maximum allowable dollar amount that can be taken by customers for prompt payment of invoices. This total is of particular importance in the cash receipts computer application.

In addition to the file-balance control totals for the invoice A/R summary file, file-balance control totals must be developed for the customer and product master files. At a minimum, a count of the records stored in each file must be maintained. The change reports produced by the two master-file backup programs then verify these counts. The equation is simply

$$\text{New record count} = \text{Old record count} + \text{Additions} - \text{Deletions}$$

Although transaction and batch control totals help to ensure accurate processing, a number of invoices should also be checked by hand before they are mailed to customers, to make certain that all data to be printed appear on each invoice and that processing totals are correct. In a manual test of processing, the invoice dollar total amount should be computed and checked against the computer-determined dollar total. Unless this is done, problems such as rounding errors will not be discovered. For example, 2 percent times $6.98 (.02 × 6.98 = .1396) is rounded to $.13 instead of $.14.

4-5 MANAGEMENT IMPLICATIONS

To most business people, a customer-invoice computer application means one thing: producing an accurate and professional-looking invoice document. This, however, is a short-term benefit. In the longer term, the application yields improved management of customer billing and extension of customer credit. Such an improvement can be traced to several factors.

First, the customer-invoice application reduces the time between the shipment of goods and the delivery of the invoice to the customer. Business firms have discovered that customers are often 20 percent faster in making their payments when bills can be delivered promptly. Moreover, the advantage of faster customer payment is that firms are able to dramatically reduce the total dollar amount owed to them.

Second, the application improves the overall accuracy of processing and, correspondingly, the clerical costs associated with processing. With manual and even with batch methods of processing invoices, a sizable amount of clerical time is spent in working with customers to clarify their bills. With an online method of processing, clerical cost savings are substantial. Much of the savings results from the capability to find a customer's record quickly and to correct a simple mistake, such as billing a customer for a quantity larger than was shipped. Processing controls are invaluable in pointing out these mistakes, and interactive processing methods greatly simplify the making of corrections.

Third, the application standardizes customer and product records. The importance of standardizing business data will be emphasized throughout this book. For now, a brief look at the procedures for pricing products will help to clarify why standards are needed. Consider a business in which prices can be adjusted by sales personnel. Consider next that the salesperson decides to shave a price slightly at first and sharply later on in order to make a sales quota. If this practice of making price concessions is permitted to continue, the unit selling price often becomes lower than the unit cost of the merchandise. Moreover, this practice frequently goes unchecked because people preparing bills by hand have little idea of the recommended selling price of merchandise. Clearly, the design of master files with standard prices, quantity discounts, and terms of payments prohibits attempts by members of the sales force to shave prices and to promise especially favorable terms, such as 5 to 10 percent cash discounts.

Fourth, the application decentralizes the authority and responsibility for producing customer invoices, for revising company records, and for preparing invoice summary data. With an interactive system, departmental rather than data processing personnel are able to control what information is entered into processing. In times past, with either manual methods or batch computing methods, people in departments were responsible for passing along needed changes to billing or data processing departments; however, they were never given the authority to make these changes. With online processing, responsibility and authority are brought more into balance. Besides being responsible for determining changes to customer and product files, departments now have the authority to make changes. To some managers this is the most significant aspect of the online customer-invoicing computer application.

REVIEW OF IMPORTANT IDEAS

A basic objective of invoice processing is to speed the delivery of invoices to customers. An online method of processing streamlines processing procedures. Interactive methods of processing permit data to be keyed, inspected, and corrected by order-processing and billing personnel.

Information that must be keyed as input to processing is contained on shipping documents and customer return slips. Shipping documents show what merchandise is ordered and what is actually shipped to customers. Customer return slips explain why merchandise is being returned for credit.

Outputs from customer invoicing include printed invoices and credit memos and several processing lists and reports. Since customer invoices and credit memos are sent to customers, they must be prepared on custom business forms. Internal working documents such as the invoice register and the invoice A/R summary provide a detailed record of processing.

The interactive portion of invoice processing consists of entering invoices into processing, adjusting and revising the customer and product master files, and displaying records stored on these two master files. The invoice processing menu calls these as well as batch programs into processing.

Building the invoice transaction file requires an interactive processing dialogue that permits customer and product information to be transferred from master files and combined with data keyed to processing. Throughout processing, transaction controls are maintained to ensure that the data keyed and transmitted are correct.

Following the building of the invoice transaction file, batch programs are used to produce the invoice register, print customer invoices, and produce special reports, such as the back-order report. A final batch-processed step is the producing of an invoice A/R summary file, suitable as input to accounts receivable processing.

Each record written to the invoice transaction file contains a header and trailing portion. The trailing portion is variable: it varies by the number of products shipped. The invoice A/R summary file is a condensed version of the transaction file. It contains fixed-length records: it is limited to invoice identification information and the total invoice charge.

The customer and product master files must be readied before data from shipping papers are keyed into processing. Interactive methods permit file records to be added, changed, and deleted, using easy-to-follow master-file processing menus. Each time a file is changed, the change must be reported. Change reports produced by file backup programs provide this information.

Besides updating master-file records, online display programs are used to permit the ad hoc search of stored data. Online display capabilities greatly improve a business's capability to respond to customer inquiries.

Both transaction and batch processing controls are required by the invoicing computer application. Initially, quantity-only totals are compared. When dollars are computed, total quantity and total dollar controls are maintained.

The longer-term implication of processing customer invoices by computer is improved management of customer billing and of extending credit. Invoices are processed much more quickly, with improved methods of control. Distributed processing provides departmental personnel with the capabilities to effect change directly.

KEY WORDS

Invoice	Cash discount
Monthly statement	Service charge
Sales draft	Customer remittance slip
Packing slip	Customer credit memo
Bill of lading	Invoice A/R summary file
Customer return slip	Invoice transaction file
Customer master file	Flag
Primary record key	Customer register
Product master file	Product register
Secondary key	Ad hoc questions
Back order	Transaction-control procedure
Terms of sale	

REVIEW QUESTIONS

1. Why is the invoice so important to large business firms?

2. List the benefits of the customer-invoice computer application.

3. What five types of information are printed on the packing slip?

4. What is a bill of lading?

5. Name the master files required by this computer application.

6. How is the record code used in processing?

7. Describe the three types of output produced by this computer application.

8. Why is an invoice generally a two-part form?

9. Name the three interactive processing functions of this application.

10. What is a split-screen design?

11. What types of control information are printed on the invoice register?

12. Why is restart important in processing?

13. What is a back order, and what information is contained on a back-order report?

14. What information is contained on the header portion of an invoice transaction record? On the trailing portion of the record?

15. Why must an invoice summary file be created?

16. Why are file-processing menus required by this application?

17. What registers and reports are produced in backing up master files?

18. Why are display programs important in processing?

19. Why should some invoices be checked by hand before they are mailed to customers?

20. What are the long-term management implications of this computer application?

EXERCISES

1. Design a product master-file processing menu. Explain what each menu selection would accomplish.

2. A customer complains that a charge was placed on his account, instead of a credit. How could this problem be checked by a customer representative? If the customer's claim is correct, what corrective actions should be taken?

3. Using Figure 4-14 as a guide, list the data elements contained on the
   (a) header portion of an invoice transaction file record
   (b) trailing portion of an invoice transaction file record

4. Suppose credit memo processing is to be kept separate from invoice processing.
   (a) What new computer programs will be required?
   (b) How must the program-processing menu be modified?
   (c) What new computer files will be created?
   (d) What new reports will be printed?
   (e) How will file-backup and reporting procedures change?

5

Customer Cash Receipts

A *cash receipt* is a payment from a customer. As we will discuss in this chapter, cash receipts are processed when payments are made by customers at the time of sale, or when payments are received from customers by mail. In most instances, customer payments received by mail are made to offset a single outstanding or "open" invoice balance. By making a payment against a specific invoice, the customer removes the invoice charge from his or her account. In other instances, payments are made with the understanding that they be applied to a customer's account. These *payment-on-account* transactions may reduce to zero several outstanding invoices. They are not difficult to process provided that procedures have been clearly thought out in advance.

The design of an online customer cash-receipts computer application is very similar to the design for customer-invoice processing—especially when a business processes cash payments that follow from computer-prepared invoices and monthly statements. The application uses two types of input to processing: information contained on remittance slips from invoices and monthly statements and on customer checks, and information previously stored on the customer master file. Only the one master file, the customer master file, is required; since dollars rather than quantities must be accounted for, the product master file is not needed in processing cash receipts.

The online customer cash-receipts design is more complex when a business accepts payments at the time of purchase *and* accepts payments by mail. Cash payments received at the time of purchase require *point-of-sale* (POS) equipment, such as online cash registers. In contrast, cash payments received by mail are processed by other computer terminals, such as video display terminals. This chapter is divided into two parts to compare these two methods of processing cash receipts. The first part examines a cash-receipts application designed to operate in parallel with the customer-invoicing computer application. The second part shows what is required to process POS transactions as well as invoice-related transactions.

The objectives of the cash-receipts application are actually very much like those associated with customer invoicing. This application can enable a business to shorten the time between the receipt of a customer payment and the deposit of the payment in the bank, cut the number of clerical errors, improve processing controls, and project the amount of cash available to offset current business expenses and other liabilities. As with invoicing, time is a critical factor. If a business is able to process customer receipts faster, dollars can be immediately applied to meet business expenses. This improved cash flow, in turn, reduces the need by a business to obtain short- or long-term loans.

Improved processing control is also critical. Large business firms, in particular, require a method of processing which will ensure that cash discounting by customers is done properly and that all cash-discount funds can be accounted for. If customers, for example, are taking discounts larger than authorized, or much later than the date permitted as shown on the invoice, this situation must be brought to the attention of management.

5-1 PRELIMINARY OVERVIEW OF PROCESSING

Figure 5-1 illustrates the four steps required in the handling of customer cash receipts. Compared with customer invoicing, receipts processing is relatively easy. The steps involved are as follows:

1. *Ready customer file* to ensure that all customer accounts stored on the customer master file are correct.
2. *Enter receipts transactions* to record the customer payment and to verify the correctness of the cash totals.
3. *Print daily register* to document the contents of the receipts transaction file and to produce a bank-deposit register.
4. *Print summary reports* to provide a summary of receipts that are to be added to the receipts A/R summary file.

An advantage of this design is that it is simple. It enables a business to quickly process all incoming receipts and to produce a cash-receipts register. One copy of the register indicates the cash payment amounts that are to be added during accounts receivable processing; another copy records the cash deposit to be made at the bank. You will notice that the design does not attempt to match a payment against an outstanding customer invoice. This step is accomplished by the accounts receivable computer application, discussed in Chapter 6.

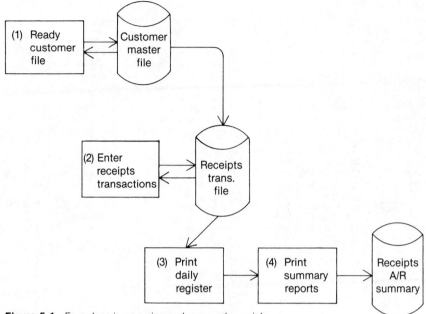

Figure 5-1   Four steps in preparing customer cash receipts

Inputs to Processing

Inputs to the cash-receipts application are limited to payment information from invoice remittance and monthly-statement remittance slips, the customer check, and the customer master file designed for processing customer invoices. Figure 5-2 shows invoice remittance and monthly-statement remittance slips. Both slips contain similar types of information, but there are important differences. For example, the invoice remittance offsets a single invoice, whereas the monthly-statement remittance typically offsets several outstanding invoices. In addition, the invoice remittance indicates any cash discount taken by the customer for prompt payment; the monthly-statement remittance does not indicate a discount amount. Other than these differences, both remittances contain the following types of information:

- *Customer invoice information* to identify the invoice or invoices to be fully paid or partially paid.
- *Customer account information* to show the customer account number.
- *Customer payment information* to show the dollar amount due, the date when the payment is due, and the cash discount if one applies.

As in customer invoicing, the cash-receipts application requires several code numbers to permit documents to be identified and related to other business

STATEMENT

REMIT TO
ELIASON AND ASSOCIATES
175 EAST 39TH PLACE
EUGENE, OR 97405

Return this portion with payment

Customer acct. no.	Month ending
35214	08-31-8x

Invoice no.	Amount	Date
24636	$135.40	06-20-8x
25810	69.20	07-05-8x
26123	93.42	07-10-8x
26205	148.72	07-12-8x
Total Due	$446.74	

Monthly statement remittance stub

INVOICE

REMIT TO
ELIASON AND ASSOCIATES
175 EAST 39TH PLACE
EUGENE, OR 97405

Customer acct. no.	Invoice no.
35214	26205

If paid by _07-12-8x_

You may deduct _2.97_

From total due _148.72_

To issue proper credit to
your account, please return
this portion with your payment

Thank you

Invoice remittance stub

Figure 5-2 Customer remittance stubs

documents. Five numbers important to customer cash receipts are the remittance number, record code number, invoice reference number, general ledger number, and customer check number.

- The *remittance number* keeps each cash receipt unique. It must be different from the invoice number because the customer may make several payments before the outstanding invoice charge is fully paid.

- The *record code number* separates invoice remittances from monthly-statement remittances, and invoice-related payments from other types of cash payments. Another purpose of the record code is to permit a customer cash payment to be adjusted. If a cash payment is entered into processing incorrectly, for example, there must be some method for correcting the error.

- The *invoice reference number* is the number of the invoice mailed to the customer. It is needed to match the receipt against an outstanding invoice.

- The *general ledger number* separates different types of cash receipts. For example, cash payments for earned interest would be entered into processing under one general ledger number; cash payments for shipped goods would be entered under another general ledger number.

- The *check number* provides a point of reference if the customer questions whether a particular check has been processed.

At times, a customer payment will be received without a remittance. When this occurs, a business must identify the customer by number and prepare a remittance slip. The entry of this information into processing together with the amount of payment is controlled by a record code and interpreted by the computer as a *payment on account*. The payment must then be applied to outstanding invoice charges. In processing, the computer is instructed to follow prescribed decision rules, such as these:

1. Use the cash payment to offset the oldest outstanding charge. If a cash balance remains, use the remainder to offset the next oldest charge.
2. Continue to offset outstanding charges until the entire payment has been applied or until all outstanding charges have been paid.
3. Record any remaining cash balance as a *credit on account*.

Figure 5-3 shows that the data keyed into processing consist of customer invoice information, customer account information, and payment information. A close inspection of these data elements shows that only numerics are keyed; approximately forty keystrokes are used. For an invoice remittance, the data-entry operator is required to key all data shown, unless the general ledger code is optional. For a monthly-payment remittance, the operator is required to key each invoice number and the cash payment to be applied to each invoice, in addition to keying in all other data shown.

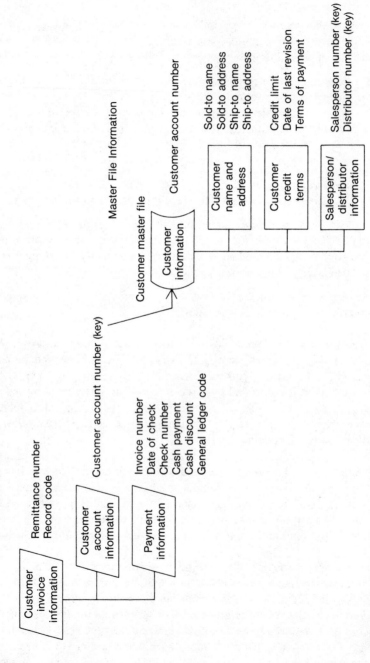

Figure 5-3 Relationships between cash-receipts data sets

Only the customer master file is required by the cash-receipts application. The file segments and data elements shown for this file are identical to those used in the customer-invoicing application. Thus, once the file is readied for customer invoicing, it is also readied for customer cash receipts. As you will observe in later chapters, the sharing of data between applications is not unusual. It simply means that the applications must be carefully designed. As you might expect, it also helps to explain why data base processing is so popular.

Outputs from Processing

The customer cash-receipts application differs from many other business computer applications in that transaction documents are not produced. Instead, the return of the canceled check to the customer by the customer's bank acknowledges the receipt and acceptance of payment. The single output file produced, the *receipts A/R summary file,* contains the condensed version of the records created during processing. The two output documents of importance are the *cash-receipts register* and the *receipts A/R summary.* Both list the customer payments processed by a business.

Because the cash-receipts register shows the totals to be posted to the accounts receivable file, some firms see little need to prepare a separate receipts A/R summary. They contend that the information contained in the summary is identical to the register, except that the customer name is missing. When the two reports are indeed this similar, they can be consolidated. Processing controls, however, should remain separate, and, when the customer name is removed from the receipts transaction file, record counts and amounts should be printed and compared with record counts and amounts printed prior to processing. There is much to be said, on the other hand, for printing both the cash-receipts register and the receipts A/R summary. The register is usually printed following remittance-number sequence, which provides an easy-to-follow list of processed receipts. This sequence also simplifies the maintainance of invoice and monthly-statement remittance totals. The receipts A/R summary, in contrast, is generally prepared by customer-number sequence, which makes it easier to locate a customer account. Moreover, as you will learn in the next chapter, this sequence is usually required in processing receivable accounts.

5-2 CASH-RECEIPTS PROCESSING

Figure 5-4 illustrates the systems organization chart for the cash-receipts application. The shaded areas show processing functions and programs that are the same as those in customer invoicing. The three new programs to be designed for this application are the programs to enter cash-receipts transactions, print the cash-receipts register, and print the receipts A/R summary.

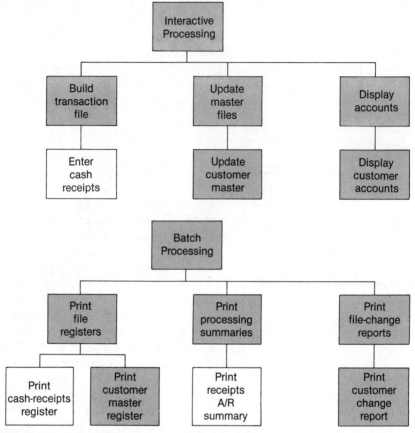

Figure 5-4 Cash-receipts systems organization chart

Figure 5-5 shows the processing menu developed from the organization chart. Three interactive programs must be developed to enter transaction data into processing, to update the customer master file, and to display accounts stored on the customer master file. The single update program is of particular importance. It alters customer records stored on file—in particular, customer name-and-address information. These changes are often reported by customers when making their cash payments.

Besides three interactive programs, four batch processing programs are needed in processing cash receipts. Two of these print registers, one prints a summary report, and one prints a change report. Since the printing of the customer master register and customer change report were discussed in Chapter 4, they need not be described again. The programs designed to print the cash-receipts register and the receipts A/R summary, however, are different. These enable a business to produce a bank-deposit register of all customer checks and to build a summary file for use in accounts receivable processing.

I.1   ENTER CASH RECEIPTS
I.2   UPDATE CUSTOMER MASTER
I.3   DISPLAY CUSTOMER ACCOUNTS

B.1   PRINT CASH-RECEIPTS REGISTER
B.2   PRINT CUSTOMER MASTER REGISTER
B.3   PRINT RECEIPTS A/R SUMMARY
B.4   PRINT CUSTOMER CHANGE REPORT
⟨5⟩   EXIT

Figure 5-5   Cash-receipts processing menu

The Enter Cash-Receipts Program

The flowchart in Figure 5-6 shows the main steps associated with the daily processing of customer cash receipts. Data from invoice and monthly-statement remittance slips are keyed into processing. At this point, the program to enter cash receipts edits cash-receipt details and permits keyed data to be visually verified by the terminal operator. Once data are verified as correct, the completed transaction is written to the *receipts transaction file*, which remains open until all receipts have been brought into processing. After the entry of receipts, batch programs produce the cash-receipts register and the receipts A/R summary.

A split-screen display is often used in entering cash-receipt transactions. This screen format requires the operator to key in the cash-receipts remittance number, the record code, and the customer number (see Figure 5-7). A record code of 1, for example, could indicate that an invoice remittance is to be keyed into processing. Once a 1 is entered, the computer responds by completing the display screen. As Figure 5-8 shows, the bottom portion of the screen is designed for the entry of invoice-remittance details. Input requirements are thus minimal: keyed data consist of the invoice number, the date of the customer check, the customer check number, the cash payment amount, the cash discount (if taken), the balance due (if it differs from the payment), and the general ledger code (if appropriate). A record code of 2 instructs the computer to accommodate the entry of monthly-statement remittance details (see Figure 5-9). The

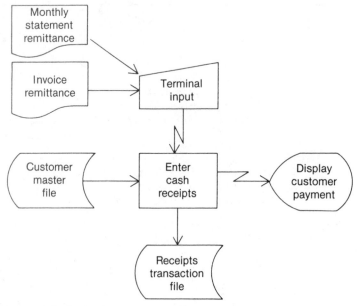

Figure 5-6 Building the cash-receipts file

keystroke requirements for this display consist of the invoice number, cash payment amount, and general ledger code (if appropriate) for each invoice to be paid by the customer check. This information is in addition to the date of the customer check, the customer check number, and the cash payment amount.

Besides serving as a way of entering data into processing, the program to enter cash receipts verifies the correctness of the customer number and confirms the correctness of transaction control totals, for each transaction keyed into processing. The customer number is verified by comparing the number keyed into processing with the number stored on file. Once a match is made, the computer assumes that the customer number is correct and continues processing; if a match cannot be made, the computer displays this information. To check transaction control totals for each invoice remittance, the computer determines the balance due by adding the cash payment to the cash discount; it then compares the computed balance-due total to the balance-due total keyed into processing. If a difference is found, an error message is displayed, so that the terminal operator can visually determine why the error occurred and make the necessary corrections. To check control totals for each monthly-statement remittance, the computer adds the cash payment amount keyed for each invoice and compares this sum to the cash payment total, which must also be keyed. If the two are not in agreement, the computer responds:

THE CASH PAYMENT TOTAL IS NOT IN BALANCE

The computer then waits for a cash payment line entry to be corrected, or for the cash payment total to be changed. A second attempt is then made to determine if the information is in balance.

```
REMITTANCE NO.:        XXXXXXX
RECORD CODE (1,2,3,4):  1

CUSTOMER ACCOUNT NO.:  XXXXXXX
```

Figure 5-7 Initial remittance display

```
REMITTANCE NO.:        XXXXXXX
RECORD CODE (1,2,3,4):  1

CUSTOMER ACCOUNT NO.:  XXXXXXX

INVOICE NUMBER     DATE OF CHECK    CHECK NUMBER
  XXXXXXX            XX-XX-XX       XXXXXXXXXXXX

CASH PAYMENT:    $XXXXXXXXX.XX

CASH DISCOUNT:   $XXXXXXXXX.XX

BALANCE DUE:     $XXXXXXXXX.XX

GENERAL LEDGER CODE:  XXXXXXX
```

Figure 5-8 Invoice remittance display

```
      REMITTANCE NO.:          XXXXXXX
      RECORD CODE (1,2,3,4):   2

      CUSTOMER ACCOUNT NO.:  XXXXXXX
      DATE OF CHECK:  XX-XX-XX      CHECK NUMBER:  XXXXXXXXXXXX

      INVOICE NUMBER            CASH PAYMENT        GENERAL LEDGER CODE
        XXXXXXX                 $XXXXXXXXX.XX          XXXXXXX
        XXXXXXX                 $XXXXXXXXX.XX          XXXXXXX
        XXXXXXX                 $XXXXXXXXX.XX          XXXXXXX
        XXXXXXX                 $XXXXXXXXX.XX          XXXXXXX
        XXXXXXX                 $XXXXXXXXX.XX          XXXXXXX
        XXXXXXX                 $XXXXXXXXX.XX          XXXXXXX
        XXXXXXX                 $XXXXXXXXX.XX          XXXXXXX
        XXXXXXX                 $XXXXXXXXX.XX          XXXXXXX
      TOTAL CASH PAYMENT                             $XXXXXXXXX.XX
```

Figure 5-9 Monthly-statement remittance display

The last function of the enter receipts program is to establish control balances for the receipts transaction file and for maintaining the receipts audit trail. The file control totals consist of the number of invoices to be fully or partially paid and their dollar amounts, and the uncommitted dollar amounts to be applied as payments on account. In addition to these file balance totals, invoice and monthly-statement remittance dollar totals are carried forward in processing. For invoice remittances, the number of receipts processed is saved, as are the dollar amounts of the cash payments, cash discounts, and balances due. For monthly statements, the number of receipts processed is saved, as are the number of invoices noted as being paid and the receipts dollar amount.

The Print Cash-Receipts Register Program

After all control totals have been approved, the records stored on the receipts transaction file are processed as a batch. The first batch processing program produces the *cash-receipts register:* a listing of the records stored on the transaction file (see Figure 5-10). To make this listing easier to read, the records on file are generally sorted to separate monthly-statement remittances from invoice remittances and to place each type of remittance in numerical sequence (see Figure 5-11). One way to simplify this process is to presort remittances as much as possible before keying in data to the computer. If two receipts are to be keyed, for example, the one with the lower remittance number would be keyed

---

Cash Receipts Register			Date 05-June-8X		Page 1

Remit. No.	Cust No.	Cust Sold To Name	Date of Check	Check Number
6321	39662	Home Stores, Inc.	03-06-8X	139214

No	Invoice No.	Cash Payment	Net $	General Ledger Code
1	11345	365.42		2000
2	11390	121.60		2000
3	11491	89.45	576.47	2000

Remit. No.	Cust No.	Cust Sold To Name	Date of Check	Check Number
11532	44831	International Supply	01-06-8X	368-9240

No	Invoice No.	Cash Payment	Cash Discount	Balance Due	General Ledger Code
1	11532	965.15	29.85	995.00	2000

Remit. No.	Cust No.	Cust Sold To Name	Date of Check	Check Number
11535	34522	Parsons and Sons	30-05-8X	22-14/910

No	Invoice No.	Cash Payment	Cash Discount	Balance Due	General Ledger Code
1	09332	89.14	0.00	89.14	2000

Total Monthly Statement Remittances	18	
Total Invoices Processed		72
Total Invoice Remittances	212	212
Total Remittances	230	284

Total Monthly Statement Cash Receipts	3,489.02
Total Invoice Cash Receipts	$29,480.00
Total Cash Discounts	1,070.60
Total Cash Receipts (Including Discounts)	$34,039.62
Total Cash Receipts (Excluding Discounts)	$32,969.02

Figure 5-10 Cash-receipts register

first. Another way to simplify the sort requirement is to create two online receipts transaction files—monthly-statement remittances would be written to one, invoice remittances to the other. The difficulty with this option is that two sets of control totals must then be maintained.

Although the main purpose of the cash-receipts register program is to provide a listing of the contents of the receipts transaction file, an important second purpose is to print receipts control totals. Figure 5-10 shows that the register program counts the number of invoice remittances, the number of monthly-statement remittances, and the number of invoices to be partially or fully paid by both types of remittance. In addition, the program separates the monthly-statement dollar amounts from the invoice dollar amounts, accumulates the cash discounts taken by customers, and adds cash receipts to show total dollars including and excluding cash discounts. These figures are compared with the receipts-transaction-file control totals. In so doing, the correctness of the receipts audit trail is preserved.

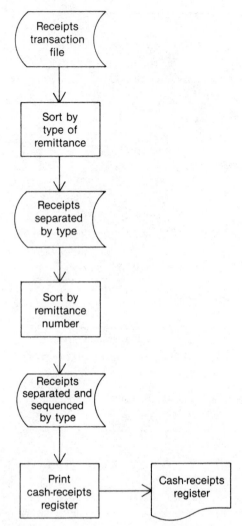

Figure 5-11 Printing the cash-receipts register

The cash-receipts register program may contain too much information to be suitable for the *bank-deposit register,* and, for this reason, a batch program can be written to print this register (see Figure 5-12). Actually, the bank-deposit register is very similar to the cash-receipts register. Its purpose is to document the number of checks and the total dollar amount of the checks taken to the bank for deposit. If the bank discovers that the sum of the individual checks differs from the total deposit amount shown at the bottom of the register, the checks must be matched against the register to determine if all checks have been accounted for or if all check amounts have been properly registered.

Bank Deposit Register			Account Number:	96-5434		Page 1
No.	Remit. No.	Cust No.	Cust Sold To Name	Date	Number	Amount
006	6321	39662	Home Stores, Inc.	03-06-8X	139214	576.47
007	6355	26877	Franklin and Masters	25-05-8X	12-14/995	1044.56
145	11532	44831	International Supply	01-06-8X	368-9240	965.15
146	11535	34522	Parsons and Sons	30-05-8X	22-14/910	89.14
Total Checks		230				
Total Deposit		$32,969.02				

Figure 5-12   Bank-deposit register

The Print Receipts A/R Summary Program

Another batch program prints a *receipts A/R summary,* which shows the cash receipts and cash discounts to be applied to outstanding customer receivables. Before the summary is printed, the customer name and check number are deleted from the receipts transaction file. In addition, the file is sorted by customer number and invoice number within customer number. This sort is necessary because customers may submit more than one cash payment.

The layout of the receipts A/R summary helps to explain some of the previous processing steps. As Figure 5-13 shows, the summary lists the lowest invoice number for a customer, followed by the next lowest number, and so forth. Because these lower numbers are found on monthly-statement remittances rather than invoice remittances, monthly-statement remittances are placed first in the receipts transaction file. Placing the lowest number first permits large code numbers (such as 99999) to be used to indicate such things as a payment on account. Since the large number will always be greater than an invoice-related number, a payment on account would not be mistakenly applied to a customer account before all invoice-directed dollar amounts. Note, too, that the summary includes control totals that are to be carried forward to accounts receivable processing. These totals must be identical to those for the cash-receipts register program; for example, the dollar amount placed in the summary file must be the same as the dollar amount contained in the transaction file.

Receipts Transaction and A/R Summary Files

Figure 5-14 shows the typical contents of the receipts transaction and A/R summary files. When monthly-statement remittances are entered into processing, variable-length receipts transaction records are created. Following the check number, the first invoice number is stored, followed by the cash payment

Receipts Summary

Cust. No.	Invoice No.	Remit. No.	Record	Remit Date	Check Date	Cash Payment	Cash Discount	G.L. Code
26877	10764	6355	2	05-06-8X	25-05-8X	544.66	0.00	2000
26877	10814	6355	2	05-06-8X	25-05-8X	199.00	0.00	2000
26877	10998	6355	2	05-06-8X	25-05-8X	300.90	0.00	2000
34522	11535	11535	1	05-06-8X	30-05-8X	89.14	0.00	2000
39662	11345	6321	2	05-06-8X	03-06-8X	365.42	0.00	2000
39662	11390	6321	2	05-06-8X	03-06-8X	121.60	0.00	2000
39662	11491	6321	2	05-06-8X	03-06-8X	89.45	0.00	2000
44831	11532	11532	1	05-06-8X	01-06-8X	965.15	29.85	2000

Total Monthly Statement Remittances	18	
Total Invoices Processed		72
Total Invoice Remittances	212	212
Total Remittances	230	284

Total Monthly Statement Cash Receipts	3,489.02
Total Invoice Cash Receipts	$29,480.00
Total Cash Discounts	1,070.60
Total Cash Receipts (Including Discounts)	$34,039.62
Total Cash Receipts (Excluding Discounts)	$32,969.02

Figure 5-13 Receipts A/R summary

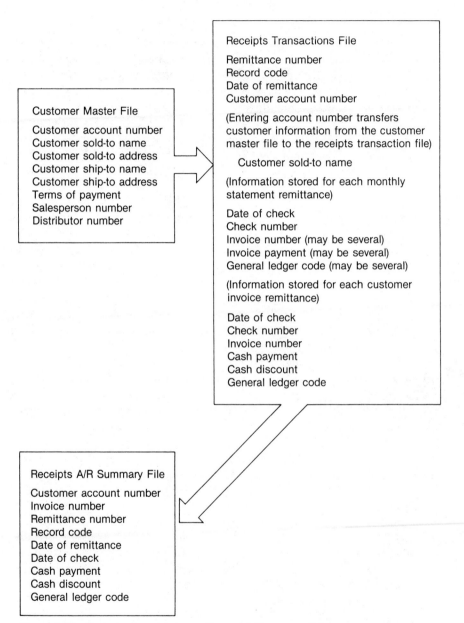

Figure 5-14 Contents of receipts transaction and A/R summary files

amount and the general ledger number. After the information for the first invoice is stored, information for each additional invoice follows, until the entire cash payment amount has been placed in the transaction file. In contrast to the monthly-statement transaction record, when invoice remittances are processed, each record is of a fixed length and contains a cash discount amount as well as a cash payment amount.

The records in the receipts A/R summary file are similar to those in the receipts transaction file, except that all variable-length records have now been changed into fixed-length records. This transformation is accomplished by deleting the customer sold-to name and the customer check number from the file and by adding the remittance number, record code, date of remittance, and date of check to each invoice identified as being paid. The summary file is also arranged differently from the transaction file. Instead of being arranged by remittance number, the file is now arranged by customer number, followed by invoice number. As was shown in Figure 5-13, this sequence leads to several summary records for a monthly-statement remittance.

5-3 CASH-RECEIPTS AND POINT-OF-SALE (POS) PROCESSING

Besides processing customer checks received by mail, most business firms accept cash payment at time of sale. This is especially true of retail establishments and businesses that combine store sales with mail-order sales. Having to deal only with cash at the time of sale greatly simplifies the processing of cash-receipts information. With cash, the need to prepare an invoice can be avoided; the applying of customer payments to outstanding invoices is not required. In practice, however, most POS systems provide for a variety of payment options besides cash. Customers can charge either part or the total amount of the sale, with one of several credit options. One option, for example, is the use of a bank credit card in lieu of cash payment. Payment by *bank credit,* a line of personal credit provided to the customer by the customer's bank, requires more complex processing than cash payment: each transaction involves the preparing of a sales draft, which is handed to the customer, and, later on, the preparing of a sales draft (and credit voucher) bank deposit slip. One advantage of this payment option is that a business avoids billing its customers directly. Instead, the customer's bank is responsible for this activity.

Another billing option is the use of store credit. In contrast to bank credit, *store credit* consists of a line of credit provided by the store or business rather than by the bank. Consequently, the store must bill its customers directly. Still other customer payment possibilities include the 30-day or 30/60/90-day interest-free payment plans, revolving charge plans, and unique types of customer installment charge plans. Today these options are common in both retailing and wholesaling businesses.

Because of the complexity brought about by several payment options and the large number of transactions to be handled daily, POS processing systems often employ large numbers of online cash register terminals. Figure 5-15 shows how terminals might be distributed throughout a large retail store: besides being located at each checkout lane, terminals are placed within each major department. As cash registers, these terminals must be able to safely store cash as well as to process and transmit the details of cash-receipts processing directly to the computer.

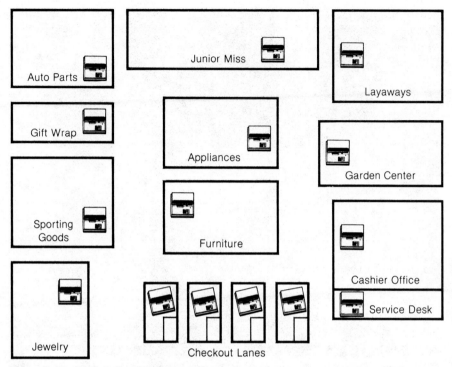

Figure 5-15 Distributed cash-receipts processing

POS terminals permit interactive processing to take place, much like video display terminals. Some POS terminals feature multiple-line displays, whereas others display only a single line of information. Still other POS terminals do not include a display screen as such; instead, they feature a light-emitting display panel designed to show the terminal operator the proper sequence of processing steps (see Figure 5-16). Regardless of the type of POS terminal, the terminal operator is required to follow a standard set of instructions in entering the details associated with a customer sale. Different instruction sets are possible when a POS terminal features a programmable terminal keyboard. With programming capabilities, special keyboard operating codes, or *qualification codes,* can be developed (see Figure 5-16). The programmable keyboard contains a ten-key numeric pad and special *function keys,* each of which is assigned a specific processing task, such as "enter data into processing," "process cash payment," or "enter customer discount." Programming capabilities also make it possible to define new payment options or to substitute one payment option for another. This flexibility explains why function keys designed for one business will differ considerably from function keys designed for another business. Instruction sets determined by the business rather than preset instructions fixed by the manufacturer determine the specific processing steps of each function key.

Figure 5-16 Point-of-sale (POS) terminal, terminal keyboard, and qualification codes

Qualification codes simplify the entry of data into processing and qualify the type of transaction to be processed by the computer. For example, after the terminal operator indicates that the details of a sale are to be transmitted, the computer will ask that a qualification code be keyed into processing. As illustrated, codes 1 and 2 are reserved for a cash sale; codes 3 and 4 are reserved for a credit sale. The computer can also be programmed to permit the details of a customer return to be recorded. As illustrated, codes 20 through 27 have been reserved for entering customer return information into processing.

POS Processing Options

The flowchart in Figure 5-17 shows several program options that can be performed by a POS computer system. The first option is to use the POS computer to verify a customer's credit. The procedure followed by the terminal operator in seeking verification of customer credit is as follows:

1. The operator enters the qualification code to tell the computer that the purchase is to be charged to a customer's store credit account. This instruction activates the program to enter customer information.

2. When the customer account number is keyed into processing, the computer matches it against the customer's master-file record and checks to determine if the customer's credit limit is higher or lower than the current balance-due amount stored on file, plus the dollar amount to be charged. If the credit limit is higher, the computer responds by telling the terminal operator to move to the next processing step. If lower, the computer indicates a credit problem—for example, that the credit limit is exceeded or will be exceeded with the additional charge.

3. The operator calls the credit department for further clarification when a credit problem is indicated.

Another popular processing option is to use the POS computer system to verify personal-checking account numbers. The processing steps associated with the second program illustrated, to enter check information, are as follows:

1. The operator enters qualification codes to tell the computer that a cash sale is to be made and that a personal check has been tendered.

2. The check number is keyed into processing, and computer compares it against a file of bad check numbers (check numbers that the store has experienced problems with in the recent past). If the customer's check number matches one stored on file, the computer informs the terminal operator that there is a problem with the personal check.

3. The operator calls the credit department for further clarification when the computer signals that there is a potential problem.

Besides verifying customer credit, the POS computer system keeps a running record of all cash-receipts transactions. Regardless of the type of transaction, the terminal operator is required to key into processing his or her clerk and department number, the transaction code, and the dollar amounts of the transaction—the dollar charges for goods and services, the sales tax (if appropriate), and the final amount of the sale. In addition, the terminal operator must indicate how payment is to be made. All of this information is transmitted to the computer.

Another important step in POS receipts processing is to create a file of all transactions and to properly document cash-receipts information. As Figure 5-17 shows, transaction information is stored on both magnetic-disk and tape files. A tape copy is made of all data transmitted from an in-store terminal to a central computer. Should data be lost in transmission or otherwise destroyed, the tape file becomes an important backup to processing. Likewise, a paper copy of all information transmitted is saved. At each terminal, a small sales journal is revised with each customer sale. This is in addition to the sales receipt handed to the customer (see Figure 5-18). The journal, located inside the POS

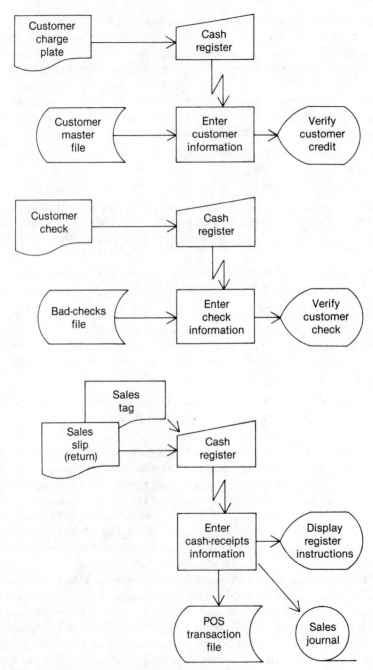

Figure 5-17 Point-of-sale (POS) systems flowcharts

```
▓▒▒ EMPORIUM INC.▒▓
  ::      WILLAMETTE PLAZA
  ::      EUGENE, OR. 97405
  ::        PHONE 342-6387


   4/20/8-   1/106    45097     30

          2888                  5.00
  SUBTOTAL                      5.00
  AMT TEND                      5.00
  CHANGE DUE                     .00

  TL    1 CASH SALE             5.00


   ▓      THANK YOU        ▓
   ::   FOR SHOPPING EMPORIUM INC.
```

Figure 5-18 Sales receipt

terminal, is perhaps better known as a *journal tape*. It can be seen by the terminal operator and checked should a question in processing be raised by the customer; it is saved in case questions arise regarding a set of customer transactions.

Finally, once the online POS transaction file is closed, a batch processing computer program is activated. The program, entitled "print cash-receipts recap," is designed to audit and summarize cash-receipts processing. Before it is run, a preliminary sort of the POS transaction file is scheduled. This sort sequences all transactions within a store by terminal number. Neither the terminal nor the store number is entered into processing by the terminal operator; instead, they are added automatically by the POS terminal. Following the sort, the terminal operator is requested to enter into processing the cash register close-out dollar total and the transaction total. Both sets of figures are printed on the POS terminal sales journal when the cash register is closed for the day. Next, the computer program summarizes receipts totals and compares dollar and transaction totals keyed into processing with those computed, to note any differences. Last, the program prints the daily audit report.

As Figure 5-19 shows, the *daily audit report* is a complex document, showing by POS terminal, for each store, several cash-receipt totals. A main purpose of this report is to identify dollar differences between cash register close-out totals (reset totals) and computer-calculated totals, for both customer sales and customer returns. Because both sales and returns are taken into account, one part of the daily audit report is the *terminal balance report* (see the lower righthand side of the daily audit report). Besides these control totals, the *miscellaneous data report* indicates whether any transactions are missing (see the lower lefthand side of the report).

TERMINAL TOTALS RECAPS

EMPORIUM, INC.

STORE NO 2101
ALL TERMINALS

CASH REPORT	SALES(TOT) CNT $ AMOUNT	RETURNS(TOT) CNT $ AMOUNT	EXCHANGES(NET) CNT $ AMOUNT	DISC/PYMT CNT $ AMOUNT	VOIDS CNT $ AMOUNT	ABORTS + REJ. CNT $ AMOUNT	SLE-RTN $ AMOUNT
CASH SALE 01	0 0.00	0 0.00	0 0.00	0 0.00	0 0.00	0 0.00	0.00
BANK CRD SALE 7	0 0.00	0 0.00	0 0.00	0 0.00	0 0.00	0 0.00	0.00
GIFT CERT-CA 14	0 0.00	0 0.00	0 0.00	**PAYMENTS**	0 0.00	0 0.00	0.00
PAID ON ACCT 9	0 0.00	0 0.00	0 0.00	0 0.00	0 0.00	0 0.00	0.00
LAYAWAY DEP 11	0 0.00	0 0.00	0 0.00	0 0.00	0 0.00	0 0.00	0.00
LAYAWAY PYMT 8	0 0.00	0 0.00	0 0.00	0 0.00	0 0.00	0 0.00	0.00
CASH TOTALS	0 0.00	0 0.00	0 0.00	0 0.00	0 0.00	0 0.00	0.00

CHARGE REPORT	QUAL CODE	SALES(X=0) CNT $ AMOUNT	RETURNS(X=2) CNT $ AMOUNT	EXCHANGES(X=3) CNT $ AMOUNT	DISCOUNTS CNT $ AMOUNT	VOIDS CNT $ AMOUNT	ABORTS + REJ. CNT $ AMOUNT	SLE-RTN $ AMOUNT
CHARGE SALE	3	0 0.00	0 0.00	0 0.00	0 0.00	0 0.00	0 0.00	0.00
LWY PYMT CHG 40		0 0.00	0 0.00	0 0.00	0 0.00	0 0.00	0 0.00	0.00
STORE CREDIT 26		0 0.00	0 0.00	0 0.00	0 0.00	0 0.00	0 0.00	0.00
GIFT CERT CH 41		0 0.00	0 0.00	0 0.00	0 0.00	0 0.00	0 0.00	0.00
LAYAWAY 11		0 0.00	0 0.00	0 0.00	0 0.00	0 0.00	0 0.00	0.00
CHARGE TOTALS		0 0.00	0 0.00	0 0.00	0 0.00	0 0.00	0 0.00	0.00
CASH+CHG TOTALS		0 0.00	0 0.00	0 0.00	0 0.00	0 0.00	0 0.00	0.00

FEES REPORT

TYPE	QTY	$ AMOUNT
ALTERATIONS 20	0	0.00
GIFT-WRAP 21	0	0.00
CURRENCY DIS 22	0	0.00
POSTAGE 23	0	0.00
TOTALS	0	0.00

MISC CREDITS

TYPE	QTY	$ AMOUNT
GIFT CERT	32	0.00
COUPONS	33	0.00
STORE CREDIT	34	0.00
LAYAWAY CR	35	0.00
TOTALS	0	0.00

ADJUSTED SALES TOTALS

	SALES	RETURNED
NON-TAXABLE	0.00	0.00
TAXABLE	0.00	0.00
TAX COLLECTED	0.00	0.00
TOTALS	0.00	

TERMINAL BALANCE REPORT

	SALES	RETURNS	CASH
	0.00	0.00	0.00
	0.00	0.00	0.00
	0.00	0.00	0.00

TERMINAL RESET TOTALS	0.00	
COMPUTED TOTALS	0.00	
DIFFERENCE	0.00	

MISC DATA REPORT

NO SALES	0
TOTAL TRANSACTIONS	1
MISSING TRANSACTIONS	0
NUMBER OF ERRORS	0

Figure 5-19 Daily audit report

Store number
Terminal number
Clerk number
Department number
Qualification code (one or more)
Nontaxable dollar amount
Taxable dollar amount
Sales tax collected
Total POS dollar total

Figure 5-20   Point-of-sale (POS) transaction file

The POS Transaction File

In marked contrast to the daily audit report, the contents of the POS transaction file are quite easy to understand. As Figure 5-20 shows, each record in the file must include several types of identification: store number, terminal number, clerk number, and department number. Next, each record must include one or more qualification codes. If you examine the daily audit report closely, you will see nineteen different codes. These codes should help you to develop some understanding of how business firms classify cash-receipts information. Dollar amounts are also included in each record. When sales tax is calculated, nontaxable dollar amounts must be kept separate from taxable dollar amounts. The dollar sales-tax total and the total POS dollar amount then complete the information to be stored on file.

5-4   PROCESSING CONTROLS

As was pointed out earlier in this chapter, different types of processing controls must be designed for monitoring cash receipts. The first type consists of control totals to monitor customer payments that are accompanied by customer invoice and monthly-statement remittance stubs. For invoice remittances, control totals are the cash payment, cash discount, and balance-due amounts. Besides accounting for cash-receipt dollar amounts, these totals are compared with outstanding invoice dollar amounts. (Why this is done will become more clear in the next chapter.) For monthly-statement remittances, control totals include committed and uncommitted cash payment amounts. In processing uncommitted cash payments, a control total is needed only for the dollar amount of the remittance; in processing committed cash payments, however, control totals are maintained both for this amount and for the dollar amounts to be applied to each invoice. Monthly-statement controls are essential for ensuring that information keyed into processing is correct; they show the number of customers, the number of invoices, and the total dollar amount to be applied against outstanding customer invoices.

Another type of processing control monitors POS processing totals. As we noted in our discussion of POS processing options, dollar control totals must be maintained for both cash and charge sales. *Cash-sale control totals* document the amount of cash contained in company cash registers. A count of the money in a register is compared with the dollar total shown on the sales journal, and, if the difference is significant, the people responsible for maintaining the register are held accountable. To resolve any discrepancy, either the journal tape for the day must be reviewed, transaction by transaction, or further testing by computer is required. A common test is to check for duplicate entries (double payments, returns, and so forth). *Charge-sale control totals* include dollar totals for several charge categories, including bank-credit and store-charge totals and the in-store credit total. Each of these controls is used differently. Bank-credit control totals, for example, show the dollar amount of sales and credits using bank credit cards. This amount should be identical to the amount shown on the *merchant summary deposit ticket*: the deposit slip taken to the bank to document bank-credit-card sales drafts and credit vouchers. Store-charge control totals are the same as invoice control totals. When customer invoices are prepared, store-charge dollar control totals should be identical to the totals printed on the computer-prepared invoice register. Last, *in-store credit* allows employees to charge for store purchases. Instead of billing employees, however, the dollar amount charged is deducted from an employee's paycheck. Accordingly, in-store control totals should be identical to the total for employee-purchase deductions that appears on the summary page of the employee payroll register (see Chapter 12).

POS processing systems require several sets of cash controls to deter employees from embezzlement. Shortages in cash, for example, can be hidden by ringing up a customer sale as a charge when the sale was for cash, and pocketing the cash. Later on, the fictitious charge can be removed from the receipts file by entering a fictitious customer return. Comparing a record of merchandise with a record of sales should point up missing items for which there is no record of sale. Typically, however, these discrepancies are explained as shoplifting losses. The only way in which this type of embezzlement can effectively be stopped is for customers to question any fictitious charges or returns printed on their monthly statement. Even then, the more inventive embezzler can protect against discovery by using a "safe account": either a personal account or an account held by an accomplice.

Customer charge slips (sales drafts) and return slips (credit vouchers) made out by hand and processed separately from POS processing help guard against employee embezzlement. For the charge slip to be valid, it must contain the customer's account number and signature, a description of the sale, and the dollar amount of the charge or return. In processing charge and return slips by computer, the running totals of the count and amount are compared with the total number and dollar amount indicated by POS processing. Any significant difference leads to a larger-scale audit of POS processing.

5-5 MANAGEMENT IMPLICATIONS

Cash-receipts computer applications have become much more important in recent years due to the ever-increasing use of customer credit in place of cash. Widespread use of credit has lead to what is commonly known as the "cashless society." This chapter should make it clear, however, that "cashless" does not mean "paperless"; nor does it mean greater simplicity in processing. Quite the contrary. Credit sales add complexity to processing and increase the chance of employee embezzlement and human error. Business firms have thus found it necessary to give greater management attention to receipts processing. Management is required to see that the time between the delivery and deposit of cash payments from customers is reduced as much as possible. Management is required to see that all receipts are accounted for.

There are several ways to gain even faster use of cash receipts than those discussed thus far. Commercial banks feature "lock-box" systems, for example. These systems instruct the customers of a business to send their payments directly to the seller's bank (or to one of its branches), instead of to the seller's business address. Once the bank receives payment, it credits the amount to the seller's account. Soon thereafter, the bank supplies the seller with the customer receipts and bank-deposit information. This information is needed to process cash receipts by computer; however, since customer payments have already been deposited, there is no need to print a bank-deposit register.

Another commercial banking service provides for automatic withdrawal of customer payments. In this system, customers are requested to authorize their bank to pay a bill. For example, by written agreement a bank might be instructed to withdraw a designated amount, say $100, and to send this amount to the seller's bank on a designated date, such as the first of the month. Generally, the bill is a recurring charge—a quarterly insurance premium, a monthly loan, or a lease payment. To the customer, the advantage of automatic withdrawal is that the bank does the work of writing checks. The real advantage is the seller's, however. With automatic withdrawal, the amount and date of a cash payment are known in advance; the payment is deposited immediately in the seller's account.

POS receipts-processing systems provide vital cash-management information in addition to keeping track of daily cash and charge transactions. Week-to-week comparisons of total cash sales to total charge sales, for example, clarify how customers are planning to pay for their purchases. If the ratio of cash sales to credit sales is changing over time, say from 3:2 to 2:3, this information suggests one of two things: either customers are forced to use credit (because times are tight), or they prefer to use credit (because credit is cheap). In terms of cash management, the most important information is the ability to anticipate the level of cash and credit sales in the near term. If the level of cash sales can be estimated with a high degree of reliability, a business knows the amount of money that will be made available for payment of business expenses and for financing business receivables. Likewise, if the level of charge sales can be estimated, a business knows the amount of money that will be needed to finance its sales on credit.

REVIEW OF IMPORTANT IDEAS

The way in which customer cash receipts are received depends upon how customers are billed. The most clear and least expensive method of billing is to disallow charge sales: to require customers to pay in cash at the time of sale. The most complex method of billing permits customers to select from one of many customer credit plans, in addition to the option of paying in cash. Online point-of-sale (POS) systems simplify complex methods of billing. These systems permit both cash and credit sales transactions to be processed. They separate sales from returns, and returns from exchanges.

The processing of customer payments that follow from store charges requires customers to return remittance slips to document how payments are to be applied. An invoice remittance slip shows how a payment will offset a single invoice, whereas a monthly-statement remittance slip shows how a payment will offset several outstanding invoices. In addition to inputting data printed on a remittance slip, the cash-receipts application must be able to accept payments for which a remittance slip is not included. These are treated as payments on account.

The cash-receipts computer application is neither complicated nor long and involved. The products of processing consist of two registers and the receipts A/R summary. Only the customer master file is needed to support processing. Provided that this file was designed for customer-invoice processing, it can be used without modification in receipts processing.

POS systems are designed to process cash and charge sales transactions. In addition, most POS systems are designed to permit online checking of customer credit and verification of customer personal checks. Both of these options are designed to stop transactions in which the customer's credit is suspect. The most complex part of POS processing is the design and analysis of the daily audit report, a document that balances cash-register close-out totals to computer-calculated totals. It summarizes the dollar volumes of various sales activities processed during the day.

Receipts processing requires careful attention by management. Because of the added complexity brought on by various cash and credit payment options, management must develop safeguards to ensure that all receipts are accounted for. Management must pay careful attention to changing customer payment trends. If credit sales are on the increase, management must be able to project the amount of money needed to finance this increase.

KEY WORDS

Cash receipt
Payment on account
Point-of-sale (POS)
Credit on account
Receipts A/R summary file
Cash-receipts register
Receipts transaction file
Bank-deposit register

Bank credit
Store credit
Qualification code
Function key
Journal tape
Daily audit report
Merchant summary deposit ticket
In-store credit

REVIEW QUESTIONS

1. Why should a business develop the cash-receipts computer application?

2. What are the three types of input to processing?

3. What is the difference between an invoice remittance and a monthly-statement remittance?

4. How is a customer payment processed if it is received without a remittance?

5. What two outputs are printed by processing?

6. What processing tasks are accomplished by the "enter cash receipts" program?

7. How are transaction control totals checked during data entry?

8. What information is printed on the cash-receipts register?

9. What layout is recommended in the design of the receipts A/R summary?

10. Why are monthly-statement receipt records variable in length and invoice receipt records fixed in length?

11. What types of transactions must online cash registers process?

12. How do function keys simplify the entry of data in a POS processing environment?

13. Name three POS processing options.

14. In a POS system, what information is contained on the daily audit report?

15. How do POS systems guard against employee embezzlement?

16. How does a lock-box system work?

17. How are POS systems able to provide vital cash-management information?

EXERCISES

1. Some POS environments are designed to verify and update a customer's credit balance.

    (a) Using Figure 5-17 as a guide, design a flowchart of the interactive portion of this revised processing system.

    (b) Explain any changes to the customer master file that would be required to implement this design.

    (c) List the advantages and disadvantages of this more complex processing design.

2. An argument against using POS receipts processing is that this method makes it easier for employees to steal from a company. How would you respond to this criticism?

3. The cash-receipts register can be designed to provide different types of management information, besides showing all the details of cash-receipts processing. List and explain the difference types of management summary totals that might be calculated in processing and printed on the register. Some of this information is already shown at the bottom of Figure 5-10.

Accounts Receivable

Besides billing customers for goods that are shipped and processing payments received in return, business firms must keep accurate records of all paid invoices and those that remain to be paid. This record keeping is accomplished by the accounts receivable computer application. By definition, *accounts receivable* represent legal claims against customers for amounts due. Receivables are also defined as *current assets,* where the assets of a business specify what is owned. At first glance, the mixing of legal claims and current assets may seem contradictory, but remember that assets can take a physical form, such as an adding machine or a building, or a legal form, such as an outstanding customer invoice. Also remember that accounts receivable are current assets: all amounts due are expected to be converted into cash within a period of less than one year.

An online accounts receivable application can do more for a business than simply keep a record of current assets and of all legal claims against customers, however. This application can provide greater accuracy in processing, timely release of attractive monthly statements, improved handling of customer account inquiries, and better customer collection procedures. It can also improve a business's ability to age customer accounts and to determine customer payment patterns. Viewed in total, the accounts receivable application is designed to improve customer service and administrative control of customer accounts. Thus, the application furthers the main objective of accounts receivable processing: to hold customer credit balances to a minimum, consistent with the prompt delivery of goods and services.

6-1 TYPES OF ACCOUNTS RECEIVABLE SYSTEMS

There are three main types of accounts receivable systems: balance only, balance forward, and open item. Up to this point, the last two chapters have examined in some detail the most complex of these, namely, the open-item system of billing. Before going further, we should examine the differences between these three receivable systems.

Balance Only

The most simple of the accounts receivable systems, the balance-only system, is designed to process minimal amounts of billing information; it produces a customer bill that shows only the current amount due, past-due charges, and the current balance. Most utility companies produce balance-only customer statements. A utility bill typically contains a current statement of charges, the previous balance, and the payments received. Current charges are generally explained in terms of kilowatt hours of electricity or thousands of gallons of water consumed. Other than this information, the statement contains customer account information (customer number and name, and home address), but little else. The past-due amount is rarely broken down to show the number of months the charges have been outstanding.

Balance Forward

The balance-forward system is similar to the balance-only system, except that it provides considerably more information about current charges and typically "ages" past-due amounts. Commercial banks and retail stores that feature credit cards generally design "revolving" balance-forward systems. With a revolving system, a company does not expect a bill to be paid in full each month. Instead, the customer is expected to make partial payment and, at the very least, to pay the minimum amount due printed on the statement. A bank credit card statement, for example, lists, by date of transaction, each sales draft, credit voucher, and payment. The statement also contains an account summary section and a minimum amount-due section. The account summary is represented by the following formula:

$$\text{Past-due balance} - \text{Payments} - \text{Returns} + \text{Purchases} + \text{Cash advances} + \text{Finance charges} = \text{New balance}$$

The minimum amount-due section is printed without explanation. If, for example, the new balance were $569.71, the minimum payment shown might be only $39.00—approximately 7 percent of the outstanding balance.

Another type of balance-forward system is designed to give customers 30 days in which to pay an outstanding balance. This system is appropriate if customers are expected to pay their bills in full. Medical clinics and legal firms, for example, are typical users of 30-day balance-forward systems. Figure 6-1 shows a balance-forward monthly statement prepared by a medical clinic. The credit policy of the clinic states that the patient is to pay the total balance within 30 days following the statement closing date. The statement itself contains current and past-due information: it shows the previous balance and lists the current charges in date-order sequence, and it ages the past-due amount. As shown at

STATEMENT

ANY CHARGES OR PAYMENTS RECEIVED AFTER
THE DATE BELOW WILL APPEAR ON YOUR NEXT STATEMENT

ACCOUNT NUMBER 00825-19538024   PAGE   1 OF 1   CG* CLOSING DATE 05/31/8-

EUGENE HOSPITAL & CLINIC
EUGENE HOSPITAL COMPANY
1162 WILLAMETTE STREET
EUGENE, OREGON 97401

F.I.D. NO. 93-0349770

TOTAL BALANCE   180.40

AMOUNT REMITTED

SEND INQUIRIES TO

ALAN L ELIASON
175 EAST 39TH PLACE
EUGENE OR 97405

EUGENE HOSPITAL & CLINIC
EUGENE HOSPITAL COMPANY
1162 WILLAMETTE STREET
EUGENE, OREGON 97401

IMPORTANT! SEE REVERSE SIDE

DETACH AND RETURN THIS PORTION WITH
YOUR REMITTANCE TO THE ABOVE ADDRESS

BILLED FROM
EUGENE HOSPITAL & CLINIC

* CLOSING DATE
05/31/8-

BILLED TO
ALAN L ELIASON

ACCOUNT NUMBER
19538024

MO	DAY	YR	DR. NO.	DESCRIPTION	PROCEDURE NUMBER	CHARGE	CREDIT
				********* PAYMENT-INSURANCE BILLING NOTIFICATION **********			
				ALL CHARGES OVER 1 MONTH, WITHOUT PRIOR ARRANGEMENTS FOR			
				PAYMENT, ARE PAST DUE AND PAYABLE, IN FULL, BY THE 20TH.			
				PRIMARY INSURANCES BILLED ON ACCOUNTS SET-UP FOR AUTOMATIC			
				BILLING. ATTACHED FORM FOR SECONDARY INSURANCES OR ACCOUNTS			
				NOT SET-UP. BUSINESS HOURS FOR CALLS, 10AM TO 5PM MON-FRI.			
				MEDICARE ACCOUNTS WILL RECEIVE MEDICARE FORMS TO BILL WITH.			
				PREVIOUS BALANCE		102 55	
				M JANE ELIASON			
05	29	8-	73	LAB CULTURE BETA-STREP	87999	11 50	
05	29	8-	73	OFFICE VISIT LIMITED	90050	20 65	
				EDWARD ANDREW ELIASON			
				INSURANCE BILLED			
05	01	8-	22	OFFICE VISIT LIMITED	90050	20 65	
05	05	8-	22	CAST MATERIAL	99070	5 00	
05	05	8-	22	CAST REPAIR	29799	5 00	
05	22	8-	22	OFFICE VISIT BRIEF	90040	15 05	
05	22	8-	22	CAST REMOVAL	29700		
				SERVICES PERFORMED BY			
			73	H W WONG MD ENT			
			22	R E MATTERI MD ORTHOPEDIC			

DATE OF LAST PAYMT   04/16/8-

FINANCE CHARGE is computed by a periodic rate of 1.38% per month, **ANNUAL PERCENTAGE RATE 18%**. Before next month's closing date *pay the portion of your new balance which has been outstanding more than 90 days in order to avoid additional **FINANCE CHARGE**.
CREDIT OR INSURANCE INFORMATION (503) 687-6231. Keep this portion of statement for tax and record purposes.

CURRENT MO.	OVER 1 MO.	OVER 2 MO.	OVER 3 MO.	OVER 4 MO.	TOTAL AMOUNT	TOTAL BALANCE
77 85	102 55				180 40	180 40

Figure 6-1 Balance-forward statement

the bottom of this statement, current charges are $77.85, and charges over a month (30 days) are $102.55. Finally, observe that finance charges are applied to the past-due amount. As shown, any amount outstanding by more than 90 days will be subjected to a finance charge of 1.38 percent per month. Thus, even though this is a 30-day balance-forward statement, a finance charge is not levied unless a past-due amount is older than 90 days.

Open Item

In contrast to the balance-forward accounts receivable system, the open-item system does not summarize past-due charges, but instead continues to list any invoice that has not been completely paid. Then, to add even more billing information, each outstanding invoice is aged. The aging categories, or *aging buckets,* show when an invoice is less than 30 days old, 30 but less than 60 days old, 60 but less than 90 days old, and over 90 days old. This aging procedure provides the customer with a clear reminder of the length of time an invoice has been outstanding. It permits business firms to determine which customer accounts are excessively past due. For long-overdue accounts, special reminder letters, known as *dunning letters,* are prepared by computer. These letters become more demanding as the account balance gets older. Besides letters, dunning messages transmitted by telephone are becoming more popular. The computer assists in this instance, also. Billing-collection operators use online displays to show the name of the customer and the name and telephone number of the person to contact. With more advanced online designs, displays provide the operator with access to recent billing information and to the payment history for the customer's account.

The value of an open-item system, compared with others, is that a complete accounting is provided for each sales transaction. Both customers and businesses are able to benefit from this complete picture of processing. Customers, for example, are able to decide which invoices to pay and when, and whether to take advantage of a cash discount; they are able to contest a single charge and ask that the paperwork supporting the charge be reviewed. Businesses, likewise, are able to apply a customer credit or exchange to a specific invoice; they are able to bring a single invoice balance due or credit amount to the attention of the customer. Indeed, the most important advantage of an open-item system is that a clear audit trail is maintained for each transaction. The system provides a documented record of each and every invoice, and how it is offset—by a credit, payment, or billing adjustment.

6-2 PRELIMINARY OVERVIEW OF PROCESSING

In this chapter we will examine an open-item accounts receivable application. Consequently, the two main inputs to processing are the invoice and the receipts A/R summary files. Following input, five steps are associated with the processing of accounts receivable information (see Figure 6-2). The first two update the *consolidated A/R master file:* the file designed to store all customer accounts receivable information. After this consolidated file is readied, the third step matches charges with payments, to delete invoice and receipts information from the file and to allow the printing of monthly statements.

The five steps and their purposes are as follows:

1. *Post invoices charges and credits* to transfer information from the invoice A/R summary to the consolidated A/R master file.

2. *Post cash receipts* to transfer information from the receipts A/R summary file to the consolidated A/R master file.

3. *Delete paid invoices* to remove paid-in-full invoice and receipts information from the consolidated A/R master file.

4. *Age customer accounts* to show delinquent customer accounts and the age of uncollected amounts.

5. *Print customer statements* to produce customer monthly bills.

The A/R Master File

Updating the A/R master file is a major step in accounts receivable processing. Before any invoice can be removed from the file or before any monthly statement can be printed, the A/R master file must be in proper sequence and in balance. Figure 6-3 shows the arrangement of invoice, credit, and payment (cash-receipts) summary information in the file, according to the following rules.

- All records are arranged by account number, such as by customer account number.

- Within each account number, customer invoice information is stored first, credit information is stored second, and payment information is stored third.

- Within each account number, the lowest invoice number (the oldest outstanding invoice) is stored first, the next lowest invoice number is stored second, and so forth.

- Each record contains one invoice summary segment, one or more credit segments, and one or more payment segments.

- Each record segment is headed by the same unique identification number, such as invoice number, to tie together the record segments.

- Record codes separate the different accounts receivable record segments.

You might observe that the record segments designed for the consolidated A/R master file follow from the records contained in the invoice A/R summary file and the receipts A/R summary file (see Figures 4-15 and 5-14). Thus, no new

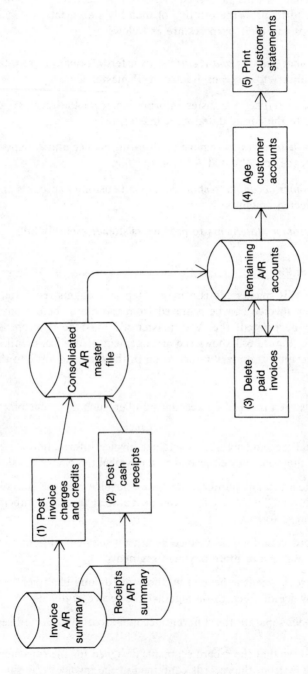

Figure 6-2 Five steps in processing accounts receivable information

---

Customer account number

  Invoice number (customer charge)
    Record code
    Date of invoice
    Product charge
    Sales tax
    Freight charge
    Insurance charge
    Cash discount
    Total invoice charge

  Credit number (customer credit)
    Record code
    Date of credit
    Product credit
    Sales tax credit
    Freight credit
    Insurance credit
    Cash discount
    Total customer credit

  Invoice number (customer payment)
    Remittance number
    Record code
    Date of remittance
    Date of check
    Cash payment
    Cash discount
    General ledger code

(*file continues*)

Figure 6-3   Accounts receivable master file

data elements need to be added in creating this file. Second, the file is organized so that credits are applied first to offset an invoice charge. If credits do not exist, customer payments are applied to offset a charge. Finally, if neither credits nor payments exist, only the invoice record segment is stored on file.

The consolidated A/R master file must be in balance as well as in proper sequence before it is used. Both total dollar amounts and total transaction counts must be accounted for. For example, the total dollar amount equation is:

Old A/R dollar total + Invoice dollar total − Credit dollar total
− Payment dollar total − Cash discounts = New A/R dollar total

In this equation, the "old A/R dollar total" represents the dollars stored in the A/R master file before invoice and receipts A/R summary dollar totals were added. Moreover, the invoice, credit, and payment dollar totals represent the file-balance-control dollar amounts previously stored on the invoice and receipts A/R summary files.

The first equation used in balancing the count of transactions is similar to the equation used in accounting for dollars, except that all parts of the equation are positive. The equation reads:

Transaction Count 1

Old number of transactions + Invoice transactions + Credit transactions + Payment transactions = New number of transactions

At this stage in processing, no attempt is made to apply credit and payment dollars to outstanding invoices. Instead, the important facts to retain are the counts of all transaction stored on the A/R master file. Later on, when invoices are deleted from the file, the number of transactions reported as being deleted from the file must be balanced against the number of transactions remaining on file. This second transaction-count balance equation reads:

Transaction Count 2

Old number of transactions − Invoice transactions deleted − Credit transactions deleted − Payment transactions deleted = New number of transactions

Thus, the first transaction count verifies that all transactions from the A/R summary files have been successfully accounted for; the second count verifies that the correct number of transactions have been successfully deleted from the A/R master file.

Outputs from Processing

The information produced by the A/R computer application includes one or more printed registers, customer monthly statements, and one or more receivable summary reports. Unlike the previous two computer applications, this one does not create a summary file for still another computer application. The following important types of printed documents are produced in processing:

- The *accounts receivable register,* which lists the contents of the A/R master file.

- The *deleted invoice report,* which shows invoices that net to zero (that have been paid in full) and invoices, credits, and payments removed from the A/R master file.

- *Customer monthly statements,* billing documents sent to customers that show which invoices are outstanding and the ages of the invoices.

- The *aging schedule,* which shows the balance-due amount and the aged subtotals for each customer.

Besides printed documents, several visual displays must be designed. Among them are the *consolidated customer receivable display,* which shows the customer's complete receivable record, and the *aged customer receivable display,* which shows the current balance-due amount and amounts past due by 31 to 60 days, 61 to 90 days, and over 90 days. The consolidated customer receivable display is used primarily in adjusting customer accounts. The most frequent adjustment removes small invoice balances from a customer's account. In contrast, the aged customer receivable display is used only for inquiries, the most frequent of which is to determine whether a credit or a payment has been applied to an account. Such an inquiry generally follows a customer's request to check the status of an account.

Figure 6-4 shows one possible design format for a *customer monthly statement.* In many ways this design, or most any other, is very similar to the customer invoice (see Figure 4-4). It must show the statement date, customer account number, and customer sold-to name and address; provide a brief description of each transaction; and show the dollar amount of each transaction.

STATEMENT

YOUR FIRM NAME HERE
123 Main Street
YOUR TOWN, STATE AND ZIP

DATE	
	11/28
ACCOUNT NUMBER	
	46S

Phone 123-4567

Star Auto Supply
145 Park St.
Town, State, Zip

AMOUNT ENCLOSED $ _____

RETURN THIS PORTION WITH PAYMENT

DATE	CHARGES AND CREDITS	AMOUNT
10/15	Invoice #4022	$ 250.32
11/3	Payment - Thank you	250.32
11/14	Invoice #4123	$ 157.80
11/22	Invoice #4230	$ 45.30
	Balance	$ 203.10

PAY LAST AMOUNT
IN THIS COLUMN

Thank You

YOUR FIRM NAME HERE

Figure 6-4   Customer monthly statement

A monthly statement does differ from a customer invoice, however. First, it generally provides only a reference to the original invoice, credit, or payment. Second, it may use codes to separate different types of transactions. (The letter A, for example, might indicate "discount allowed," and the letter F denote "finance charge.") Third, the description part of the statement supplements the reference number with a brief statement such as "balance remaining," or a numerical description to aid in tracing the transaction. The description "Re: 3264; 6-18-83," for example, could be printed to show a monthly-statement remittance number and the date of the customer check. Still another possibility is to use the description to identify a store location. A numeric code interpreted by the computer provides this information. Consider a three-digit code in which the first digit indicates the type of transaction and the second and third digits show the number of the store. The number 116 would be interpreted as meaning an invoice (1 equals invoice) prepared by store 16; the number 208 would be interpreted as a credit (2 equals credit) prepared by store 08.

6-3 ACCOUNTS RECEIVABLE PROCESSING

Figure 6-5 illustrates the systems organization chart for accounts receivable processing. Compared with the previous charts, the batch portion of this application is somewhat more complex. A new function, entitled "sort/merge files," has been added to acknowledge that processing must merge data from different files into a sequenced consolidated file—the *consolidated A/R master file*. Other than this new function, the remaining batch functions should be familiar. They are identical to those required in invoice processing.

As Figure 6-5 shows, the interactive portion of processing contains two new programs: adjust receivable master and display receivable accounts. Of particular interest is the program designed to adjust the A/R master file. One kind of adjustment eliminates small balances from the file (such as all invoices with a balance of $.50 or less). Another follows from a review of an account. Suppose a customer claims, correctly, that a debit rather than a credit has been applied to his account. An online review in this situation should spot the difficulty immediately. Once spotted, an adjustment to the account can be made. There are also times when accounts simply need review. One type of review is to examine all accounts when the current and past-due amounts have been projected by the computer to exceed customer credit limits. Through review, a business is able to determine which customer accounts require special attention.

The A/R systems chart of organization, much like charts shown earlier, should be viewed as a minimal processing design. Several other print programs, such as intermediate file-balance reports, error handling reports, and automatic dunning letters, could be added to the design. Even though the design is minimal, however, it should not be considered deficient. It is several times more advanced than designs common to smaller business firms.

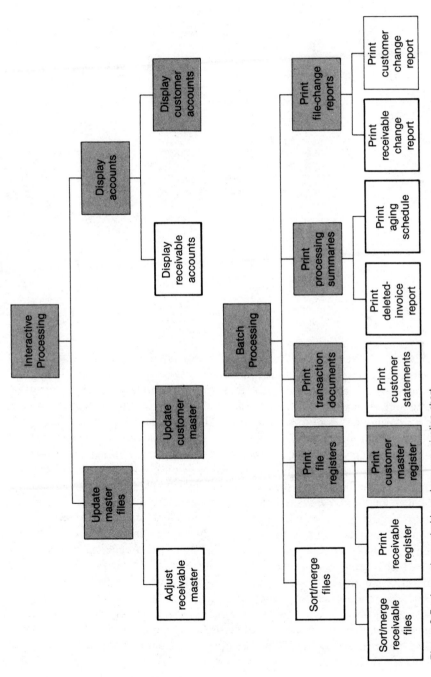

Figure 6-5 Accounts receivable systems organization chart

```
        I.1   ADJUST RECEIVABLE MASTER
        I.2   UPDATE CUSTOMER MASTER
        I.3   DISPLAY RECEIVABLE ACCOUNTS
        I.4   DISPLAY CUSTOMER ACCOUNTS

        B.1   SORT/MERGE RECEIVABLE FILES
        B.2   PRINT RECEIVABLE REGISTER
        B.3   PRINT DELETED-INVOICE REPORT
        B.4   PRINT AGING SCHEDULE
        B.5   PRINT CUSTOMER STATEMENTS
        B.6   PRINT CUSTOMER MASTER REGISTER
        B.7   PRINT RECEIVABLE CHANGE REPORT
        B.8   PRINT CUSTOMER CHANGE REPORT
        (9)   EXIT
```

Figure 6-6 Accounts receivable processing menu

Figure 6-6 illustrates the processing menu that follows from this chart of systems organization. The four interactive programs and the nine batch programs permit a terminal operator to examine accounts stored in the consolidated A/R master file and to schedule the batch processing of accounts receivable information. In times past, processing would be scheduled once each month, leading to the production of what are commonly known as month-end customer statements. With computer processing, *cycle billing* has tended to replace month-end billing. With cycle billing, monthly statements for groups of accounts are produced at different times during the month. For example, a business might divide its accounts receivable accounts into six groups and produce statements six times each month. Likewise, a company with a large number of accounts might produce monthly statements daily. In this instance, either the account number or a specific billing-cycle code appended to the account determines the *account cycle time* (the time during the month when a monthly statement is to be prepared). Last, with computer processing it is also possible to produce customer monthly statements "on demand." Here the processing cycle is controlled by the terminal operator rather than by computer. Typically, on-demand production of statements follows the adjustment of computer statements. Following adjustment, the customer is supplied with a revised billing statement.

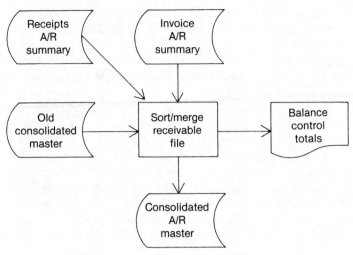

Figure 6-7 Updating the consolidated A/R master file

The Sort/Merge Receivable Files Program

The sort/merge receivable files program is required to update the consolidated A/R master file. As Figure 6-7 shows, the update is accomplished by combining invoice, credit, and payment transactions stored on the invoice A/R summary and the receipts A/R summary files, with transactions stored on the old consolidated A/R master file. A new consolidated A/R master file is created as a result of processing. The records stored on this file are sequenced, first, by customer number and, second, by type of transaction.

Since sort/merge utility software packages exist for most computer systems, business firms are able to avoid designing complex sort/merge computer programs. As with any type of computer program, however, problems in processing are usually experienced. Thus, the sort/merge program must be carefully monitored. At a minimum, batch-balance-control totals of counts and amounts should be printed to ensure that all records have been accounted for.

The Print Receivable Register Program

Figure 6-8 shows an abbreviated *accounts receivable register.* Besides listing the invoice, customer credit, and customer-receipts activity for each customer account, the register prints dollar and transaction-count file-balance totals. For example, the totals on the righthand side of the register illustrate total dollar controls. The beginning A/R balance represents the "old A/R dollar total," whereas the ending A/R balance now represents the "new A/R dollar total." Likewise, beginning and ending transactions shown on the lefthand side indicate the change in the number of transactions following the update of the file. These totals follow from the file-balance-control equation previously shown as Transaction Count 1.

Close review of the accounts receivable register reveals one additional processing feature: the program determines the remaining balance on any invoice older than 30 days, and any balance following the application of a customer credit or payment. In Figure 6-8, a remaining balance of $29.85 is shown for customer account number 44831. On examination, we see that the reason for this balance is that the customer took the cash discount; however, the computer determined the discount should not have been taken. This situation would occur if the terms of payment required payment within 10 days. In processing, the computer would add 10 to the date of the invoice (the invoice posting date) and compare this date with the date of the cash receipt (the receipt posting date). In this example, it should be clear why the computer would not permit the discount: the customer receipt was posted 20 days after the posting of the invoice.

The Print Deleted-Invoice Report Program

Prior to printing customer monthly statements, invoices that net to zero must be deleted from the consolidated A/R master file. During processing, invoice transactions are matched against credit and payment transactions to arrive at a balance-due total. When a balance of $0.00 is achieved, the invoice, all offsetting credit and payment record segments, and all other record adjustments are deleted from the master file.

As illustrated by Figure 6-9, deleting invoices changes the consolidated A/R master file once again. However, instead of enlarging the file, as is the case when files are merged, the consolidated A/R master file is made smaller by this update. As with other file updates, the effects of processing must be documented. The *deleted-invoice report* meets this need. It shows all record segments deleted from the file and the dollar amounts used to arrive at each $0.00 balance-due total. In addition, the report provides new balance-control totals for audit purposes. For example, it provides the dollar value of invoices removed from the file and the count of transactions that remain on file. This adjustment of the transaction count was shown earlier as Transaction Count 2.

A considerable amount of detail work must precede and follow the deletion of invoices from the A/R master file. Small account balances, for example, must be removed from the file to avoid embarrassing statements to customers. (Billing a customer for six cents would be embarrassing; moreover, its cost to prepare is more than the balance due.) To eliminate these balances, the amounts to be removed must be entered into processing as adjustments. Likewise, some cash discounts are allowed even though they are taken by customers later than the date shown in the terms of payment. These discounts represent another type of receivable adjustment.

The problem with making adjustments after the deleted-invoice program has been run is that a change will reduce to zero invoices stored on file. If they are

Accounts Receivable Register

Date 16-May-8X　　Page 1

No.	Cust No.	Type	Number	Apply To	Posted	Check	Charge	Discount	G.L.	Payment	Discount	Balance
0131	39662	Inv.	11345		180482		346.47	7.31				
0132	39662	C.R.	6321	11345	050682	030682			2000	346.47	0.00	0.00
0133	39662	Inv.	11390		200482		121.60	2.43				
0134	39662	C.R.	6321	11390	050682	030682			2000	121.60	0.00	0.00
0135	39662	Inv.	11491		280482		89.45	1.79				
0136	39662	C.R.	6321	11491	050682	030682			2000	89.45	0.00	0.00
0137	39662	Inv.	11538		100582		365.00	7.30				
0138	39662	Inv.	11573		060582		430.60	8.61				
0139	39662	Inv.	11680		150582		82.14	1.64				
0187	44831	Inv.	11532		150582		995.00	29.85				
0188	44831	C.R.	11532	11532	050682	010682			2000	965.15	29.85	29.85

Beginning Transactions	1076
Total Invoices Processed	241
Total Credits Processed	12
Total Payments Processed	233
Ending Transactions	1562

Beginning Accounts Receivable	$159,643.26
Plus: Invoice Charges	48,326.42
Less: Customer Credits	532.16
Customer Payments	46,842.16
Cash Discounts	389.76
Ending Accounts Receivable	$160,205.60

Figure 6-8　Accounts receivable register

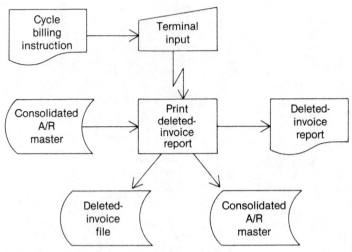

Figure 6-9 Deleting paid-in-full invoices

allowed to remain on file, they lead to the printing of $0.00 balance-due statements—another type of statement to avoid. The only way to treat this particular problem is to rerun the deleted-invoice program. The rerun, in turn, produces another deleted-invoice report and a second set of file-control balances.

The Adjust Receivable Master Program

Interactive methods of processing are especially useful in making adjustments to the consolidated A/R master file. To begin processing, the program, adjust receivable master, is selected. As Figure 6-10 shows, this program permits the operator to review both the customer and receivable account and to adjust the consolidated A/R master file accordingly. In processing, a customer's account is displayed page by page to show how invoices will be reduced to zero by follow-on processing.

Figure 6-11 shows the first page of a consolidated customer receivable display. The entire customer account can thus be examined before invoices have been deleted from the file. Suppose that the reason for examining this particular account is to determine if the cash discount for invoice number 11225 has been allowed. On inspection it can be determined that it has: there is a difference of $1.03 between the invoice charge and the cash payment.

A file-processing menu controls the types of adjustments that can be made to a customer's account. Figure 6-12 shows an abbreviated menu. Of the processing selections, the first two deal with the analysis of receivable accounts. Selection 1, "Adjust small-balance totals," for example, is used to determine the number and total dollar value of invoices that are less than a specified amount.

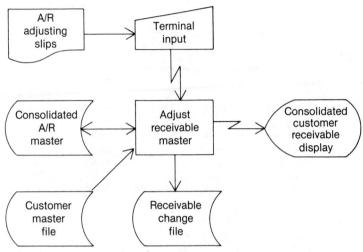

Figure 6-10   Adjusting receivable accounts

Processing instructions might include:

1. WHAT SMALL-BALANCE AMOUNT IS TO BE EXAMINED? $XX.XX
   (Enter the dollar amount.)

2. WHAT ACCOUNTS ARE TO BE EXAMINED?   _____
   (Enter "All" or specify "Account cycle number.")

Following a summary showing the effects of making all adjustments, the computer will ask,

3. SHOULD THE SMALL-BALANCE ADJUSTMENT BE MADE (Y or N)?   _____

Thus, if $0.50 is entered initially, this amount becomes the small-balance *cutoff point*. If all accounts are to be analyzed, the computer will search through the entire A/R master file to identify the invoices whose balance-due amounts are less than the cutoff. After summarizing the effects of deleting these small-balance invoices, the computer will ask whether to go ahead or not. If a Y is entered, the small-balance invoices of $0.50 or less will be adjusted, thus bringing their balance-due amounts to zero.

Selection 2, "Adjust cash discounts," is similar to Selection 1. When placed in this processing mode, the computer identifies all invoices with balance-due amounts equaling the cash discount amount. Such invoices usually result when the customer has taken the discount and the computer has disallowed the discount when processing the payment. Each case must be investigated to ensure that the action taken by the computer is correct. Suppose, for example, that the terms of an invoice are 2 percent 10, net 30; that the invoice was posted on

CUSTOMER NO.: 48316   PAGE 1
        NAME: INTERNATIONAL PAPER PRODUCTS, LTD.

NO.	INVOICE DATE	CHARGE	DATE PAID	CASH PAYMENT	BALANCE DUE
10354	XX-XX-XX	54.00	XX-XX-XX	54.00	0.00
10822	XX-XX-XX	66.00		66.00 CR	0.00
10873	XX-XX-XX	86.40	XX-XX-XX	50.00	36.40
10965	XX-XX-XX	762.00			762.00
11225	XX-XX-XX	51.40	XX-XX-XX	50.37*	0.00
TOTAL		1019.80		220.37	798.40

NOTE: $1,019.80 − $220.37 − $1.03 = $798.40.
(The $1.03 is the cash discount taken by the customer.)

Figure 6-11 Consolidated customer receivable display

June 1; that the customer check was written on June 9; and that the payment was posted by the company on June 15. As these figures show, the customer payment was made seven working days after the invoice was posted; however, the payment was posted eleven working days afterwards. In such a situation, the cash discount is usually allowed.

Selections 3 and 4, "Credit customer account" and "Debit customer account," are required in making subtractions from or additions to customer accounts. A *credit adjustment* is the same as a customer credit: it subtracts a dollar amount from an outstanding account. Removing a small balance, such as $.40, for instance, illustrates a credit adjustment. A *debit adjustment* is the reverse of a credit adjustment: it adds a dollar amount to an outstanding account. Suppose a customer's check is returned to a business because of insufficient funds in the customer's checking account. By now, the payment information would have passed through the cash-receipts computer application and would either show up as a payment on a customer's account or be applied to delete an invoice from the file. In either case, a dollar charge in the form of a debit adjustment must be added to processing. The charge will either offset a payment or reinstate an invoice previously deleted from the file.

Selections 5 and 6 are similar to those discussed in earlier chapters. "Display account," for instance, is an inquiry-only command designed to permit an ac-

1. ADJUST SMALL-BALANCE TOTALS

2. ADJUST CASH DISCOUNTS

3. CREDIT CUSTOMER ACCOUNT

4. DEBIT CUSTOMER ACCOUNT

5. DISPLAY ACCOUNT

6. RETURN TO MAIN MENU

Figure 6-12   Accounts receivable file-processing menu

count to be examined but not changed. Following an examination, the terminal operator usually enters additional processing instructions to show whether the account requires adjustment. The last selection, "Return to main menu," is self-explanatory. This processing option provides an exit from the file-processing menu; it returns control to the main processing menu.

The Print Aging Schedule Program

One additional file-processing selection generally associated with the interactive update of the receivable file is "Age customer account." Figure 6-13 illustrates the display that might follow this command. For each outstanding invoice, it shows the invoice number, date, and charge; any payment and the date of payment; and the balance due. At the bottom of the display the amount due is subdivided into one or more aging buckets: current, 31–60 (days past due), 61–90 (days past due), and over 91 (days past due). Thus, the purpose of aging an account is to show the length of time that different dollar amounts are past due. As shown, the fictitious International Paper Products, Ltd., is slow in making payment. Invoice 10873 has a remaining balance of $36.40 that is past due by more than 90 days.

Besides aging accounts on request, a batch program is used to age each account stored on file. The purpose of processing is twofold: to print a *receivable aging schedule,* a report used to show accounts past due, and to create a

```
        CUSTOMER NO.:   48316                                        PAGE 2
                 NAME:   INTERNATIONAL PAPER PRODUCTS, LTD.
          CREDIT LIMIT:  $2500

                        INVOICE                 DATE      CASH      BALANCE
            NO.         DATE      CHARGE         PAID      PAYMENT   DUE

          10873         XX-XX-XX    86.40      XX-XX-XX     50.00     36.40
          10965         XX-XX-XX   762.00                            762.00




          CURRENT                  31–60                 61–90      OVER 90
                                   762.00                            36.40
```

Figure 6-13   Aged accounts receivable display

print file suitable for printing customer statements. Figure 6-14 illustrates an aging schedule, entitled "Accounts Receivable Aged Trial Balance Summary." The term *aged trial balance* is a carryover from precomputer days: controls are designed to ensure that aged accounts are in balance. To arrive at a balance, all aged subtotals are summed to arrive at an aged total. This total must be the same as the amount-due total written to the consolidated A/R master file. If the totals differ, adjustments must be made and a second "trial" conducted.

The aging schedule is used in several ways: to determine whether outstanding receivables are becoming more or less past due, to spot problem and delinquent accounts, and to project the amount of money that should be received by a business in the short term. Of these, we will examine how the schedule is used to spot problem accounts. In processing, several rules are generally followed to mark accounts to be carefully examined—for example, accounts in which the total amount due exceeds the credit limit. As illustrated, no accounts have exceeded their assigned credit limits. When a limit is exceeded, the credit department must decide whether to forbid future sales to these customers, until payment is made, or to increase their credit limits. Another rule is to identify all accounts whose past-due total exceeds current sales. Account 19543 would be identified if this rule were enforced. Current sales of $135.72 are less than past-due sales of $410.07. Still another rule is to identify all accounts whose past-due balance is over 60 days and above a dollar amount, such as $1,000. Account 347958 would be flagged using this rule.

AGE ANALYSIS REPORT

GENERAL OFFICE PRODUCTS

5/31/8-

6/ 2/8-
PAGE 1

CUSTOMER NUMBER	CUSTOMER NAME	SLS MAN	BALANCE	CURRENT	31-60 DAYS	61-90 DAYS	91-120 DAYS	OVER 120 DAYS	CREDIT LIMIT	PHONE
11257	NORTH STAR SPECIALTI	4	463.19			203.27	173.45	86.47	2000.00	715-898-5805
19543	CROSBY MANUFACTURING	4	410.07	135.72	162.02	112.33				608-435-5960
	SLS MAN TOTAL		873.26	135.72	162.02	315.60	173.45	86.47		
347958	AWARD REALTY	12	1704.18	289.95	397.04	178.26	431.82	407.11	3000.00	507-447-4700
	SLS MAN TOTAL		1704.18	289.95	397.04	178.26	431.82	407.11		
110	STANDBY SYSTEMS INC.	15	300.10	244.40	55.70				2500.00	612-564-2315
1008	EDINA LAWN & LANDSCA	15	958.48	958.48					2000.00	612-874-3900
225479	SENTRY ENAMELING CO.	15	887.18	462.80	286.51	137.87			2500.00	612-882-8673
5683296	ART WILLIAM & SON TRU	15	154.05	154.05					1500.00	612-333-6431
	SLS MAN TOTAL		2299.81	1819.73	342.21	137.87				
285	SEASONAL CONTROL INC	23	825.89	7.84	475.95	325.25	16.85		2000.00	612-854-7838
1050	BLACK & KUEHN	23	70.24	55.12	15.12					612-371-4504
77864329	BROCK - WHITE CO.	23	236.75	177.32	59.43				2000.00	612-646-4008
	SLS MAN TOTAL		1132.88	240.28	550.50	325.25	16.85			
	TOTALS		6010.13	2485.68	1451.77	956.98	622.12	493.58		

Figure 6-14   Receivable aging schedule

The Print Customer Statements Program

As Figure 6-15 shows, the print aging schedule program creates a *receivable print file* in addition to printing the receivable aging schedule. Once the aging schedule is approved, the next step is to begin printing customer statements.

As Figure 6-16 shows, the receivable print file is somewhat similar to the file used in printing customer invoices: several differences can be noted, however. First, only customer sold-to information is needed in printing the monthly statement, whereas both sold-to and ship-to information are printed on the customer invoice. Second, details describing each outstanding invoice are placed on the statement. These details show the original total charge and the current balance-due amount. Third, aging information is important to the statement. This information is calculated by the aging schedule program and explains why this program is run prior to producing customer statements.

The printing of customer statements is similar to the printing of customer invoices. Even with cycle billing, the print program requires considerable time to complete. Some business firms, for example, must set aside several hours to complete this processing step; others use more than one eight-hour shift. Because of the time requirements, it is essential that the program include a restart provision. With restart, it is possible to begin a rerun and to resume printing customer statements at the point at which a problem in processing was identified.

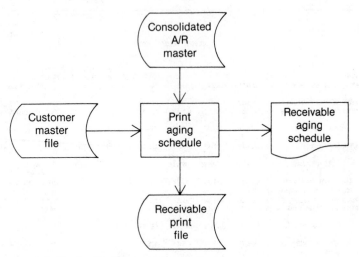

Figure 6-15 Creating the receivable print file

Besides producing customer statements as a batch, the printing of statements "on demand" is required if a customer is to be able to request that a statement be sent in advance of a monthly statement. On-demand printing adds another selection on the file-processing menu developed for updating the A/R master file. This selection is entitled "Print customer statement." Continuous computer forms that allow the removal of one or more forms from a terminal printer without loss or wastage of the next form have contributed to the increase in on-demand printing. Even then, caution is advised; one-at-a-time statement printing is not advisable as a common practice. Because of the high cost of on-demand printing, considerable judgment is needed to determine when to use this option.

6-4 ADDING COMPLEXITY TO RECEIVABLES PROCESSING

The accounts receivable computer application, as discussed thus far, is not very complex or difficult to understand. The major conceptual difficulties perhaps lie in seeing how records are placed in the consolidated A/R master file and how these records are adjusted and eventually deleted. In this section we will consider two areas that contribute to making receivables processing more complex than it may initially appear. The first of these, automatic cash application, results from customer behavior that is the exception rather than the rule. The second of these, month-end closing, results from conflicting choices. One choice is to print customer statements well in advance in order to maximize payments by customers. Another choice is to delay printing as long as possible in order to include as many outstanding invoices as possible on each customer statement.

Customer account number

(Entering account number transfers
information from the customer master
file to the receivables print file)

    Customer sold-to name
    Customer sold-to address
    Salesperson number
    Distributor number

Invoice 1
    Record code
    Date of transaction
    Description (optional)
    Total invoice charge
    Balance due

Invoice 2
    .
    .
    .

Invoice 3
    .
    .
    .

Current
31–60
61–90
Over 90

(*file continues*)

Figure 6-16 Receivable print file

Automatic Cash Application

As we saw in the last chapter, some customers make payments on account
instead of using the invoice or monthly-statement remittance to indicate how a
payment is to be applied. Although this behavior is unusual, it nonetheless must
be handled by the accounts receivable application. Typically, automatic-cash-
application processing instructions are included in the print receivable register
program, or a cash application program is added to processing. This new program is placed between the sort/merge receivable files program and the print
receivable register program.

    Automatic cash application can best be understood by using an illustration.
Figure 6-17 shows how a $600 payment on account would be applied to the

```
        CUSTOMER NO.:  48316                                    PAGE 3
             NAME:  INTERNATIONAL PAPER PRODUCTS, LTD.


                INVOICE              DATE        CASH      BALANCE
         NO.     DATE     CHARGE     PAID      PAYMENT       DUE

        10354  XX-XX-XX    54.00   XX-XX-XX   54.00 POA      0.00
        10822  XX-XX-XX    66.00              66.00 CR       0.00
        10873  XX-XX-XX    86.40   XX-XX-XX   86.40 POA      0.00
        10965  XX-XX-XX   762.00   XX-XX-XX  459.60 POA    302.40
        11225  XX-XX-XX    51.40                            51.40




        TOTAL             1019.80             666.00       353.80
```

Figure 6-17 Automatic-cash-application display

International Paper Production, Ltd., account illustrated earlier. Notice that the lowest invoice number is paid first, followed by the next lowest, until the entire payment has been exhausted. Pay attention to the assumption. It was assumed that the lowest invoice number is also the oldest invoice. This assumption holds, provided invoice numbers follow a date-ordered sequence. When they do not, a sort by date is needed to identify the oldest invoice.

A problem with automatic cash application is that it is difficult to explain to customers how a payment has been applied—especially if a customer decides to make a payment on account early in the month and another later payment in which a remittance stub is enclosed. (In this instance, the customer usually attempts to make payment on an invoice that has been reduced to zero.) To make payment-on-account information more understandable to all, a payment-on-account code is appended to each affected transaction. The code tells where cash was applied. Even then the customer may not understand, however. Situations in which the customer disagrees with the way in which payment is applied are even more difficult. Suppose that, as before, a cash discount of $1.03 is permitted if invoice 11225 is paid first. As illustrated, invoice 11225 is the newest invoice. According to the earlier rule used in applying cash to an account, this invoice would always be paid last—much to the dismay of the customer.

Obviously one way of dealing with many of the problems that result from automatic cash application is to use only one method of applying a payment on account and to never deviate from this method. If a customer attempts to pay an invoice that already has been reduced to zero, the payment would be treated as yet another payment on account. Or, if a customer complains that a discount was not allowed when it might have been, he or she is simply informed that the rules cannot be changed.

A more prudent way of handling payment-on-account problems is by the design of interactive routines that permit adjustments to be made quickly. For example, if a payment on account has reduced an outstanding invoice balance to zero and another payment instructs the company to do the same, the double payment can be flagged for online review. During the review the account is usually adjusted so that the application of payments is consistent with the customer's instructions.

Month-End Closing

As with automatic cash application, month-end closing decisions must be set carefully to minimize internal conflict and friction. When sales commissions are based on sales, paid in full, marketing and sales personnel want to see receivables month-end closing dates delayed as long as possible, so that the maximum number of outstanding invoices will be included in customer statements. Financial officers and data processing managers, on the other hand, both view any cutoff date as the absolute deadline. To protect their interests, they like to see processing completed well in advance of the month-end closing deadline. By processing in advance, financial officers can be sure that bills will reach customers as scheduled. Likewise, processing in advance protects the data processing manager by providing recovery time if errors turn up. Sufficient time remains so that reruns of programs can be made before a month-end deadline.

To avoid the conflict inherent in this situation, business firms limit the time between closing the A/R master file and printing customer statements. This makes it necessary to assign a high priority to the printing of customer statements. Another method of reducing conflict is to establish different closing dates for different groups of customers or for different types of accounts. For example, it is common to divide accounts by store or by regional sales office. This division defines the way in which cycle billing is performed. With cycle billing, massive runs of month-end statements are avoided, and recovery problems are simplified. The only area more difficult to manage is the maintenance of financial controls.

Automatic cash application and month-end closing are but two areas affecting the design of the accounts receivable application. They show that the design of an application must take into consideration a variety of things. In particular, because designs specify the ways in which business transactions are to be handled, they must be carefully reviewed and evaluated to avoid conflicts in business procedures. This task of review and evaluation does not belong only to the data processing manager. Rather, the impact of data processing must be determined by all managers whose areas are affected by a computer design.

6-5 MANAGEMENT IMPLICATIONS

In recent years business firms have realized that efficient use of assets is a key factor in determining profitability. As a consequence, the management of accounts receivable has received considerable attention. With receivables, a closely watched activity ratio is the *average collection period:*

$$\text{Average collection period} = \frac{\text{Average accounts receivable in dollars}}{\text{Sales per day in dollars}}$$

To clarify how this ratio is applied, assume that the accounts receivable average is $1,000,000 and that total sales per day is $40,000. These figures permit the financial manager to compute the average collection period. In this example, the period is 25 days ($1,000,000 ÷ $40,000 per day = 25 days). Now suppose that the collection period considered normal for the industry within which the company belongs is 35 days. Since 25 is clearly better than 35, the financial manager is able to state that collections are well within the normal time frame.

The amount of money saved by lowering the average collection period can be substantial. Suppose all receivables must be financed with short-term loans at an interest rate of 12 percent per year. Suppose further that the average collection period is reduced by 10 days, from 35 days to 25 days, but that sales remain constant at $40,000 per day. From these data, yearly interest savings of $48,000 are possible. Instead of having to finance an average receivables of $1,400,000 (35 days × $40,000 per day), the company need only finance average receivables totaling $1,000,000 (25 days × $40,000). Annual interest costs are thus reduced from $168,000 to $120,000.

With savings as high as twenty cents on the dollar (depending on the cost of short-term financing), companies have been willing to invest large amounts in automating their accounts receivable operations. Some of these investments have produced even larger gains than expected. One firm, ranked near the bottom (61st out of 70 firms) in managing its receivables, realized a complete turnaround following the installation of an online accounts receivable application. At a cost of less than $200,000 for equipment and personnel, the company automated all receivables processing. With this system in operation the firm was able to improve its industry ranking from 61 to 12. In so doing, it also lowered its average collection period by 18 days and reduced average receivables by more than $850,000.

Besides direct dollar savings, an online accounts receivable system leads to improved customer service. A major form of improvement is the capability to respond quickly to a customer's or salesperson's questioning of an account. Suppose, for example, that a customer payment must be received before an additional sale can be made. In a strictly batch processing environment, it can take several days to report customer payment information to district sales offices. In an interactive processing environment, however, information is reported as it becomes known. For instance, a company can provide a daily display of customer accounts that have been suspended as well as accounts that are no longer suspended.

Last, improved collection procedures typically follow from a modern, online accounts receivable system. A major collections stumbling block with batch-processed receivables is that aging reports are not designed for ease of use by collections personnel. What collections people are most concerned about is the capability to let customers know that payments are past due and to stop further sales from taking place before an even larger amount becomes past due. With online processing, these concerns are dealt with directly. If a customer account is to be limited to cash-only sales, this information can be entered by terminal and placed immediately in the customer master file. Since this file must be checked before a credit sale is permitted, the credit adjustment takes place immediately—not several days or weeks after the decision to change a customer's terms of payment.

REVIEW OF IMPORTANT IDEAS

The main objective of accounts receivable processing is to hold customer credit balances to a minimum, consistent with the prompt delivery of goods and services. This objective is achieved in part by the timely release of customer monthly statements and by improved customer collection procedures.

There are three types of accounts receivable systems: balance only, balance forward, and open item. The simplest of these is the balance-only system; the most complex is the open-item system. Both the balance-forward and the open-item systems age past-due amounts; however, the open-item system is the only type that lists each invoice past due. An important advantage of the open-item system is that it provides a complete accounting of each sales transaction.

The preliminary overview of accounts receivable processing shows that the update of the consolidated A/R master file is an involved process. Before processing can begin, the file must be in proper sequence and in balance. After the file is consolidated, invoices that net to zero can be identified and later removed from the file. Following this, the remaining open invoices are aged; month-end statements are printed. Because the consolidated A/R master file is first expanded and later reduced in size, different file-balance-control equations help to ensure that all transactions are accounted for.

Different registers are used in monitoring accounts receivable processing. The accounts receivable register lists all transactions stored on the consolidated A/R master file and prints dollar and transaction-count file-balance totals. The deleted-invoice report is another register. It lists all invoices that net to zero and that have been deleted from the consolidated A/R master file. Several copies of this report may be prepared to account for all file adjustments.

Customer accounts are aged to remind the customer of past-due amounts and to identify customers who are slow in making payments. Accounts can be aged on request and as a batch. Programmed rules are used to pinpoint problem accounts. One rule, for example, is to flag all accounts in which the past-due total exceeds current sales.

Deleting invoices from the A/R master file, making account adjustments, and aging accounts should occur before month-end statements are prepared. Doing this work in advance protects against having to rerun the statements program. Although the program itself is not difficult, it takes considerable time to complete.

Automatic cash application and month-end closing represent two areas that add complexity to accounts receivable processing. Automatic cash application requires programmed instructions to show how payments on account are to be applied. With month-end closing, management must clearly specify receivable cutoff dates. Failure to do so leads to internal conflict and friction.

Sizable benefits can be derived from an online accounts receivable application. Besides direct dollar savings resulting from lower interest payments, companies benefit from improved customer service and collection procedures. Customers are made to feel that a business fully understands its billing activities. Thus, when questions are asked, they are answered quickly; when billing mistakes are pointed out, they are easily resolved.

KEY WORDS

Accounts receivable

Current assets

Balance-only A/R system

Balance-forward A/R system

Open-item A/R system

Aging buckets

Dunning letters

Consolidated A/R master file

Customer monthly statement

Cycle billing

Account cycle time

Accounts receivable register

Deleted-invoice report

Cutoff point

Credit adjustment

Debit adjustment

Receivable aging schedule

Aged trial balance

Receivable print file

Automatic cash application

Month-end closing

Average collection period

REVIEW QUESTIONS

1. Besides keeping a record of current assets, why should a company develop an online A/R application?

2. What are the three types of A/R systems and how do they differ?

3. What is an "aging bucket"?

4. What is a "dunning letter"?

5. How are records arranged in the A/R master file?

6. Explain the equation needed to balance the total dollar amount stored on the A/R master file.

7. Name the four types of printed output produced by this application.

8. How does a monthly statement differ from a customer invoice?

9. What is cycle billing and how does it work?

10. What processing function is performed by the sort/merge receivable files program?

11. How does the deleted-invoice report differ from the accounts receivable register?

12. Why do some customer accounts require adjustment prior to printing monthly statements?

13. What types of customer account adjustments can be made online?

14. What information is printed on the receivable aging schedule?

15. How does the receivable print file differ from the print file used in producing customer invoices?

16. What is on-demand printing?

17. Explain automatic cash application.

18. Why must business firms use care in setting month-end closing deadlines?

19. Explain an average collection period and discuss why it receives close attention by management.

20. How can an online A/R system improve customer service?

EXERCISES

1. Explain the types of data that are stored on the following computer files:
   (a) The invoice A/R summary file
   (b) The receipts A/R summary file
   (c) The old consolidated A/R master file
   (d) The consolidated A/R master file (before deletion)
   (e) The consolidated A/R master file (after deletion)
   (f) The receivable print file
   (g) The receivable change file

2. Draft flowcharts for the following interactive programs and explain how each program might be designed:

   (a) The update customer master program

   (b) The display customer account program

   (c) The display receivable account program

   Why is the customer master file needed in the design of the display receivable account program?

3. Using Figure 6-3 as a guide, show how the accounts receivable master file would be designed for a balance-forward A/R system. In your design show which data elements would be stored for each invoice, customer credit, and customer payment.

CASE

Integrated Receivables Processing

Instead of designing separate customer-invoicing, customer cash-receipts, and accounts receivable computer applications, many business firms design all three at once. They then call their finished design an *integrated accounts receivable system.* An integrated design offers several advantages. Only a single organization chart and one set of system flowcharts are needed. Likewise, the system requires a single program-processing menu, unified sets of file-processing menus for the customer and product master files, and unified file-balance-control procedures. Fewer programs need to be written and fewer summary files processed. File backup procedures are simplified, as is online updating of the consolidated A/R master file. Last, an integrated design makes it easier to understand how the system works.

Figure A-1 provides a preliminary overview of an integrated accounts receivable system. Twelve steps in processing are illustrated—three less than the fifteen-step total of the six steps needed for processing customer invoices, the four steps for customer cash receipts, and the five steps for accounts receivable (see Figures 4-1, 5-1, and 6-2). More important, neither the invoice nor the cash-receipts A/R summary file is required. Instead, Steps 3 and 4, "Enter invoice transactions" and "Enter receipts transactions," update the consolidated A/R master file directly. Concurrently, each transaction entered into processing is either added to the invoice transaction file or to the receipts transaction file.

The twelve preliminary processing steps shown in Figure A-1 can be summarized as follows:

1. *Ready customer file* ensures that all customer accounts stored on the customer master file are correct.

2. *Ready product file* ensures that all product accounts stored on the product master file are correct.

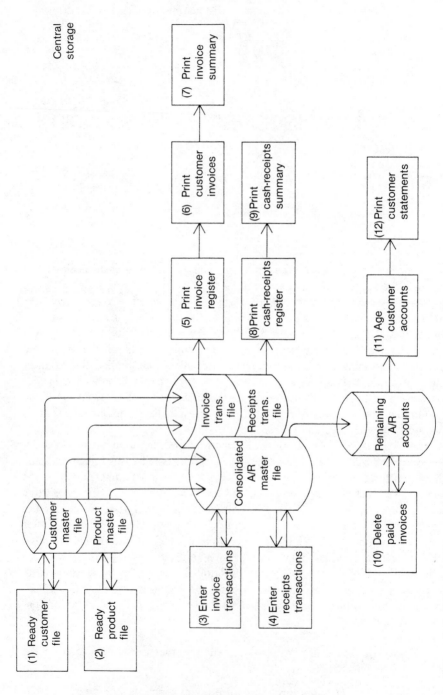

Figure A-1 Integrated A/R processing: preliminary overview

3. *Enter invoice transactions* records what items are shipped to a customer, calculates customer charges, posts items shipped and customer charges to the invoice transaction file, and posts customer charges to the consolidated A/R master file.

4. *Enter receipts transactions* records the cash payment received from the customer, posts the payment to the receipts transaction file, and posts the payment to the consolidated A/R master file.

5. *Print invoice register* documents the contents of the invoice transaction file.

6. *Print customer invoices* produces customer invoices (or credit memos).

7. *Print invoice summary* provides a summary of customer charges (or credits).

8. *Print cash-receipts register* documents the contents of the receipts transaction file and produces a bank deposit slip.

9. *Print cash-receipts summary* provides a summary of cash-receipts processing.

10. *Delete paid invoices* removes paid-in-full invoice and cash-receipts information from the A/R master file.

11. *Age customer accounts* shows delinquent customer accounts and the age of uncollected amounts.

12. *Print customer statements* produces customer monthly bills.

REQUIREMENTS

Prepare system organization charts and systems flowcharts for an integrated accounts receivable system.

1. Prepare an organization chart for the entire system. Because of the number of processing functions and computer programs, place interactive functions and programs on one page; place batch functions and programs on a second page.

2. Prepare ten of the twenty-two systems flowcharts required by an integrated accounts receivable system. The programs to be charted are shown below. Use standard symbols in preparing each flowchart. Two flowcharts will fit on each 8½-by-11-inch sheet of paper.

    (a) Enter (edit/update) invoice transactions

    (b) Enter cash-receipts transactions

    (c) Update customer master file

(d)   Update product master file

(e)   Print invoice register

(f)   Print cash-receipts register

(g)   Adjust receivable master file

(h)   Print deleted-invoice report

(i)   Print aging schedule

(j)   Print customer (monthly) statements

PART

MATERIALS-CONTROL
APPLICATIONS

In this three-chapter section, we will examine applications that stress ways to improve materials management. We begin with an application designed to process and speed the filling of customer orders. An important objective of this application is to provide fast response to customer requirements for goods and services. Next, we look at an inventory-control application developed, in part, to keep track of all goods stored in inventory and, in part, to help determine proper inventory stocking levels. We then finish this section with a two-stage application designed to process purchase orders and to verify the receipt of goods from suppliers. The objective in this instance is the development of formal processing procedures for reordering and accepting goods into stock.

Of the three materials-control applications, we will examine the second, finished-goods inventory, in more detail. It is this application that points to the problems of balancing the demand for inventory (which is recorded by the processing of customer orders), with its supply (which is regulated by the purchasing of additional goods from suppliers). It is this application that most clearly demonstrates the true value of improved materials control.

CHAPTER

7

Customer Order Entry

Customer order entry is an application that businesses use to reduce the time between the receipt of a customer order, the processing and filling of the order, and the shipment of goods to a customer. By quickly translating a customer's order for goods and services into instructions for filling the order from stock, the application provides the capability to improve order turnaround. Businesses have come to rely on fast turnaround as an important part of their customer service programs. With help from the customer order-entry application, they are able to promise the customer "same day" service in filling requests for goods and services. Because the application serves to tell others how to fill customer orders, it is often known as *order filling*. This name is somewhat misleading, however, because order entry actually includes three types of processing activities: customer order processing, order filling, and customer order packing and shipping.

- *Customer order processing* consists of the steps needed to verify customer accounts, including the verification of each customer's credit; it requires maintaining the customer master file.

- *Order filling* consists of the steps showing how the items ordered by a customer are to be picked from inventory; it requires maintaining the product master file and verifying that stock is carried in inventory.

- *Customer order packing and shipping* consists of the steps leading to the printing of packing slips and bills of lading; it creates summary file records required in billing customer for goods shipped.

These three sets of activities make customer order entry one of the more complex data processing applications. Fortunately, it is also one of the more valuable applications developed for business.

Online customer order entry is required by companies that warehouse and distribute large quantities of stock carried in *finished-goods inventory* (inventory that is ready for sale). These companies must often process hundreds of customer orders daily, stock thousands of items, and maintain thousands of square feet of warehouse space. Very large distributors, for example, may process 1,000 or more orders each day, carry 50,000 products in stock, and maintain 100,000 square feet of warehouse space. From an administrative point of view, the key to managing this complex environment is an automated system that moves orders in and moves goods out as accurately and as efficiently as possible. With online processing, for instance, orders received before two in the afternoon can be packed and shipped before five o'clock the same day. In addition to prompt service, the order is filled and shipped correctly: the customer receives the correct quantity, size runs, and colors; the merchandise is shipped to the correct customer and the correct address.

There are other reasons for developing this application besides providing faster and more accurate customer order processing. Three of these reasons follow:

- Customer order entry simplifies order processing. One of the most difficult aspects of processing customer orders is keeping track of all needed details: each order to be filled, each filled order, each customer account, each product account, each product location, and the stock carried at each location. With online processing, the computer keeps track of all of these details.

- Customer order entry standardizes customer and product inventory records. With standard records, it becomes possible to undertake different types of customer and product analyses. By definition, *customer analyses* deal with the study of customer buying habits, whereas *product analyses* deal with the study of product demand. Understanding the characteristics of both is vital to the management of business firms.

- Customer order entry integrates administrative and operational groups in an organization. An administrative group is commonly referred to as a "white collar" group: the people who keep the records and process the paperwork in a business. An operations group represents a "blue collar" group: the people who run the machines and operate the warehouse or plant. For this application, customer order processing is performed by an administrative group, and order filling and shipping are performed by an operations group. With online processing, the computer is able to better integrate the work of both groups.

Finally, compared to a batch design, an interactive, online design of processing can simplify edit and file-update procedures, improve account-inquiry capabilities, reduce clerical costs, improve processing controls, and offer decentralized data processing capabilities. As with invoicing, an online design builds checks and balances into the interactive portion of processing. These help to ensure that each customer order is processed correctly.

7-1 PRELIMINARY OVERVIEW OF PROCESSING

Figure 7-1 provides a preliminary overview of order-entry processing. The following six steps describe the main parts of the application. (Notice that the first three are similar to customer invoicing.)

1. *Ready customer file* to ensure that all customer accounts stored on the customer master file are correct.

2. *Ready product master file* to ensure that all product accounts stored on the product master file are correct.

3. *Enter customer orders* to record what items are ordered by a customer, to determine if each line item contained on the order can be filled from stock, and to determine how best to pick the items from stock.

4. *Print picking documents* to show what items are ordered by a customer, where the stock is located, and in what order to pick the items from stock.

5. *Prepare shipping papers* to document what items were ordered, picked, and packed for shipment.

6. *Prepare summary reports* to provide a summary of items picked from stock and shipped and to create an invoice transaction file.

Inputs to Processing

The main input to processing is the customer order. As Figure 7-2 illustrates, a *customer order* can look quite different from either a customer invoice or a shipping document (see Chapter 4). Close inspection shows, however, that an order form contains the same types of information as a customer invoice.

- *Business order information* documents the business order number (the number assigned to a customer order).

- *Customer order information* identifies the customer account number (if one exists), the customer P.O. number (when appropriate), the date, and the method of payment.

- *Packing information* identifies each product or catalog number, the quantity ordered, the order-fill date, and how the goods are to be shipped.

- *Customer information* provides customer name and address, customer credit details, and salesperson/distributor number/codes.

- *Product information* provides product name, product description details, pricing and discount information, product inventory counts, and product location details.

Figure 7-3 shows how these five types of data are brought together in processing. Data keyed into processing consist of business order, customer order,

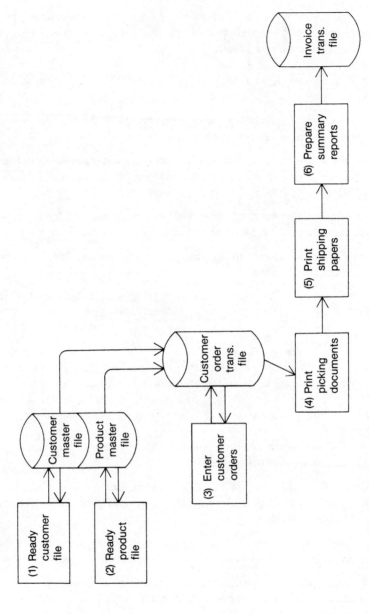

Figure 7-1 Six steps in processing customer orders

PLEASE FILL OUT THIS ORDER FORM CAREFULLY.
ERRORS WILL CAUSE A DELAY IN PROCESSING YOUR ORDER.

IN A HURRY? PHONE IN
YOUR ORDER - 800/258-1710

Customer Contact	Phone Number	Date
ALAN L. ELIASON	345 - 2005	JUNE 21, 19XX

BILLING ADDRESS:

COMPANY: ELIASON and ASSOCIATES
DEPT/ATTN: SOFTWARE DEVELOPMENT
STREET: 175 EAST 39TH PLACE
CITY: EUGENE STATE OR ZIP 97405

Purchase Order No.
9432

Partial Shipment Allowed?
☒ YES ☐ NO

SHIPPING ADDRESS:

COMPANY: ELIASON and ASSOCIATES
DEPT/ATTN: BILLING DEPARTMENT
STREET: 175 EAST 39TH PLACE
CITY: EUGENE STATE OR ZIP 97405

Taxable: ☐ YES ☐ NO
Tax Bond or
Exempt No. (if applicable):

Delivery Requirement:
☒ ASAP

Special Instructions:

☐ Not Before: _____

Digital Intransit Insurance?
(50¢ per $100 Order Value)
☒ YES ☐ NO

Order Item No.	DECdirect Ordering No.	Page Number	Quantity	Unit Price	Extended Amount
1	F- VT 18X - AC	64	1	2,400.00	2,400.00
2	F- QV001 - C2	64	1	250.00	250.00
3	F-				
4	F-				
5	F-				
6	F-				
7	F-				

Sub-Total	2,650.00
Discount	- 132.50
Tax	—
Total	2,517.50

METHOD OF PAYMENT
Cash/Money Order or Charge Card required on all orders less than $35.00*.

Make checks payable to DIGITAL EQUIPMENT CORP.

Invoice upon shipment __X__
Check/Money Order with order _____
Master Card _____ Visa _____
　Charge Card Account No. _____
　Card Assignee _____
　Expiration Date _____

MAIL ORDER TO:
DIGITAL EQUIPMENT CORP.
P.O. BOX CS2008
NASHUA, NH 03061

By executing this order, I acknowledge that I have read, understood and accept the terms and conditions on the reverse side of this order form.

Alan L. Eliason

← **Please Sign Here**

Authorized Signature　　　　　　　　Date

*Puerto Rico customers: Orders less than $35.00 must be placed at the Digital facility (809) 754-7575.

Figure 7-2 Customer order form

and packing information. Data-entry requirements are similar to those for invoicing, but not identical. With order entry, a business is able to determine the method of payment *prior to* the actual shipment of goods. Likewise, the "order-fill date" allows the customer to specify in advance when goods should be packed and shipped: today, as soon as possible, next week, or within the next six months.

Information stored on master files and brought into processing consists of customer and product details. As Figure 7-3 shows, customer records for order entry are the same as customer records for invoicing. Product records, in contrast, must be enlarged for order-entry processing: two new record segments, for product inventory and product location, must be added to each record. The *product inventory segment* is required to store four types of counts and the "estimated date of delivery of new stock." The difference between these four counts of inventory can be explained as follows:

- *Quantity on hand* is the count (the quantity) of finished goods carried in stock (on hand) and available for sale.
- *Quantity on order* is the count of stock previously ordered by a business but not yet delivered.
- *Quantity on back order* is the count of stock needed to fill customer orders that for lack of stock were not filled earlier.
- *Quantity on future order* is the count of stock needed to fill customer orders that specify delivery at a future date.

The *product location segment* stores indicators to tell where stock is located in the warehouse and provides picking instructions. For example, B-6543, a bin location code, means that stock is located in row B, bin number 6543. A distance code of D83-954 states that bin B-6543 is 83 feet from a main traffic aisle, which, in turn, is 954 feet from the main packing area. Last, packing instructions tell order pickers how stock is to be drawn. Code AAA might indicate that a package in a bin cannot be opened, whereas code AAP might mean just the reverse.

Since an online system permits data stored on master files to be retrieved and displayed, a *customer order display* often provides a suitable substitute for the customer order form. In this option, customer order details are keyed directly by clerical operators (order takers) in a business's order-fulfillment department. Later, all keyed input is printed on a customer order form. Figure 7-4 illustrates one possible customer order display. Page 1 shows how information stored on the customer master file is displayed and verified. After an operator has entered the customer account number (an essential input for this option), the record code, and the method of payment, the computer is instructed to retrieve and display the customer's name and address and to warn if there is a credit problem. Additional display pages record customer order details. For each item ordered, the product number, quantity desired, order-fill date required, and method of shipment are entered by an operator into processing.

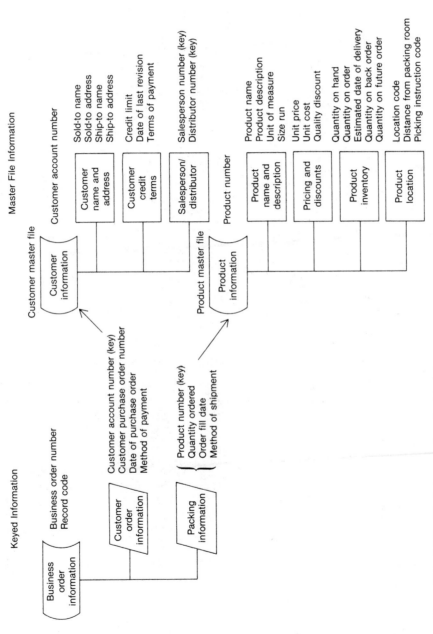

Figure 7-3 Relationships between order-entry data sets

```
CUSTOMER ACCOUNT NO:   XXXXXXX      RECORD CODE:  X
METHOD OF PAYMENT:      XXXXXX


----------------------------------------------------------------------------
THE SOLD-TO AND SHIP-TO NAME AND ADDRESS OF THE CUSTOMER IS:
SOLD TO:
    XXXXXXXXXXXXXXXXXXXXXXXXXXXXXXXXXXXXXXXXXX
    XXXXXXXXXXXXXXXXXXXXXXXXXXXXXXXXXXXXXXXXXX
    XXXXXXXXXXXXXXXXXXXXXXXXXXXXXXXXXXXXXXXXXX
    XXXXXXXXXXXXXXXXXXXXXXXXXXXXXXXXXXXXXXXXXX        CORRECT?
SHIP TO:
    XXXXXXXXXXXXXXXXXXXXXXXXXXXXXXXXXXXXXXXXXX
    XXXXXXXXXXXXXXXXXXXXXXXXXXXXXXXXXXXXXXXXXX
    XXXXXXXXXXXXXXXXXXXXXXXXXXXXXXXXXXXXXXXXXX
    XXXXXXXXXXXXXXXXXXXXXXXXXXXXXXXXXXXXXXXXXX        CORRECT?
```

```
CUSTOMER NAME:   XXXXXXXXXXXXXXXXXXXXXXXXXXXXXXXXXXXXXXXXXX

LINE     PRODUCT NO.      QUANTITY      FILL DATE      SHIP VIA
  1       XXXXXXXX         XXXXXXX       XX-XX-XX      XXXXXXXXX
  2       XXXXXXXX         XXXXXXX       XX-XX-XX      XXXXXXXXX
  3
  4
  5
  6
  7
  8
  9
 10
----------------------------------------------------------------------------

TOTAL QUANTITY ORDERED:   XXXXXXXXXX
```

Figure 7-4 Customer order-entry display

Outputs from Processing

The order-entry application can produce a variety of printed working documents, including picking slips and packing slips. *Picking slips* (or tickets) tell the warehouse crew what stock has been ordered, the quantity ordered, where it is located in the warehouse, and in what sequence it should be picked from stock. The picking slip is organized, for example, so that all stock located in row B is picked before moving to row D. We will examine how this is done later in the chapter. *Packing slips* show what items are being shipped, rather than what was ordered. Figure 7-5 illustrates one type of packing slip: the quantity picked is shown, as is the name of the originator, the bill of lading number, and the date the order was shipped.

There are some very good reasons why the customer invoice is not packed, replacing the packing slip. First, invoices are always sent to the sold-to address, not the ship-to address. With larger businesses, these two addresses often differ. Second, shipping documents, such as packing slips and bills of lading, often become soiled in the course of a shipment's movement through various warehouses and loading docks. It may thus be acceptable for these documents to be difficult to read, but it is not acceptable for an invoice to be difficult to read. Third, many business firms enclose merchandising literature with their invoices. A release describing a special sale of office supplies might be included with a bill, for example. It is assumed that the people paying the bill will be interested in "special sale" literature, or will pass it to the appropriate people in their organization.

Printed outputs other than picking and packing slips include three registers, three change reports, and a variety of processing summaries. The register of most interest is the *open-order register,* which lists all orders to be filled. The *daily order-filling report,* in contrast, is a valuable processing summary that lists all orders filled during the day. Information contained on the open-order register is combined with information on the order-filling report to calculate the *order-fill rate,* which is computed as follows:

$$\text{Order-fill rate} = \frac{\text{Orders filled}}{\text{Orders to be filled}}$$

Accurate and efficient order-entry processing leads to order-fill rates in excess of 95 percent. This means that if 100 orders were received during the day, 95 or more would be filled and shipped before five the same day.

A summary file is the final type of output. The *invoice transaction file,* produced as a final step in processing, contains the condensed version of order-filling details. It is identical to the file created by the program to enter invoice transactions, developed for the customer-invoicing application. Thus, once again we discover how computer applications are related to one another.

apple computer inc.

10260 BANDLEY DRIVE CUPERTINO, CALIFORNIA 95014   (408) 996-1010

SHIPPING AUTHORIZATION

TO DEPARTMENT OF COMPUTER AND INFORMATION SCIENCE
COLLEGE OF ARTS AND SCIENCE
ANYTOWN, U.S.A.

S/A NO.	DATE	REJECT NO.
27090	5/20/8x	

SHIP: PREPAID ☒   COLLECT ☐

1	A2M0011	CENTRONICS 779	2

CHARGE 9500-0541

REASON FOR SHIPMENT

REJECTED MATERIAL ☐	PRODUCTION KIT ☐	OTHER			
P.O. NO.	REQ. NO.	VENDOR		DATE REC'D.	ORIG. QTY. REC'D.

FREIGHT TO BE PAID BY:	VENDOR ☐	APPLE COMPUTER ☐	RETURN FOR:	CREDIT ONLY ☐	CREDIT AND REPLACEMENT ☐

SHIP VIA

VENDOR RETURN AUTHORIZATION NO.		SHIP VIA		INSURED YES ☐ NO ☐	VALUE $
ORIGINATOR'S NAME *M. C. REDFORD*	EXT. *2975*	VENDOR'S AUTHORIZATION BY			DATE
DEPT. (CIRCLE 1) IQC MRB OTHER _____ INTERNAL USE SHIPPER ONLY *9500*	DATE *5/20/8X*	SIGNATURE (PURCH. OR ACCTG.)			DATE

DATE SHIPPED *5/26/8X*	CARRIER *PIE*	B/L NO: W/B NO: *22161*	NO. PCS. *4*	WEIGHT *136*	PPD. CHGS.	RECEIVED BY

P 1002   10/81

PACKING SLIP

Figure 7-5 Packing slip

7-2 ORDER-ENTRY PROCESSING

Figure 7-6 shows the systems organization chart for customer order entry. As illustrated, the first program in the interactive part of processing is used to "enter customer orders." This program builds a *customer order file,* transaction by transaction. Three interactive programs also update or adjust computer files. They serve to ready the customer master file, ready the product master file, and adjust the customer order file. The need to update or adjust results from a variety of situations: the customer decides to cancel an order, to increase the quantity to order, to change the ship-to location, or to change the order-fill date. Likewise, internal business adjustments must be made: to change the quantity-shipped total, to cancel a line item on an order, or to substitute one product for another. Finally, three display programs are indicated. The first, "display customer order," permits a company to track each unfilled order. Should a customer question whether an order has been filled, the answer can be determined in seconds. The second, "display customer account," provides direct access to each customer account. The third, "display product account," also permits direct access. This display permits the status of each product carried in inventory to be reviewed.

The batch portion of the application, as charted, consists of eleven print programs. The print requirements for registers and change reports show what types of online files are maintained in processing. For example, since the records of the customer master file can be modified online, a copy of the file (the customer master file register) and all changes made to the file (the customer change report) must be printed. In addition to registers and change reports, the two transaction documents printed are picking slips and packing slips. Last, several processing summaries are included in the design. These lead to a future-order report, a back-order report, and a daily order-filling report.

Figure 7-7 shows the program menu that follows from the chart of organization. The seven interactive and eleven batch programs make order entry one of the larger computer applications. As before, the computer operator begins processing by selecting one of these programs from the menu.

The Ready Customer Master File Program

Before customer orders can be processed, both the customer and the product master files must be current. The flowchart in Figure 7-8 shows the steps needed to ready the customer master file. As illustrated, the documents used in processing are the new customer form and the customer change form. The *new customer form* is completed in large part by the salesperson assigned to the customer's account. Details such as customer name and address are usually completed while the salesperson is working his or her sales territory. Before an order from a new customer is accepted, however, the customer's credit rating must be checked. This work is done by the credit department. Generally, more than one credit reference is required. Two popular reference sources are the customer's bank and the firm of Dun and Bradstreet, which estimates the finan-

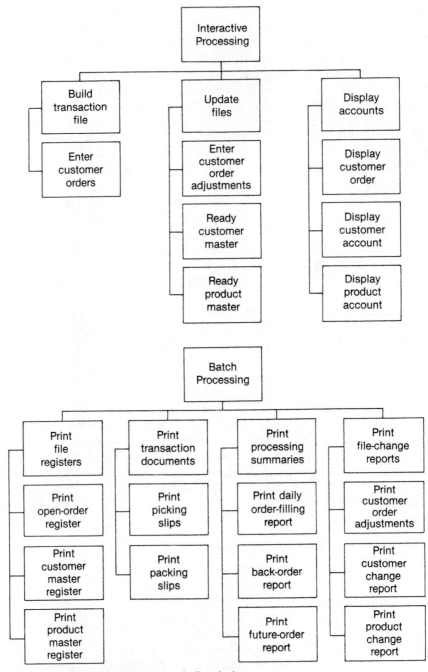

Figure 7-6 Order-entry systems organization chart

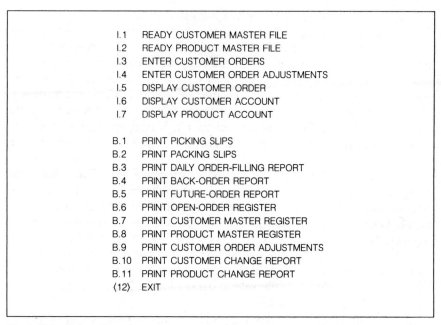

```
I.1    READY CUSTOMER MASTER FILE
I.2    READY PRODUCT MASTER FILE
I.3    ENTER CUSTOMER ORDERS
I.4    ENTER CUSTOMER ORDER ADJUSTMENTS
I.5    DISPLAY CUSTOMER ORDER
I.6    DISPLAY CUSTOMER ACCOUNT
I.7    DISPLAY PRODUCT ACCOUNT

B.1    PRINT PICKING SLIPS
B.2    PRINT PACKING SLIPS
B.3    PRINT DAILY ORDER-FILLING REPORT
B.4    PRINT BACK-ORDER REPORT
B.5    PRINT FUTURE-ORDER REPORT
B.6    PRINT OPEN-ORDER REGISTER
B.7    PRINT CUSTOMER MASTER REGISTER
B.8    PRINT PRODUCT MASTER REGISTER
B.9    PRINT CUSTOMER ORDER ADJUSTMENTS
B.10   PRINT CUSTOMER CHANGE REPORT
B.11   PRINT PRODUCT CHANGE REPORT
(12)   EXIT
```

Figure 7-7 Order-entry main program menu

cial strength of a customer and provides a composite credit appraisal. When the credit rating for a customer is not high, credit managers usually require a more detailed credit report to document specific financial items such as the customer's payment experience.

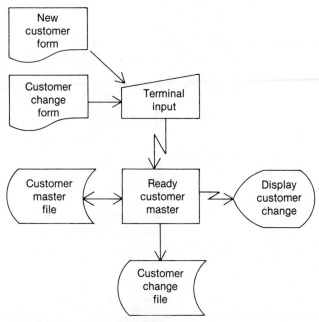

Figure 7-8 Ready customer master file

The *customer change form* contains less information than the new customer form. It is used to change information stored on file about the customer. Figure 7-9 illustrates a display page for checking off items to be changed. To begin processing, the operator must enter the customer account number. Following input, the computer locates the customer's account and displays the customer name. After visual verification of the name, the operator keys in the fields to be changed. Initially, the cursor is placed to the left of the sold-to name. If this field is to be changed, a character, such as a 1, is inserted. Tapping the directional key moves the cursor to the next item. This continues until the return key is depressed.

Often changes to the customer master file are made immediately before the entry of customer order details. Consider the following example. Instead of sending an order by mail, a customer decides to place a direct order by telephone. On receiving the call, the order taker asks for the customer's account number; the customer responds, "612554." The order taker keys in the account number to display the sold-to and ship-to names and addresses and asks the customer to verify each name and address, whereupon the customer replies, "We have made a change in our sold-to street address. Our new address is 3564 Cardinalle Road."

In such a situation, one processing procedure, rather than two, could be used both to change the customer master and to process the details of the customer order. There are two good reasons for using separate programs, however. First, any change to the customer master file must be carefully documented. As Figure 7-8 shows, all changes to the customer master file are written to a

```
CUSTOMER ACCOUNT NUMBER XXXXXXXXX
CUSTOMER NAME IS XXXXXXXXXXXXXXXXXXXXXXXXXXXXXXXXXXXXXXXXXXXXX

CUSTOMER NAME AND ADDRESS:
                                    ■ SOLD-TO NAME
                                    ■ SOLD-TO ADDRESS
                                    ■ SHIP-TO NAME
                                    ■ SHIP-TO ADDRESS
CUSTOMER CREDIT TERMS:
                                    ■ CREDIT LIMIT
                                    ■ DATE OF LAST REVISION
                                    ■ TERMS OF PAYMENT
SALESPERSON/DISTRIBUTOR:
                                    ■ SALESPERSON NUMBER
                                    ■ DISTRIBUTOR NUMBER

EXIT    ----------------------------------    ■
```

Figure 7-9 Customer change display

customer change file; later, the contents of the change file are printed to produce a register of all customer changes. Second, using separate programs means that many changes to the customer master file can be made in advance of processing the customer order. Most companies ask their customers to record name-and-address changes on customer order forms. When change information is received in this way, it can be entered into processing in advance of customer order details.

The Ready Product Master File Program

The flowchart in Figure 7-10 shows the steps required to make the product master file ready for processing. Although this procedure resembles that used to ready the customer file, it is not actually identical. The documents used to record changes to the product master file are the new product form and several types of product change forms. New product forms are required for all new or improved products carried in inventory. An improved product, for example, might be the second edition of a textbook. This product would be assigned a unique product number. Considerably more new products are added to inventory than most people expect: it is not unusual for a business to replace 20 to 25 percent of the items carried in stock each year with new or improved items. For each addition, a product number must be assigned. Following this, product name and description, pricing and discounts, product inventory, and product location information must be keyed into processing.

Product change forms, in contrast to the new product form, generally contain a minimal amount of information. They are used to show new product prices

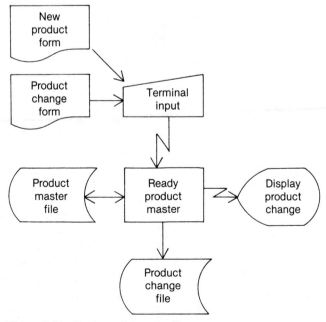

Figure 7-10   Ready product master file

NOTICE OF COST CHANGE

BRANCH _____WESTFIR_____

DATE _____04 - 08 - XX_____

_____Martin A. Mitchell_____
Signed

_____Helen Matthews_____
Approved

PRODUCT NUMBER	NEW COST
22222	7.90
36859	11.46
89734	19.13

Figure 7-11 A product change form: Notice of cost change

and discounts, additions to inventory, and changes in product location. Figure 7-11 illustrates a "notice of cost change" form. This form, like many others, provides room for the product number and the change to be keyed into processing.

Product changes must always be completed before customer order processing begins. The objective is to make the product master file as accurate as possible, that is, consistent with the latest changes in the warehouse. As might be expected, completing all changes on time tends to be difficult when large shipments of new stock are received or when a major reorganization of the warehouse is undertaken. It is common to find terminal operators making changes to the product master file as early as six in the morning, in order to complete all changes by ten. Generally, pricing and discount changes are entered into processing first. Later, after stock has been received, counted, and stored, product inventory and location changes are made.

Making all changes of one kind, one after another, simplifies data-entry procedures. Suppose, for example, that only price changes are to be made. After the operator selects "price change" from the file-selection menu, the program displays a *change table,* which lists by product number all price changes (see Figure 7-12). In some cases, both the old and new prices are shown to provide the operator with a point of reference. Special edit checks help the operator to

PRODUCT	NEW	OLD
NUMBER	PRICE	PRICE
22222	8.99	8.49
36859	12.22	11.98
89734	44.46	24.46 •••

THE PRICE DIFFERENCE IS TOO GREAT.
PLEASE VERIFY.

Figure 7-12   Change table

isolate errors. If the old price is $6.99 and the new price is $79.90, the computer will respond with:

THE PRICE DIFFERENCE IS TOO GREAT.
PLEASE VERIFY AND ENTER AGAIN.

Entering the different types of changes separately also makes it easier to spot and correct input errors and clerical mistakes. As Figure 7-10 shows, all changes to the product master file are displayed. At this point in processing, a visual inspection is required. Following this initial inspection, all changes are written to a product change file, which is used later in printing the change report for the product master file. The change file is sequentially organized, and unless it is sorted prior to printing the change report, the report will list the first change entered into processing, the second change entered into processing, and so forth, regardless of the type of change (price, cost, quantity, or location). The way around this problem is to enter all price changes at one time, followed by all cost changes, and so on. In this way, the change report will list all price changes followed by all cost changes.

The Enter Customer Orders Program

After all product changes have been completed and a customer account has been verified, customer order details are entered into processing (see the flowchart in Figure 7-13). As with invoicing, the customer master file serves as a reference file. Customer information, such as sold-to and ship-to addresses, is read into processing and is added to the customer order record. The product

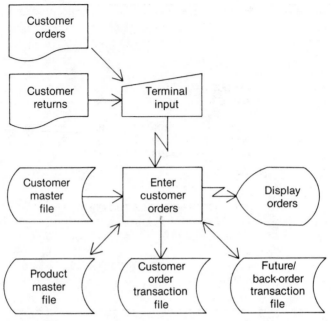

Figure 7-13 Enter customer orders

master file, in addition to serving as a reference file, is updated by processing. The actual update is simple: the field for on-hand quantity is changed to correspond to the quantity ordered by the customer. If, for example, the on-hand field shows 100 units and the customer orders 10, then 10 units are transferred to the customer order record and the on-hand field is reduced to show a remaining balance of 90 units.

Input documents to customer order processing include customer returns as well as orders. As a general rule, all customer returns are processed before customer orders, so that quantity-on-hand totals can be increased, since returns add to stock. Following the processing of customer returns, different types of customer orders are processed; these include preshipped orders, future orders, back orders, and current orders.

Preshipped orders consist of orders for which stock has been picked from inventory in advance of processing the order against the product master file. Such orders are ill advised in an automated order-entry processing environment: every preshipment violates the objective of keeping the product master file accurate. There are times, however, when preshipped orders cannot be avoided. Suppose the president of the company decides to give away six dozen shirts; or suppose a rush order is received while the computer is being serviced. These situations would lead to preshipped orders.

Future orders consist of orders that have been held to be filled according to a customer's request for a shipment on a specific future date. Processing future orders requires that a file be checked daily to determine which ones should be filled. This file might be manually maintained, or, as Figure 7-13 shows, information from the file of future orders can be brought into processing by keying the file-processing selection to "process future orders." Still another alternative is to immediately add all future orders to the customer order file. With this option, each order-fill date is compared with the current date; if the dates match, the order is scheduled for picking.

Back orders, as stated in Chapter 4, represent orders for which the on-hand quantity of a particular stock is less than the quantity desired by the customer. They are to be filled once sufficient stock is available. Processing back orders is similar to processing future orders: a file must be reviewed daily to determine which orders, if any, can be filled. This file can be maintained by hand or, as Figure 7-13 shows, can be updated in processing. In the latter method, the operator activates the "process back orders" selection, and the computer is instructed to compare back-order requirements to the latest version of the product master file. Once it is determined that an order can be filled, the order is written to the customer order file. The back order, in turn, is deleted from the back-order file.

Current orders are orders received for the first time. Generally, they are filled after future and back orders have been processed. In processing, the customer account is initially verified; customer information is added to the customer order transaction. Where necessary, new customer information must be added to the customer master file. Following customer verification, the order-fill date is checked to determine if the order (or some part of the order) should be filled as soon as possible, or at some future date. When the order is to be filled as soon as possible, product information is verified, the field for on-hand quantity of the product record is updated, product information is transferred to the customer order file, and the completed transaction is written to the customer order file. When the order is to be filled at some future date, product information is verified and transferred; however, the product master file is not updated. Instead, the now verified order is written to the future order transaction file or, as Figure 7-13 shows, to a combined transaction file of future orders and back orders.

The Print Picking Document Program

Picking slips are printed following the entry of customer orders into processing. As Figure 7-14 shows, the program to print packing slips may be preceded by a sort program that sequences the items in each customer order in the file by bin (or warehouse) location code. Suppose, for example, that business order 6345 contains three items. If the order were not properly sequenced, an order picker might walk to the back of the warehouse to pick the first item, then to the front to pick the second item, then again to the back to pick the third item. To avoid such an inefficient situation, the computer is programmed to rearrange the items to be picked. Most often the objective sought is to *minimize travel time.* Thus, in our example, a computer sort would sequence the order so that the first and third items, located at the back of the warehouse, would be picked first, followed by the second item, at the front of the building.

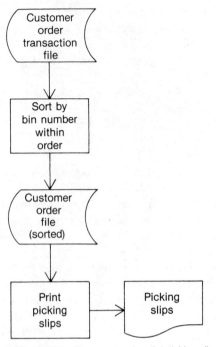

Figure 7-14 The program to print picking slips

A time-consuming sort of the entire customer order file can be avoided if the customer order is arranged in the most efficient way before writing the order to the customer order file. The program to enter customer orders is designed to manage a table of the items to be ordered and their locations. After the final item is entered, the computer identifies the most efficient picking route and, following this route, writes the order—line item by line item—to the customer order file.

Figure 7-15 illustrates one type of picking slip. Not surprisingly, the layout and content of the slip are the same as the shipping document shown in Chapter 4 (see Figure 4-2). The difference between the two documents is that the picking slip shows the quantity to be picked, not the quantity shipped. This information must be filled in later, because the quantity known by the computer as being in stock is unfortunately not always identical to the quantity actually carried in stock. In addition, the order picker might not be able to find the stock. The computer printout might show that the stock is located in bin 356. On inspection, however, the order picker might discover that bin 356 contains items that are quite different from those described on the picking sheet.

The Customer Order Adjustments Program

Adjustments must be made to the customer order file to resolve any differences between items indicated by the computer as held in stock and items actually picked. The flowchart in Figure 7-16 shows this interactive processing routine.

Footwear International
622 West 5th
St. Paul, MN/55113

OUR ORDER NO.		
4635		
NEW □	CONFIRM □	

SALESPERSON NO./NAME	ORDER DATE
15 Pierson	11-5-8X
CUSTOMER NO.	CUST. P.O. NO.
5264	P32456
DEPT.	SHIP BY	SHIP VIA
12	11-8-8X	Truck

SOLD TO
Kid Togs
1526 Pearl
Eugene, OR 97402

SHIP TO
Kid Togs
1526 Pearl
Eugene, OR 97402

BIN NO.	ITEM NO.	DESCRIPTION	C	W	QUANTITY ORDERED	PRESHIPPED	1	1½	2	2½	3	3½	4	4½	5	5½	6	6½	7	7½	8	8½	9	9½	10	10½	11
43GL	3924	Little Foxes	B	M	5			1		1	2			1			1										
124R	4410	Speed Trims	R	M	4							2			2													

TOTALS THIS PAGE

SPECIAL INSTRUCTIONS

ALL CLAIMS MUST BE MADE WITHIN TEN
(10) DAYS AFTER RECEIPT OF GOODS.

Figure 7-15 Picking slip

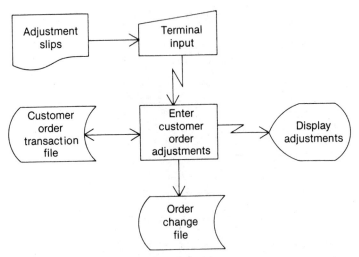

Figure 7-16 Enter customer order adjustments

Typically, a member of the warehouse office staff prepares adjustment slips and enters adjustment data into processing; this practice avoids sending all paperwork to a centralized order-entry staff. The entry of adjustments updates the customer order file directly. As with other interactive programs, all changes are recorded on a separate file for later printing and review.

Only limited types of adjustments are permitted at this late stage in processing. It is possible, for example, to change the quantity picked figure to show an actual count. It is possible, too, to adjust the shipping and insurance charges. Other adjustments, such as entering different product account numbers, product location codes, on-hand quantities, and so forth, are never made part of the adjustment program. Problems such as an incorrect count of inventory require different business procedures. (In the next chapter we will examine online applications to assist in the management and control of inventory.)

After a quantity-picked total has been adjusted, the question remains, Should the difference between the quantity ordered and the quantity actually picked be canceled or back ordered? If the quantity is canceled, processing is straightforward: the customer order is simply revised. If the quantity difference is to be treated as a back order, processing becomes more complex: the back-order file must be updated. As might be expected, there are alternative ways of handling back orders. The back-order file can be updated as part of the adjustments program, for example, or it can be updated during the printing of the order change report. (We will examine this second option later in this chapter.)

The adjustments program performs one more task other than changing order-picked totals: it posts shipping weight and charges and insurance charges to the customer order file. This information cannot be determined until goods are packed and made ready for shipment. Whenever possible, however, tables of shipping and insurance charges should be built into the adjustments program,

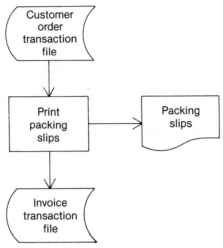

Figure 7-17 Print packing slips

in order to simplify data entry. Then only the actual shipping weight remains to be keyed into processing; table look-up procedures determine actual shipping and insurance costs.

The Print Packing Slip Program

After the customer order transaction file is adjusted, packing slips are printed (see Figure 7-17). As with the entry of adjustments, processing is monitored by a member of the warehouse staff, who loads a remote printer with packing slips and initiates printing. The adjusting of orders and the printing of packing slips close to the area where they are needed illustrate two key features of online systems: the ability of individuals to communicate directly with the computer from remote locations and the capability to distribute the authority for data processing. These concepts of *remote job entry* and *distributed data processing* are highly visible in the customer order-entry computer application.

It should be clear that the packing slip program does little more than print out the contents of the customer order transaction file. At this point in processing, adjustments should not be required. As Figure 7-17 shows, the unique feature of the packing-slip program is that it produces an invoice transaction file. This file can be used directly in billing customers for goods picked, packed, and shipped.

Customer Order Transaction File

The actual layout of the customer order transaction file is highly similar to the layout of the customer invoice transaction file produced by the packing-slip program. As Figure 7-18 shows, each record in the file contains business order

Business order number (invoice number)
Record code
Date of business order
Customer account number
    Customer sold-to name
    Customer sold-to address
    Customer ship-to name
    Customer ship-to address
    Credit limit
    Date of last revision
    Terms of payment
    Salesperson number
    Distributor number
Customer purchase order number
Date of purchase order
Method of payment

> Product number (1)
>   Product name
>   Product description
>   Unit of measure
>   Size run
>   Unit price
>   Unit cost
>   Quantity discount
>   Location code
>   Distance from packing room
>   Packing-instruction code
> Quantity ordered
> Quantity shipped
> Quantity back ordered
> Quantity canceled

Order-fill date
Date of shipment
Method of shipment
Shipping weight
Freight charge
Insurance charge

Figure 7-18 Customer order transaction file

information, customer information, product information, and packing and shipping information. Indeed, the order transaction file differs from the invoice transaction file (see Figure 4-13) only in the following ways:

- Each customer order transaction record begins with a business order number. (This number is assigned by the business and may become the invoice number, however, during the processing of invoices.)

- Each record contains product location data (bin location, picking instructions, and so forth) that are not needed when processing the customer invoice.

- Each record contains an order-fill date and the method of shipment desired by the customer—items that may or may not be placed on the invoice.

- Each record *does not* contain line-item charges or the total invoice charge. These financial totals are computed during the processing of invoices.

Because these differences are minor, the customer order and the customer invoice transaction files should be designed at the same time, even if only one application is to be implemented at this time. Suppose, for example, that a business decides first to design a customer-invoicing computer application, to be followed by the more complicated order-entry application. The chances are that if a business designs the invoicing file without considering the layout of the customer order file, it will be forced to redesign the invoicing file when thinking about order entry.

Even though order transaction records vary in length, an indexed sequential method of file organization is recommended. This organization permits direct access to customer orders, so that they can be examined and, where necessary, adjusted. It avoids having to sort the transaction file whenever a record is to be examined. Business order numbers are the primary keys when the file is organized to permit direct access. In addition, some order-entry systems maintain secondary key indexes that permit the retrieval of records by customer or by product number. In so doing, they greatly simplify locating records stored on the customer order transaction file.

7-3 PROCESSING SUMMARIES AND REGISTERS

Besides printing picking and packing slips, the order-entry computer application produces important summary reports and several file registers. The summary reports of greatest interest are those that are used to recap order-entry performance and show order-filling requirements for back orders and future orders. The *daily order-filling report,* for instance, is designed to list all orders filled during the day and to show several performance measures. We have already discussed one of these measures, the order-fill rate (the number of orders filled divided by the number of orders to be filled). Other performance measures include the following:

$$\text{Distance traveled per order} = \frac{\text{Total distance traveled}}{\text{Number of orders filled}}$$

$$\text{Items per customer order} = \frac{\text{Number of line items ordered}}{\text{Number of orders filled}}$$

$$\text{Value of average order} = \frac{\text{Dollar value of orders filled}}{\text{Number of orders filled}}$$

$$\text{Weight of average order} = \frac{\text{Total weight of orders filled}}{\text{Number of orders filled}}$$

$$\text{Quantity shipped of average order} = \frac{\text{Total quantity shipped}}{\text{Number of orders filled}}$$

The reports of back orders and future orders are similar in design to the daily order-filling report. The *back-order report* lists all orders that cannot be filled due to insufficient stock. As discussed in Chapter 4, this report also provides several kinds of performance measures, including the back-order percentage (the number of line items ordered divided by the number of line items filled) and the back-order fill rate (the number of back orders filled divided by the number of back orders to be filled). The flowchart in Figure 7-19 shows the steps required in printing the back-order report. Prior to printing, the transaction file of future and back orders is updated as part of the program to print customer order adjustments (see Figure 7-19). Remember that if a customer order is adjusted and if company policy is to back order the difference between the quantity ordered and the quantity shipped, this difference will be written to

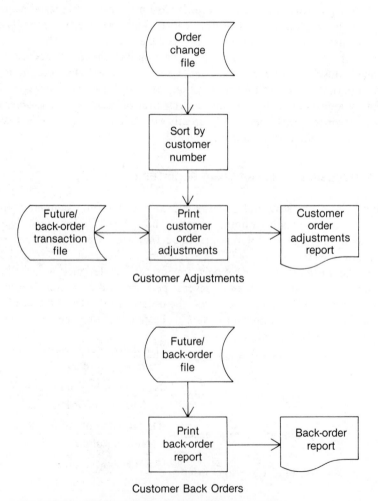

Figure 7-19 Printing customer adjustments and back orders

the order change file. As now illustrated, processing the change file is required to update the future/back-order file and to provide a printed record of all customer order changes. This printed record, the *customer order adjustments report,* must be carefully reviewed, and if adjustments leading to back orders appear to be overly high, members of the warehouse crew are dispatched to doublecheck inventory stock counts. After the customer order adjustments report is approved, the back-order report is printed (see Figure 7-19), usually in the sequence of customer account numbers or product or item numbers. Figure 7-20 shows a listing by item number. A third alternative is to sequence back orders by business order number; the difficulty with this choice, however, is that it fails to group multiple back orders for either customers or products.

The *future-order report* is usually printed after the back-order report, with which it is identical in format. Some firms, in fact, see little need to keep the two reports separate, since both list orders to be filled at some future date. Whereas businesses discourage back orders, future orders are encouraged because they help to refine estimates of product demand.

Still another processing summary often prepared at this time is the *sales-analysis summary report.* By now it should be evident that customer order entry, combined with customer invoicing, captures valuable sales information. Besides showing sales by customer and by product, the profit and percentage of profit by customer order, by customer, by salesperson, by distributor, by product, and by product line can all be determined. Because of the importance of sales analysis (and profit analysis), we will devote a separate chapter to this subject (see Chapter 15). Until then, remember that the sales-analysis computer application is made possible by the order-entry and customer-invoicing applications.

The order-entry application produces several file registers in addition to processing summaries. Three of these are the open-order register, the customer master register, and the product master register. The *open-order register,* which lists the contents of the customer order transaction file *before* picking slips are

```
WED, MAR 25, 198-                         MCBA Demonstration Furniture Company                              PAGE 0001
8:56 AM
                                       B A C K   O R D E R S   B Y   I T E M

ITEM NO      DESCRIPTION              CUST   NAME                     ORDER    ORDER    CUST-PO NO   QTY    UNIT  DIS
                                      NO                              NO       DATE                  B/O    PRICE  %

300          EXECUTIVE CHAIR          000100 Sunnyside Furniture      10030  03/25/8 -              1     151.00   5
                                      000200 21st. Century Enterprises 10016  03/09/8 -             11     188.00   5
                                                                      ITEM TOTALS:     2 ORDERS     12 B/O QTY

400          SECRETARIAL CHAIR, METAL 000100 Sunnyside Furniture      10021  03/06/8 -              150    32.50    5
                                      500000 Fieldings Office Emporium 10012  03/05/8 -             9      32.50    5
                                                                      ITEM TOTALS:     2 ORDERS    159 B/O QTY

DP600        DESK PAD, EXECUTIVE TYPE 500000 Fieldings Office Emporium 10012  03/05/8 -             16     28.91    5
             PEN & PENCIL SET
                                                                      ITEM TOTALS:     1 ORDERS    16 B/O QTY

      3 ITEMS ON B/O     TOTAL UNIT QTY ON B/O =    187    TOTAL SALE VALUE OF ALL B/O ITEMS =    7,456.61
```

Figure 7-20   Order-entry back-order report

produced, is printed infrequently. It becomes important whenever there is some question about the accuracy of the file, such as when file-balance controls are inaccurate, or when there appear to be problems with computing equipment. The other two registers should be familiar by now. The *customer master register,* as discussed in Chapter 4, lists all customer accounts stored on the customer master file; it serves as a backup to processing. If there are questions regarding the accuracy and completeness of customer information, the register provides a point of reference. The *product master register,* another backup listing, shows what information is stored in the product master file. Like the customer register, the product register is printed to provide a reference, if stored information is questioned.

7-4 INTERACTIVE DISPLAY PROGRAMS

A well-designed customer order-entry computer application will feature easy-to-use interactive display programs. An important design objective is to develop a responsive system that is capable of handling several types of inquiries. If, for example, a customer wants to know the status of a particular order, it should be possible to conduct a search by terminal to answer this question in seconds. Or suppose a member of the sales force asks, "Do we have in stock 50 Halon 1211 fire extinguishers?" Direct inquiry should return a response almost immediately.

Generally, an interactive order-entry design provides, at a minimum, three interactive display programs: the customer order, customer account, and product account display programs. The customer order display program, by far the most complex of the three, is designed to provide fast response to the question, Where is a particular order? Imagine a large 1,000-order-per-day warehousing facility that sometimes has difficulty in filling orders. Customers soon begin to call, asking for the latest information. The problem with locating a single order, however, is that it may be stored in one of several locations—for example, in the customer order transaction file (it is scheduled to be filled), the future/back-order transaction file (it is waiting to be filled), or the invoice transaction file (it has been filled). There are other possibilities: the order may not have been received, or, if received, it might be held by the credit department.

To make it easier to locate customer orders, order-entry computer applications often feature an *order-status file,* the contents of which are limited to three or four data elements (business order number, customer account number, and customer P.O. number) and the order status code. This code may be as simple as:

1 = customer order transaction file
2 = future/back-order transaction file
3 = invoice transaction file
4 = received, but held by the credit department

After a request is received, the status file is searched. Once the order status is known, several actions can take place: the customer can be told that the order was shipped, the customer's call can be transferred to the credit department, or the details of the order stored on the customer order transaction file can be displayed and reviewed directly.

Customer and product display programs also provide valuable information. When a customer account is questioned, entry of the customer number provides an immediate display of the customer's account. Suppose a customer asks: "Do you have our correct address?" This information can be checked in seconds. Product account displays are equally important. Since the on-hand amount of inventory is now stored in the product master records, the question of whether an order can be filled can be answered directly. No longer is it necessary to dispatch a member of the warehouse crew to find, count, and bring back an accounting of the stock available for sale.

7-5 PROCESSING CONTROLS

The use of an order-status file represents a different approach to establishing processing controls. By maintaining such a file, an accounting is kept of all transactions internal and external to processing. Transactions that have been held for review, for example, and transactions that have been transferred to the customer-invoicing application represent types of transactions external to processing. The *master control equation* developed to explain this accounting is as follows:

$$
\begin{aligned}
\text{Total orders} = {} & \text{Orders, customer order transaction file} \\
& + \text{Orders, future/back-order transaction file} \\
& + \text{Orders, invoice transaction file} \\
& + \text{Orders, held}
\end{aligned}
$$

As with other control equations, the numbers used must be revised daily, at a minimum. In addition, parts of the master control equation are made up of one or more smaller equations. The "orders held" component, for instance, must be changed as decisions are made to delay new orders or to release orders from the "orders held" category. The equation describing this activity is

$$\text{Orders held} = \text{Orders held, yesterday} + \text{Additions} - \text{Deletions}$$

Similar types of equations control the count of orders stored in the future/back-order transaction file.

The count of orders in the customer order transaction file will vary throughout the day. Each time an order is entered successfully into processing, the count is increased by one. The count continues to increase until the file is closed and packing slips are printed. Later on, the count may be modified by the enter adjustments program—as problems are discovered, it may be necessary to place some orders in the back-order category. Next, the count is reduced to zero, as filled orders are written to the invoice transaction file. Reducing this count to zero is offset, however, by increasing the count of records stored in the invoice transaction file by the same amount.

To complicate matters somewhat, it is sometimes necessary to process more than one customer order transaction file at the same time. Suppose the daily order file is closed at two o'clock in the afternoon each day: orders received after two can still be entered into processing, provided they are written to a new customer order transaction file. This second file is often kept open until the next day. To establish processing controls for two or more files with the same name, each file must be numbered in a way that allows counts to be kept separate. One method of numbering, for example, might list 875 orders for customer order transaction file #206 and 116 orders for customer order transaction file #207. Provided that the open-order file is always assigned the next larger number, these counts can be interpreted to mean that file #206 is a closed file that contains 875 orders, whereas file #207, an open file, contains, at present, 116 orders.

Besides keeping track of the count of orders (to ensure that no order is lost), processing controls must balance quantity totals (to ensure that no item ordered is lost). The type of control used, in this instance, is the same as the control required in customer invoicing, with minor modifications. The control equation is:

$$\text{Quantity ordered} = \text{Quantity shipped} + \text{Quantity, future ordered}$$
$$+ \text{Quantity, back ordered} + \text{Quantity, canceled} + \text{Quantity, held}$$

Unless this equation is in balance, there is a serious problem with computer processing.

Last, in addition to keeping balance-control totals for customer orders, processing controls must be kept for the customer and product master files. At the very minimum, a record count must be maintained for the customer master file. Processing controls for the product master file require more attention. Besides a count of all records, the count of the on-hand quantity of inventory must be carefully monitored. This activity is discussed in detail in the next chapter.

7-6 MANAGEMENT IMPLICATIONS

Even though the order-entry application is difficult to design and implement, management is rarely disappointed with the results that follow from it. Improved customer service is a major benefit: less than a twenty-four-hour turnaround between the receipt of an order and its shipment, for example, tends to impress customers. Such fast service indicates that a business is responsive to meeting the needs of its customers. Two closely related benefits are the ability to "track" customer orders and to provide greater accuracy in processing and filling orders. In a large order-entry facility, a major headache is keeping track of customer orders. With inadequate processing procedures, some companies lose orders; others pack and ship the correct amount but send it to the wrong customer. With an automated approach, the details of processing are controlled, in large part, by the computer. If an adjustment to an order is made, for instance, the computer is programmed to respond:

```
IS THE DIFFERENCE TO BE
   1. BACK ORDERED?
   2. CANCELED?
   3. EXIT
```

The computer is further instructed to refuse to process the adjustment further until one of these choices is made.

A computer-based order-entry application often permits better use of human and material resources. Worker productivity is improved all along the line, for example, because less time is needed to pick goods from stock, to respond to customer inquiries, to process an order, to make adjustments to an order, and to enter customer and product changes. The interactive features of the order-entry design contribute to other improvements in worker productivity. Because work can be distributed much more easily, the people who are most familiar with the details of processing are able to make needed changes; this result is a major advantage of interactive methods. For example, managers familiar with processing orders for a designated regional sales area can be assigned this responsibility. Likewise, managers who discover that adjustments to an order are required can be responsible for entering these adjustments.

Savings in material resources also result. As discussed in the next chapter, proper controls on inventory help to lower the total quantity of stock carried. Controls also lead to less pilferage and other types of stock losses. Performance reporting is another important product of the order-entry application. By tracking order-fill rates, back-order and future-order percentages, stock loss percentages, order adjustment rates, and the like, management is able to determine whether the order-entry system is working smoothly or not. Equipped with appropriate tracking measurements, management can take corrective action before problems become serious.

REVIEW OF IMPORTANT IDEAS

The customer order-entry computer application contains three types of processing activities: customer order processing, order filling, and order packing and shipping. The main input to processing is the customer order. After the details of an order have been successfully entered into processing, the computer determines whether the order can be filled. The filling of an order reduces the count of stock and produces a picking slip showing where stock is located and how many items to pick from each location. Customer order packing and shipping follows order filling. Packing slips show what items were shipped compared with what items were ordered.

Before customer orders are processed, the customer and product master files must be readied, in order to make both files as accurate as possible. Customer changes generally consist of name-and-address changes or the adding of new customer information to the customer master file. Product changes show all changes in the warehouse, including receipt of new merchandise, movements of goods from one location to another, price and cost changes, and stock adjustments. Change tables are used whenever possible to simplify these numerous changes.

After preshipped orders, future orders, and back orders have been processed, current orders are filled. This type of scheduling helps to ensure that all customers are treated fairly.

Even though the computer indicates that stock is on hand, there will be times when computer-printed information is wrong. Thus, adjustments must be made to quantity-picked figures. The difference between the quantity to be picked and the quantity actually picked must be canceled or back ordered.

Besides picking and packing slips, the customer order-entry application produces a number of processing summaries, registers, and change reports. The three processing summaries of special interest are the daily order-filling report and the reports listing back orders and the future orders.

Maintaining control of order-entry processing is simplified by the use of a single master control equation. The parts of this equation are made up of several, smaller file-balance equations.

A well-designed order-entry application contains easy-to-use interactive display programs that help to identify the status of a customer's order and whether information stored on the customer and product master files is correct. A major benefit is the ability to track customer orders.

KEY WORDS

Order filling	Packing slip
Finished-goods inventory	Open-order register
Customer analyses	Order-fill rate
Product analyses	Customer order file
Customer order	Change table
Quantity on hand	Preshipped orders
Quantity on order	Future orders
Quantity on back order	Back orders
Quantity on future order	Daily order-filling report
Picking slip	Order-status file

REVIEW QUESTIONS

1. What are the main reasons for developing the customer order-entry application?

2. What benefits result from an interactive approach to processing?

3. What is the main input to the customer order-entry application?

4. Compared with customer invoicing, how does the product master file differ in terms of its makeup?

5. How are bin location codes used in order-entry processing?

6. Why is a packing slip instead of a customer invoice placed with goods shipped to customers?

7. Why must master files be current before customer orders are processed?

8. Why is one computer program required for changing the customer master file and another required for processing the details of a customer order, when all processing could be done using a single computer program?

9. Why are change tables recommended in making changes to the product master file?

10. What are the differences between preshipped orders, future orders, back orders, and current orders?

11. What objective is sought by programming the computer to specify how orders should be picked from stock?

12. How does the packing slip differ from the picking slip?

13. What information may be changed by the customer order-adjustments program?

14. Why is an indexed sequential organization recommended for the customer order transaction file?

15. Why is it important to track the order-fill rate?

16. Why should the order-entry application include easy-to-use interactive display programs?

17. Explain how an order-status file can simplify the search for a customer's order.

18. Why is a master control equation important for this application?

19. How does an order-entry application help to improve worker productivity?

20. Why is distributed data processing an important consideration in the design of this application?

EXERCISES

1. Suppose a company decides to adopt a policy to cancel rather than back order any differences between items specified by the computer as to be picked and items actually picked. Suppose further that the company wants a record of all items canceled. How would the order-entry system be modified to handle this policy decision?

2. A merchandising manager indicates that she would like the following activities incorporated into the order-entry application:

    At the time the warehouse picking list is prepared, the computer is to prepare a postcard for mailing to the customer. The postcard will show any invalid size, style, or color, along with suggestions on how to reorder. Explain the design implications of this processing requirement.

3. Some business firms practice what might be called a "favored customer rule." The rule reads: Orders received from favored customers are filled before all others (including future orders and back orders). How would this policy decision be incorporated into an order-entry design?

4. A standard customer purchase agreement involves shipping a predetermined quantity of stock to customers on a scheduled basis, such as 100 units every 30 days. Explain how this variation would be included in an order-entry design.

5. Suppose items are returned by a customer for credit. Suppose next that the price for the goods has increased between the filling of the order and the request for credit. How must the order-entry application be designed to avoid granting a credit at the higher price?

Finished-Goods Inventory

Closely related to the customer order-entry computer application is the application for finished-goods inventory. As we discussed in the last chapter, an essential requirement for successful order-entry processing is an accurate, complete product master file. Lacking such a file, an order-entry system is bound to fail. In this chapter, we will more closely examine the maintenance of the product master file. In particular, we will show how to plan for and control onhand stocks of inventory. To simplify the subject as much as possible, we will focus on one business environment—warehousing—as in the last chapter.

In the design of the finished-goods inventory application, the product master file used previously by the customer-invoicing computer application and, following its modification, by the customer order-entry computer application is once again enlarged. Besides showing the inventory on hand, the larger file shows when to order more stock (the *order frequency*), how much to order (the *order quantity*), and from whom to order (the *approved vendor*). These three decisions of when to order, in what quantity, and from whom, are fundamental to *inventory management*.

The finished-goods application differs from other applications in an important way: it is designed to maximize the return on capital invested in inventory. To realize this objective, management must carefully balance the demand for inventory with the supply to inventory. A common saying is that inventory management tries to always keep as little stock on hand as possible, to order new stock at the best possible prices, and to never run out of stock. In practice, it is difficult to do all three things at once.

One way better to appreciate the objective of maximizing the return on capital invested in inventory is to examine the factors that contribute to a favorable return. The *return-on-investment* (R.O.I.) equation tells us, for example, that for a given profit margin on sales (percentage earned), the resulting R.O.I. is determined by turnover:

$$R.O.I. = \text{Percentage earned on sales} \times \text{Turnover}$$

where

$$\text{Turnover} = \frac{\text{Yearly sales}}{\text{Total investment in inventory}}$$

$$\frac{\text{Percentage earned}}{\text{on sales}} = \frac{\text{Earnings}}{\text{Sales}}$$

As the equation shows, *inventory turnover* refers to the number of times the stock carried in inventory can be sold during the year. Suppose, for instance, that the percentage earned on sales is 15 percent and turnover is three times per year. The resulting R.O.I. would be 45 percent—which means that if every product carried in stock is turned three times during the year, every dollar invested in this product returns 45 cents. Clearly, if a firm can reduce its total investment in inventory, while holding sales and earnings constant, the benefits can be most dramatic. A chemical distributor, for example, discovered that a finished-goods computer application greatly enhanced its ability to reduce its investment in inventory. A detailed cost comparison revealed that the application led to an overall investment reduction of $100,000. As another example, a small manufacturing company increased inventory turnover by 33 percent (from 2.9 to 3.8 times per year) and cut stocks by $500,000; in addition, the computer was found to be 99 percent accurate in reporting on-hand stocks. Such results are not uncommon and explain why interactive methods of inventory control have become so popular.

In addition to maximizing the return on invested capital, a well-designed finished-goods inventory application offers these five important advantages:

- The taking of a *physical inventory* is simplified, because manual counts of stock can be checked and verified, by computer, on a controlled basis, such as once every month, every two months, or every six months.

- The number of stockouts and stock losses can be reduced by using the computer to pinpoint areas where running out of stock (stockouts) and "shorts" or "shrinkage" (stock losses) are common.

- Warehouse stocking procedures can be improved because space requirements and storage locations for stocks can more easily be determined.

- Management can spot interesting sales trends and areas of strong (and weak) customer demand and, as a consequence, can develop more realistic product-stocking plans.

- Reliable sources of supply can be identified. To achieve control of the demand for finished-goods stocks, the supply of stock must be adequate. Shortages in supply obviously upset even the best designed finished-goods inventory or order-entry applications.

Finally, there are several more good reasons for designing an interactive finished-goods inventory application. Most important, interactive processing simplifies the maintaining of the product master file by making it easier to add, change, or delete records stored on file. Second, interactive processing improves inquiry capabilities. No longer is it necessary to search through page after page of stock-keeping reports and registers. Various types of search routines can be built in to perform product-inquiry tasks. Third, an interactive design simplifies the study of an individual product or of a *product line*—several products, all of which are similar. This type of study and inspection can lead to dramatic improvements in inventory turnover as well as in product earnings and sales totals. Fourth, an interactive design allows inventory management tasks to be better distributed. Members of the warehouse crew, for example, can be made responsible for taking and verifying a physical count of inventory.

8-1 PRELIMINARY OVERVIEW OF PROCESSING

Figure 8-1 shows the main processing steps associated with the finished-goods inventory application. The heart of processing is the update of the product master file. Because this file update is so extensive, it can best be understood by examining three of its parts:

1. *Enter stock-keeping information* to add, revise, or delete from the file, information about product name and description, pricing and discount, inventory, and location.

2. *Enter product-requirements information* to document the estimated demand for products in future periods and to store the actual historical demand for products in previous periods.

3. *Enter stock-replenishment information* to show when to order stock, in what quantity, and from whom, and to store information about product performance.

After the product master file has been updated, it can be used in a variety of ways, two of which are shown in Figure 8-1:

1. *Print/display stock-status reports* to show the status of items held in inventory relative to the expected demand for merchandise. (Any difference is then compared with the anticipated supply of merchandise.)

2. *Print/display purchase-advice reports* to show what items need to be ordered, the suggested reorder quantity, the lead time associated with delivery (the time between the placing of the order and the receipt of goods), and the preferred source of supply.

A unique feature of an interactive finished-goods inventory design is that information can be either printed or displayed. Typically, the status of a product held in inventory is displayed for review. If a decision is made to take some action, such as the placing of an order or checking the count stored in the warehouse, displayed information can be saved by producing printed hard copy.

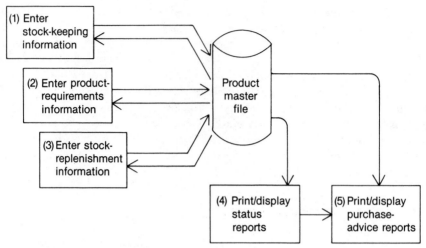

Figure 8-1 Five steps in processing inventory transactions

Inputs to Processing

The primary input to the finished-goods inventory application is the product master file—the file used in customer invoicing and customer order entry, except that now we consider additional data elements required in the management of inventory. Figure 8-2 shows this enlarged file; the shaded areas show data elements used previously. The three main sections of the file, stock-keeping information, stock-requirements information, and stock-replenishment information, help to clarify the types of data stored in the eight record segments. The organization of the file can thus be outlined as follows:

- *Stock-keeping information:*
  1. Product name and description
  2. Pricing and discount
  3. Product inventory
  4. Product location

- *Product-requirements information:*
  5. Product forecast
  6. Sales history

- *Stock-replenishment information:*
  7. Product reorder
  8. Product performance

Stock-keeping information consists of descriptive, pricing, and inventory-control information, the last of which is of primary importance. In checking the status of products carried in inventory it is essential to know what quantity is on hand and what quantity is on order. Otherwise duplicate orders will be placed.

Product Master File

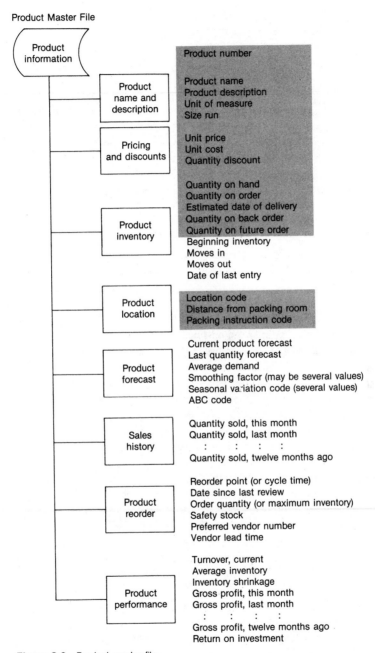

Figure 8-2 Product master file

Likewise, it is essential to know the difference between beginning and ending inventory, which is calculated as follows:

Beginning inventory + Moves in − Moves out = Ending inventory

If a physical count of inventory does equal the computed ending-inventory total, *inventory shrinkage* has occurred. Shrinkage can result from a variety of factors, including unreported wastage or loss, improper reporting of parts added to inventory, physical inventory errors, and pilferage. Regardless of the cause, managers must keep a watchful eye on any differences between stock thought to be available for sale and stock actually available for sale.

Product-requirements information concerns product forecast and sales history. The product-forecast record segment establishes the requirements for a product for a specified time period, such as next month, next two months, or next six months. It uses an *ABC code* to indicate whether a product is classified as high-value (A), medium-value (B), or low-value (C). Other data important for determining product requirements are product-forecast coefficients and historical sales figures. If a forecasting technique known as exponential smoothing is employed, for example, smoothing factor and seasonal variation codes must be stored. Sales history information is usually kept for an entire calendar year (although some firms insist that sales data be stored for five years). The value of historical data is that it permits individuals to study how customer demand changes.

Stock-replenishment information deals with product reorders and product performance. The amount to be ordered (the order quantity) and the point at which stock is to be ordered (the reorder point) describe conditions under which stock is to be replenished. Performance data help to show whether or not product stock-replenishment decisions are correct. By tracking inventory turnover, average inventory, inventory shrinkage, product profitability and return on investment, managers are able to determine how well a particular product or product line is controlled.

Outputs from Processing

A wide variety of displays and printed reports can be designed for the finished-goods inventory application. These displays and reports are used to verify stock-keeping information and to present product-requirement plans and stock-replenishment decisions. Suppose, for example, that an inventory planner wants to list all product accounts for which no demand is shown over the next six months. To process this request, the current product-forecast field would be checked. If the forecast for a product account number were zero, the stock carried in inventory under this number might be classified as *obsolete inventory*. A list of all such numbers could be displayed or printed, to document the inventory value of obsolete goods (see Figure 8-3). Most obsolete-inventory reports break down summary counts to show on-hand and on-order amounts. Likewise, an ABC analysis, which itemizes inventory amounts by class, helps the inventory planner to visualize the impact of removing obsolete items from stock.

The most common types of output are a series of displays or reports designed to show the status of goods held in stock and what items to order for stock. *Stock-status reports,* for instance, permit inventory planners to review information stored in the product master file and, as a result of their review, to solidify

```
           Obsolete Inventory          10/20/XX
      Planner: A4                       Page 10

  Item      Inv.  Unit   Date Last  On      On
  Number    Class Cost   Activity   Hand    Order

  07518     B     8.50   3/15/XX    23,600
  A7791     B    27.50   5/01/XX    18,400  1,000
  05687     C     4.30   2/03/XX    15,000
  32702     C    12.00  10/01/XX     9,000
  ─────────────────────────────────────────────
                                   267,700  22,100

  Summary   A                       98,000  12,100
    By      B                      100,700   1,000
  Category  C                       69,000   9,000
```

Figure 8-3   Obsolete-inventory report

inventory plans. Changes to a plan can include revised product forecasts, product prices and discounts, and product counts and locations. *Purchase-advice displays* are used to specify how items should be reordered. As Figure 8-4 shows, a purchase advice clarifies which products carried in inventory are at a stock level lower than the reorder point. As indicated, the reorder point for product 65349 is 85, whereas the quantity on hand is 82. Thus, this stock item should be reordered.

PURCHASE ADVICE

ITEM NO.	PRODUCT DESCRIPTION	ON HAND	ON ORDER	RE ORDER	ORDER SIZE	ITEM COST
65349	TRAIL FUEL PACKS	82	0	85	160	$ 5.63
44361	SWITCHING LIGHTS	22	16	25	16	$211.15

Figure 8-4   Purchase-advice display

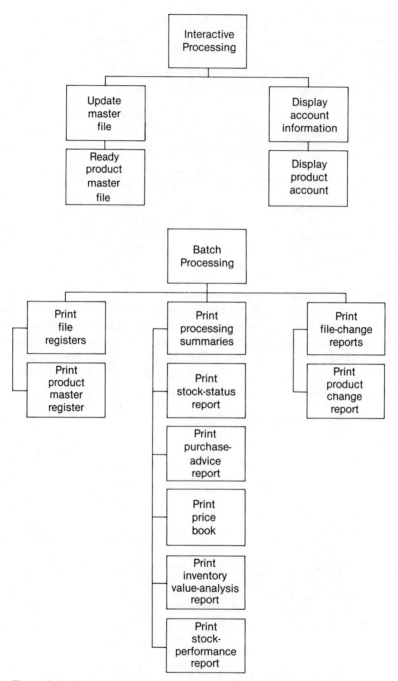

Figure 8-5 Finished-goods inventory systems organization chart

8-2   FINISHED-GOODS INVENTORY PROCESSING

Figure 8-5 shows the systems organization chart for the finished-goods inventory application; Figure 8-6 shows the corresponding program-processing menu. The interactive part of processing appears to be simple enough: it consists of only two programs. This simplicity is misleading, however. Figure 8-7, a modified organization chart of the interactive portion of processing, shows how product update and display routines have been subdivided into specific file-processing tasks. One task is to "update product location" information; another is to "update product reorder" information. Each update program is matched by a display program. If an update is not required (or permitted), the same segment of the product master file can be displayed for review.

The batch portion of processing is more straightforward than the interactive portion. As Figure 8-6 shows, processing summaries make up the main part of the design. Of these, the *stock-status report,* the *purchase-advice report,* and the *price book* are hard-copy printings of information stored on file. The *inventory-value analysis* shows the dollar value of stock carried in inventory. Inventory planners use this information in determining annual product requirements. *Stock-performance reports,* of which there are several, show facts and figures about obsolete inventory, month's supply of inventory, turnover rates, return on investment, distance traveled, space requirements, and inventory shrinkage. These reports are important guides for inventory management.

I.1   READY PRODUCT MASTER FILE
I.2   DISPLAY PRODUCT ACCOUNT

B.1   PRINT STOCK-STATUS REPORT
B.2   PRINT PURCHASE ORDER ADVICE
B.3   PRINT PRICE BOOK
B.4   PRINT VALUE-ANALYSIS REPORT
B.5   PRINT STOCK-PERFORMANCE REPORTS
B.6   PRINT PRODUCT MASTER REGISTER
B.7   PRINT PRODUCT CHANGE REPORT
(8)   EXIT

Figure 8-6   Finished-goods inventory program-processing menu

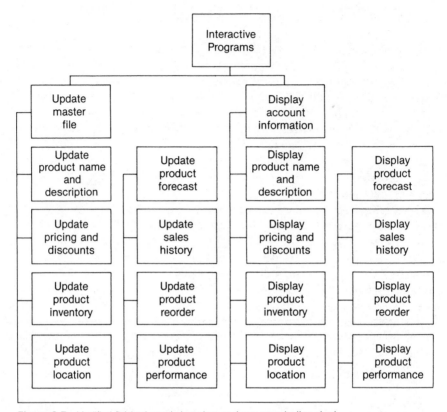

Figure 8-7 Modified finished-goods inventory systems organization chart

Adding Stock-Keeping Information

Typically, fifty or more pieces of information must be kept for each item stored in inventory. In an effort to streamline the entering and maintenance of product information, some inventory designs combine file-processing menus with data-input display screens (see Figure 8-8). The particular display shown in Figure 8-8 permits different types of inventory information to be entered when a new part is added to inventory. For example, besides the number and description for the part, information concerning its location, product line, part status, purchase agreement, and order policy are entered using a single screen. The menu appearing at the top of the screen shows what additional tasks can be performed. For example, the terminal operator might choose to change the description of the part or to delete the part from the file.

Although adding stock-keeping information to the product master file is time-consuming, it is not difficult. Inputs to processing consist of new or change notification sheets, such as the item-change notification sheet illustrated in Figure 8-9. Efficiency of data entry can be greatly improved by entering changes of the same kind one after another. Easy-to-follow change notification sheets also simplify the design of processing controls.

```
  Add a New Part                                                    ADD PART
     Change    Change     Add      Add          Add     Review   Delete    EXIT
     Desc      Plan      Struct    Rout        Remark   Desc     Part

                                    Part Number
                                     300015

     Prime      Prime                                    Unit of   Product
   Warehouse  Location    Ctlr          Description      Measure   Line
      01       B1-474       20    FLANGED THRUST WASHER, REINFOR     EA

     Document            Part    Date     Date     Aging   Purchase    ABC    Part
   Responsibility       Status  In Prod  Obsolete  Policy  Agreement   Code   Class
     ENGR                 A     040680                6                 C      P


    Order     Order    Safety    Order   Quantity                           Action
    Policy    Point    Stock   Quantity  Multiple   Shrinkage   Yield       Report
      L                                                 %        100%         Y
```

Figure 8-8   Combined menu and data-entry display

Revising Product-Requirements Information

From a systems designer's viewpoint, a difficult part of processing is the construction of a set of displays that will help managers review inventory plans and, where necessary, adjust product-requirement forecasts. To aid in this process of inventory planning, the computer is used to forecast future product sales. Managers must review these forecasts to decide if they are realistic—that is, if they are consistent with sales promotion programs and changes in market demand.

The computer can be used to prepare both extrinsic and intrinsic product forecasts. An *extrinsic forecast* assumes that a correlation exists between an external event, such as housing starts or birth rates, and internal company sales. By knowing what is happening outside the firm, planners are better able to predict how internal sales will be affected. This approach to forecasting is particularly useful when attempting to estimate the demand for an entire product line, such as infant shoes.

An *intrinsic forecast* assumes that the best way to forecast the demand for a product is to examine past sales trends. This historical data-analysis approach is appropriate when attempting to determine the demand for a single product, such as product number 5543, a down-filled sleeping bag. To begin the forecasting process, inventory planners generally classify products by demand pattern (see Figure 8-10). Of the three basic patterns—constant, trend, and seasonal—the first is the easiest to calculate (and also the least common). The following equation is used to prepare a forecast for a *constant-demand* pattern.

$$F_n = F_{n-1}$$

where

$$F_n = \text{Forecast in period } n$$
$$F_{n-1} = \text{Last forecast in period } n$$

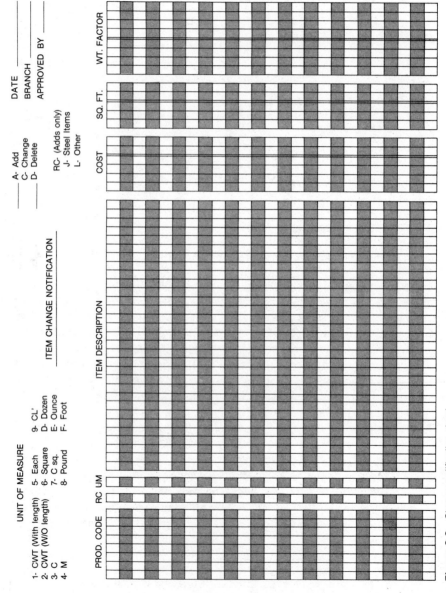

Figure 8-9 Change notification sheet

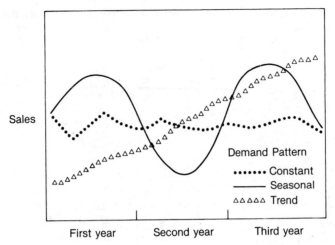

Figure 8-10 Three demand patterns

Thus, if period *n* were July, its forecast would be the same as the forecast for June (period *n* − 1).

Trend analysis is used to forecast sales when demand is either increasing or decreasing. Two popular mathematical approaches used frequently in tracking trend-demand patterns are *least squares regression analysis,* which yields a straight line of "best fit" and is used primarily in market-analysis studies, and *exponential smoothing,* which produces a forecast trend line and is preferred in setting forecasts based on historical sales trends. Of the two, we will consider only exponential smoothing.

Exponential smoothing is a weighted-average approach to forecasting, in which some weight (known as alpha) is applied to the latest actual demand information and another weight (known as one minus alpha) is applied to the last forecast information. The exponential smoothing formula is as follows:

$$F_n = \alpha D_{n-1} + (1 - \alpha) F_{n-1}$$

where

$$F_n = \text{New forecast}$$
$$F_{n-1} = \text{Last forecast}$$
$$D_{n-1} = \text{Last demand}$$
$$\alpha = \text{Smoothing factor}$$

Assume, for example, that sales in March for product 5543, down-filled sleeping bags, were 1,050, compared with the sales forecast for March of 1,100. When alpha (α) is set at .10, the new, April forecast can be set:

$$F_{\text{April}} = (.10)(1,050) + (.90)(1,100) = 1,095$$

Stating the equation somewhat differently, we can see that exponential smoothing is a weighted average.

$$F = \underbrace{105}_{\substack{\text{Weight given} \\ \text{to the last} \\ \text{actual demand} \\ \text{(10 percent)}}} + \underbrace{990}_{\substack{\text{Weight given} \\ \text{to the last} \\ \text{product forecast} \\ \text{(90 percent)}}}$$

The advantage of exponential smoothing over other weighted-average forecasting methods is that little historical sales information needs to be retained and stored on the product master file—only the last forecast and current demand (plus the value for alpha). This advantage is viewed by many as quite a disadvantage, however: people often feel uncomfortable examining sales data unless they have several sales periods to consider. For this reason, twelve or more months of historical data are usually kept for each product carried in inventory. Some companies even store years of sales data, so that they can examine both short- and long-term sales trends.

A difficult feature of exponential smoothing is the setting of alpha, the smoothing factor. The general rule is that alpha should be set low, to give more weight to previous forecasts. Close study of the smoothing formula shows that the last forecast is made up of all previous forecasts—although they are smoothed. Consider the following:

$$F_n = \alpha D_{n-1} + (1 - \alpha) F_{n-1}$$

However,

$$F_{n-1} = \alpha D_{n-2} + (1 - \alpha) F_{n-2}$$

and

$$F_{n-2} = \alpha D_{n-3} + (1 - \alpha) F_{n-3}$$

and so on.

Another general rule is that when demand is increasing (or decreasing) rapidly, the value of alpha should be set higher. This practice means that forecasts will always be lower than actual sales when demand is increasing rapidly and higher than actual sales when demand is decreasing rapidly. Unfortunately, when demand is increasing or decreasing rapidly, no value of alpha between 0 and 1 will accurately predict next month's sales. Such inaccuracies occur with *any* weighted average forecasting method based on historical data.

Because of the problems with any mathematical approach to forecasting, inventory planners are always permitted to override computer-generated forecasts. Although never easy to make, these override decisions are easier when planners are able to use interactive graphics terminals equipped with powerful curve-fitting techniques. As Figure 8-11 shows, these techniques allow the plan-

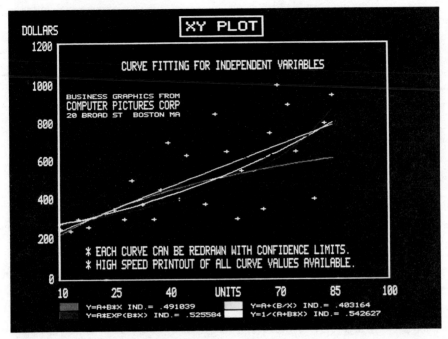

Figure 8-11 Curve-fitting technique

ner to compare forecast curves with actual sales curves and to change the shape of the forecast curve to reduce the overall forecasting error. Unfortunately, curve-fitting technology is expensive to implement and to maintain. Special graphics terminals and software must often be acquired. More important, massive amounts of sales-history and forecast data must be stored in order to compare historical predictions and events.

Estimating sales in which demand follows a seasonal pattern is the most difficult forecasting assignment. Here, too, curve-fitting techniques are used. *Seasonal variation graphs*—graphs that depict expected shifts in demand from one period to another—are prepared according to more advanced exponential smoothing formulas than those used in trend analysis. The new forecast, adjusted for seasonal trends, becomes:

$$F_n = \beta_n \times D_{\text{average}}$$

where

$$F_n = \text{New forecast}$$
$$\beta_n = \text{Seasonal coefficient base index}$$
$$D_{\text{average}} = \text{Average demand}$$

As an example, suppose the average demand for down-filled sleeping bags is 840: this is the number of bags that could be expected to be sold during an average month. Now suppose that the seasonal coefficient for April (β_4) is 1.50. (It is higher than 1.00 because sleeping bags sell better in the spring than during the winter months.) Applying this coefficient to average demand yields the April forecast:

$$F_{\text{April}} = (1.50)(840) + 1,260 \text{ sleeping bags}$$

Although this formula is easy to understand, its simplicity is misleading. Both the average demand and the seasonal coefficient base index must be smoothed to show changes in seasonal patterns. As demand increases, for example, average demand will increase. The smoothed equation becomes:

$$D_{\text{new average}} = \alpha_1 \left(D_{\text{current deseasonal demand}}\right) + (1 - \alpha_1) D_{\text{old average}}$$

Likewise, as seasonal demand changes, so must the seasonal-variation base index. The smoothed base index equation typically requires a different value for alpha and is computed as follows:

$$\beta_{\text{new seasonal coefficient}} = \alpha_2 \left(\beta_{\text{current base index}}\right) + (1 - \alpha_2) \beta_{\text{old base index}}$$

Adjusting Stock-Replenishment Information

Estimating the demand for each product carried in stock is one part of the inventory-planning and control puzzle. Other parts involve stock-replenishment considerations: determining when to reorder (the reorder point), how much to order (the order quantity), how much extra inventory to carry in stock (the safety stock), who to order from (the preferred vendor), and when to expect a new shipment (the vendor lead time). Designing a system to enable managers to make these stock-replenishment decisions is not an easy matter. A brief overview of how the quantity to order and the reorder point are set will illustrate some of the mathematical complexity involved.

The quantity to order can be expressed as:

Quantity to order = (Estimated quantity to be sold)
\qquad\qquad − (Quantity on hand + Quantity on order)

Suppose 1,260 sleeping bags are estimated to be sold; the quantity on hand is 500 and the quantity on order is 300. We would assume that the quantity to order would be 460 (1,260 − 500 − 300). In actuality, however, if the manufacturer of the bags is offering a 15 percent reduction of the cost per unit for orders of 500 or more, the solution is not so straightforward. It would make more sense to order 500 sleeping bags rather than 460. To account for such conditions, inventory managers use analytic expressions to help them determine the most economic order quantity. The most familiar expression for *economic order quantity* (E.O.Q.) is:

$$\hat{Q} = \sqrt{2(R)(S) \div (C)(I)}$$

where

$$R = \text{Annual demand}$$
$$S = \text{Purchase order cost}$$
$$C = \text{Cost per unit}$$
$$I = \text{Cost of capital}$$
$$\hat{Q} = \text{Economic order quantity}$$

This formula is designed to minimize the costs associated with purchasing and carrying stock in inventory.

When price breaks are permitted, such as those shown in Figure 8-12, the calculation of order quantity must take into consideration three factors: the cost of purchasing, the cost of carrying stock in inventory, and the changing unit cost of the item. The total cost equation must recognize all of these variable costs:

$$T = RC + S(R) \div Q + C(I) \times (Q/2)$$

where

$$T = \text{Total cost}$$
$$RC = \text{Annual demand times the cost per item}$$
$$\text{(annual payment to the vendor)}$$
$$S(R) \div Q = \text{Total purchase order cost}$$
$$C(I) \times (Q/2) = \text{Total inventory carrying cost}$$

To determine the most appropriate order quantity, the computer must be programmed to evaluate the effects of the product discount on the annual payment to the vendor. Following this procedure, the cost of maintaining inventory at various stock levels is determined. Typically, these relationships are plotted for review.

Once the quantity to order has been determined, the reorder point can be set. Expressed in units, the *reorder point* (R.O.P.) is equal to the vendor lead time (the time in days that it takes a vendor to fill an order) times average daily demand, plus safety stock (the stock held in reserve to offset higher than normal demand):

R.O.P. = (Vendor lead time)(Average demand) + Safety stock

Quantity Purchase	Unit Price	Discount
1–11	$1.00	none
12–23	.90	10 percent
24–47	.75	25 percent
48 and above	.60	40 percent

Figure 8-12 Quantity price breaks

Suppose, for example, that it takes 30 days to receive new sleeping bags and that 200 bags are carried in inventory as safety stock. The reorder point is determined by first calculating the average demand, which is equal to the forecasted demand divided by the number of days in the month.

$$D_{average} = F_n \div \text{Days in the month}$$

Assume that average demand is 42 bags per day. Inserting this value into the R.O.P. equation shows that the point at which stock should be reordered is 1,460 bags (30 days $\times$ 42 bags per day + 200 bags = 1,460 bags). When the on-hand and the on-order stock reach this quantity level, the computer will indicate that a new order should be placed with a vendor.

Setting Reorder Cycles

Some business firms calculate the order frequency instead of the reorder point. The *order frequency* states in days rather than in units when an item carried in stock should be reviewed. Determining the order frequency requires that the number of orders to be placed during the year be calculated.

$$\text{Number of orders} = \text{Annual demand} \div \hat{Q} \text{ (Economic order quantity)}$$

Once the number of orders is known, the order frequency is determined by dividing the number of working days by the number of orders.

$$\text{Order frequency} = \text{Annual working days} \div \text{Number of orders}$$

For instance, assume annual demand is 10,000 units and the E.O.Q. ($\hat{Q}$) is 800. At this order quantity, the number of orders per year would be 12.5 (10,000 $\div$ 800). When the number of working days per year is 250, the order frequency is every 20 days (250 working days per year $\div$ 12.5 orders per year = 20 days per order). Thus, the level of stock should be checked by a member of the warehouse crew every 20 days. Checking involves comparing the quantity on hand with the computer-projected quantity on hand. The quantity-to-order decision then follows as before.

Cycle buying follows directly from the calculation of order frequency points. With cycle buying, the computer checks each item stored on the product master file to determine which stock items should be scheduled for review. This schedule is set daily. In processing, the date of the last review is matched against the current date, and the difference is then compared with the cycle time stored on file. When the time between reviews equals the cycle time, product review information is written to an output file. This small file typically contains the number and name of the product, where it is located in inventory, and the quantity on hand.

Cycle buying is advantageous for a variety of reasons. First, it combines the taking of a physical inventory with the reordering of stock. If a manual check reveals a difference between the actual and computer-predicted amount on hand, adjustments to the product master file can be made. Second, and closely related to the first advantage, cycle buying helps to control inventory shrinkage. A stock-loss tolerance standard can be set for each product carried in inventory. If losses are greater than the standard, steps can be taken to determine what is wrong. Third, cycle buying permits higher-valued items to be reviewed more often than lower-valued items. In this instance, the usage value of the product is calculated to determine how often the product should be reviewed. *Usage value* is simply the average demand for the product times its unit cost:

$$\text{Usage value} = \text{Quantity sold} \times \text{Unit cost}$$

Figure 8-13 shows the results of a stock review based on usage value, when cycle buying is implemented. As illustrated, all A items are scheduled for review weekly, because they are the most highly valued stock items carried in inventory. All C items, in contrast, are reviewed twice a year. The reason for such infrequent review is that it costs more to review C items than the cost associated with running out of stock. Since B items are of medium value, they are reviewed more frequently than C items, but less frequently than A items.

Reporting Stock-Status and Reorder Information

Stock-status and purchase-advice displays and reports provide inventory managers with a recap of stock-keeping information and of decisions about product requirements and stock replenishment. With several online display screens, an inventory manager is able to review the actions taken by the computer or the effects of override decisions in regulating the quantity to carry in inventory. One display, for example, shows how the product forecast was determined, or how it was determined and later modified. Another display screen shows how product-reorder decisions were made by the computer, or how they were initially made and later modified. Still another display screen permits inventory planners to study the sales history for a product and to fit various curves to sales trends and seasonal variations. Figure 8-14 for example, illustrates the sales trend for a single item over the past twelve months. As indicated, sales of this post lantern reveal a downward trend, but they also show a six- to seven-month cycle.

Item Category	No. of Items	Count Frequency	Items Each Week
A	2000	Weekly	2000
B	6000	Monthly	1500
C	12000	Semi-annually	500
Total	20000		4000

Figure 8-13 Results of cycle buying

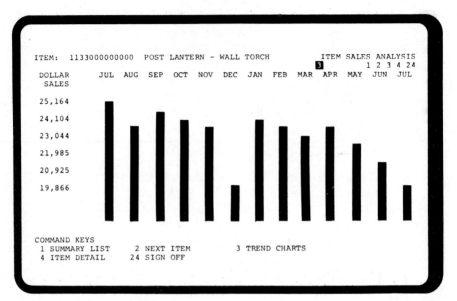

Figure 8-14 Sales history display

The *stock-status report* provides a summary of inventory activity for the current period (see Figure 8-15). Although this report contains several types of product information, its main use is to show the quantity on hand and on order, the quantity on hand that has been allocated, the remaining quantity available for sale, and the on-hand cost of the item.

The inventory-balance display is similar to the stock-status report (see Figure 8-16). This particular display shows inventory location and other inventory information, and provides a complete accounting of the quantity on hand, on order, on reserve (safety stock), and on back order.

Another important summary is the purchase-order advice report, or the *product-reorder report*. In addition to showing product-inventory information, this report describes reorder decisions: the order point, the E.O.Q., the safety stock, and vendor lead time. Generally, the purchase-order advice report is made available on request. Inventory managers can choose to review product-reorder decisions for a warehouse, a class of products, or a range of vendors. Any changes to reorder decisions are noted, so that they can be entered directly into processing later on (see Figure 8-17).

8-3 FINISHED-GOODS INVENTORY ANALYSIS

Besides reviewing items held in stock to determine their current status and pending reorder decisions, inventory planners must carefully evaluate overall inventory performance. When a program of evaluation is combined with stock

Report sequence selection   Report content slection   Can be standard, average, or last cost

GATEWAY MFG CO   PERIOD END INVENTORY STOCK STATUS   DATE 12/11/   TIME 13.46.17   PAGE   1   AM16C

ALL WAREHOUSES   SEQUENCE BY ITEM

ITEMS FROM 27002   TO 27006-80
ALL CLASSES
ALL VENDORS

ITEM CLASS	ITEM NUMBER	ITEM TYPE	ITEM DESCRIPTION		U/M						
WHSE NO.	VENDOR NUMBER	BEGIN BAL	----- PERIOD TO DATE ----- ISS/SALE RECEIPTS	ADJ.	QTY ON-HAND	QTY ON-ORDER	QTY ALLOC.	QTY AVAIL.	AVERAGE UNIT COST	ON HAND COST	BASE PRICE
70	27002-01	4	ADAPTER PLATE		EA						
1	036657	0	3042	0	0	3256	9000	225	11031	.2400	741.44	.000
20	27003-20	1	PUMP ASSEMBLY		EA						
1		0	3125	3334	0	267	250	225	292	27.9590	7,462.55	49.000
50	27004-01	2	HANDLE		EA						
1		0	3034	4099	0	316	0	0	316	2.600	821.60	6.250
	27005-A	1	PUMPING UNIT		EA						
A		0	0	0	0	13	0	0	13	37.7368	490.57	75.000
1		0	3042	4105	0	144	225	0	369	38.0150	5,474.16	75.000
		0	12243	11538	0	3996	8475	-50	12021		15,030.42	
	27006-F2	F	TANK SIZE FEATURE		EA						
A		0	0	0	0	0	0	0	0	.0000	.00	.000
1		0	0	0	0	0	0	0	0	.0000	.00	.000
		0	0	0	0	0	0	0	0		.00	
	27006-00	2	TANK TOP 8 INCHES		EA						
A		0	0	0	0	12	0	0	12	2.4316	29.17	.000
B		0	0	0	0	187	0	0	187	2.4316	454.79	.000
1		0	1575	1602	0	216	0	2200	1984-	2.3905	516.34	.000
		0	1575	1602	0	415	0	2200	1785-		1,000.21	
50	27006-10	2	TANK TOP 10 INCHES		EA						
1		0	2419	920	0	1392-	0	0	1392-	3.0050	4,182.96-	.000
50	27006-20	2	TANK TOP 12 INCHES		EA						
1		0	656	660	0	99	0	1000	901-	4.7200	467.28	.000
	27006-70	2	TANK BOTTOM 8 INCHES		EA						
A		0	0	0	0	0	0	0	0	1.5103	.00	.000
B		0	0	0	0	0	0	0	0	1.5123	.00	.000
1		0	1575	1591	0	209	0	2200	1991-	2.0132	420.13	.000
		0	4650	3171	0	1084-	0	3200	4284-		3,295.55-	
50	27006-80	2	TANK BOTTOM 10 INCH		EA						
1		0	2419	918	0	1393-	0	0	1393-	1.6005	2,229.49-	.000

REPORT TOTAL   10,505.59

Figure 8-15   Stock-status report

review, a company is better able to meet its inventory investment, stock performance, and order-filling objectives. In this section we will examine three types of analysis important to such a program of evaluation.

Inventory-Value Analysis

Inventory-value analysis provides the basis for an ABC approach to inventory control. In this type of analysis, the initial step in processing is to determine the usage value (average demand times unit price) of each item carried in inventory. Returning to an earlier example, suppose that the average demand for down-filled sleeping bags is 840 and that each bag sells for $50.00. The usage value for down-filled bags is thus $42,000. Now suppose the average demand for polyester-filled bags is 1,760 and each of these bags costs $25.00. The usage value would be $44,000, or approximately the same as that for down-filled bags, even though demand is more than twice as great.

After usage value has been determined, the next step in processing is to rank all products from highest to lowest usage value and to calculate the cumulative cost associated with this ranking. As Figure 8-18 shows, this procedure is required to produce a *value-analysis report*—a listing of all items carried in stock, ranked in order of their usage value. This report often reveals interesting

```
 9201000000000    POWER HAND DRYER                       ITEM INQUIRY
                                              2 3 4 5 6 7 8 24
 ITEM CLASS .......... 09           INVENTORY GROUP ...... 2
 VENDOR NUMBER ........ 8620AR      MFR NUMBER QR-44DRYR-02
 UNIT OF MEASURE ...... CTN         ALTERNATE U/M ........ EA
 CONVERSION:      6 EA PER CTN


                     --- INVENTORY BALANCE ---

    W/H      FULL UNITS ON HAND    ON    ON   ON   ODD EA   ON HAND
 W/H LOC     COUNT / ALLOC / NET  ORDER  RSV  B/O  COUNT / ALLOC / NET

  1 A-703     10      4      6      0     0    0     3         0      3

  3 BN 19     21      3     18     12     0    0     0         0      0


            UNIT COST-   96.710 CTN   ALT COST-   97.000 CTN


 COMMAND KEYS-
 2 NEW SEARCH     3 BILLING DATA     4 INV BALANCE    5 SALES DATA
 6 PRICE INQUIRY 7 PURCHASING DATA 8 P/O LOOKUP    24 SIGN OFF
```

Figure 8-16   Inventory-balance display

findings. It is common, for example, to discover that 20 percent of all items stored make up 80 percent of the cumulative usage value!

The final step in inventory-value analysis is to assign an A code to the items of highest value, a B code to items of medium value, and a C code to those of lowest value. As Figure 8-18 shows, C items tend to account for more than 50 percent of all items carried in stock.

One important use of the value-analysis report is that it helps the controller (the chief financial officer) of a company project inventory cash requirements. If, for example, the cumulative cost of inventory is increasing by 5 percent a month, this percentage increase can be used in estimating future cash requirements. This report is also valuable in setting the value of inventory for insurance purposes. By comparing the value of inventory with the dollar amount of insured coverage, a business is able to determine whether or not it is adequately protected.

Inventory-Investment Analysis

Inventory-investment analysis examines the performance of stock items to determine whether the supply of stock appears high, whether the turnover of stock appears low, and whether the return on investment (R.O.I.) is acceptable. To answer the first question—whether the supply of stock appears high—the "month's supply" of stock must be calculated and printed. In calculating the month's supply of inventory for a product, current inventory is divided by average demand.

VENDOR ITEM ITEM NUMBER CLASS NUMBER	WH NO	U/M	QTY ON-HAND	QTY ON-ORDER	QTY ALLOCATED	QTY AVAILABLE	ORDER POINT	E.O.Q.	SAFETY STOCK	LEAD TIME	L/T ADJ	AVERAGE PERIOD USE
NUT 001011 80 07243	1	EA	5,087	0	0	5,087	7,000 *	10,182 *	0	030P	02	665
PLATED CYLINDER 12 IN 006592 30 99239-RM	1	EA	1,017	0	0	1,017	2,500 *	109 *	0	120P	10	76
CASTING 015772 30 99990-RM	1	EA	11,247	0	0	11,247	15,000 *	414 *	0	150P	10	357
HINGE WASHER 018834 80 03587	1	EA	12,631	0	0	12,631	72,000 *	6,961 *	0	015P	02	665
HINGE WASHER 018834 80 03640	1	EA	4,871	0	0	4,871	6,000 *	12,000 *	0	015P	02	665
ROUND STOCK 5/8 DIA - CRS 024775 30 99544-RM	1	FT	5,327	0	0	5,327	8,000 *	1,476 *	0	030P	02	712
1/8 SHEET METAL 024775 30 99750-RM	1	SF	10,851	0	0	10,851	20,000 *	1,435 *	0	060P	02	1,201
IRON PLATE 1/4 IN - HRS 024775 30 99910-RM	1	LB	6,445	0	0	6,445	10,000 *	902 *	0	060P	02	567
BAR STOCK 1 X 3/8 - CRS 024775 30 99950-RM	1	FT	1,261	0	0	1,261	15,000 *	1,204 *	0	090P	02	526
VALVE 030716 80 03021	1	EA	93-	0	0	93-	1,063	9,000	0	060P	02	332
CONTROL BOX 042598 70 33480-A	1	EA	4,898	0	225	4,673	6,000 *	544 *	308	060P	05	342
WRENCH 072303 80 03385	1	EA	7,927	0	0	7,927	9,500 *	1,208 *	0	030P	02	337
RUBBER TUBE 1 X 3 096267 80 34180-A	1	EA	3,143	0	0	3,143	6,000 *	2,977 *	0	030X	05	332
RUBBER TUBE 3/4 X 2 096267 80 34180-B	1	EA	3,267	0	0	3,267	6,000 *	3,220 *	0	030X	02	332
RUBBER TUBE 1/4 X 4 096267 80 46800-C	1	EA	5,232	0	0	5,232	7,000 *	2,629 *	0	030X	02	332

GATEWAY MFG CO — INVENTORY REORDER REPORT — DATE 12/11/ TIME 8.42.07 PAGE 1 AMI2P
SEQUENCE BY VENDOR
VENDORS FROM 001011 TO 096267
DESCRIPTION

TOTAL NUMBER OF RECORDS SELECTED   15

NOTE- * -MANUALLY ENTERED
M -LEAD TIME MANUFACTURING
P -LEAD TIME PURCHASING
X -OTHER LEAD TIME

Figure 8-17 Purchase-advice report

$$\text{Month's supply} = \text{Current inventory} \div \text{Average demand}$$

(If, for example, the average demand is 1,000 units and 6,500 units are stored in inventory, the month's supply is 6.5.) The calculations are collected in a *month's supply report* (see Figure 8-19), which permits inventory managers to evaluate all stock items with a high month's supply. Once it is decided that inventory is too large, managers can adjust stock-replenishment decisions. For example, the reorder point can be lowered and the order quantity can be reduced in size.

Inventory-turnover analysis is similar to month's supply analysis. The summary produced, the *inventory-turnover report,* provides a ranking of inventory-turnover ratios (see Figure 8-20). Each ratio is calculated by dividing annual requirements for a product by average inventory:

$$\text{Turnover} = \text{Annual requirements} \div \text{Average inventory}$$

Thus, for part number 07688-1, the annual requirement of 1,110 would be divided by the average inventory, 1,850, to yield a turnover ratio of 0.6. You might observe that this equation differs slightly from the turnover equation discussed earlier.

ITEM NUMBER	DESCRIPTION	ITEM COUNT	%	ANNUAL USAGE QTY	UNIT COST	ANNUAL USAGE VALUE	CUMULATIVE COST	%
8300007-80	PUMP ASSM	1	.9	6,250	185.90	1,161,875	1,161,875	9.4
8300004-81	TANK ASSM	2	1.9	5,107	224.73	1,147,696	2,309,571	18.7
07085	HOUSING ASSM	3	2.8	10,000	97.74	977,400	3,286,971	26.6
8300005-20	PUMPING UNIT	4	3.7	3,762	216.93	816,090	4,103,061	33.1
8300005-23	PUMPING UNIT	5	4.6	2,488	210.63	524,047	4,627,108	37.4
8300005-21	PUMPING UNIT	6	5.6	2,045	233.07	476,628	5,103,736	41.2
8300004-80	TANK ASSM	7	6.5	2,493	182.23	454,299	5,558,035	44.9
8300004-01	TANK TOP	8	7.4	5,819	77.05	448,353	6,006,388	48.5
8300007-81	PUMP ASSM	9	8.3	2,045	202.04	413,171	6,419,559	51.9
8300005-22	PUMPING UNIT	10	9.3	1,705	241.39	411,569	6,831,128	55.9
8300007-8	PUMP ASSM	11	10.2	1,705	210.36	358,663	7,189,791	58.1
A7685	COVER ASSM	12	11.1	10,200	32.49	331,398	7,521,189	60.8
07106	PUMP SHAFT	13	12.0	10,200	28.00	285,600	7,806,789	63.1
07087	DISCHARGE FERRULE	14	13.0	10,000	28.18	281,800	8,088,589	65.3
8300004-83	TANK ASSM	15	13.9	1,431	180.87	258,824	8,347,413	67.4
8300004-84	TANK ASSM	16	14.8	1,003	223.37	224,040	8,571,453	69.2
8300004-20	TANK BOTTOM	17	15.7	7,512	28.60	214,843	8,786,296	71.0
07685	COVER	18	16.7	10,200	20.41	208,182	8,994,478	72.7
8300004-00	TANK TOP	19	17.6	3,737	50.39	188,307	9,182,785	74.2
07730	MOTOR	20	18.5	6,250	28.45	177,812	9,360,597	75.6
8300003-80	FRAME	21	19.4	4,601	35.00	161,035	9,521,632	76.9
A7666	STAND PIPE ASSM	22	20.4	10,000	16.00	160,000	9,681,632	78.2
A7761	PROBE	23	21.3	7,512	20.30	152,493	9,834,125	79.4
07086	SHELL	24	22.2	10,000	12.50	125,000	9,959,125	80.5
07682-2	STAND	25	23.1	5,819	20.52	119,405	10,078,530	81.4
07686-2	TREADLE ASSM	26	24.1	5,819	19.35	112,597	10,191,127	82.3
8300006-01	HANDLE	27	25.0	10,100	10.69	107,696	10,298,823	83.2
07090	SEALING PLATE	28	25.9	11,000	9.63	105,930	10,404,753	84.1
8300003-21	BASE	29	26.9	1,649	57.16	95,256	10,500,009	84.8
07730-1	MOTOR	30	27.7	2,045	44.59	91,186	10,591,195	85.6
A7696	CLAMP	31	28.7	10,000	9.06	90,600	10,681,795	86.3
07730-2	MOTOR	32	29.6	1,705	52.91	90,211	10,772,006	87.0
8300003-22	BASE	33	30.6	1,487	56.92	84,640	10,856,646	87.7
05785	CONNECTION	34	31.5	10,000	7.50	75,000	10,931,646	88.3
07686	TREADLE ASSM	35	32.4	3,737	18.83	70,367	11,002,013	88.9
8300003-24	BASE	36	33.3	1,203	56.92	68,474	11,070,487	89.4
8300004-23	TANK BOTTOM	37	34.3	2,488	27.24	67,773	11,138,260	90.0
07689	HINGE ARM	38	35.2	10,000	6.54	65,400	11,203,660	90.5
03867	CONNECTION NUT	39	36.1	10,000	6.30	63,000	11,266,660	91.0
05810	FERRULE	40	37.0	10,000	5.90	59,000	11,325,660	91.5
8300003-81	FRAME	41	38.0	1,649	35.60	58,704	11,384,364	92.0
8300004-82	TANK ASSM	42	38.9	288	201.75	58,104	11,442,468	92.4
07682	STAND	43	39.8	3,737	15.00	56,055	11,498,523	92.9
8300003-84	FRAME	44	40.7	1,487	36.00	53,532	11,552,055	93.3
07687	TREADLE	45	41.7	10,000	5.12	51,200	11,603,255	93.7
8300003-86	FRAME	46	42.6	1,203	36.00	43,308	11,646,563	94.1
8300004-85	TANK ASSM	47	43.5	179	200.39	35,869	11,682,432	94.4
07510	10" WHEEL	48	44.4	14,582	2.36	34,413	11,716,845	94.7
A7762	CONTROL BOX	49	45.4	2,488	210.63	34,160	11,751,005	94.9
07688-2	LEVER ARM	50	46.3	14,548	2.29	33,314	11,784,319	95.2
8300003-23	BASE	51	47.2	558	58.16	32,453	11,816,772	95.5
07690	HINGE BRACKET	52	48.1	10,500	2.91	30,555	11,847,327	95.7
A7641	FILTER SLEEVE	53	49.1	10,000	3.00	30,000	11,877,327	96.0
07725	WRENCH	54	50.0	10,000	3.00	30,000	11,907,327	96.2
8300003-25	BASE	55	50.9	502	58.16	29,196	11,936,523	96.4
8300004-02	TANK TOP	56	51.9	444	62.70	27,838	11,964,361	96.7
07186	TUBE	57	52.8	10,000	2.69	26,900	11,991,261	96.9
07198	ADAPTOR PLATE	58	53.7	10,000	2.62	26,200	12,017,461	97.1
8300008-01	ADAPTOR PLATE	59	54.6	10,000	2.62	26,200	12,043,661	97.3
07693	WHEEL BOLT	60	55.6	21,000	1.12	23,520	12,067,181	97.5
07105	WEARING COLLAR	61	56.5	10,000	2.08	20,800	12,087,981	97.7
8300003-85	FRAME	62	57.4	558	36.60	20,422	12,108,403	97.8
07104	DRIVING COLLAR	63	58.3	10,000	1.98	19,800	12,128,203	98.0
07688	LEVER ARM	64	59.3	9,343	2.03	18,966	12,147,169	98.1
8300003-87	FRAME	65	60.2	502	36.60	18,373	12,165,542	98.3
07523	HINGE SCREW	97	89.8	20,000	.10	2,000	12,366,985	99.9
21928	HANDLE SCREW	98	90.7	40,000	.05	2,000	12,368,985	99.9
33427	PUMP SCREW	99	91.7	20,000	.09	1,800	12,370,785	99.0
33527	BKT. WASHER	100	92.6	20,000	.07	1,400	12,372,185	100.0
32057	WHEEL NUT	101	93.5	20,000	.05	1,000	12,373,185	100.0
A7600	OWNERS PKG.	102	94.4	10,000	.10	1,000	12,374,185	100.0
07108	PIN	103	95.4	10,200	.09	918	12,375,103	100.0
21896	HINGE NUT	104	96.3	20,000	.04	800	12,375,903	100.0
12102	WASHER	105	97.2	70,000	.01	700	12,376,603	100.0
07109	SET SCREW	106	98.1	10,000	.07	700	12,377,303	100.0
06478	WHEEL WASHER	107	99.1	40,000	.01	400	12,377,703	100.0
07460	HINGE WASHER	108	100.0	20,000	.01	200	12,377,903	100.0

Figure 8-18 Value-analysis report

Inventory Investment — Month's Supply 10/01/XX				
Finished Goods				
Part Number	ABC Code	Current Inventory	Unit Cost	Month's Supply
8300007-80	A	$ 500,600	$185.90	6.6
8300004-81	A	23,000	224.73	6.2
8300003-21	B	44,560	57.16	6.0
8300004-82	B			
No. Items — 375		$1,939,500	Average	2.7
Summary	A	$ 755,000		5.6
by	B	500,000		2.9
Category	C	684,000		1.8

Figure 8-19 Month's supply report

The inventory-turnover report helps inventory planners to review the order policy and order-quantity decisions set for products. Typically, if order quantities are too high, turnover will be too low. Suppose, for example, that following review it is determined that the order quantity for part number 07688-1 must be reduced to 500 units. This action increases the turnover rate by 0.5 (from 0.6

Inventory Investment — Turns per Year 10/01/XX						
Fabricated Parts:						
Part Number	ABC Code	Order Policy	Order Quantity	Average Inventory	Annual Reqmts	Turnover Ratio
07688-1	C	Fixed	1000	1850	1110	0.6
07682-1	C	Fixed	700	555	444	0.8
8300004-85	B	Period	30 days	163	179	1.1
8300003-25	C	Period	180 days	418	502	1.2
No. of Items — 5,164					Average	2.8
Summary	A					4.8
by	B					2.6
Category	C					1.1

Figure 8-20 Inventory-turnover report

Inventory Investment—Return on Investment					10/1/XX
Part Number	ABC Code	Total Sales	Turnover Ratio	Percent Earned	Return on Investment
		Finished Goods			
0893167	C	5000	1.1	.034	.0374
0996524	B	40000	2.6	.045	.1170
0439621	A	160000	4.8	.055	.2640
Number of Items		4316		Average	.1524
Summary	A Items				.3236
	B Items				.1564
	C Items				.0451

Figure 8-21   Return-on-investment report

to 1.1). As Figure 8-20 shows, a turnover ratio of 1.1 is the average rate for class C items.

Return-on-investment analysis determines which product returns are higher or lower than average. This information is printed on a *return-on-investment report* (see Figure 8-21). R.O.I. is determined by multiplying the turnover ratio times the percent earned on a product. As the figure shows, part number 0893167, a C item, provides a small return of .0374 (3.74 percent on sales), whereas part number 0439621, an A item, provides a much higher return of .2640 (26.4 percent on sales). In addition, even though R.O.I. is high for part number 0439621, it is low compared with the average for all A items (32.36 percent on sales).

Analyses such as month's supply, inventory turnover, and return on investment help inventory managers visualize the performance characteristics of products carried in inventory. As important, they isolate products that are above and below average. Careful review of these products combined with corrective action, when necessary, is the basis underlying the concept of *inventory control*. A vital objective is to maximize the return on investment in inventory in a way that is consistent with the prompt delivery of goods and services to customers.

Inventory-Location Analysis

Inventory-location analysis examines the location of items in inventory to determine if they should be relocated to save travel time, to reduce stock items stored in multiple locations, to free inventory space, or to reduce inventory shrinkage. Several types of reports help inventory planners make these determinations. For example, travel-time figures are printed on a *distance-traveled report* (see Figure 8-22), which shows the computed distance traveled by the

Inventory Location—Bin Location   10/1/XX

Finished Goods

Part Number	ABC Code	Total Sales	Total Orders	Distance Each Trip	Distance Traveled
064100	C	500	75	850	12.07
095450	B	18000	380	85	6.12
069340	B	10000	212.5	112	4.51
069086	A	46000	35	516	3.42

Number of Items   2354   Average   3.8

Summary   A Items   2.4
          B Items   3.3
          C Items   5.4

Figure 8-22   Distance-traveled report

warehouse crew in stocking parts and in filling customer orders. The total distance travel time is arrived at by multiplying the distance traveled per trip times the number of orders received and the number of orders picked:

Distance traveled = Distance each trip × (Number of orders received
+ Number of orders picked)

Suppose, for instance, that the annual demand for product number 069340 is 10,000 units, the order quantity is 800 units, and the average customer order is 50 units. If the warehouse crew must walk 112 feet to stock this product or to fill a customer order, the total distance traveled can be calculated as follows:

$$N_1 = \text{Number of orders received} = \text{Annual demand} \div \hat{Q}$$
$$= 10{,}000 \div 800 = 12.5$$

$$N_2 = \text{Number of orders filled} = \text{Annual demand} \div \text{Average sale}$$
$$= 10{,}000 \div 50 = 200$$

Distance traveled = 112 ft × (12.5 + 200) = 23,800 ft.
= 23,800 ft. ÷ 5,280 ft. per mile = 4.51 miles

Information printed on the distance-traveled report isolates cases in which total travel time appears to be much higher than normal. To equalize travel time, inventory planners must make tradeoffs: the distance associated with high order counts (high N_1 and N_2) is reduced, and the distance associated with low order counts (low N_1 and N_2) is increased. By thus coordinating changes in bin location, inventory planners attempt to minimize overall travel time.

Reducing the number of stock items stored in multiple locations is often accomplished by reducing the space requirements of slower-moving items and giving this space to faster-moving items. This solution addresses what is sometimes called the "grocery shelving" problem: shelf space is constant, but product demand is variable. The objective of managing shelf space is to increase the amount of space for faster-selling items to maximize sales and to avoid running out of stock. Because space is limited, this increase must be achieved either by eliminating slower-moving items or by reducing the shelf space previously assigned to them. Juggling a fixed amount of inventory space is especially difficult when a firm maintains several warehouse locations. With several locations, stored-product-location data must be expanded, and online displays must be designed to show the various storage locations. A display must show the quantity stored at each location, and whether the quantity is unreleased and can be used to fill customer orders (see Figure 8-23).

Multiple stock locations can be avoided, although not completely eliminated—unless, of course, a business has excess storage space. To maximize the use of available space, inventory managers must conduct space-analysis studies. The report needed for these studies is the *space-requirements report*. As Figure 8-24 shows, this document compares the space assigned with the space required by products carried in inventory. Suppose, for example, that a product measures 5 by 5 by 5 inches, or 125 cubic inches, and that, at most, 6,000 of these items will be carried in stock. The space required (in cubic feet) is calculated as follows:

$$\begin{aligned}\text{Space required} &= (\text{Maximum inventory})(\text{Cubic inch requirements}) \\ &\quad \div 1{,}728 \text{ cubic inches per cubic foot} \\ &= (6{,}000)(125) \div 1{,}728 = 434.03 \text{ cubic feet}\end{aligned}$$

Thus, the product would require a total storage space of approximately 7.6 by 7.6 by 7.6 feet (439 cubic feet).

```
Review Inventory Locations for a Part                                    REVIEW LOCN
 Add      Change    Delete    Issues          Stop    Printed    Both      EXIT
 Locn      Locn      Locn    Receipts                 Report

                    Part Number          Warehouse    Location
                   300008

                                               Total                          Total
             Description              UM Ctlr On Hand  In Insp Allocated Unreleased
------------------------------        -- --   -------  ------- -------   -------
BUSHING                               EA  20       70        0        0        70

                                      Unreleased  Locn
Warehouse Location     Quantity        Quantity   Type          Location Remarks
   --     --------      -------        -------     --    ------------------------------
   01      74330           15             15        P    PRIME LOCATION
   02      96147           30             30        P    EXPANSION TO A NEW WAREHOUSE
   02      43444           25             25        T    TEMPORARY LOCATION
```

Figure 8-23 Inventory-location review

Inventory Location—Space Requirements　　　　　　　　　　10/1/XX

Finished Goods

Part Number	Part Location	Maximum Stock	Cubic Inch	Assigned Space	Required Space	Diff
30008	7433			3.0		
	96147			4.0		
	43444			3.5		
Total		160	125	10.5	11.57	(1.07)

Figure 8-24　Space-requirements report

The final type of inventory-location analysis common to business deals with tracking inventory shrinkage. As discussed earlier, shrinkage can result from a number of factors, such as pilferage or errors in physical inventory. The formula used in determining shrinkage is as follows:

$$\text{Shrinkage} = \text{Beginning inventory} + \text{Moves in}$$
$$- \text{Moves out} - \text{Ending inventory}$$

Thus, if beginning inventory for an item is 500 units, ending inventory is 650 units, moves in equals 600 units, and moves out equals 400 units, the shrinkage during the month would be 50 units (500 + 600 − 400 − 650).

Figure 8-25 illustrates an abbreviated inventory-shrinkage report. A unique feature of shrinkage is that it can be positive as well as negative. As shown, part number 93214 reveals a surplus of 70 units. The typical reason for such a surplus is that 70 units were stocked incorrectly—in the wrong bin location. Inspection of all accounts often shows that "surplus items" can be matched against outstanding losses, called "shorts." As the figure shows, product number 93214 has a surplus of 70 items, whereas product number 93241 has a reported "short" of 70 items. Because these two counts are the same, the odds are high that the two products were switched.

Inventory Location—Shrinkage Analysis　　　　　　　　　　10/1/XX

Finished Goods

Part Number	Part Location	Begin Invt	Moves In	Moves Out	End Invt	Shrinkage
31124	85AJ	500	600	400	650	(50)
43694	54BP	900	100	300	500	(200)
93214	654R	1820	850	1240	1500	70
93241	896J	625	70	225	400	(70)

Figure 8-25　Inventory-shrinkage report

8-4 MANAGEMENT IMPLICATIONS

Finished-goods inventory is a popular computer application because it provides inventory planners with a wealth of record-keeping and stock-performance information. Another review of the contents of the product master file (see Figure 8-2) illustrates that this single application is able to describe, locate, and provide an accounting and forecast for each product carried in inventory. This capability is much more important than it might initially appear. If, for example, a business attempts to keep in stock 100,000 or more items, some automated method must be found to assist in record-keeping and in making routine inventory decisions. Otherwise the sheer task of inventory management is enormous.

Besides its benefits for record-keeping and record maintenance, this computer application is also extremely popular because it allows inventory planners to monitor computer-based decisions, substituting, where appropriate, programmed decisions with their own. Moreover, with an online design, inventory management can be decentralized. People familiar with the characteristics of items carried in inventory are able to rule on inventory decisions. Online designs also simplify file-update procedures and improve processing controls, so that people familiar with the types of updates required are responsible for making these updates. Through visual review of all updates, processing control can be markedly improved.

Producing various types of inventory-analyses displays and reports is another major managerial benefit of an automated approach to inventory management. By closely monitoring stock value, supply, turnover, and return on investment, inventory planners are better able to make more objective inventory plans. Combining these studies with different types of inventory-location analyses, business firms discover that they are able to carry smaller quantities of stock while increasing sales volume and overall product profitability. This ability to operate at higher leverage (less investment in relation to sales) can dramatically improve the financial well-being of a business. Reducing the funds needed for inventory permits funds to be released for use in more profitable operations.

REVIEW OF IMPORTANT IDEAS

The finished-goods inventory application must provide product inventory counts (quantity on hand, on order, on back order, and so forth) and show all product-reorder decisions (when to order, how much to order, and from whom to order). Careful review of both types of information leads to better understanding of how to make inventory decisions.

The finished-goods inventory application is designed to maximize the return on capital invested in inventory. By improving inventory turnover while holding the percentage earned on sales constant, companies are able to dramatically increase their return on invested capital.

The design of the application is straightforward. The heart of processing is the update of the product master file. Once updated, the file is used in a variety of ways. Two common products of processing are stock-status and purchase-advice reports and displays. Stock-status reports show the current status of items held in stock relative to future supply and demand for these items. Purchase-advice reports show product-reorder decisions: which products to order (or review), the quantity to order, and the preferred source of supply.

Planners can determine which products to order by studying computer-calculated reorder points or order frequencies. Cycle buying follows from the calculation of order frequencies. With cycle buying, the taking of a periodic physical inventory is combined with the ordering of stock. Cycle buying permits high-valued items to be checked more frequently than lower-valued items.

Inventory-value analysis, investment analysis, and location analysis are vital parts in an overall inventory-management plan. Inventory-value analysis assigns A, B, and C codes to items carried in stock. Inventory-investment analysis examines the supply of stock, product-turnover rates, and product returns on capital invested in inventory. Inventory-location analysis determines more economical ways to store products in company warehouse facilities. Collectively, these different types of analysis permit inventory planners to carefully monitor and finely adjust inventory-management decisions. In so doing, a business firm is better able to achieve its objective of maximizing the return on capital invested in inventory.

KEY WORDS

Order frequency	Extrinsic forecast
Order quantity	Intrinsic forecast
Approved vendor	Trend analysis
Inventory management	Exponential smoothing
Return on investment	Seasonal variation graph
Inventory turnover	Economic order quantity
Physical inventory	Reorder point
Product line	Cycle buying
Inventory shrinkage	Usage value
ABC code	Inventory-value analysis
Obsolete inventory	Inventory-investment analysis
Stock-status report	Inventory control
Purchase-advice displays	

REVIEW QUESTIONS

1. What three reorder decisions are fundamental to inventory management?

2. Explain how return on investment (R.O.I.) is related to inventory management.

3. What is the primary reason for developing the finished-goods inventory application? What are important secondary reasons?

4. Outline the various types of information (classes and record segments) contained in the product master file.

5. What is an ABC code? How is it used in processing?

6. What information is contained on the stock-status report? How does it differ from information contained on the purchase-advice report?

7. How does a combined menu and data-entry display differ from a program-processing-menu display?

8. Explain the difference between an extrinsic forecast and an intrinsic forecast.

9. Explain the exponential smoothing formula.

10. What is an override decision? Why are override decisions important to this application?

11. How does the seasonal coefficient base index affect the sales forecast for a product?

12. What is a reorder point? How is it calculated?

13. What is the order frequency? How is it calculated?

14. What is cycle buying? What are its main advantages?

15. Explain the difference between usage value and value analysis.

16. Name three types of inventory-investment-analysis reports.

17. Define the term "inventory control."

18. How does inventory-location analysis differ from inventory-investment analysis?

19. What types of information are contained on the space-requirements report?

20. Name three types of inventory-location studies.

21. What advantage is gained by a decentralized finished-goods inventory design?

EXERCISES

1. Design the systems flowchart for the program entitled "ready product master file" (see Figure 8-6). Compare this flowchart with the ready-product-master-file systems flowchart in Chapter 7 and explain any differences in processing.

2. Suppose product sales and the product sales forecast from June through October for product number 64521, Golden Wire Baskets, are as follows:

Month	Product Forecast	Product Sales
June	900	925
July	903	940
August	907	955
September	912	965
October	917	935
November	?	

(a) When alpha (α) equals 0.1, what is the product forecast for November?

(b) Compute the November forecast once again; however, set the value of alpha (α) at 0.3 instead of 0.1. After adjusting, the product forecast should read as follows: forecast for June equals 900, forecast for July equals 908, forecast for August equals 918, and so forth.

(c) Compare the two product forecasts. Based on this comparison, what can you say about setting the correct value of alpha? Would you change your view if the actual product sales for November were 856 units?

3. The following information is known about a product carried in inventory:

Annual demand	20,000 units
Purchase order cost	$200.00
Cost per unit	$10.00
Cost of capital	20 percent
Annual working days	250 days
Percent earned on sales	4 percent
Average inventory	1,250 units

Based on this information, calculate the

(a) economic order quantity

(b) order frequency

(c) usage value

(d) return on investment

9

Purchasing and Receiving

Purchasing and receiving is an integral part of materials management. The purchasing department of a business buys material in amounts authorized by requisitions it receives from warehouse and inventory managers. This department is responsible for four basic purchasing activities: selecting suppliers, or vendors, expediting delivery from suppliers, coordinating communications between suppliers and the departments within the company, and identifying new vendor products and services that contribute to company profits.

Surveying these activities clarifies why purchase orders should not be printed directly, as part of an inventory computer application. Selecting suppliers, for example, entails identifying vendors who are best able to deliver needed products, negotiating the most advantageous terms of purchase, and issuing necessary purchase agreements and purchase orders. The computer is able only to accomplish the last of these tasks, provided the terms of purchase have been entered into processing. Terms of purchasing must be negotiated in advance; they are determined individually, rather than set arbitrarily by the computer.

The receiving department of a business is responsible for checking vendor shipments for correctness and for moving goods from receiving areas to warehouse locations. If goods are found to be unacceptable, the receiving department notifies members of the purchasing staff, who in turn must notify the vendor and work out the problems associated with the faulty material.

Thus, as with purchasing, there are four main types of receiving activities: verifying the correctness of vendor shipments, inspecting incoming material, informing the purchasing department about materials that do not conform to company standards, and telling members of the warehouse crew where to stock newly received material.

In effect, receiving attempts to close the loop between a company's purchasing, inventory-control, and accounts payable activities. By accepting products and moving them to warehouse locations, a company is able to verify that an outstanding purchase order has been filled, an on-order quantity has been received, and a vendor invoice can be paid. Likewise, once merchandise is received (not returned), the vendor knows that shipped merchandise has been accepted and that payment of the vendor invoice should be forthcoming.

There are several good reasons for developing an online purchasing and receiving application. This application can provide a firm with (1) faster and more accurate processing of purchase requisitions and receiving reports, (2) improved inquiry capabilities, (3) improved vendor relationships, (4) better control of materials inventory, and (5) better control of accounts payable. Besides these more obvious benefits, the purchasing and receiving application helps to formalize the tasks associated with acquiring materials inventory. In times past, when supplies were abundant relative to demand, companies believed that they could afford to treat purchasing as a minor business function. Periods of material scarcity have changed this view. Today business firms realize that the supply of incoming materials must be carefully managed. Otherwise a smooth flow of production or order-entry processing will be disrupted. Clearly, even the best order-entry system will look inadequate if stock is not available. Then, instead of filling orders, a firm must place incoming requests for stock on back order.

9-1 PRELIMINARY OVERVIEW OF PROCESSING

Figures 9-1 and 9-2 provide preliminary overviews of the purchasing and receiving computer application. The purchasing portion of the design identifies the sources of supply and prints purchase orders to confirm the choice of suppliers. The receiving portion matches incoming material receipts against outstanding, or pending, purchase orders. This portion produces the receiving report and prints stock tickets to identify products stored in the warehouse.

The five main processing steps associated with purchasing can be summarized as follows:

1. *Ready vendor master file* to ensure that all vendor information, including new information, is correct.

2. *Ready product master file* to ensure that all product information, including new information, is correct.

3. *Enter purchase requirements* to specify what items are to be ordered from a supplier, in what quantity and at what price, and when delivery is expected.

4. *Prepare purchase orders* to produce formal purchase order documents.

5. *Prepare purchasing summaries* to record the charges that can be expected as a result of buying goods from vendors.

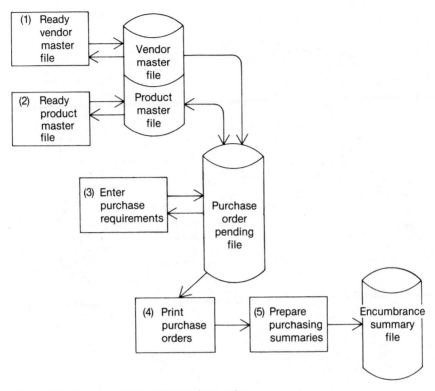

Figure 9-1 Five steps in processing purchase orders

An important product of the purchasing portion of the design is the *purchase order pending file,* which stores the details of outstanding, or open, purchase orders. Another important file created in processing is the *encumbrance summary file,* which stores the dollar amounts to be set aside to pay an outstanding purchase order.

Once a purchase order is filled, shipped, and delivered by the vendor, the receiving department processes the details of each order. As Figure 9-2 shows, five more steps are associated with receiving:

6. *Enter new receipts* to specify what items have been received and are acceptable.

7. *Post new receipts* to match incoming vendor packing slips against pending purchase orders.

8. *Print receiving report* to document goods received on a given day.

9. *Print stock tickets* to document where goods are to be stored in the warehouse.

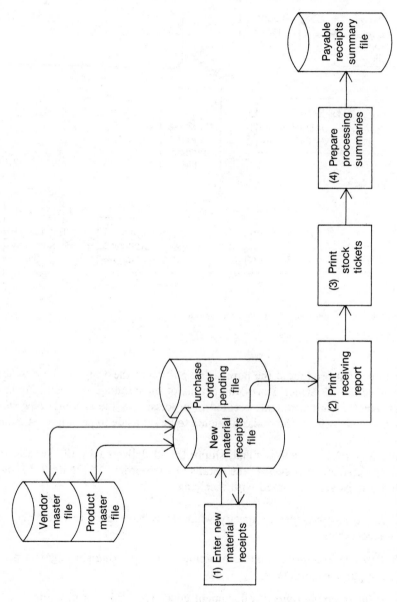

Figure 9-2 Five steps in processing new material receipts

10. *Prepare processing summaries* to record the charges to be paid as a result of buying goods from vendors.

As the figure indicates, the file of pending purchase orders that has been created by purchasing is next updated by receiving. Thus, all records contained in the pending file are "open" orders; they will remain in the pending file until goods are received and the receiving department instructs the computer to "pull," or remove, an open order.

Inputs to Processing

In this divided application, there are two main inputs to processing: purchase requisitions and receiving slips. A *purchase requisition* provides the authority to issue purchase orders to outside suppliers. As Figure 9-3 shows, a purchase requisition describes the product to be ordered, by number (if possible) and by name, and states the quantity desired and the desired date of delivery. To this information, the purchasing agent must usually add or modify the name of the vendor, the product price and terms of purchase, and the terms of shipment. In setting the terms of shipment (when goods are to be shipped by the vendor and how), the purchasing agent must factor in a number of lead times—for example, the time required by the vendor to receive and fill an order, the time required by the shipper to deliver it, and the time required by receiving to inspect and put it away. In more complicated situations, the agent must also estimate the time required to negotiate the price and terms of payment.

Receiving slips show goods delivered by suppliers and provide the authority to print stock tickets. As Figure 9-4 shows, a receiving slip verifies the correctness of the vendor's packing slip and states the quantity of incoming material that has passed company inspection. There are several counts that must be kept by receiving and reported to purchasing, including the quantity received, the number of items "short" or the number of items "long," the number of items rejected, and the number of items to be reworked. "Items short" or "items long" is simply the difference between the quantity ordered and the quantity received. "Items rejected" is the difference between the quantity received and the quantity passed by inspection. "Items reworked" is significant only if a company can repair or rework some of the rejected items rather than sending them back to the supplier. The purchasing department is responsible for determining who pays for the reworked material.

Outputs from Processing

Valued outputs produced by the purchasing and receiving application include two different transaction documents (purchase orders and stock tickets), two or more types of processing summaries, and three important summary files (the purchase order pending file, the encumbrance summary file, and the payables receipts summary file). Collectively, these documents, summaries, and files de-

ORDER REQUEST

BRANCH REQ. # _72415_

FROM: _Field Sales_   OFFICE _Eugene_   DATE _7/29/8x_

TO BE ORDERED FROM OUTSIDE VENDORS ONLY

InterWare Computer Supplies
COMPANY NAME

1540 Austin Drive
ADDRESS

Santa Clara, CA 95051
CITY   STATE   ZIP

_(408) 737-9342_
PHONE

REQUIRED SHIP DATE _9/1/8x_

SHIP TO THE ATTENTION OF:

M. Rarick

CC: _____

_____

CONFIRMING ☐ YES ☐ NO

ITEM #	QUANTITY	DESCRIPTION (include product # if possible)	UNIT PRICE	EXTENDED PRICE
1	2	12 - Platter Disk Pack 5156 - II	775.00	1550.00
2	1	5 - Platter Disk Pack 1258 FF	550.00	550.00

STATE REASON AND INTENDED USER OF ORDER: TOTAL PRICE $ _2100.00_

_____

_____

_____

CHARGE TO: ☑ CAPITAL EQUIPMENT ACCOUNT NO. _6220_   TARGETED ☑ YES ☐ NO
            ☐ EXPENSED (UNDER $1000.00)

BRANCH OFFICE #	DEPT. NUMBER	SALES FORCE	PRODUCT TYPE	PRODUCT LINE		SALES FORCE	PRODUCT TYPE
_0142_	_0017_	_80_	_19_	_0 0_	(or) ☐ SALES _____		
____	____	__	__	_0 0_	☐ SERVICE _____		

☐ DEMO   ☐ SALES FINANCE
☑ FACILITIES   ☐ ORDER PROCESSING   ☐ SEO - dept. code _____
☐ OTHER   ☐ CREDIT/COLLECTION
  (explain)

_____   AUTHORIZED SIGNATURE: _____

NSR 69 (rev. 10/81)   (Per NSR Financial Administrative Policy)

Figure 9-3 Purchase requisition

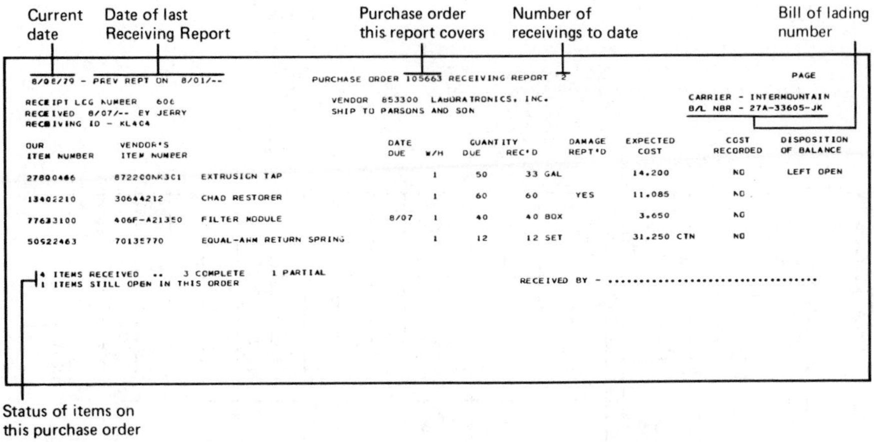
Current date
Date of last Receiving Report
Purchase order this report covers
Number of receivings to date
Bill of lading number
8/08/79 - PREV REPT ON 8/01/--
PURCHASE ORDER 105663 RECEIVING REPORT 2
PAGE
RECEIPT LOG NUMBER 606
RECEIVED 8/07/-- BY JERRY
RECEIVING ID - KL4C4
VENDOR 853300 LABORATRONICS, INC.
SHIP TO PARSONS AND SON
CARRIER - INTERMOUNTAIN
B/L NBR - 27A-33605-JK
OUR ITEM NUMBER
VENDOR'S ITEM NUMBER
DATE DUE
W/H
QUANTITY DUE REC'D
DAMAGE REPT'D
EXPECTED COST
COST RECORDED
DISPOSITION OF BALANCE
27800486 8722CONK3C1 EXTRUSION TAP 1 50 33 GAL 14.200 NO LEFT OPEN
13402210 30644212 CHAD RESTORER 1 60 60 YES 11.085 NO
77633100 406F-A21350 FILTER MODULE 8/07 1 40 40 BOX 3.650 NO
50522463 70135770 EQUAL-ARM RETURN SPRING 1 12 12 SET 31.250 CTN NO
4 ITEMS RECEIVED .. 3 COMPLETE 1 PARTIAL
1 ITEMS STILL OPEN IN THIS ORDER
RECEIVED BY - ....
Status of items on this purchase order

Figure 9-4 Receiving slip

fine all new purchase orders, purchase orders "let" but not received, and all new material receipts. This information is vital in attempting to determine the status of quantities on order; it is even more vital in deciding whether or not to pay a vendor invoice. (This second subject is discussed in the next chapter, which deals with accounts payable processing.)

Figure 9-5 illustrates a typical business purchase order. The format of this transaction document is similar to the format of the customer invoice. It must provide space for the purchase order number, the date, the vendor number, the name and address of the vendor, product information (quantity desired, product description, and price), and shipping information (ship via and by what date). The two numbers of special importance are the purchase order number and the vendor number. The *purchase order number* should be unique—to identify a single purchasing agreement. This number is also used by the vendor in referring to an order. Typically, the vendor prints the purchase order number on the packing slip and invoice, so that goods ordered can be matched against goods received and billed for.

Like the purchase order number, the *vendor number* should be unique. As with the customer account number and the product number, each vendor number should refer to a single source of supply. By using a unique vendor number and a unique purchase order number, a company is able to trace an outstanding order in one of two ways. By entering a purchase order number, for example, an outstanding order can be displayed directly. Likewise, by entering a vendor number, a listing can be produced of all purchase order numbers placed with that particular vendor.

Besides purchase orders, the purchasing portion of the application prints a *new order register,* to document which orders have been let, and a *purchase order encumbrance summary,* to show what funds should be set aside to cover outstanding purchases. The need to encumber funds is widely recognized in

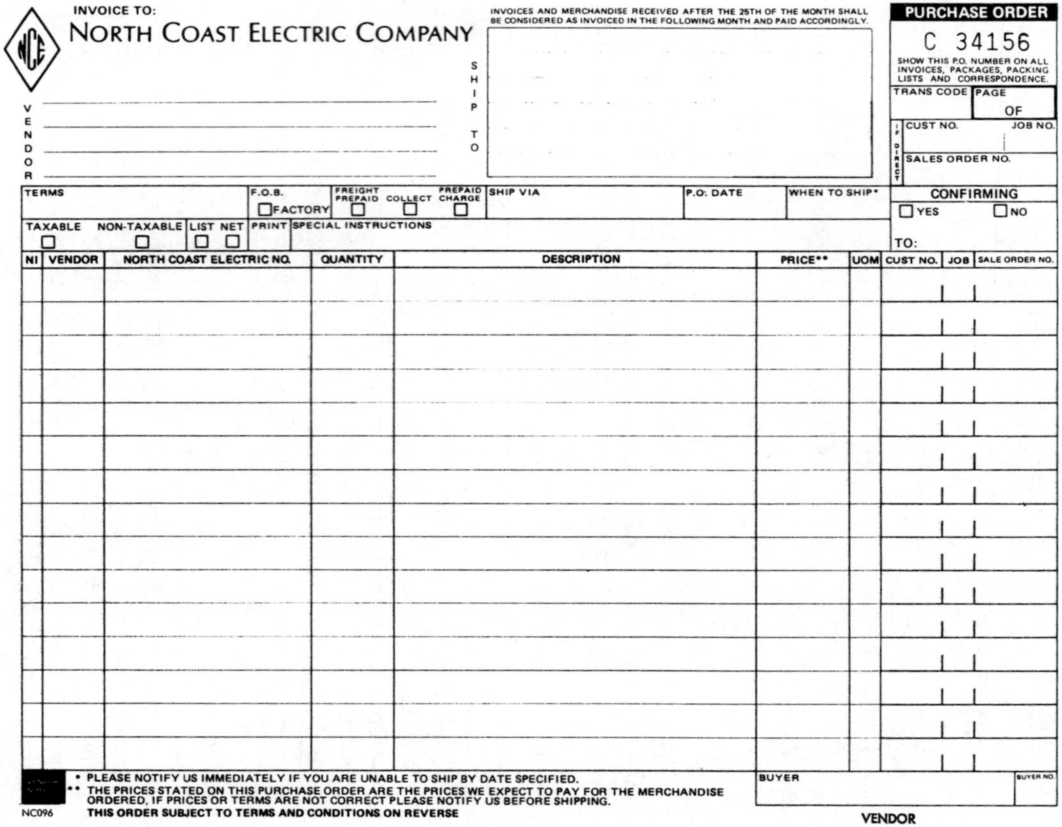

INVOICE TO:
NORTH COAST ELECTRIC COMPANY

INVOICES AND MERCHANDISE RECEIVED AFTER THE 25TH OF THE MONTH SHALL BE CONSIDERED AS INVOICED IN THE FOLLOWING MONTH AND PAID ACCORDINGLY.

PURCHASE ORDER

C 34156

SHOW THIS P.O. NUMBER ON ALL INVOICES, PACKAGES, PACKING LISTS AND CORRESPONDENCE.

TRANS CODE | PAGE OF

VENDOR

SHIP TO

IF DIRECT: CUST NO. | JOB NO. | SALES ORDER NO.

TERMS | F.O.B. ☐ FACTORY | FREIGHT PREPAID ☐ | COLLECT ☐ | PREPAID CHARGE ☐ | SHIP VIA | P.O. DATE | WHEN TO SHIP*

CONFIRMING ☐ YES ☐ NO

TAXABLE ☐ | NON-TAXABLE ☐ | LIST ☐ NET ☐ | PRINT | SPECIAL INSTRUCTIONS

TO:

NI	VENDOR	NORTH COAST ELECTRIC NO.	QUANTITY	DESCRIPTION	PRICE**	UOM	CUST NO.	JOB	SALE ORDER NO.

* PLEASE NOTIFY US IMMEDIATELY IF YOU ARE UNABLE TO SHIP BY DATE SPECIFIED.
** THE PRICES STATED ON THIS PURCHASE ORDER ARE THE PRICES WE EXPECT TO PAY FOR THE MERCHANDISE ORDERED, IF PRICES OR TERMS ARE NOT CORRECT PLEASE NOTIFY US BEFORE SHIPPING.
THIS ORDER SUBJECT TO TERMS AND CONDITIONS ON REVERSE

BUYER | BUYER NO.

NC096

VENDOR

Figure 9-5 Purchase order

business and government. By setting aside funds to cover authorized pending purchases, companies are better able to keep expenses within their yearly budgets.

The receiving portion of the application produces a receiving report and stock tickets or labels. The *receiving report* shows the quantity of material received from the vendor and the disposition of these materials (see Figure 9-6). Disposition categories might be as follows: release, return to vendor, rework in our plant, and scrap. "Release" means that goods have passed inspection and can be made ready to transport to a warehouse location. Prior to transport, some type of *stock ticket* or *move ticket* is prepared. This ticket generally contains the product number, descriptive information, and the bin location number. The ticket is attached to each shipment to indicate clearly where goods are to be placed in the warehouse.

Other products produced by the receiving portion include a report of overdue purchase orders and a payables receipts summary. The *overdue purchase order report* lists all purchase orders that should have been received at an earlier date. Equipped with this information, purchasing agents are able to directly contact vendors to determine why shipments are late. The *payables receipts summary* shows the status of received materials. This information is required to verify the correctness of the vendor invoice and the amount to pay.

9-2 PURCHASE ORDER PROCESSING

Figures 9-7 and 9-8 show the systems organization charts for the purchasing and receiving computer application. Seven interactive programs are featured: two of these create transaction files, two update master files, and three produce display programs. Thirteen batch programs are also required. These produce four different registers, two types of transaction documents, four processing summaries, and three change reports. Because this application is rather large, we will first consider the processing of purchase orders. The next section describes the receiving portion of the design.

Figure 9-9 shows the purchasing processing menu. Interactive programs are used to enter purchase requirements, to ready vendor and product master files, to display product and vendor accounts, and to display pending purchase orders. After purchase requirements have been successfully entered into processing, batch programs are needed to print the new order register and purchase orders. The remaining batch programs produce processing summaries, product and vendor registers, and change reports.

The Enter Purchase Requirements Program

Three types of purchase-requirements information must either be keyed or read to processing from computer files: purchase order information, vendor information, and product information. As Figure 9-10 shows, keyed information can be kept to a minimum, provided vendor and product master files are available.

CORPORATION 01-777 BOYD, RESEARCH GROUP   RUN   FRIDAY   8/14/3-   PAGE 1
PIX100-C   FOR   RECEIVING REPORT 8/14/8-   AT 21.26
                  14 DAYS BEFORE 8/14/8-

BUYER CODE - BH   BUYER NAME - FAWLTY   ALBERT

P.O. NUMBER	VENDOR NAME	LN IT	SB LN	RCPT NBR	PART NUMBER	DESCRIPTION	ORDERED QUANTITY	U/M	UNIT PRICE	RECEIVED QUANTITY	RECEIVED DATE	DUE DATE	EARLY /LATE	P C
CJ4298	BASTALLIO	01		LOT01 LOT02 LOT03	82103602-001	SNAP PLATE, BLK	1,500	EA	42.98	1,400 109 UNACCEPTD	8/30/8- 8/30/8-	8/30/8- 8/30/8-		N
		02		LOT04	82109206-303	CASING, PLASTIC	1,500	EA	25.12	2,000	8/30/8-	8/30/8-		N
BH4901	ELECTROL, INC.	01		LOT01 LOT02	43168999-001	BLOWER, HISPEED	800	EA	26.25	400 400	8/01/8- 8/27/8-	8/15/8- 8/15/8-	14E 12L	N
		02		LOT01 LOT02 LOT03	43168900-001	BLOWER,LOPWR	800	EA	26.25	UNACCEPTD 200 200	8/01/8- 8/15/8-	8/15/8- 8/15/8-	14E	N
BT4900	MOTO DIRECT SALES	01		LOT01 LOT02	60069555-001	GATE ARRAY	800	EA	64.40	400 400	8/01/8- 8/15/8-	8/15/8- 8/15/8-	14E	N
BT3009	TEXAS	01	06	BS006	70940118-122	TRANSISTOR	1,000	EA	1.59	1,000	7/31/8-	7/24/8-		N

Figure 9-6   Receiving report

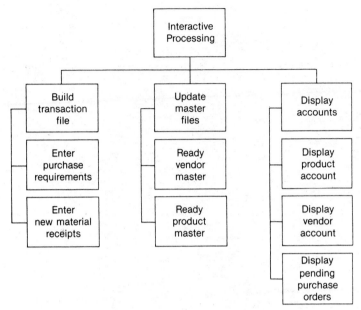

Figure 9-7 Purchasing and receiving interactive processing

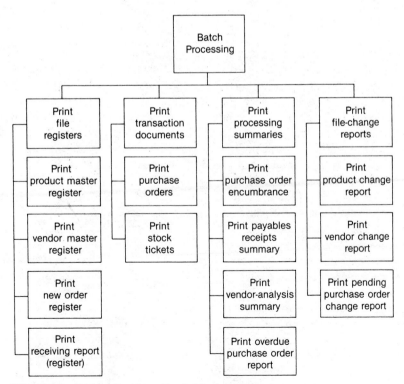

Figure 9-8 Purchasing and receiving batch processing

I.1   ENTER PURCHASE REQUIREMENTS
I.2   READY VENDOR MASTER FILE
I.3   READY PRODUCT MASTER FILE
I.4   DISPLAY PRODUCT ACCOUNT
I.5   DISPLAY VENDOR ACCOUNT
I.6   DISPLAY PENDING PURCHASE ORDER

B.1   PRINT NEW ORDER REGISTER
B.2   PRINT PURCHASE ORDERS
B.3   PRINT PURCHASE ORDER ENCUMBRANCE
B.4   PRINT VENDOR-ANALYSIS SUMMARY
B.5   PRINT PRODUCT MASTER REGISTER
B.6   PRINT VENDOR MASTER REGISTER
B.7   PRINT PRODUCT CHANGE REPORT
B.8   PRINT VENDOR CHANGE REPORT
B.9   PRINT PURCHASE ORDER CHANGE REPORT
⟨10⟩ EXIT

Figure 9-9   Purchasing menu

Following the entry of the purchase order number and record code, the vendor number is keyed and transmitted. This step transfers the vendor name and address into processing for visual verification. Next, the first product number, quantity to be ordered (if special), and unit cost (if special) are keyed and transmitted. This step transfers product name and description, pricing and discounts, and reorder information into processing. After product information has been visually verified, the computer responds by asking for the next product number. Data entry continues until all product line items have been successfully brought into processing.

This data-entry procedure calls for an override set of instructions. If the quantity to be ordered and the unit cost are the same as the computer-determined order quantity and unit cost, only the product number is keyed and transmitted. If either the quantity to be ordered or the unit price is changed, however (perhaps due to a special purchase agreement), the totals displayed must be replaced with the new figures, which override the amount or price stored on file.

A number of separate actions take place during the entry of purchase order requirements (see Figure 9-11). After purchase order information has been entered, vendor information is transferred from the vendor master file. Next, product information is transferred, and after the information is verified as correct, the product master file is updated: the on-order field is increased by the quantity ordered. Last, the completed order is written to the purchase order pending file, since this file stores all open purchase orders. Changes to the pend-

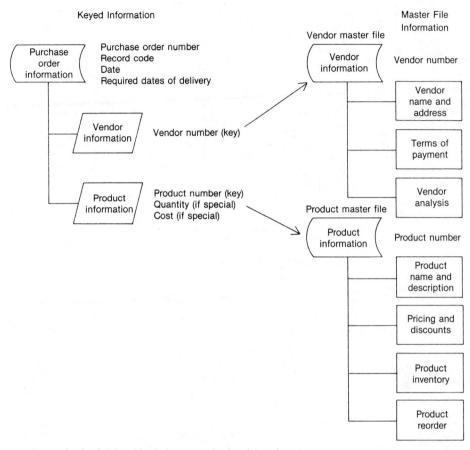

Figure 9-10 Relationships between purchasing data sets

ing file are also written to the purchase order change file, to provide a record of all new purchase order transactions.

Ready Master Files

Before purchase requirements information can be successfully processed by the computer, the vendor and product master files must be current. If, for example, a new supplier is identified, vendor information must be collected and entered prior to entering purchase requirements. As we discussed earlier, vendor information consists of three or more segments, including name and address, terms of payment, and vendor analysis. The contents of each can be summarized as follows:

- *Vendor name and address.* This segment is limited to the vendor's name for ordering and billing, vendor address (street, city, state, postal code), the name of the person to contact, and telephone number.

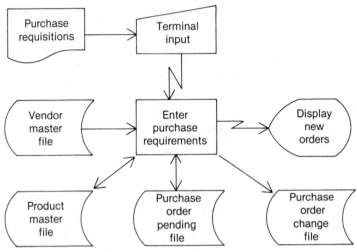

Figure 9-11 Entering purchase-order requirements

- *Terms of payment.* This segment may store specific information such as:

Vendor number	3210
Product	Type I ribbons
Price	5.75 1 to 11
schedule	5.30 12 to 35
	4.95 over 35
Terms	5% prepaid, net 30

Or, it may be limited to general information, such as 5 percent prepaid, net 30, catalog number R962. The number R962, in this instance, indicates where the item is listed in the vendor's catalog.

- *Vendor analysis.* This section contains both product and background information. *Vendor product information* specifies product delivery and quality performance averages. The details stored include the vendor's average delivery time (the time between the receipt of the purchase order and the shipment of goods), the average inventory carried by the vendor, and the product rejection rate. *Vendor background information* is more subjective than product information. It indicates the financial strength of the vendor (AAA, BB, B), the work stoppage rating, and a trade relations rating.

Entering new product information is more complicated than entering new vendor information. Each of the eight record segments discussed in the last chapter must be completed; variable fields such as the on-hand quantity must be set to their current value. Of these eight segments, four are especially vital in purchasing: product name and description, pricing and discounts, product inventory, and product reorder. For example, the product name and description is needed to explain to the vendor the product being ordered and the number assigned to that product by the business. Pricing and discount information stores the average cost of the product. If, in ordering, the unit cost indicated on the purchase order is significantly higher than the unit cost stored on file (10 percent or more), this information should be displayed for review. Inventory information shows the quantity on hand, the quantity on order, and the expected date of delivery. When an order is placed with a vendor, these last two fields must be updated. Finally, reorder information includes the preferred vendor number and the vendor lead time. In larger purchasing applications, these fields are enlarged to permit several vendor numbers and lead times to be stored. The reason for storing several numbers is that some vendors are able to deliver materials faster, but at a slightly higher price.

Printing and Reviewing Purchase Orders

After the vendor and product master files have been updated and purchase requirements have been successfully entered into processing, purchase orders are printed. As Figure 9-12 shows, the actual printing is a two-step batch process. Prior to printing purchase orders, a new order register is produced. This report lists all new orders contained on the purchase order pending file; it shows processing control totals to verify that the file is in balance.

Information shown on the new order register can also be visually reviewed directly. By calling the *display purchase order program* and by keying in the purchase order number, an open order can be examined (see Figure 9-13). There are several advantages in displaying an order rather than referring to the new order register. A vendor might call, for example, to request that a specific order be reviewed. Once the order number is known, the purchasing agent can

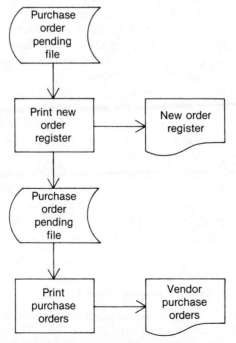

Figure 9-12 Printing purchase orders

```
Review an Entire Purchase Order                              REVIEW ALL PO
   Add      Change   Receive   Issues         Stop    Printed    Both    EXIT
  PO Hdr    PO Hdr   PO Part  Receipts                Report

                                                      Leave blank to review
       Order Number  PO0053     Part Number          all parts on order

           Vendor     Invoice to Locn          Order Remarks
           --------        --            ----------------------------------
           HANDY HDW

                                  Qty    Left To    Date      Date     Order
      Item     Part Number    UM  Ordered Receive  Received    Due     Status
      --   ----------------   --  ------- -------  --------  --------   --
       1     300000           EA    200     100    09/21/    10/17/ --    O
       2     300000           EA    500     500              10/24/ --    O
       3     300015           EA    500     500              10/14/ --    O
```

Figure 9-13   Open-order display

inquire directly. Notice however, what occurs without online inquiry capabilities. The agent would ask the vendor: On what day was the order placed? Finding this, he or she would have to search by hand through the files to find the new order report for the day in question.

In contrast, a current file of pending purchase orders shows the status of all open orders and thus permits direct status reporting. Sometimes this information is invaluable, because it can be extremely difficult to explain the status of a single order. As Figure 9-13 shows, for example, two quantities of part number 30000 were ordered, each with a different due date. Moreover, the vendor was able to ship 100 units well in advance of the first due date. This split shipment means that three shipments of product 30000 will be received and that two of these can still be expected at some future date.

After the new order register is approved (and all necessary changes have been made), purchase orders are printed. The actual printing of orders is a relatively easy processing job, even with a large number of orders. After processing, the printed batch must be burst, to separate the printed documents, deleaved, to remove the carbon copies, and mailed.

In some instances, purchase orders are placed by telephone, in advance of the printed purchase order. When this occurs, the message "written confirmation of telephone order," or a similar message, must be printed on the order. This provision avoids possible double filling and billing of the order by the vendor; the printed purchase order continues to provide written confirmation of a verbal commitment to buy.

The Print Purchase Order Encumbrance Program

A valuable summary produced by the purchasing application is the *purchase order encumbrance summary*. Since the cost of purchased goods is known (the

```
┌─────────────────────────────────────────────────────┐
│         Purchase Commitments          10/20/XX       │
│                                       Page           │
│                                                      │
│   Vendor  Vendor       Delivery  No. of              │
│   No.     Name         Week      Deliveries  Value   │
│                                                      │
│   A11678 Allen Bradley 42 10/21    16     $ 33,250   │
│                        43 10/28    21       47,500   │
│                        44 11/04    11       26,110   │
│                        45 11/11     4          580   │
│                                           ─────────  │
│                                           $107,440   │
│                                                      │
│  A76-41 Solid State Dev. 43 10/21                    │
└────────────                              ────────────┘
```

Figure 9-14 Current purchase commitments

quantity ordered times the unit cost equals the cost of purchased goods), it is possible to accurately predict the dollar amount to be encumbered. This information can be printed in sequence by purchase order or by vendor number sequence, or, as we will show in the chapter on budgeting, by department or by general ledger number.

A variation of the encumbrance summary is a listing of purchase commitments by vendor. As Figure 9-14 shows, this report summarizes the open purchase orders held by each vendor. It can be combined with a report of planned purchase commitments by vendor (see Figure 9-15). A listing of planned commitments is produced using product forecast information stored in the product master file. Product forecasts combined with cycle times are used to estimate

```
┌─────────────────────────────────────────────────────┐
│     Planned Purchase Commitments      10/20/XX       │
│                                       Page           │
│                                                      │
│   Vendor    Vendor       Planned      Receipt        │
│   No.       Name         Week         Value          │
│                                                      │
│   A11678   Allen Bradley  44 11/04   $  8,900        │
│                           45 11/11     20,600        │
│                           46 11/18     15,750        │
│                           47 11/25     28,300        │
│                           48 12/02     12,000        │
│                           49 12/09      8,070        │
│                                      ─────────       │
│                                      $190,400        │
│                                                      │
│   A76-41   Solid State Dev.  45 11/11                │
└───────────                              ─────────────┘
```

Figure 9-15 Planned purchase commitments

when purchase orders should be let. Financial officers of a company find the reports of current and planned purchase commitments extremely valuable. These reports show the dollar amount needed to cover current purchases as well as the projected dollar amount necessary to cover purchases over the next two- to three-month period. As such, purchase commitment reports help to simplify the difficult task of planning cash flow.

9-3 MATERIAL RECEIPTS PROCESSING

After stock is received from a vendor, a company must have procedures to verify a number of things: that the products received are the same as the products ordered, that the quantity received is the same as the quantity ordered, that the quality of the products received is acceptable, and that the purchase order, product, and vendor numbers recorded by the vendor are accurate. Such comparisons must be performed by hand as well as by the computer. For example, a physical examination and count of items received must be done to verify that product quality is acceptable and to determine the "actual" number of items received. Computer processing is used, however, to compare the actual count with the quantity ordered.

Figure 9-16 shows the receiving processing menu. Compared with the purchasing menu (see Figure 9-9), the interactive and batch programs are highly similar; some programs, as indicated, have the same titles. With receiving,

```
I.1   ENTER NEW MATERIAL RECEIPTS
I.2   READY VENDOR MASTER FILE
I.3   READY PRODUCT MASTER FILE
I.4   DISPLAY PRODUCT ACCOUNT
I.5   DISPLAY VENDOR ACCOUNT
I.6   DISPLAY PENDING PURCHASE ORDER

B.1   PRINT RECEIVING REPORT
B.2   PRINT STOCK TICKETS
B.3   PRINT PAYABLES RECEIPTS SUMMARY
B.4   PRINT OVERDUE PURCHASE ORDER REPORT
B.5   PRINT PRODUCT MASTER REGISTER
B.6   PRINT VENDOR MASTER REGISTER
B.7   PRINT PRODUCT CHANGE REPORT
B.8   PRINT VENDOR CHANGE REPORT
B.9   PRINT PURCHASE ORDER CHANGE REPORT
(10)  EXIT
```

Figure 9-16 Receiving menu

an "enter new material receipts" program is the only new interactive part of the purchasing and receiving design. Four new batch programs are required, however: "print receiving report," "print stock tickets," "print payables receipts summary," and "print overdue purchase order report." These batch programs fully document new materials received, their disposition, and their expected cost to the business.

The Enter New Material Receipts Program

After materials have been counted and inspected, products can be released from the receiving area in a company. Just prior to this release, new material receipts are processed. As Figure 9-17 shows, five types of information must be keyed in order to process new material receipts by computer: receiving slip, purchase order, vendor, product, and product inspection information. *Receiving slip information* includes a receiving slip number (assigned by the company), a record code (debit or credit), and the date of new material receipt. In addition, the vendor-assigned packing slip number should be entered into processing. Should

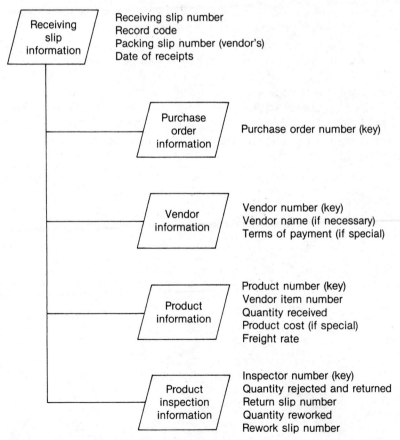

Figure 9-17 Receiving data-entry requirements

the need arise to question the vendor about a particular order, this number provides an immediate point of reference. Last, some companies keep several date fields instead of a single date field. They store the shipment arrival date, the shipment release date, and the material restocking date. If it takes several days to inspect incoming products and to transfer and restock goods in the warehouse, different dates must be kept to estimate product reorder lead times.

Figure 9-17 also shows that four keys are entered into processing; each key locates data stored on computer files. For instance, the purchase order number is entered to locate the corresponding number and open order stored on the file of pending purchase orders. The vendor and product numbers identify accounts stored on the vendor and product master files, respectively. Finally, if an inspection file is maintained, an inspection number is entered. This entry leads to the transfer of totals for the quantity rejected for return and the quantity rejected for rework. To complete the entry of inspection information, either the return or rework slip number must be keyed to explain the disposition of goods rejected by inspection.

Figure 9-18 illustrates the separate actions required in processing new material receipts. Initially, receipts information is posted against the vendor and product master files. This step verifies the correctness of the vendor's number and name and each product number and description. Following verification, several file updates are performed. These updates (1) remove open purchase orders from the pending file; (2) revise the quantity on hand, the quantity on order, the "moves in" totals, and the product lead time for a product account; (3) revise the average delivery time (vendor lead time) and product rejection rate (yield) for a vendor account; and (4) add product inspection information to previous information stored under an inspector number account. All of these updates, with the exception of the product inspection update, are shown in Figure 9-18.

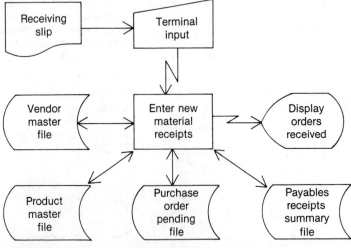

Figure 9-18 Entering new receipts

Each file update procedure must be carefully designed. Suppose, for example, that 200 items were ordered and a partial shipment of 100 was received. In this case, an open order cannot be deleted from the pending file. Instead, the amount received must be added to the record of open purchase orders. This practice permits the quantity ordered and the quantity "left to receive" to be displayed (see Figure 9-13). The design of the procedure to update the product master file must consider the timing of events. If the quantity on hand is increased by the quantity released—"in advance" of restocking the items in the warehouse—the product master file will be incorrect, at least temporarily. If the on-hand and on-order fields are changed following restocking, however, the product file records will also be incorrect. In this situation, products will be shown to be on order when, in fact, they have been received—and are awaiting someone's attention in either the receiving or the warehouse area of a company.

Besides file updates, the new material receipts program must calculate any differences between purchase orders and new receipts, such as the difference between the quantity ordered and the quantity received, and write this information together with all file updates to the payables receipts summary file. This file is used for a variety of purposes: it is carried over to accounts payable processing to test the validity of vendor claims for payment, and is used to print the receiving report and new stock tickets.

Ready Master Files

As with the purchasing portion of the application, the vendor and product master files may need to be revised before the entry of any new receipts information. In this instance, file modifications are often limited to changing the vendor master file. Several vendor changes might have occurred, for example, between the placement of the order and the receipt of new materials: the name of the company, the address, the contact person, or the telephone number might be different. Likewise, the vendor might report a more favorable price schedule than before, extending the new prices to all incoming orders. Still other possibilities include different terms of payment and different catalog numbers. Regardless of the type of change, each must be noted and entered into processing to keep the vendor master file current.

Changes to the product master file are required if the vendor decides to change the product description, such as the unit of measure, the size run of the product, the color, or the unit cost. In rare cases, the vendor might also change the product name. When this occurs, a company is faced with the decision of storing both the old and new product names, and selling products under one name while ordering replacement products using another name, or of replacing the old with the new name, and informing customers of the name change.

Printing Stock Tickets

Once the purchase order change file is complete, batch programs to prepare stock tickets can be scheduled. Figure 9-19 shows that the printing of stock

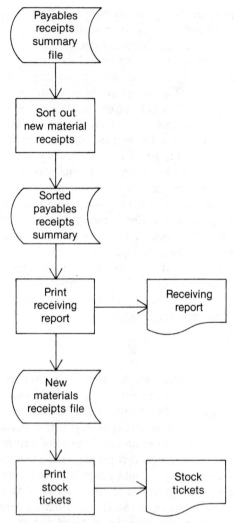

Figure 9-19 Printing stock tickets

tickets is a two-step process. Prior to printing stock tickets, the receiving report is printed. As shown earlier (see Figure 9-6), the receiving report documents the complete status of each purchase order. It compares items ordered with items received, and states the disposition of split shipments and whether any items were damaged. The receiving report also shows *extended cost totals*. These dollar totals provide an estimate of the dollar amount due on the vendor invoice. (The processing of vendor invoices is the subject of the next chapter.)

Stock tickets can take a variety of shapes and forms. Since the purchase order change file contains information previously stored on the pending file (plus information transferred from the vendor and product master files), several pieces of information can be printed on each ticket. Typically, a stock ticket contains product description and location information (product number, de-

Weber®Marking Systems
711 W. Algonquin Road   Arlington Heights, IL   60005
Phone (312) 364-8500

Sample label printed on
Weber Legitronics Printer

CONTENTS		WEIGHT	
WASHERS		**35 LBS**	

UNITS	PACKAGE NO.		
456	**3** OF	**5**	

DATE	CUSTOMER ORDER NO.
03/09/8–	**255909**

SHIP ▶
TO ▶
SAXE HARDWARE
234 APPLE STREET
DAYTON, OHIO 36678

Figure 9-20   Stock ticket

scription, and bin location number). However, some business firms have seen fit to view the stock ticket as a multipurpose document (see Figure 9-20). It is designed as a receiving and order-entry document. By perforating the ticket and attaching several ticket stubs or coupons, the ticket can be used in order-entry processing. When an order is picked from stock, a stub or coupon is detached from the stock ticket. Each stub or coupon contains detailed bar-coded information about the product, such as product number, packing and shipping requirements, insurance cost, and product weight. Scanning the bar codes prior to packing the product helps to ensure that the correct item has been picked from stock. This procedure simplifies the paperwork processing associated with preparing the order for shipment.

The Payables Receipts Summary Program

The *payables receipts summary,* a valuable summary produced by the receiving application, is in many ways similar to the purchase order encumbrance summary and, in fact, may adhere to the same reporting format. The difference between the two summaries is that the payables receipts summary shows the quantities received (and approved) and their estimated cost, compared with the quantities ordered and their estimated cost. Since the revised estimated cost is less than or equal to the dollar amount shown on the purchase order encumbrance summary, the receipts summary permits some previously encumbered funds to be released for additional expenditures. More important, the final estimate of costs is required by the accounts payable application. In processing, the quantity received and its estimated cost are compared with the quantity billed for, as recorded on the vendor invoice. If there is a significant difference, payment of the vendor invoice is delayed. Instead of payment, purchase agreements are pulled and compared against receiving slips and the receiving report. When such a trace reveals that the vendor is in error, direct contact with the vendor is required to modify the outstanding bill.

9-4 PROCESSING CONTROLS

The design of processing controls for the purchasing and receiving application is similar to the design of controls for the customer invoice application. For each, a strict accounting of quantity and cost totals must be maintained. The following summary outlines the processing control steps built into the purchasing application.

1. The program to *enter purchase requirements* must sum the "new purchase order quantity," which is the same as the total determined by the finished-goods computer application, unless modifications have been keyed into processing.

2. The program to *enter purchase requirements* must also revise the pending purchase order quantity and cost totals to reflect the new purchase order quantity and its associated cost. The pending purchase order (P/O) formulas in each case are:

$$\text{Pending P/O quantity} = \text{Old pending P/O quantity} + \text{New P/O quantity}$$

$$\text{Pending P/O expense} = \text{Old pending P/O expense} + \text{New P/O expense}$$

3. The *print new order register* program, which is designed to report both pending P/O quantity and expense totals and to show how each total was reached, permits all verification to be completed prior to the printing of purchase orders.

4. The *print purchase order encumbrance* program is also designed to print both quantity and expense totals. From this point, the totals can be brought across to the company general ledger and budgeting computer applications—to show the financial impact of outstanding purchases.

The receiving application continues to modify the pending purchase order quantity and cost totals. Once goods are received and inspected, the differences between the quantity ordered and the quantity received must be entered into the processing control formulas. The processing control steps built into the receiving application are as follows:

1. The *enter new material receipts* program is designed to sum a number of control totals: the total quantity received, the total quantity accepted, the total quantity rejected and returned, and the total quantity reworked. Each of these totals must be entered into a processing control equation. The quantity-received total, for example, changes the pending P/O formulas as shown below. Unlike purchasing, the quantity and expense totals are subtracted from the pending totals.

   Pending P/O quantity = Old pending P/O quantity − Quantity received
   − Quantity canceled by vendor

   Pending P/O expense = Old pending P/O expense
   − Quantity received estimated expense

2. The same program, *enter new material receipts,* calculates quantity and cost differences. Two variance equations are shown below. The quantity-received variance shows the difference between what was ordered and what was received; the quantity-accepted variance shows the difference between what was received and what passed inspection. Both of these variance equations can be expressed as percentages instead of actual amounts.

   Quantity-received variance = Quantity ordered − Quantity received

   Quantity-accepted variance = Quantity received − Quantity accepted

   Cost variance differences are also computed. Two of these equations are:

   Quantity-received expense variance = P/O estimated expense
   − Receiving estimated expense

   Encumbered funds variance = P/O estimated expense
   − Estimate expense of accepted goods

   As the first equation shows, if the quantity received is less than the quantity ordered, then the difference in estimated cost of goods must be determined. The second equation shows the net effect on encumbered funds. Since the firm will only pay for accepted goods, the dollar amounts must be revised.

3. The *print receiving report* program is designed to show both revised pending P/O quantity counts and dollar amounts; quantity ordered, quantity received, quantity rejected and returned, and quantity reworked totals; and quantity and expense variance totals. Each of these equations must be checked to ensure the correctness of processing. All verification must be done prior to printing stock tickets.

4. The *print payables receipts summary* program is designed to print the total quantity and expense associated with new material receipts. These totals are brought across to the accounts payable and the general ledger computer applications. They help to control the release of funds from a business.

9-5 MANAGEMENT IMPLICATIONS

There are several good reasons for developing the purchasing and receiving application besides using it to keep a strict accounting of the quantities ordered and received and their estimated costs. Some of the more obvious reasons are faster and more accurate processing of purchase requisitions and receiving slips, improved vendor information, and better file-inquiry procedures. With interactive programs a clear advantage is the improved edit and update of new purchase and material receipts transactions. The less obvious but equally important reasons include the capability to take advantage of special sales or discounts offered by vendors, to evaluate vendors, and to control the quality of incoming materials. These less obvious reasons are perhaps better known as programs: supplier selection programs, vendor evaluation programs, and quality assurance programs.

Supplier selection programs concern the selection of the best source of supply defined in terms of providing the highest quality products, for the lowest cost and the shortest delivery time (vendor lead time). Objectives such as these are difficult to achieve, all at one time, by one vendor. As a consequence, the design of supplier selection programs requires that the three dimensions of quality, cost, and lead time be weighted, so that different scores for vendors can be compared. When fully developed, supplier selection programs permit purchasing agents to ask direct questions such as:

VENDOR 65332 HAS QUOTED A 49.99 PRICE FOR MOISTURE-FREE PARKAS.
IS THIS A GOOD PRICE?

The computer will respond to this question by calculating the new weighted score for moisture-free parkas supplied by vendor number 65332, compare this weighted score with that for other firms that supply moisture-free parkas, and display the findings.

Vendor evaluation programs are also concerned with the quality, cost, and lead time associated with the purchase of items. These programs calculate and store a wide variety of vendor performance ratios and statistics, including the actual vendor lead time (difference between date of purchase and date of receipt); the product delivery fill rate (quantity received divided by the quantity ordered); the product acceptance rate (quantity accepted divided by quantity received); and the product cost change (differences between new and last vendor unit price). Such differences and ratios can be used in supplier selection programs or in quality assurance programs. They are also important in helping purchasing agents interpret market conditions. The analysis of vendor cost change, for example, helps to determine how inflation affects the product lines carried by a business. Suppose unit costs are found to be increasing by .08 percent a month. This means that either product prices must be increased to cover the cost of inflation or profit margins will be lower. In either case, vendor evaluation determines the base figures from which to make business-wide decisions.

Quality assurance programs call for the design of product quality and reliability standards and for procedures to determine whether incoming materials meet or exceed these standards. One standard, for example, might be 30 or fewer defective parts in lot sizes of 1,540. By taking a small sample from the large lot, such as a sample of 50, and noting the number of defects in the sample, it can be determined whether the entire lot of incoming materials should be accepted or rejected. In cases such as these, the computer is used to store the quality standards, the required sampling plan, the incoming percent defective and the product acceptance rate by vendor, and the percent change in vendor quality compared with previous shipments. Many firms have developed elaborate vendor quality comparison tests in their attempts to improve the overall quality of company products. Although testing was done in the past, the results of several tests were seldom compared. Today the computer makes quality comparison testing both possible and practical.

REVIEW OF IMPORTANT IDEAS

Four basic activities are associated with purchasing: selecting suppliers, expediting delivery from suppliers, coordinating communications between suppliers and departments within a company, and identifying new vendor products and services that will contribute to company profits. In addition, four activities are associated with receiving: verifying the correctness of vendor shipments, inspecting vendor materials, informing purchasing of materials failing to conform to company standards, and telling members of the warehouse crew where to stock newly received merchandise. The purchasing and receiving application helps to formalize these two sets of activities. Besides permitting faster and more accurate processing of purchase requirements and receiving slips, the application helps purchasing and receiving staff to better control the flow of products into the firm.

Purchasing begins with the processing of purchase requisitions. Following careful verification, all processed requisitions are placed on the purchase order pending file. This file stores the pending order until it is filled—until goods shipped by the vendor are received and approved by the firm. The file is also used to print the new order register and vendor purchase orders.

Receiving begins with the processing of receiving slips. Through processing, the open orders stored on the pending files are removed and transferred to the payables receipts summary (new material receipts) file. Processing also updates the product master file (to show the addition of new material), the vendor master file (to show new delivery times and product rejection rates), and the product inspection file (to show product rejections by inspector).

The receiving report and stock tickets are printed after receiving slips are processed. The receiving report documents the complete status of each product by comparing the quantity ordered with the quantity received and with the quantity approved, and by printing extended cost totals. Stock tickets serve both the receiving and order-entry computer applications. These tickets show product description and location information.

Two important summary reports produced in processing are the purchase order encumbrance summary and the payables receipts summary. The encumbrance summary lists purchase commitments by vendor in order to show the dollars necessary to cover purchases. The payables receipts summary is similar. It lists purchase commitments by vendor in order to show the dollars necessary to cover the cost of merchandise approved by inspection.

A strict accounting of quantity and cost totals is maintained by the purchasing and receiving application. These controls help to ensure that the quantity ordered is the same as the quantity received and the quantity billed for. They ensure that the charges recorded on the vendor invoice are consistent with the charges estimated for a vendor shipment.

Improved supplier selection programs, vendor evaluation programs, and quality assurance programs follow a well-designed purchasing and receiving application. With computer assistance it becomes easier to determine the best source of supply, the effects of changing market conditions on product availability and supply, and whether incoming products satisfy quality and reliability standards.

KEY WORDS

Purchasing

Receiving

Purchase order pending file

Encumbrance summary file

Purchase requisition

Receiving slip

Purchase order number

Vendor number

New order register

Purchase order
   encumbrance summary

Receiving report

Stock ticket

Overdue purchase order report

Payables receipts summary

Vendor analysis

Extended cost totals

Supplier selection program

Vendor evaluation program

Quality assurance program

REVIEW QUESTIONS

1. Name the four basic purchasing activities. Name the four basic receiving activities.

2. What are the main reasons for developing an online purchasing and receiving application?

3. What is the difference between the purchase order pending file and the encumbrance summary file?

4. Name the two main types of input for this divided application.

5. Distinguish among the terms "items short," "items long," and "items reworked."

6. Why should purchase order numbers and the vendor numbers be unique?

7. What four types of reports and documents are printed by the receiving portion of the application?

8. What is meant by "an override set of instructions"?

9. What master files are required by the purchasing and receiving application?

10. Explain the difference between vendor product file information and vendor background file information.

11. Why is it important to be able to display the status of all open orders?

12. Why do financial officers find the reports of current and planned purchase commitments valuable?

13. After stock is received, what four things must be verified?

14. Name the four keys entered in processing receiving-slip data.

15. What file updates are performed by the enter new material receipts program?

16. What information is stored on the payables receipts summary file? How is this file used in processing?

17. Why do business firms print stock tickets?

18. What types of processing controls must be maintained to ensure that records stored on the purchase order pending file are correct?

19. What is the difference between the quantity-received expense variance and the encumbered funds variance? Why are both variances important?

20. What benefits to the firm result from well-conceived supplier selection programs? From vendor evaluation programs? From quality assurance programs?

EXERCISES

1. A manager questions: "Why do we need a purchasing and receiving application when we already have a finished-goods application?" He adds: "Let's have the computer tell us how much to order, from whom, and print the purchase order automatically."

   What is wrong with this approach? Explain why the purchasing and receiving application should be developed separately.

2. Companies often contract with vendors to make split shipments. Rather than sending the entire order at one time, a vendor might agree to ship one-third immediately, one-third two months from now, and one-third four months from now. How would split shipments be accommodated by the purchasing and receiving application?

3. Suppose a company decides to centralize all purchasing activities and to decentralize receiving activities. How might this business decision be incorporated into a purchasing and receiving design?

4. Some vendors will ship a quantity slightly higher than the quantity ordered to compensate for defective items. How would this practice be handled by the purchasing and receiving application?

Product Planning

Product planning is essential if a business hopes to remain competitive. Since customer wants and needs change, companies must continually be prepared to introduce new products to better satisfy these wants and needs. And, while introducing new products, firms must retire and replace older products no longer desired by their customers.

All products that a company carries in inventory have a life cycle. Some products have an extremely short life: for example, they might show high sales almost immediately after being introduced, sell well for six months to a year, and show rapidly dropping sales thereafter. Other, longer-life products might show very low sales initially, followed by a gradual sales buildup, before they attain a respectably high sales level. Once that level is reached, high sales might continue for an extended period; when sales finally do decline, the descent is slow.

Online technology is especially valuable in examining the life cycle of a single product, a class of products, or product sales for a company as a whole. As Figure B-1 shows, computer graphics permit managers to examine product sales trends and patterns over time. Coupled with supporting data, visual displays can be extremely useful in making decisions about whether products and product lines are beginning to be accepted by customers in the marketplace, are maturing and leveling off, or are nearing the end of their product life. In addition, visual displays are able to compare the performance of different products and product groupings, to show, for example, how successful new products are in comparison with other products carried by a business firm.

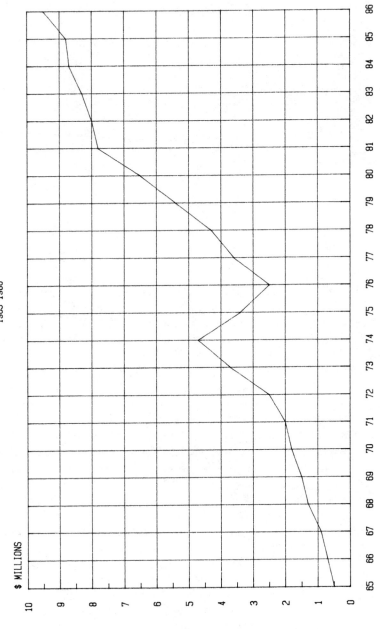

Figure B-1 Product sales trend

REQUIREMENTS

Suppose you are asked to design a new interactive program entitled "display product-planning information," to be inserted in the finished-goods program-processing menu (see Figure 8-6). Suppose further that once the program is selected, the user is immediately required to select a processing option from a more detailed, secondary menu. This menu contains the following choices:

    S.1   DISPLAY QUANTITY-SOLD PRODUCT TREND
    S.2   DISPLAY GROSS-PROFIT PRODUCT TREND
    S.3   DISPLAY FORECAST-TO-ACTUAL PRODUCT SALES TREND
    S.4   DISPLAY NEW-TO-ALL-PRODUCTS SUCCESS TREND
    S.5   DISPLAY NEW-TO-PRODUCT-LINE SUCCESS TREND
    S.6   DISPLAY NEW-TO-OLD-PRODUCT SUCCESS TREND
    S.7   DISPLAY PRODUCT VALUE-ANALYSIS TREND
    S.8   DISPLAY PRODUCT MONTH'S SOLD TREND
    S.9   DISPLAY PRODUCT TURNOVER TREND
    S.10 DISPLAY PRODUCT RETURN-ON-INVESTMENT TREND
   (11) RETURN TO MAIN MENU

1. Prepare written specifications to explain how each of these ten interactive program selections would be designed. In preparing these specifications, describe

   (a) the purpose of each program;

   (b) the information required to produce each display;

   (c) the changes (if any) to be made to the product master file (see Figure 8-2); and

   (d) the processing steps required to produce each display.

2. Prepare sample graphs (or charts) to show how information might be presented for each of the ten programs. Remember to label the x-axis and the y-axis. Show the title of each graph. Use fictitious numbers in plotting all trend lines.

IV

PAYABLES APPLICATIONS

Most firms expect to be carried "on account" by their suppliers and, to a lesser extent, by their employees, much like they carry their customers on account. In this part of the text we will examine three more accounting applications, all of which relate to the payment and processing of a firm's bills. As we will show in discussing the first application, bills can be paid and processed in different ways. A firm may decide, for example, to pay its bills promptly or to pay slowly; either approach has certain advantages and disadvantages. Our middle chapter, which deals with fixed assets, serves to remind us that some bills, even though paid in full, cannot be deducted fully by a business as an expense. Instead, a percentage of the bill must be applied to each of several years. These yearly deductions are necessary until the entire expense has been written off. Our final chapter, dealing with the payment of employees, reminds us that there are some instances in which payment choices disappear: business firms must either pay their employees promptly or face the consequences.

10

Accounts Payable

A business can expect the delivery of a vendor invoice soon after goods are shipped by a vendor. When the vendor is efficient, the invoice will reach a business even before merchandise is recorded as being received. Once invoices are in the hands of a business, several decisions must be made: when to pay, what amount to pay, whether to challenge the invoice total, and whether to take the cash discount (if one is available). Such decisions must be built into the design of the accounts payable application.

Accounts payable processing may be viewed as the inverse of accounts receivable processing. With receivables, a firm must keep records of legal claims against customers for amounts due. Since the assets of a company include what is owed to the company, we defined these amounts due as current assets. With payables, a firm must keep records of the legal claims against the business by vendors or suppliers. These claims result from the vendor's decision to supply the business with goods on credit. As opposed to an asset, an amount to be paid is defined as a *liability*. Because businesses are expected to pay their bills within a short period of time (less than one year), accounts payable are also known as *current liabilities*.

Two primary objectives of accounts payable processing are to keep credit balances with vendors within reason and to pay vendor invoices promptly. These practices protect the credit rating of the business and also take advantage of favorable trade credit and cash discounts. The *credit rating* of a business is an indicator of its financial soundness. Very financially sound business firms may receive preferential credit terms. The credit extended to a B-rated firm must be 1 percent 10, net 20, for example, whereas the credit to an A-rated firm might be 2 percent 10, net 30. The length of credit terms determines the extent to which *trade credit* may be used as a source of short-term financing. Thus, if the two firms make average purchases of $2,000 each day, terms of net 20 mean that trade credit for the first is limited to $40,000 (20 days times $2,000); terms of net 30, however, lead to trade credit of $60,000 (30 days times $2,000) for the second.

Another important objective of accounts payable processing is improved control of cash payments. In this regard, processing controls are vital. Since the accounts payable application specifies whom to pay and in what amount, there are the ever-present risks of employee embezzlement and fraud and of embarrassing financial mistakes, such as paying a vendor when goods were never received. Some payables designs almost encourage employee embezzlement, by making it so easy to steal that even the timid are tempted to try. The only mischief required is to instruct the computer to write a company check to a fictitious vendor and, later on, to delete from computer files any evidence that the check was ever written and processed.

10-1 PRELIMINARY OVERVIEW OF PROCESSING

Because the accounts payable application is fairly complex, tight financial controls are difficult to prepare. As Figure 10-1 shows, five steps can be associated with the processing of accounts payable (A/P) information. These steps either lead to the creation of records to be stored on computer files (four out of the five illustrated files), or are dependent on the direct input of information from computer files.

Careful study of Figure 10-1 shows that accounts payable processing can be separated into three major processing runs. The first run, Steps 1 and 2, creates a *consolidated payables file,* which stores all approved vendor invoices (invoices for which goods have been received and approved). The second run, Step 3, determines which vendor invoices are to be paid. Most firms make payments on approved vendor invoices two or three times each month. Much like individuals, they must decide which bills to pay and which bills to hold. As illustrated, bills to be paid are placed in a file entitled *payables this period.* Bills held over for another payment period are placed in a *payables held over* file. Finally, the third run, Steps 4 and 5, involves printing vendor voucher-checks and various types of payables summaries.

With this understanding of the entire five-step process, we can summarize the purpose of each step shown in Figure 10-1, as follows:

1. *Ready vendor master file* ensures that all vendor information stored on file is correct.

2. *Enter payables transactions* determines whether an incoming bill is legitimate and, if so, adds the vendor charge to the consolidated payables file.

3. *Enter payment instructions* determines which vendor invoices to pay and in what amount, and which vendor invoices to hold until another billing period.

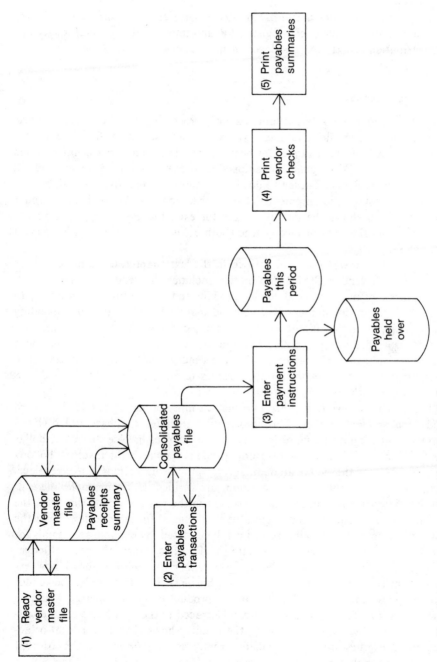

Figure 1O-1 Five steps in processing accounts payable

4. *Print vendor invoices* produces the formal *vendor voucher-check* and creates the *pending-check file.*

5. *Print purchasing summaries* produces a variety of reports, including the accounts payable check register, the accounts payable general ledger distribution report, and the departmental expense report.

Inputs to Processing

The three main inputs to accounts payable processing are the vendor invoice, the vendor master file, and the payables receipts summary file. The *vendor invoice* looks like the customer invoice: it shows the same types of information (see Chapter 4). When goods are shipped by the vendor, a packing slip and bill of lading are included. These two documents show the quantity shipped, but not the dollar cost of the shipment. That information is submitted on a vendor invoice, which shows the dollar charges for each line-item shipped, terms of payment, and the total invoice charge (both before and after the cash discount is applied).

The *vendor master file,* as described in the last chapter, contains records to describe each vendor. Stored information includes the vendor's name and address, terms of payment, and vendor product and background information. In processing, a vendor number is keyed and matched against the corresponding number stored on file. Figure 10-2, for example, shows the data-entry requirements associated with processing a vendor invoice. After a record code has been keyed (to indicate a charge or credit), the vendor number is transmitted. The matching of the two vendor numbers serves to add vendor name-and-address information to the payables transaction record.

Figure 10-2 shows that other information must be keyed beside the record code and vendor number. This information includes purchase order (P.O.) number, vendor invoice number, date of the invoice, invoice due date, dollar total of the invoice, and cash discount (if one is shown on the invoice). Following the entry of the dollar amount, several processing actions can take place. Initially, the terms offered by the vendor are verified. If, for example, the vendor has permitted a 2 percent cash discount in the past, but none this time, the invoice should be questioned. Typically, it is flagged for later review. Next the history segment of the vendor record can be updated, by changing the totals for current monthly sales and year-to-date (YTD) sales. Third, the general ledger (G/L) distribution is made. The *general ledger distribution* shows how expenses are related to major activities of a business. If, for example, the vendor invoice shows the charges for 50 units of product 6453, this charge would be coded as a *direct cost:* the cost that can be traced to the operations of a department or a product line. If, however, the invoice shows charges for legal or accounting fees, these would be coded differently, as an *indirect cost:* the cost that is associated with general business overhead. By separating costs in this way, a

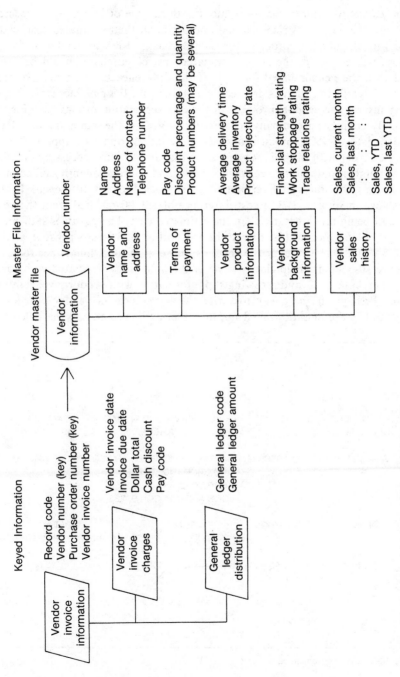

Figure 10-2 Relationships between payables data sets

business is able to determine the expenses associated with each of its major functions or activities.

The *payables receipts summary* file, the third type of input, stores records that show the quantities received and approved and their estimated cost, compared with the quantity ordered, for each purchase order, by vendor. Before a vendor invoice is paid, the stored estimated cost of purchase should be compared with the vendor billed-for cost. If the difference between the two cost figures is significant, such as greater than 10 percent, the payables staff should closely inspect the vendor invoice, using a cost-verification display (see Figure 10-3). By comparing company information stored in the summary file (P.O. number, date of P.O., product number, description, quantity approved, and estimated cost) with information keyed or transferred into processing (vendor invoice number, date of invoice, vendor name and address, quantity billed, and invoice cost), the staff can determine what factors led to cost differences. In the case shown in Figure 10-3, a cost difference of $30.00 resulted from the vendor's cost being much greater than the estimated cost. The payables staff must now determine which cost is correct: the unit cost of .055 dollars per foot, stored in the product master file, or the vendor's unit cost of .085 dollars per foot.

Figure 10-3 should help clarify some of the difficulties associated with comparing purchase order and receiving slip information with vendor invoice information. Perhaps the best way to verify the correctness of vendor charges is always to key the quantity billed for, line item by line item, and the billed-for

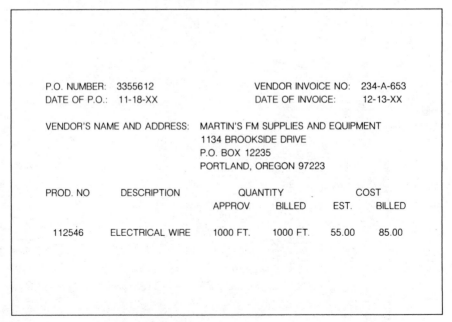

P.O. NUMBER: 3355612   VENDOR INVOICE NO: 234-A-653
DATE OF P.O.: 11-18-XX   DATE OF INVOICE: 12-13-XX

VENDOR'S NAME AND ADDRESS: MARTIN'S FM SUPPLIES AND EQUIPMENT
                             1134 BROOKSIDE DRIVE
                             P.O. BOX 12235
                             PORTLAND, OREGON 97223

PROD. NO	DESCRIPTION	QUANTITY		COST	
		APPROV	BILLED	EST.	BILLED
112546	ELECTRICAL WIRE	1000 FT.	1000 FT.	55.00	85.00

Figure 10-3 Cost-verification display

cost. Earlier we indicated that this extra data-entry work was not required (see Figure 10-2); instead, the only total entered into processing was the total invoice charge. Although it is much easier to enter into processing only the total invoice charge, it should be remembered that there is some risk with this procedure.

Outputs from Processing

The main products produced by accounts payable processing are vendor voucher-checks and payables summary reports. A *vendor voucher-check* is a two-part form, the lower portion of which (the voucher) contains information to help the vendor process the check (see Figure 10-4). The voucher provides space for printing the vendor invoice number, invoice date, amount of the invoice, amount paid, and discount taken. The upper portion, the check, is negotiable. It shows the net check amount, or the amount to be taken to the bank for deposit.

Although several reports can be printed as products of processing, two reports, the payables check register and the general ledger summary, are the most common. The *payables check register* shows the results of check writing (see Figure 10-5). As we mentioned earlier, business firms, like individuals, must decide which of their bills to pay and which to hold. The purpose of the check register is to show which outstanding invoices are to be paid by the check-printing run. The register in Figure 10-5, for example, shows that the payment of $584.00 to vendor 000100 will pay in full two outstanding invoices (vendor invoice numbers 659214 and 834733). Likewise, the payment of $238.00 to vendor 001520 will pay in full invoice 654. No discount is taken on this payment, however.

The check register illustrates one often-overlooked feature of payables processing. In processing, a business must assign its own reference or *voucher number* to each vendor invoice. In most designs this number is assigned by the computer. Should the vendor later question the payment by a business, the specific transaction is traced using the voucher number. A *check number* is also assigned to each computer-printed check. This numbering can also be done by the computer, or checks can be prenumbered. Businesses usually prefer the first alternative—assigning the number directly by computer—because it permits the check number to be stored on file, together with the voucher number. Both numbers simplify the tracing of questionable payables transactions.

The *general ledger summary* is similar to the check register except that it summarizes expenses by general ledger (G/L) code (see Figure 10-6). As illustrated, a G/L distribution cross-reference shows the amount expended for prepaid expenses. This listing is prepared by posting each charge shown on the check register to one or more general ledger accounts. It shows details such as when payables were initially received, when checks were written, what discounts were taken, and when payables were listed as paid.

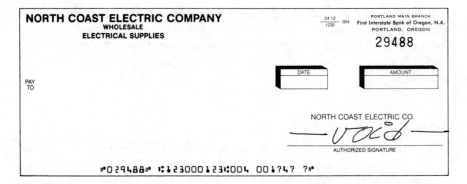

NORTH COAST ELECTRIC COMPANY
WHOLESALE
ELECTRICAL SUPPLIES

$\frac{24\text{-}12}{1230}$ 004

PORTLAND MAIN BRANCH
First Interstate Bank of Oregon, N.A.
PORTLAND, OREGON

29488

DATE

AMOUNT

PAY
TO

NORTH COAST ELECTRIC CO.

VOID

AUTHORIZED SIGNATURE

⑈0 29488⑈ ⑆123000123⑆004 001747 7⑈

REMITTANCE STATEMENT

NORTH COAST ELECTRIC COMPANY

INVOICE DATE	INVOICE NO.	P.O. NO.	STORE#	B-#	ACCT. NO.	GROSS AMOUNT	DISCOUNT	NET AMOUNT
CHECK NO.				TOTALS				

Figure 10-4 Vendor voucher-check

10-2 PAYABLES PROCESSING

Figure 10-7 illustrates the systems organization chart associated with the accounts payable design; Figure 10-8 shows the corresponding payables processing menu. As with other designs, the interactive portion of processing requires
one program to build the payables transaction file, two programs to update or

```
THU, JUL 23, 198-                      M.C.B.A. Demonstration Furniture Compan··              PAGE 000
3:32 PM
                        A C C O U N T S   P A Y A B L E   C H E C K   R E G I S T E R

CASH ACCOUNT:  10100-00100  Cash - First National Bank

CHECK    CHECK   VENDOR NAME                        VOUCH   P.O.#   INVOICE  INVOICE    AMOUNT    DISCOUNT    CHECK
 #       DATE      #                                  #               #      DATE       PAID      TAKEN      AMOUNT

122088 07/22/8- 000100 Commonplace Office Supplies  001511  MCBA-9834  654214  03/25/8-   185.00     .00      185.00
                                                    001512  MCBA-907           04/28/8-   125.00     .00      125.00
                                                    001516  MCBA-3843  834733  07/15/8-   280.00    6.00      274.00

                                                              CHECK TOTALS:   590.00    6.00      584.00


122089 07/22/8- 000200 Checker Distributors, Inc.   001513           5461    04/21/8-   250.00    2.50      247.50

                                                              CHECK TOTALS:   250.00    2.50      247.50


122090 07/22/8- 000400 General Telephone            001519  MCBA-039  837-83  07/12/8- 2,450.00     .00    2,450.00

                                                              CHECK TOTALS: 2,450.00     .00    2,450.00


122091 07/22/8- 000500 Fast Freight Company         001520           654     07/11/8-   238.00     .00      238.00

                                                              CHECK TOTALS:   238.00     .00      238.00


122092 07/22/8- 000700 Hepperwill, Stills & Stein   001522           97222   07/16/8- 3,250.00   32.50    3,217.50

                                                              CHECK TOTALS: 3,250.00   32.50    3,217.50


        5 COMPUTER CHECKS                                     CASH ACCT TOTALS: 6,778.00  41.00    6,737.00
        0 PREPAID CHECKS
        0 MANUAL CHECKS
        0 VOID CHECKS
        5 CHECKS TOTAL
```

Figure 10-5 Payables check register

adjust files, and three programs to display accounts or summary totals. Two interactive programs unique to payables processing are entitled "enter payment instructions" and "display cash requirements."

The *enter payment instructions* program permits payables staff members to decide how many vendor invoices to pay, when to hold a vendor invoice for payment, when to remove the hold placed on an invoice, and when to make a partial payment. It computes how to maximize cash discount allowances. If, for example, $50,000 is available to pay outstanding bills of $75,000, the computer will determine which bills to pay in order to receive the greatest discount. Because computer-based decisions are not always best, flexibility must be built in. As in the purchasing application, the program must permit the payables staff to override automated decisions. If the materials shipped by a vendor are found to be unsatisfactory, for example, the payables staff must be able to override a computer decision to pay by transmitting instructions to hold the invoice.

```
TUE, AUG 11, 198-                      M.C.B.A. Demonstration Furniture Compan··              PAGE 0001
3:54 PM
          A C C O U N T S   P A Y A B L E   D I S T R I B U T I O N   T O   G E N E R A L   L E D G E R   R E P O R T

FOR THE PERIOD:  EARLIEST TO 08/11/-

ACCOUNT-NO  DESCRIPTION              VOUCHR  VENDOR  INVOICE     AMOUNT
                                       #       #      DATE    DISTRIBUTED

EXPENSE DISTRIBUTIONS:

11500-80100  Prepaid Expenses        001110  000100  03/21/8-    33.00
                                     001111  000300  03/22/8-    15.50
                                     001113  000600  04/06/8-   111.00
                                     001521  000600  07/05/8-    55.00
                                     001523  000800  07/10/8-    65.00
                                     001517  000300  07/17/8-   180.00
                                     001518  000200  07/20/8-    15.00

                                             ACCOUNT TOTAL:     474.50

11500-80200  Prepaid Expenses        001522  000700  07/16/     200.00
                                     001526  000100  07/21/8-   185.00
                                                         8-
                                             ACCOUNT TOTAL:     385.00
```

Figure 10-6 General ledger summary

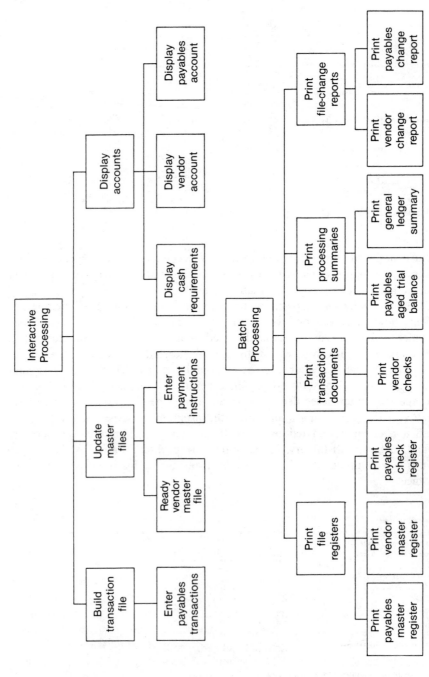

Figure 10-7 Accounts payable systems organization chart

```
        I.1  ENTER PAYABLES TRANSACTIONS
        I.2  READY VENDOR MASTER FILE
        I.3  ENTER PAYMENT INSTRUCTIONS
        I.4  DISPLAY CASH REQUIREMENTS
        I.5  DISPLAY VENDOR ACCOUNT
        I.6  DISPLAY PAYABLES ACCOUNT

        B.1  PRINT PAYABLES CHECK REGISTER
        B.2  PRINT VENDOR CHECKS
        B.3  PRINT GENERAL LEDGER SUMMARY
        B.4  PRINT PAYABLES MASTER REGISTER
        B.5  PRINT PAYABLES AGED TRIAL BALANCE
        B.6  PRINT VENDOR MASTER REGISTER
        B.7  PRINT VENDOR CHANGE REPORT
        B.8  PRINT PAYABLES CHANGE REPORT
        (9)  EXIT
```

Figure 10-8 Payables processing menu

The *display cash requirements* program permits payables staff to determine the dollar value of outstanding invoices. Most cash requirement programs feature several types of display listings and summaries. One commonly used display lists, in date sequence, the invoices to be paid to take advantage of all cash discounts; another date-sequenced display lists invoices to be paid in order to meet invoice due dates when the cash discounts are not taken. Thus, an invoice received on the first of the month with the terms 2 percent 20, net 30, would be listed after an invoice received on the fifth of the month with the terms 2 percent 10, net 20.

The batch portion of the payables design is also similar to other online computer applications. Besides vendor voucher-checks, products of processing include three registers, two or more processing summaries, and two file-change programs. The differences between the printed file registers and processing summaries produced by the payables application are often minor. As previously illustrated, the payables check register and the general ledger summary are both listings of invoices paid (see Figures 10-5 and 10-6). Likewise, the *consolidated payables register* shows a complete listing of all invoices to be paid, whereas the *payables aged trial balance* places all outstanding invoices in one of several aging brackets or "buckets." As with accounts receivable processing, aging is done to determine the current and past-due dollar amounts. In most instances, aging tracks how many invoices are older than 90 days, 61 and 90 days, and 31 and 60 days, and how many invoices are current or less than 31 days old.

The Enter Payables Transactions Program

The enter payables transactions program is a multipurpose interactive processing routine. As Figure 10-9 shows, this entry program is required to key vendor invoice and credit memo information to processing and to display vendor charges (or credits). In addition, the program creates or updates four online computer files: the vendor master file, the payables receipts summary file, the consolidated payables file, and the payables change file. The processing sequence is as follows.

First, the record code and vendor number are keyed. Following their transmission, the computer determines whether the vendor's record is stored on the vendor master file. If the record exists, vendor information is transferred into processing; the vendor's name and address are displayed for visual review. If the computer discovers that the vendor's record does not exist, it is programmed to respond with a message such as, "The vendor's record cannot be located"; this message blocks further invoice information from entry into processing. The problem associated with the vendor number must be corrected before the invoice in question can be processed further. Likewise, if the terminal operator discovers that the vendor's name and address are different from the name and address displayed, processing can be stopped. In this case the operator must copy by hand the name and address shown on the screen or direct the computer to prepare a hard-copy print of the information shown on the display screen.

For the next step, the operator keys in the purchase order number, the entry of which (in combination with the vendor number) serves to locate the outstanding purchase order stored on the payables receipts summary file. Once located, the record is read into processing. If the outstanding purchase order

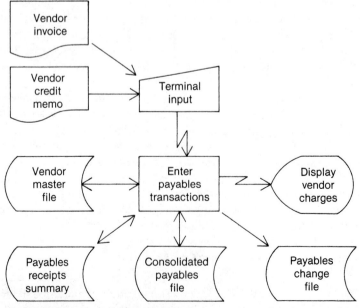

Figure 10-9 Entering payables information

cannot be located, several possibilities exist: first, the order was placed, but the goods never arrived or are in transit; second, the order was not placed and the invoice is in error; third, the order was placed, but was never entered into the purchasing and receiving application; and, fourth, the purchase order number keyed to processing is in error. Regardless of which of the above conditions exists, processing of the vendor invoice must be stopped to permit further investigation.

In the third step in processing, vendor invoice charges are keyed (see Figure 10-2), after which the computer compares and displays the vendor billed-for charges and the estimated cost of the purchase. If the two costs are identical, or are within a reasonable range, the decision to pay can be made. The trouble begins if the two costs are not identical (or within a reasonable range). In this instance, one of two actions can be taken, depending on the design of the interactive program. First, the operator can instruct the computer to move ahead, while placing a provisional "hold" on the vendor invoice. This hold, which indicates that the invoice is not to be paid, must later be removed by an additional processing step. The other option is to block processing from moving ahead, which is safer than the first action but also requires more work. It means pulling copies of the original purchase order and receiving report from office files and comparing them with the vendor invoice to determine the reasons for any differences between the quantity ordered and the quantity received and accepted, and between the estimated costs and the quantity billed-for totals. Once the differences can be explained, it becomes safe to process the vendor invoice.

The fourth and final step in processing entails keying of general ledger information (see Figure 10-2). This step requires display space to permit the entry of several G/L account codes and dollar amounts (see Figure 10-10). Business firms must often break down each purchased item into two or more G/L categories; this breakdown is known as the *general ledger distribution.* It is common, for example, to code and keep separate the sales taxes paid from the coded cost of merchandise. Different codes are also required for different types of merchandise. Office furniture, for instance, requires one code; office supplies, another.

After the G/L distribution has been entered into processing and reconciled, the operator can make the final "go ahead" decision, which tells the computer to assign a voucher number to the invoice transaction and to perform three computer file updates: to update the payables receipts summary file, by deleting the outstanding purchase order from the file, to update the consolidated payables file, by adding the approved vendor invoice information, and to update the vendor master file, by adding sales history information. As a record of these updates, all information deleted from the summary file and all information added to the consolidated file is written to the payables change file.

The Consolidated Payables File

Each vendor invoice entered into processing adds an additional record to the consolidated payables file. As Figure 10-11 shows, the contents of this file

```
        P.O. NUMBER:        3355612          VENDOR INVOICE NO:  234-A-653
        VENDOR NUMBER:   2456               DATE OF INVOICE:       12-13-XX
                                                                   DUE DATE:              01-12-XX


        VENDOR NAME:   MARTIN'S FM SUPPLIES AND EQUIPMENT


        INVOICE TOTAL   $ _____       CASH DISCOUNT   $ _____


        G.L. ACCOUNT NO.   _____       AMOUNT   _____
        G.L. ACCOUNT NO.   _____       AMOUNT   _____
        G.L. ACCOUNT NO.   _____       AMOUNT   _____
        G.L. ACCOUNT NO.   _____       AMOUNT   _____
        G.L. ACCOUNT NO.   _____       AMOUNT   _____
        G.L. ACCOUNT NO.   _____       AMOUNT   _____
        G.L. ACCOUNT NO.   _____       AMOUNT   _____
        G.L. ACCOUNT NO.   _____       AMOUNT   _____
```

Figure 10-10   Entry of general ledger information

consists of groups of outstanding payable vouchers within a vendor number. Thus, there may be one or more vouchers for each vendor number. Grouping outstanding payables in this manner makes it easier to identify invoices for each supplier, and means that a single check can be written for the entire amount due.

The information stored for each outstanding payable includes data that are keyed to processing, assigned during processing, or transferred from computer files. The vendor number is keyed, for example, whereas the vendor name, address, contact person, and telephone number are transferred into processing from the vendor master file. Likewise, the purchase order number is keyed; however, the date of the purchase order is transferred.

Three data fields that require special attention are the pay code, the hold instruction code, and the dollar amount paid. The *pay code* refers to the vendor's stated terms of payment. For example, 1 percent 10, net 20, might be coded 101020; 2 percent 10, net 30, might be coded 201030. The *hold instruction code* is set by the payables staff to specify whether an invoice is to be paid and, if so, the dollar amount of payment. A code of 000P might indicate that the entire invoice is to be paid as soon as possible, whereas a code of 025M might indicate that a partial payment of 25 percent is to be paid by the end of the month. The *dollar amount paid* field stores the partial payment made on an outstanding invoice. A 50 percent partial payment on an outstanding invoice of $2,250 would be stored as $1,125 in the dollar amount paid field.

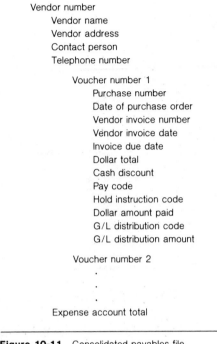

Vendor number
　Vendor name
　Vendor address
　Contact person
　Telephone number

　　Voucher number 1
　　　Purchase number
　　　Date of purchase order
　　　Vendor invoice number
　　　Vendor invoice date
　　　Invoice due date
　　　Dollar total
　　　Cash discount
　　　Pay code
　　　Hold instruction code
　　　Dollar amount paid
　　　G/L distribution code
　　　G/L distribution amount

　　Voucher number 2
　　　·
　　　·
　　　·

　Expense account total

Figure 10-11　Consolidated payables file

The Enter Payment Instructions Program

Determining which vendor invoices to pay and which to hold is as difficult for a business as it is for most individuals. Under perfect conditions, a business pays all of its bills, receives the full benefit of all cash discounts, and meets the terms specified by all vendors. Usually, however, firms attempt to take advantage of cash discounts, but also find that there are times when the availability of cash falls short of outstanding payables. Then, too, some bills should be disputed, such as when a vendor bills for goods that were returned or for a purchase order that was canceled. Some vendors will intermix charges with credits improperly, which erroneously leads to the printing of an invoice instead of a credit memo. Still other bills should be negotiated. If a vendor has indicated that one set of terms is to be used, yet places a different set on the invoice, it is necessary to contact the vendor and to work out a satisfactory solution.

To simplify the difficult task of deciding who to pay, in what amount, and when, the enter payment instruction program initially selects which invoices to pay, using standard programmed decision rules. To begin processing, the operator must enter a *cutoff date* (see Figure 10-12), which the computer matches to invoice due dates (cash discount due dates or end-of-term due dates) in order to decide which invoices to pay. (In practice, as we will discuss in the next section,

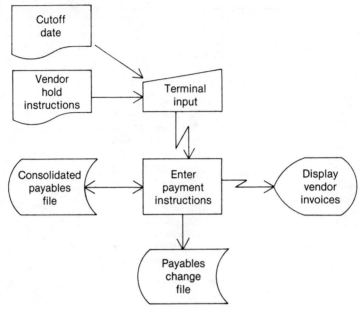

Figure 10-12 Payment instruction processing flowchart

the availability of cash determines the most appropriate cutoff date.) When cash becomes insufficient to cover all outstanding vendor invoices, the computer is programmed to indicate which vendor invoices to hold—even though their due dates are reached. This stage in processing begins by instructing the computer to identify the largest invoice dollar amount outstanding combined with the smallest cash discount percentage. The invoice selected is flagged for later review, and the computer tests once again to determine if funds are now sufficient.

Besides using the computer to select invoices to be paid and to flag invoices to be held, the payment instruction program permits the payables staff to override these automated decisions. As Figure 10-13 shows, payment instruction displays permit the operator to hold payment (halt code), specify the amount of a partial payment, or to stop payment altogether. Payment instruction programs also typically permit page-forward or -backward processing, which works as follows:

1. The operator makes a file selection, with a command such as "display all invoices with an expected payment date of today."
2. The computer responds by displaying the first open invoice that meets this condition.
3. The operator transmits a page-forward message.
4. The computer displays the second open invoice that meets this condition.
5. The operator transmits a page-forward or -backward message.

```
DATE    8/14/--            VENDOR OPEN INVOICES  INQUIRY        F  AMA203  W2
COMPANY NO.  01            EXPECTED PAYMENT DATE 8/14/--


VENDOR NUMBER                     000600
VENDOR NAME    HEAVY SUPPLY CO.
TELEPHONE NO.                 415-332-1234


PAYMENT SELECTION NO.          9
INVOICE NUMBER       141733         DESCRIPTION    SUPPLIES
INVOICE DATE          3/10/--        DUE DATE             4/10/--
GROSS AMOUNT        2,100.00         DISCOUNT AMOUNT          .00
PAID TO DATE            .00         NET DUE            2,100.00

HALT CODE <R/0-9>
PAY? <YES/NO>                  NO
PARTIAL PAYMENT AMT.          .00
FORCE DISCOUNT CODE<FD>

                                     CK02 PAGE FORWARD
                                     CK03 PAGE BACKWARD
                                     CK19 RETURN TO SELECT
                                     CK24 END OF JOB
```

Figure 10-13 Open invoices display

6. The computer displays the third open invoice (page-forward) or the first open invoice (page-backward).

As this process illustrates, the combining of computer-based decisions with visual review, verification, and modification of these decisions by members of the payables staff is the underlying basis of the payables selection and payment process. In effect, individuals are required to monitor the actions of the computer. Where necessary, they are to override actions believed improper or in need of some adjustment.

The Display Cash Requirements Program

The program to display cash requirements is often selected prior to entering payment instructions. This interactive program is designed to show how much cash is needed to pay all open invoices and how much cash is required to take full advantage of all cash discounts. For example, a popular cash-requirements display, the aged-analysis display of open invoices, helps to determine what cash will be needed to meet present and near-term financial obligations (see Figure 10-14). In addition to the dollar amount due for the next cutoff date (09/01/8X), the display shows payables totals for several payables periods.

Like the program to enter payment instructions, the cash requirements program must also be flexible. One option is to permit payables staff to select different aging dates. Another is to have the computer determine the effects of extending the cutoff date by one or two days, or of reducing the cutoff date by one or two days. Still a third option is to show the cash discounts lost by extending the cutoff date or the cash discount realized by reducing the date.

```
DATE   8/14/--    AGED OPEN PAYABLES INQUIRY    OPTIONS    AMA802       W2


              COMPANY NO.    1

              AS OF DATE     8/14/--

              AGING DATE              NET AMOUNT DUE
                9/01/                   30,605.90
                9/15/                   33,942.00
               10/01/                   11,534.74
               11/01/                   12,113.35
               12/01/                    3,337.04

                 TOTAL DUE             91,533.03




                                     CK10   SELECT OPTIONS
                                     CK24   END OF JOB
```

Figure 10-14   Aged-analysis display

Printing Vendor Voucher-Checks

Figures 10-15 and 10-16 show the processing differences between the cash requirements program and the program to print the payables check register. The cash requirements program is an inquiry-only program. The computer is instructed to compute different cash requirement totals based upon *tentative* cutoff dates, to display these totals, and to ask whether a different cutoff date is to be tested next. The check register program is a batch program that uses a *firm* cutoff date. As Figure 10-16 shows, this date is entered by the terminal operator into processing. Once the cutoff date is specified, vendor invoices to be paid are written from the consolidated payables file and added to the *payables pending-check file*. As shown earlier (see Figure 10-1), the payables pending-check file might be called the *payables this period* file (that is, it contains invoices to be paid this period). Likewise, after deleting the invoices to be paid, the considerably smaller consolidated payables file might be called the *payables held over* file. This smaller file now contains invoices to be paid at some later date.

Once the payables pending-check file is complete, the *payables check register* is printed. This valuable register lists each invoice to be paid (see Figure 10-5); it must be carefully reviewed before vendor voucher-checks are printed. This review helps to determine if vendor invoices deleted from the consolidated payables file were transferred to the pending-check file as specified, if cash discounts were processed correctly, and if the total dollar amount to be paid is consistent with the cash amount presently available.

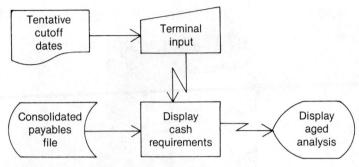

Figure 10-15   Cash requirements flowchart

Finally, printing of vendor voucher-checks begins after the check register is approved. Information that appears on the register also appears on the voucher portion of the check (see Figure 10-4). Following the printing of the voucher, the computer is instructed to print the check. The only data not printed by the computer is the signature. Because of the risks associated with producing and storing continuous sheets of presigned checks, businesses use special equipment to add the signature to each check and to separate the sheets into individual checks. The forms-handling machine shown in Figure 10-17, for example, is known as an *imprinter.* It requires that a *signature die* be inserted prior to processing; the die, in turn, imprints the signature on each check, as well as other information such as remittance location, postal indicia, or even special messages. After imprinting, another machine, known as a *detacher,* separates single- or multiple-part continuous forms of checks (see Figure 10-18).

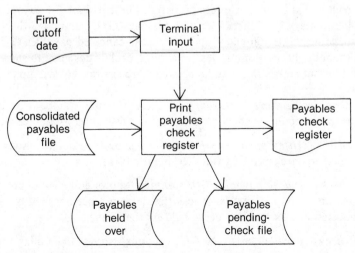

Figure 10-16   Check register flowchart

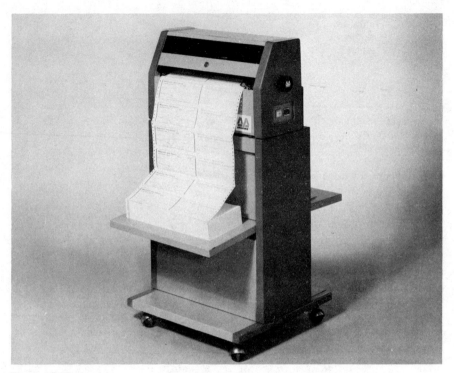

Figure 10-17   Imprinter

Printing General Ledger Summaries

General ledger distributions, such as the distribution shown in Figure 10-6, are important products of accounts payable processing. Several different types of general ledger (G/L) summaries are prepared. These include the payables held-over G/L summary, the checks-written payables G/L summary, the checks-pending payables G/L summary, and the checks-canceled payables G/L summary. Although all these summaries are similar, each is designed to show dollar totals at different stages in accounts payables processing. For example:

- The *payables held-over G/L summary* shows the dollar amounts to be paid by expense account, such as for advertising, insurance, and office supplies.

- The *checks-written payables G/L summary* shows the dollar amounts paid by a specific check-printing run (see Figure 10-6).

- The *checks-pending payables G/L summary* shows dollar amounts paid to vendors and pending (that is, checks that have not been cashed by vendors or canceled checks that are being held by the bank).

- The *checks-canceled payables G/L summary* shows the dollar amounts fully paid to vendors (that is, checks that have been deposited by vendors, returned by the bank, and reconciled by the business).

Figure 10-18 Detacher

Figure 10-19 illustrates the processing differences associated with printing these four types of G/L summaries. Each run requires a different input file. Otherwise, the steps are the same: the G/L report is printed following a sort of the input file by G/L code.

The final steps in payables processing take place after paid checks are returned from the bank. Then *check reconciliation* programs ensure that canceled check dollar amounts are in balance with the dollar amounts printed on the face of each vendor-voucher check. Through check reconciliation processing, canceled checks are deleted from the pending-check file; reconciliation reports identify the checks deleted from the file.

10-3 FILE PROCESSING

Several file-processing activities must be carried out in conjunction with accounts payable processing. These include adjusting the vendor master file, the consolidated payables files, and the consolidated pending-check file. In addition, several additional programs are needed to backup master, consolidated, and change files. Fortunately, most of these programs are simple in their design.

Adjusting Computer Files

Before payables transactions are entered into processing, the vendor master file must be made current. Information closely monitored at this time includes any changes in vendor name and address and terms of payment (see Figure 10-2).

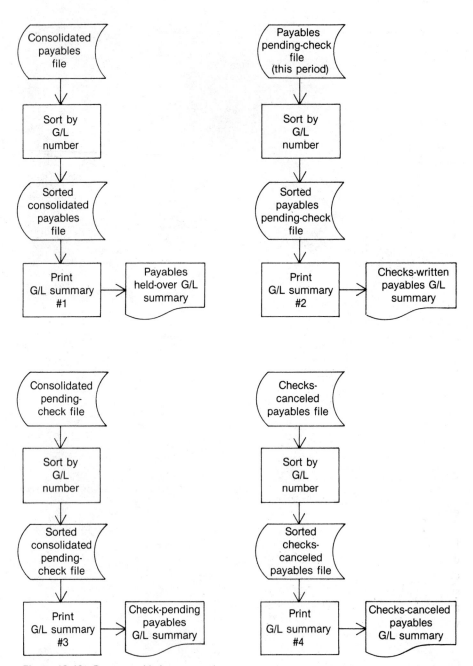

Figure 10-19 Four general ledger processing runs

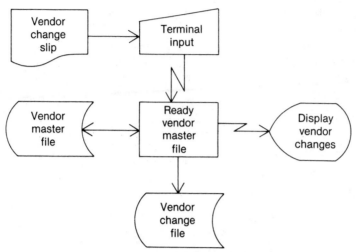

Figure 10-20   Updating the vendor master file

When a change is noted, a vendor change slip is prepared; then the new vendor information is entered into processing and the master file is updated, according to the steps shown in Figure 10-20. As with other file updates, all changes must be initially displayed for review. If the review indicates that the revised information is correct, the computer is instructed to update the file. To provide a permanent record of the update, the change is also written to the *vendor change file*.

The consolidated payables file must also be updated, on those occasions when it becomes necessary to delete an invoice in error. If, for example, a vendor invoice is found to be in error and the vendor sends a corrected statement, the business receiving the correction must fill in an *adjusting entry slip* or a *credit memo*. In processing, the enter payables transactions program must be capable of handling either type of transaction.

Finally, adjustments to the consolidated pending-check file must be made from time to time. These updates result when checks are not cashed by vendors—an unusual circumstance, but one that does occur, for example, when a check is returned by the postal service with a message printed on the envelope stating that the vendor has moved and left no forwarding address. In such cases, a business must be able to remove the pending check from the file. Otherwise, it will remain in the file forever.

File Backup and Reporting

Several file backup and reporting programs must be written in support of accounts payable processing. Each program creates a backup copy of a computer file; each is written to print a listing of the contents of the file. Besides the payables check register, three additional backup registers must be printed: the vendor register, the consolidated accounts payable register, and the consolidated pending-check register.

- The *vendor register,* produced by the print vendor master register program, lists all vendors contained on the vendor master file. This register is particularly helpful if a vendor account cannot be located.

- The *consolidated payables register,* produced by the print payables master register program, lists all invoices that remain to be paid. It is generally printed before and after the printing of the payables check register. Thus, the consolidated payables register shows invoices to be paid and invoices held over, whereas the check register shows invoices to be paid this period.

- The *consolidated pending-check register,* produced by the program to print outstanding checks, lists all checks not yet cashed by vendors. This register is printed soon after checks have been returned from the bank and posted against the consolidated pending-check file.

Besides these three additional registers, three change reports also serve to backup processing.

- The *vendor change report,* produced by the print vendor change report program, lists all changes to the vendor master file, including when a change was made (the time and date), by whom (the person), and what parts of the vendor record were altered (the content).

- The *payables change report,* produced by the print payables change report program, lists all vendor invoices added to the consolidated payables file and deleted from the payables receipts summary file (see Figure 10-9). In addition, the report shows how the vendor master file was updated by processing.

- The *checks-pending change report,* produced by the checks-reconciled change report program, lists all checks deleted from the consolidated pending-checks file. This listing tells when (the time and date) a check was reconciled by a business.

Collectively, these registers and reports provide an important backup to processing. Suppose, for example, that a company believes that it has paid an invoice but that the vendor believes otherwise. To determine who is correct, the first step is to activate the display payables accounts program, which can determine whether or not an invoice to be paid is stored on the consolidated payables file. If the invoice is not stored on file, its absence means either that the invoice was never entered into processing or that it was deleted for payment. To see which of the two explanations is correct, back copies of the consolidated payables register can be reviewed, to determine whether the vendor invoice was entered into processing and whether the invoice was scheduled to be paid. If the invoice was to be paid, the check register, the consolidated pending-check register, and the checks-pending change report can all be inspected. These will tell when a check was written, whether it was returned from the bank or is still outstanding, and, if it was returned, the date it was processed.

Besides allowing invoice payments to be traced, backup copies of computer files and reports are invaluable because they make it possible to reconstruct the entire accounts payable application, should entire files of data be lost or destroyed. Three files in particular provide a clear record of payables processing: the payables receipts summary file shows which vendor invoices are to be expected; the consolidated payables file shows which invoices were received and are yet to be paid; and the consolidated pending-check file shows which checks were written but are yet to be returned. Because of their importance, copies of all three files should be stored off-site in fireproof vaults, as insurance against unforeseen computing center disasters.

10-4 PROCESSING CONTROLS

The design of a series of printed registers and change reports, showing before-and-after versions of payables files, is one method of securing control over processing. If a vendor, a member of the payables staff, or a financial officer of the business questions the status of an invoice, it should be possible to immediately identify an invoice being held and stored on file, or to quickly trace an invoice that has been paid. In addition to the paper trail of processing provided by these documents, transaction- and batch-control balances must also be maintained. The design of these control balances can be summarized by major payables program.

The *enter payables transactions program* maintains both transaction- and batch-balance controls. A transaction-control balance is established during the checking of general ledger distributions. The sum of the general ledger entries is compared with the total invoice amount; if the sum differs from the total, the transaction is out of balance. Unless corrected, the transaction is blocked from further processing and cannot be added to the consolidated payables file.

Besides this balance, several batch-control balances are maintained. The payables register must show that the dollars entered into processing equal the sum of the dollars stored on the payables change file, the dollars added to the consolidated payables file, the dollars added to the vendor master file, and the dollars subtracted from the payables receipts summary file (see Figure 10-9). In addition, the program must keep a separate accounting of the invoice total with and without cash discounts. The batch-balance equation is

Total discounted invoice total = Total invoice charge (net amount)
− Cash discount available

The *print payables check register program* alters the dollar amount stored on the consolidated payables file. When the decision is made to pay an invoice, dollars must be subtracted from the consolidated file and added to the payables pending-check file (see Figure 10-16). The equation maintained by this program is

$$\text{Total check amount} = \text{Total invoice charge (net amount)} - \text{Cash discounts taken}$$

Because it is important to carefully review cash discounting, most companies require cash discount percentages to be calculated. One ratio is:

$$\text{Cash discount percentage} = \frac{(\text{Discounts available} - \text{Discounts taken})}{\text{Discounts available}}$$

Unless this ratio is high, managers should question individual vendor payment instructions.

The *vendor check program* should compute and print the same amount as the total determined by the program to print the payables check register. Printed checks should not be signed and released unless the totals are identical.

The *print general ledger summary program* provides a final check on the accuracy of processing. A *trial balance* is obtained by matching expense-account totals to the total check amount. If the totals do not agree, adjusting entries must be prepared and keyed to processing. Either a general ledger entry will have to be revised or a vendor invoice (debit or credit) adjustment will have to be made.

Manual audits should be conducted to supplement programmed transaction- and batch-balance tests. After checks are printed, a random sample of payables should be selected for audit. The check amount should be compared, first, with the total printed on the check register and, next, with the total printed on the consolidated payables register. As a further audit, the check amount should be compared with the amount shown on the original vendor invoice. Finally, a full test would trace the vendor charge back through the purchasing and receiving application. The check amount should be compared both with the estimated dollar amount printed on the payables receipts summary (the receiving portion of the application) and with the dollar amount printed on the purchase order encumbrance summary (the purchasing portion of the application).

10-5 MANAGEMENT IMPLICATIONS

An automated accounts payable application offers two main benefits. The first is the most obvious: prompt payment of vendor invoices. With computer assistance the process of making payments is simplified. The computer helps to determine when to pay, what amount to pay, whether to challenge the invoice total, and whether to take the cash discount. The second benefit is not so self-evident: improved control of cash payments. Within large businesses, it becomes difficult to know whether all invoices submitted by vendors or all checks written to vendors are legitimate. The computer helps to make this determination.

Substantial savings can result when a firm is able to process vendor invoices quickly. First, prompt payment enables a business to take the cash discount. When the terms 2/10, n/30 (2 percent 10 day, net 30 days), are quoted, for example, the cost of credit is 36 percent if the cash discount is not taken; forgoing the discount is expensive. Promptness also often leads to more favorable terms of payment and to a resulting important improvement in *trade credit*. For instance, if a business sells on the average $2,000 of goods per day, with an average collection period of 40 days, outstanding receivables will approximate $80,000. If the firm then buys $1,000 worth of goods from vendors per day, with an average payables period of 10 days, accounts payables will approximate $10,000. The $70,000 difference between accounts receivable and accounts payable thus would indicate the *net credit amount* that the business must finance. If, however, instead of 10 days, the average payables period is extended to 25 days, the dollar amount of trade credit would be increased from $10,000 to $25,000, and the net credit amount would be reduced significantly— from $70,000 to $55,000.

The savings from improved control over processing are more difficult to document. Most business firms never attempt to cost-justify this particular area of processing. Instead, the objective of a design should be to reduce the probability of employee embezzlement by providing for well-planned processing controls, to be backed up by scheduled and nonscheduled manual audits. Lacking the best of controls, payables processing is extremely vulnerable to embezzling. Shortages in cash can be hidden by writing checks to fictitious vendor accounts, followed by deleting all traces of the accounts. Some organizations are especially vulnerable to fraudulent vendor invoices. A large branch of the military, for example, makes no attempt to match vendor invoices to purchase orders or receiving documents. When an invoice is received, it is paid; not until several weeks later does the branch attempt to match the paid invoice to the original purchase order and to investigate if a match cannot be made. Unfortunately, this type of processing is not limited to a few instances. Far too many firms have weak to nonexistent payables controls.

A final savings to be realized through using the accounts payable application lies in being able to predict the cash required to pay current and future bills. Financial officers of a business need this type of information. It helps them to estimate the demand for capital and to determine the implications of demand on cash flow. With better understanding and time to make decisions, financial officers are able to achieve a most desired objective: to minimize the cost to finance their net credit amount.

REVIEW OF IMPORTANT IDEAS

Several decisions must be incorporated into the design of the accounts payable application. These include when to pay, what amount to pay, whether to challenge the invoice total, and whether to take the cash discount. Correct decisions help a business to attain two main objectives of payables processing: to pay vendor invoices promptly and to keep vendor credit balances within reason.

Improved control of cash payments is another important objective of payables processing. Since this application specifies who to pay and in what amount, safeguards must be developed to reduce the risk of embezzlement and fraud.

Three processing runs are required by the payables application. The first run consists of making the vendor master file current and creating a file of approved vendor invoices. In creating the approved-invoice file, vendor invoice information must be keyed and displayed. If the information is verified as correct, the program continues by updating four online computer files (the vendor master file, the payables receipts file, the consolidated payables file, and the payables change file).

The second processing run determines which vendor invoices to pay and which invoices to hold. In processing, one computer program applies a cutoff date to all dated, open invoices in deciding which invoices to pay. When cash is insufficient to cover all open charges, the computer determines which invoices to hold—even though their due dates are reached. A separate program determines how much cash is needed to pay all open invoices and to take advantage of all cash discounts. Likewise, this program assists financial officers in setting the cutoff date.

The third processing run consists of batch programs to split the consolidated payables file and to print vendor voucher-checks, registers, and summary reports. Vendor voucher-checks contain a voucher portion to show why the check was written and a negotiable check portion. Prior to the printing of checks, a check register is prepared and reviewed. This register helps to determine if vendor invoices have been processed correctly. After checks are printed, a general ledger summary is produced. This summary provides a further check on the accuracy of processing.

Vendor voucher-check information is also written to a consolidated pending-check file. Here the information remains, awaiting the return of checks by the bank. A check-reconciliation processing run deletes checks from the pending file and reports the results of processing.

A variety of registers and change reports are printed in addition to the check register and G/L summary. The vendor register, the consolidated payables register, and the consolidated pending-check register help to track the status of vendor invoices. The vendor change report, the payables change report, and the checks-pending change report show the movement of payables information. Although the paperwork associated with payables processing may appear extreme, registers, reports, and G/L summaries permit the entire payables process to be reconstructed if files of data are lost or destroyed. This paper trail is required for a manual audit of processing. Audits must be conducted to supplement automated transaction- and batch-balance tests of processing.

Substantial savings result from a well-designed payables application. Prompt payment of vendor invoices enables a business to improve its credit rating, take advantage of cash discounts, and reduce the net credit amount to be financed. Besides direct savings, indirect savings result from improved processing control and the ability to better estimate the demand for capital and its implications.

KEY WORDS

Current liability	Pay code
Credit rating	Hold-instruction code
Trade credit	Cutoff date
Consolidated payables file	Payables pending-check file
Vendor invoice	Payables check register
Vendor master file	Imprinter
Direct cost	Signature die
Indirect cost	Detacher
Vendor voucher-check	Check reconciliation
Voucher number	Vendor register
Check number	Trial balance
General ledger (G/L) distribution	Net credit amount

REVIEW QUESTIONS

1. Explain why accounts payable processing is sometimes viewed as the inverse of accounts receivable processing.

2. What are the two main objectives of payables processing?

3. How does trade credit differ from a cash credit?

4. What invoices are placed in a "payables this period" file, and what invoices are placed in a "payables held over" file?

5. Briefly describe the three main inputs to accounts payable processing.

6. What is the difference between a direct cost and an indirect cost?

7. Why is the vendor voucher-check a two-part form?

8. Why is a voucher number assigned in processing? Why is a check number assigned?

9. What is the main difference between the check register and the general ledger summary?

10. Name the four online files updated by the enter payables transaction program.

11. What is a general ledger distribution, and why is it important to processing?

12. How does the pay code field differ from the hold instruction field? From the dollar amount paid field?

13. What is a cutoff date? Why is such a date important to payables processing? Why are several cutoff dates tested before a firm date is established?

14. Of what value is a display of aged open invoices?

15. What is the difference between an imprinter and a detacher?

16. What four G/L summaries are important to payables processing?

17. How does the process of check reconciliation differ from the process of check writing?

18. What is the difference between the consolidated payables register and the consolidated pending-check register? Between the payables change report and the checks-pending change report?

19. Describe the transaction- and batch-control balances maintained by the enter payables transaction program.

20. If control balance tests are working correctly, why are manual audits necessary?

21. What is a net credit amount? Why should a company be concerned about such an amount?

22. Explain how payables processing helps financial managers to determine their cash-flow requirements.

EXERCISES

1. It is necessary at times for a business to pay in advance for goods and services. For example, a vendor might require a down payment of 50 percent before agreeing to begin work on an order. Explain how the payables application would have to be modified to handle prepaid expenses.

2. Compare the accounts payable application with the accounts receivable application. In what ways are the two applications similar? In what ways are they different?

3. Suppose a company is able to negotiate yearly installment plans with vendors. Under this agreement, the company would pay an outstanding balance in twelve equal installments. How must the payables application be modified to support this requirement?

4. Design the systems flowcharts for an online check-reconciliation application. The program menu to be followed is shown below. Attach a short descriptive statement with each program (flowchart) to describe how processing is supposed to work. If sort programs are required prior to processing, these too should be shown.

    > ENTER CANCELED CHECKS
    > PRINT PAID CHECKS REGISTER
    > PRINT OUTSTANDING CHECKS REGISTER
    > PRINT G/L SUMMARIES (MAY BE SEVERAL)
    > EXIT

5. There are several ways to create the payables pending-check file besides the way described and illustrated in this chapter (see Figure 10-16). Here are two possible options:

    Option 1: Create the file as part of the enter payment instruction program. Use a cutoff date and vendor hold instructions to determine which payables are to be added to the payables pending-check file and which are to remain in the consolidated payables file (see Figure 10-21).

    Option 2: Create the file as part of the print payables check register program, as described in the chapter. Update the consolidated payables file, however, instead of dividing it into two smaller files (see Figure 10-22).

    Explain the advantages and disadvantages of each of these processing options compared with the design presented in the chapter.

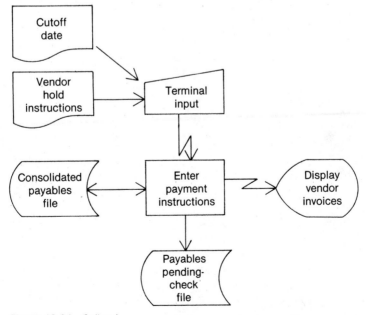

Figure 10-21 Option 1

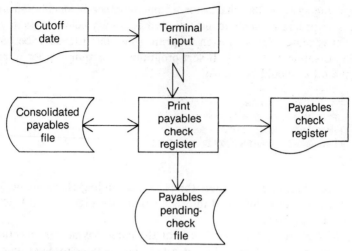

Figure 10-22 Option 2

11

Fixed Assets

If a company acquires business property, such as plant and equipment, that has a useful life of more than one year, it cannot by law deduct the cost of such property as an expense in a single year. Instead, the company must spread the cost over several years. This is called *depreciation* of business property. Since the dollar amount deducted each year for business expenses offsets taxable income, it is often referred to as a *tax write-off*.

Property is depreciable if it meets requirements specified by federal government law. Four such requirements are, first, that the property must be used (or held) for the production of income; second, that it must have a useful life of more than one year; third, that the span of its useful life can be determined; and, fourth, that it must be something that wears out or loses its value. For example, tangible property with a useful life of several years, such as equipment or machinery, would be depreciable since it wears out. In contrast, real property, such as land, can never be depreciated.

Property with a useful life of more than one year is also known as a *fixed asset*. It is fixed because it makes up the permanent part of a business. In processing fixed-assets information, procedures must be developed to do two things: first, collect and record fixed-assets information and determine the depreciation schedule of the property and, second, maintain the depreciation schedule and determine the yearly tax write-off. In this chapter we examine both sets of activities.

11-1 FIXED-ASSETS ACCOUNTING SYSTEMS

One of the major difficulties associated with the design of fixed-assets accounting systems is that they are greatly affected by ever-changing federal and state tax legislation. Thus, before we examine the preliminary processing overview for this application, we will need to review the current status of methods of depreciation, as well as the basic procedures of each method.

The Accelerated Cost Recovery System (ACRS) introduced by the federal government in 1981 has greatly simplified the reporting of depreciation for new purchases; however, it has also meant that firms need to keep at least two sets of records—one for assets obtained on or before December 31, 1980, and one for property acquired in or after January 1981. Under ACRS, assets acquired after January 1981 are grouped into four recovery periods of three, five, ten, and fifteen years. Within each period, a percentage of the total value of the asset can be written off. These write-off percentages are shown in Figure 11-1. As illustrated, 15 percent of the value of a five-year property item can be written off the first year, or the first *recovery period*. Following this initial write-off, 22 percent can be written off in the second year, and 21 percent can be written off in each of the next three years.

Assets acquired on or before December 31, 1980, must continue to be depreciated using one of three methods (with some exceptions): straight line, declining balance, and sum of the years digits.

A *straight-line method* of depreciation permits the same percentage (or dollar amount) to be deducted each year. The deduction is calculated as follows:

$$\text{Straight-line depreciation (in dollars)} = \frac{(\text{Investment} - \text{Salvage value})}{\text{Useful life of asset}}$$

Suppose, for example, that a business buys a used machine for $2,000. If the machine has a useful life of 10 years and will have no salvage value (meaning that it cannot be sold as salvage 10 years from now and thus has no residual value), the straight-line depreciation for the machine is $200 ($2,000 ÷ 10 years). In other words, $200 can be deducted as depreciation, each year, for 10 years.

The *declining-balance method* of depreciation is more complex than the straight-line method. Several steps are required in calculating yearly depreciation.

1. The straight-line rate of depreciation must be determined by dividing the number 1 by the useful life of the investment. Returning to the example above, we can calculate the straight-line rate as 10 percent (1 ÷ 10 years).

2. The accelerated rate of depreciation must be determined by multiplying the straight-line rate times the declining-balance rate (1.25, 1.5, or 2). In the example above, if the declining-balance rate were 1.5, the accelerated rate of depreciation would be 15 percent (1.5 × 10 percent).

3. The first-year depreciation is calculated by multiplying the fixed investment times the accelerated rate of depreciation. Continuing our example, first-year depreciation is $300 (or 15 percent × $2,000).

ACCELERATED COST RECOVERY TABLE

Applicable Percentage for Class of Property:

Recovery Year	Three Years	Five Years	Ten Years	Fifteen Years
1	25	15	8	5
2	38	22	14	10
3	37	21	12	9
4		21	10	8
5		21	10	7
6			10	7
7			9	6
8			9	6
9			9	6
10			9	6
11				6
12				6
13				6
14				6
15				6
	100	100	100	100

Property placed in service after Dec. 31, 1980, and before Jan. 1, 1985.

Figure 11-1 Accelerated Cost Recovery System (ACRS)

4. The second-year depreciation is calculated by subtracting the previous depreciation from the investment and multiplying the balance times the accelerated rate of depreciation. The second-year depreciation for our $2,000 example investment would thus be $255 ($2,000 − $300 first-year depreciation × .15 = $255).

5. The third-year depreciation is calculated in the same way as the second year. All previous depreciations must be subtracted before the balance is multiplied by the accelerated rate of depreciation. In our example, the third year of depreciation is $216.75.

The double-declining-balance method of depreciation uses a 2.0 declining-balance rate, or a rate that is twice the straight-line rate. With double declining balance, it is thus possible to depreciate an asset at 200 percent of the straight-line rate. Using the figures from the previous example, first-year depreciation is $400, or 20 percent times $2,000. The 20 percent accelerated rate of depreciation is twice the 10 percent straight-line rate. Second-year depreciation is $320 ($2,000 − $400 × .20 = $320). As before, depreciation is calculated by subtracting the previous depreciation from the remaining investment balance and multiplying this balance times the accelerated rate of depreciation.

The *sum-of-the-years-digits method* of depreciation, like the declining-balance method, permits a faster tax write-off than does the straight-line method. Several steps are also required in calculating yearly depreciation.

1. The adjusted investment must be determined by subtracting the salvage value from the investment. Thus, if the salvage value of a $25,000 investment is $4,000, the adjusted investment would be $21,000.

2. The years of useful life of the investment must be added to arrive at the sum of the years digits. For example, the sum of the years digits for an asset with a useful life of 6 years is 21 (6 + 5 + 4 + 3 + 2 + 1).

3. The first-year depreciation is calculated by multiplying the adjusted investment times the sum of the years fraction.

$$\text{Sum of the years fraction} = \frac{\text{Years remaining in useful life}}{\text{Sum of the years digits}}$$

Thus, in our example, we would multiply the adjusted investment, $21,000, times 6/21, to arrive at a first-year depreciation of $6,000.

4. The second-year depreciation is calculated in the same way as the first-year depreciation, except that the sum of the years fraction is different because the number of years remaining in the useful life of the property has been reduced by 1. Returning to the example once more, we can calculate second-year depreciation as $5,000 ($21,000 × 5/21).

The tables presented in Figure 11-2 compare the three methods of depreciation for a new machine costing $10,000. The machine has a useful life of five years and no salvage value. Notice that the straight-line percentage rate is the same for each of the five years. The double-declining-balance and sum-of-the-years-digits methods, in contrast, feature accelerated rates. For the first year, the percentage rate for double declining balance is twice that of the straight-line rate. The sum-of-the-years-digits method begins with a rate of 33 1/3 percent.

In addition to these three basic methods of depreciation, still other provisions in federal legislation complicate accounting procedures for fixed assets. For instance, tangible personal property with a useful life of 6 years or more qualifies for *additional first-year depreciation*. This provision permits a business to deduct 20 percent of the cost of an investment during the first year in addition to regular depreciation. If, for example, the machine that is depreciated in Figure 11-2 has a useful life of six years instead of five years, the depreciation during the first year, using a straight-line method, becomes:

First-year straight-line depreciation = $10,000 ÷ 6   = $1,667
Additional first-year depreciation   = $10,000 × .20 = $2,000
Total first-year depreciation   = $3,667

Straight-line

Year	Cost	Rate	Deduction	Reserve Dec. 31
First	$10,000	20%	$2,000	$ 2,000
Second	10,000	20%	2,000	4,000
Third	10,000	20%	2,000	6,000
Fourth	10,000	20%	2,000	8,000
Fifth	10,000	20%	2,000	10,000

Double-declining-balance

Year	Unrecovered cost Jan. 1	Rate	Deduction	Reserve Dec. 31
First	$10,000	40%	$4,000	$ 4,000
Second	6,000	40%	2,400	6,400
Third	3,600	40%	1,440	7,840
Fourth	2,160	40%	864	8,704
Fifth	1,296	40%	518	9,222

Sum-of-years digits

Year	Cost	Fraction	Deduction	Reserve Dec. 31
First	$10,000	5/15	$3,333	$ 3,333
Second	10,000	4/15	2,667	6,000
Third	10,000	3/15	2,000	8,000
Fourth	10,000	2/15	1,333	9,333
Fifth	10,000	1/15	667	10,000

Figure 11-2 Comparing methods of depreciation

Finally, for assets purchased after 1970, federal legislation allows a Class Life Asset Depreciation Range (CLADR) system to be used in calculating depreciation. This system is similar to the Accelerated Cost Recovery System (ACRS) discussed earlier (see Figure 11-1). The main differences between the two are that the CLADR system provides guidelines; it does not show what method of depreciation or what amount of depreciation can be recovered in a single year. As Figure 11-3 shows, the CLADR system provides a depreciation-period (useful life) guideline for different classes of assets. The expected useful life for computers, for example, is six years, whereas the expected useful life for office equipment is ten years. In addition, the upper and lower limits for depreciation periods are listed. These limits can be interpreted as follows: the useful life for office equipment is ten years, plus or minus two years. The CLADR system also shows the repair-allowance guideline, which is a percentage. If the cost of repairs for a computer during the year is less than 7.5 percent of the value of the asset, the cost of repairs can be treated as a business expense and deducted the same year. If the cost exceeds 7.5 percent, however, the additional

	Asset depreciation range (in years)			Annual repair allowance guideline (percentage)
	Lower limit	Period guideline	Upper limit	
Office equipment	8	10	12	2.0
Computers	5	6	7	7.5
Typewriters	5	6	7	15.0

Figure 11-3   Class Life Asset Depreciation Range (CLADR) system

expense cannot be deducted in the same year. Rather, the balance of the expense must be *capitalized* after deducting for the repair allowance—that is, the property must be classified as a fixed asset and the expense must be recovered through annual depreciation deductions.

11-2   PRELIMINARY OVERVIEW OF PROCESSING

In order for the computer to calculate the depreciation schedule for fixed assets, information describing each fixed asset must be entered into processing. As Figure 11-4 shows, some fixed-assets information is provided by the accounts payable application. When payables transactions are entered into processing, *payables to be capitalized* are separated and written to a computer file.

Following the extraction of fixed assets from other payables, the steps in fixed-assets processing include the following (see Figure 11-4):

1. *Enter new property information* to combine new fixed-assets information keyed to processing with information stored on the file of payables to be capitalized. Each new property record is added to the *fixed-assets master file.*

2. *Print depreciation schedule* to determine which method of depreciation is appropriate and to set the depreciation schedule for the asset.

3. *Print identification labels* to produce labels or tags that are attached to the property for purposes of control.

4. *Print fixed-assets summaries* to produce a variety of depreciation projections, property-control reports, and tax depreciation reports.

One step not shown in Figure 11-4 is the adjusting of the fixed-assets master file. If changes occur in the value or the disposition of an asset, for example, the useful life and salvage value of the asset can be modified. The reporting requirement is that there must be a clear reason for making the change. It is also

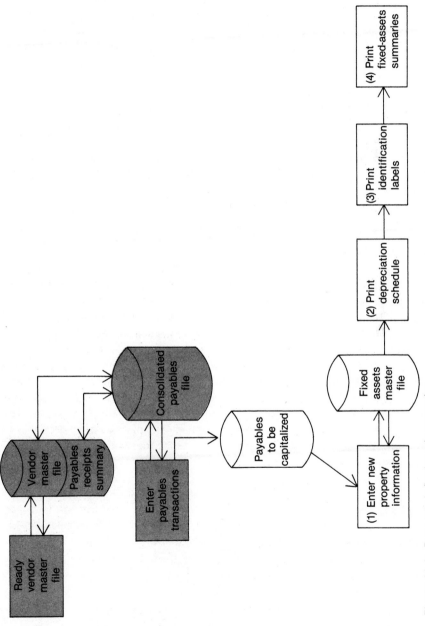

Figure 11-4 Four steps in fixed-assets processing

possible to change the method of computing depreciation. A company can make the change from a declining-balance method to a straight-line method at any time without permission from the Internal Revenue Service. Other adjustments permitted include changing from the straight-line method or from the declining-balance method to the sum-of-the-years-digits method. As a consequence, the fixed-assets computer application should include provisions for testing different depreciation methods to determine which method or combination of methods will lead to an optimum cash flow over the life of an asset.

Inputs to Processing

The main input to fixed-assets processing is the *new property report*. This report is prepared by accounting and lists each piece of property to be capitalized. It contains three types of information to be keyed into processing: property-control information, insurance and replacement information, and depreciation and tax information (see Figure 11-5).

Property-control information identifies fixed assets stored on the fixed-assets master file. Each asset is assigned a unique number and a classification code; each asset is briefly described. The location of the asset (department, room number, and so forth) must also be specified.

Insurance and replacement information protects a business against the unforeseen loss of or damage to an asset. Included in this category are the useful life (for tax-reporting purposes) and the retirement life of an asset. For example, for tax-reporting purposes, the useful life of an asset might be five years, even though the asset might actually be kept in service for seven years.

Besides different lives, the insurable value of an asset is stored. New property is generally valued at cost, whereas used property is assigned an appraised value. Independent appraisals are performed by insurance agents. To this end, maintenance and appraisal schedules are stored. The maintenance schedule shows how and when the property is to be serviced; the appraisal schedule shows how often the property is to be inspected. The purpose of inspection is to determine the degree to which the insurable value must be modified.

Department and tax information shows how the property is to be depreciated. Both tax and book depreciation methods are specified. The *tax depreciation method* indicates how the asset will be depreciated for purposes of tax reporting. The *book depreciation method* indicates how the asset will be depreciated for purposes of company-asset reporting. Under new IRS rules, for example, a building can be fully depreciated in fifteen years, but this does not mean that the building has zero value for its owners. Quite the contrary. For this reason, the *book value*, which shows the true value of property, is kept separately from the tax depreciation value.

Depreciation and tax information also include dollar values for tax credits and additional first-year depreciation. An *investment tax credit* is a direct credit against taxes that applies when a business acquires property. The credit can range from 7 to 11.5 percent of the cost of the property and is applied in

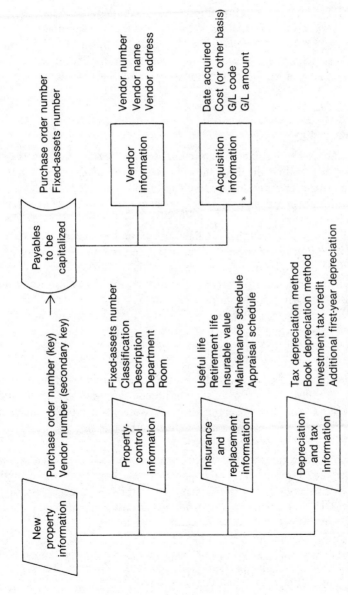

Figure 11-5 Relationships between fixed-assets data sets

filing the tax forms for the year in which the asset was acquired. Additional first-year depreciation, discussed above, offers extra incentive for businesses to acquire depreciable property.

To create fixed-asset records, keyed information is combined with information extracted from payables and stored on the file of payables to be capitalized. As Figure 11-5 shows, information important to fixed-assets processing includes vendor and acquisition information. Vendor information (number, name, and address) shows where the property was acquired. Acquisition information includes the date acquired, the cost of the property, and general ledger assignments. These facts substantiate the dollar value of the asset and its financial disposition.

Outputs from Processing

Outputs produced by the fixed-assets computer application include the fixed-assets master file; online displays showing the status of fixed-asset accounts, depreciation projections, and tax write-off totals; printed property identification labels; and printed reports showing new property acquisitions, tax depreciation schedules, depreciation projections, and property and insurance schedules.

Figure 11-6 shows an abbreviated fixed-assets master record. A fixed-assets number identifies a particular piece of property, and the purchase order number permits the property to be traced back to the initial requisition. Each file record is made up of property-control, vendor, acquisition, insurance and replacement, and depreciation and tax information, plus one new segment containing depreciation-history information. Tax and book values and current and accumulated tax and book depreciation totals are stored under this category.

A variety of reports and displays can be prepared after new property information has been added to the fixed-assets master file and depreciation totals have been calculated. As an example, Figure 11-7 illustrates a *book depreciation expense report,* which provides a comprehensive summary of the current, year-to-date, and cumulative depreciation for each asset stored on the fixed-assets master file. It also provides user-defined subtotals: for example, the current depreciation for the Atlanta plant is $137,522.91.

With an online design, the fixed-assets information appearing on a report can also be displayed. Figure 11-8, for instance, shows how book value might be compared with tax value for a fixed asset. Here the tax value is less than the book value. This difference results from using different methods of depreciation: a straight-line (1.0 S/L) method for calculating book value and a declining-balance method (2.0 S/L) for calculating tax value.

Displays showing different groups of assets (such as groups arranged by asset class, department, or general ledger code) are also part of a fixed-assets design. Like the display in Figure 11-8, these displays also compare book and tax values. They provide financial officers with the capability to page through the fixed assets of a company. Thus, at any point in time financial officers can determine the dollar value of major classes of business investments.

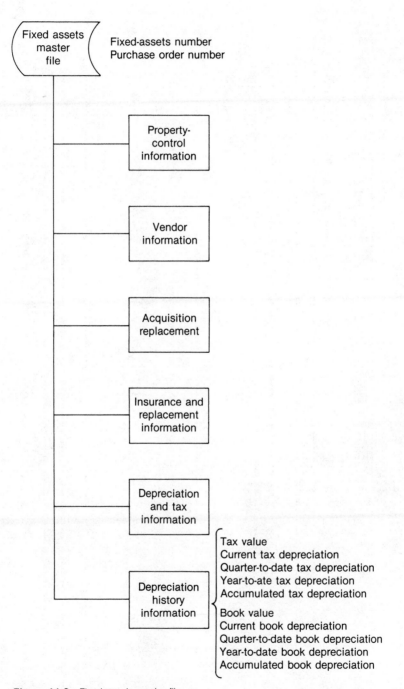

Figure 11-6 Fixed-assets master file

CORP 0/1 ABEL CORPORATION — B O O K   D E P R E C I A T I O N — REL 5.02 PAGE 2
FA050-A FINANCIAL BOOK 0 — FROM 7-8- THRU 1-8- FOR 6 PERIODS — REPT DATE 7-13-8-

REGION — PLANT ATLANTA — DEPT SHP0012

ITEM NUMBER	DESCRIPT	BEGIN DEPR	ASSET LIFE	DEPR METH	INSTALLED COST	DEPRECIATION CUMULATIVE	DEPRECIATION YEAR TO DATE	DEPRECIATION CURRENT	SALVAGE VALUE	REMAINING VALUE
10CD00100009	ADDING MAC	3-76	05-00	P10000	1,465.13	695.94	85.46	42.73	146.51	769.19
10HD00100014	HEAVYDUTY	*RETIRED*					1,887.34			
10HD00100015	HEAVYDUTY	11-77	07-00	RSYD	45,000.00	20,848.61	10,176.61	5,088.30	4,500.00	24,151.39
10HD00100017	HEAVYDUTY	4-77	07-00	RSTL	20,000.00	7,408.82	3,258.82	1,629.41	2,000.00	12,591.18
PLANT	ATLANTA	T O T A L			2368,136.84	310,749.53	214,617.28	137,522.91	26,931.45	2057,387.31

REGION — PLANT BOSTON — DEPT CUT0012

ITEM NUMBER	DESCRIPT	BEGIN DEPR	ASSET LIFE	DEPR METH	INSTALLED COST	DEPRECIATION CUMULATIVE	DEPRECIATION YEAR TO DATE	DEPRECIATION CURRENT	SALVAGE VALUE	REMAINING VALUE
20CDB0200033	PLANT BUIL	5-80	15-00	STL	293,359.07	13,162.40	9,774.30	9,774.30		280,196.67
20HDB0200015	CUTTING MA	*RETIRED*								
20HDB0200016	CUTTING MA	10-77	07-00	RSTL	4,200.00	2,276.31	512.98	256.49		1,923.69
20HDB0200017	CUTTING MA	7-77	07-00	RSTL	55,000.00	29,769.08	7,208.84	3,604.42		25,230.92
20MD00200018	COMPUTERIZ	*TRANSFERRED*					146,066.67			
20MD00200019	LEFT-HANDE	8-75	05-00	RSTL	3,100.00	3,100.00	205.58	29.37		
20MD00200020	HAND TRIMM	3-75	05-00	RSTL	5,000.00	5,000.00	92.31			
20MD00200023	COMPUTERIZ	11-75	05-00	STL	156,500.00	156,500.00	10,433.33	10,433.33		

REGION — PLANT BOSTON — DEPT JHD0012

ITEM NUMBER	DESCRIPT	BEGIN DEPR	ASSET LIFE	DEPR METH	INSTALLED COST	DEPRECIATION CUMULATIVE	DEPRECIATION YEAR TO DATE	DEPRECIATION CURRENT	SALVAGE VALUE	REMAINING VALUE
20CDB0200023	PLANT BUIL	*TRANSFERRED*				.01-	5,212.46			.01
20CDB0200034	PLANT BUIL	5-80	15-00	STL	45,132.17	2,024.99	1,503.74	1,503.74		43,107.18
20CDB0200043	PLANT BUIL	5-80	15-00	STL	112,830.42	5,062.46	3,759.34	3,759.34		107,767.96
20CF00200010	DESK	*TRANSFERRED*								
20CF00200012	TYPEWRITER	6-68	10-00	STL	405.00	405.00				
20CF00200030	DESK	2-68	10-00	STL	445.00	445.00				
20CN00200007	OIL PAINTI	4-79	60-00	NON	10,100.00					10,100.00
20CN00200008	PAINTING W	3-75	60-00	NON	2,130.00					2,130.00
20CN00200009	SCULPTURE	2-75	60-00	NON	3,270.00					3,270.00
20DD00200022	TRUCKING C	5-80	12-00	STL	124,120.00	6,895.56	6,895.56	5,171.67		117,224.44

REGION — PLANT BOSTON — DEPT PCK0012

ITEM NUMBER	DESCRIPT	BEGIN DEPR	ASSET LIFE	DEPR METH	INSTALLED COST	DEPRECIATION CUMULATIVE	DEPRECIATION YEAR TO DATE	DEPRECIATION CURRENT	SALVAGE VALUE	REMAINING VALUE
20CDB0200001	STACKER	7-77	08-00	STL	7,000.00	3,107.19	1,028.76	547.81	650.00	3,892.81
20CDB0200002	STACKER	8-78	08-00	D2SL	16,480.00	8,679.54	2,600.16	1,300.08		7,800.46
20CD00200003	STACKER	4-78	08-00	RSYD	16,480.00	6,759.74	3,113.74	1,556.87	1,500.00	9,720.26
20CD00200004	ANNEX-NORT	6-67	30-00	SYD	185,000.00	128,074.38	39,671.16	37,032.45		56,925.62
20CD00200100	SMOKE FILT	6-72	25-00	STL	25,000.00	8,583.33	1,000.00	500.00		16,416.67
20CD00200200	POLLUTION	6-74	20-00	STL	50,000.00	16,458.33	2,500.00	1,250.00		33,541.67

Figure 11-7 Book depreciation expense report

```
FIXED-ASSET NUMBER:    34521            P.O. NUMBER:    984361


CLASS:    00.12              DESCRIPTION:    OPTICAL READER
DATE ACQUIRED:     12-14-8X      DEPT.:    B12      ROOM:    468

                                    VALUE
                              BOOK       TAX
LIFE                          10 YEAR    8 YEAR
DEPRECIATION METHOD           S/L        2.0 S/L
DATE OF LAST UPDATE           1-15-8X    1-15-8X

INSTALLED COST                $5,800     $5,800
SALVAGE VALUE                   800        800
CURRENT DEPRECIATION            500        591
ACCUMULATED DEPRECIATION      2,000      3,417
REMAINING VALUE               3,800      2,383
```

Figure 11-8   Comparing book and tax values

Other information produced by the fixed-assets application includes a variety of registers, tax depreciation reports, and accounting summaries. Four printed registers are the *new property register,* which lists all new property added to the fixed-assets master file; the *assets retirement register,* which lists all property retired (deleted) from the fixed-assets master file; the *fixed-assets master register,* which includes all properties stored on the fixed-assets master file; and the *fixed-assets change register,* which enumerates all changes (changes to the useful life, salvage value, and so forth) to properties stored on the fixed-assets master file.

Still other outputs include a variety of tax reports, the formats of which are largely determined by federal reporting requirements. Three of the several reports to be prepared by a business are the *tax depreciation report* (Form 4562), which lists tax depreciation expenses by type of asset for a fiscal year (see Figure 11-9); the *Class Life Asset Depreciation Range* (CLADR) *report* (Form 4832), which lists class life calculations to reach the total shown on Form 4562 (see Figure 11-9); and the *investment tax credit report* (Form 3468), which lists property that qualifies for an investment tax credit.

Last, depreciation projections, annual depreciation summaries, and insurance-value and replacement cost analyses are prepared by processing. *Depreciation projections* show year-by-year depreciation totals for individual assets, for different classes of assets, and for the company as a whole. These projections and

Form **4562**		**Depreciation**					19
Department of the Treasury Internal Revenue Service		▶ See instructions on back. ▶ Attach this form to your return.					

Name(s) as shown on return — **Identifying number**

For grouping assets, see instructions for line 3.

a. Description of property	b. Date acquired	c. Cost or other basis	d. Depreciation allowed or allowable in earlier years	e. Method of figuring depreciation	f. Life or rate	g. Depreciation for this year
1 Total additional first-year depreciation. See instructions for limitation. ▶						
2 Class Life Asset Depreciation Range (CLADR) System depreciation from Form 4832 . .						
3 Other depreciation: Buildings						
Furniture and fixtures . . .						
Transportation equipment . .						
Machinery and other equipment .						
Computer	1-5-	$60,000	$20,000	S/L	6	$10,000
Other (Specify)						
4 a Totals (add amounts in columns c and g) .		$60,000				$10,000
b Total current year acquisitions (included in line 4a, column c)		θ				

Individual and partnership filers enter the totals from line 4a on the corresponding lines of their regular depreciation schedule. Other filers should attach Form 4562 to their return and enter line 4a, column g, on the depreciation expense line in the "Deductions" section of their return.

Form **4562** '19

Figure 11-9 Tax depreciation report

annual summaries are useful in short-term budgeting and in planning future acquisitions. *Insurance-value analysis* shows the current and replacement costs of fixed assets. This information is used to determine how much insurance should be carried by a business. Current-value costs are stored in the fixed-assets master file and can be reported with little difficulty. Replacement-value costs are more difficult to compute. Either a replacement cost field must be added to each fixed-asset record, thus providing for an itemized reporting of the replacement value, or replacement costs must be projected. Replacement cost projections are generally applied to an entire class of assets rather than to a single fixed asset.

11-3 FIXED-ASSETS PROCESSING

The flowchart in Figure 11-10 shows a modified accounts payables processing design, in which a new file entitled *payables to be capitalized* is created. The extraction of fixed-assets information to make up the file is simple and straight-forward. Prior to processing, a *fixed-assets extract slip* is prepared and attached to the vendor invoice (or acquisition slip). Information recorded on the slip includes a fixed-assets identification number and the dollar total to be capitalized. The fixed-assets number permits the property to be identified later on during fixed-assets processing. The dollar total is required to allow the new

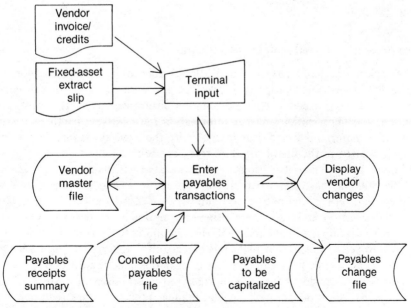

Figure 11-10 Modified payables processing

file to be audited. Routine checks must be made to determine if the dollar amount extracted from accounts payable is consistent with the dollar amount held in the file of payables to be capitalized.

After fixed-assets information has been extracted, processing begins. As Figure 11-11 shows, the interactive part of the application consists of six programs; the batch part consists of eight programs. Three of the six interactive programs enter or adjust fixed-assets information; the other three display individual account information and project book or tax depreciation schedules. A special feature of the display program is that book and tax depreciation projections can generally be made for a single fixed-asset account or for an entire class of fixed assets. This capability to review depreciation projections in different ways is of vital importance to property managers. It helps them to formulate equipment-replacement plans and policies based on up-to-date plant and equipment book and tax values.

Figure 11-12 shows the processing menu for fixed-assets processing. As will soon be apparent, there is a close correspondence between the interactive and the batch programs. For example, the program to enter new property information creates a *new property file,* which consists of new property records added to the fixed-assets master file; these records are required to print the *new property report* (program B.1) and *property identification labels* (program B.2). The program to adjust property information creates a *property change file,* which contains changes to the fixed-assets master file, other than the addition of new property; these change records are needed to show which fixed assets have been retired (program B.7) and how book and tax values have been modified (program B.8).

The Enter New Property Information Program

Although the accounts payable application is able to provide some of the data needed to describe new property, it does not provide all of it. As we saw earlier in Figure 11-5, property-control information, insurance and replacement information, and depreciation and tax information must be keyed into processing. Once this material is keyed, it is merged with the fixed-assets information previously written to the file of payables to be capitalized.

Figure 11-13 shows the systems flow associated with adding information to the fixed-assets master file. If multiple keys are built into the design, the purchase order, vendor, and fixed-assets numbers are keyed and transmitted. These numbers transfer vendor and acquisition information into processing. Once they have been visually verified as correct, the remaining fixed-assets information is keyed. Property-control information is entered first, followed by insurance and replacement, and depreciation and tax information (see Figure 11-13).

If it becomes impossible to merge the keyed information with the previously stored fixed-assets information, special manual procedures are required. As a first step, the payables master register must be inspected to determine if the property was processed by the payables application and, if so, if it was coded as

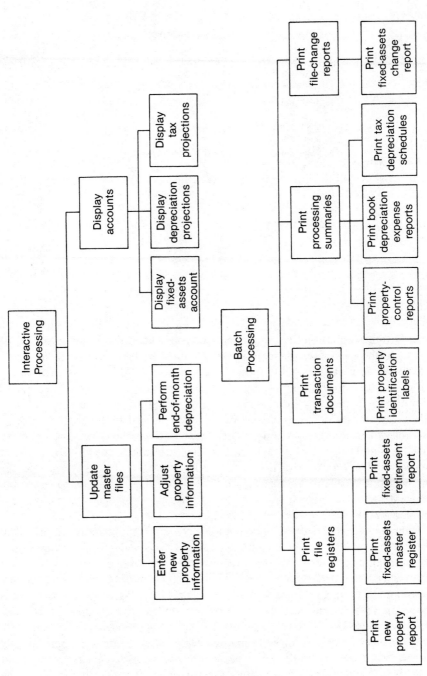

Figure 11-11 Fixed-assets systems organization chart

I.1   ENTER NEW PROPERTY INFORMATION
I.2   ADJUST PROPERTY INFORMATION
I.3   PERFORM END-OF-MONTH DEPRECIATION
I.4   DISPLAY FIXED-ASSETS ACCOUNT
I.5   DISPLAY DEPRECIATION PROJECTIONS
I.6   DISPLAY TAX PROJECTIONS

B.1   PRINT NEW PROPERTY REPORT
B.2   PRINT PROPERTY IDENTIFICATION LABELS
B.3   PRINT PROPERTY-CONTROL REPORTS
B.4   PRINT BOOK DEPRECIATION EXPENSE REPORTS
B.5   PRINT TAX DEPRECIATION SCHEDULES
B.6   PRINT FIXED-ASSETS MASTER REGISTER
B.7   PRINT FIXED-ASSETS RETIREMENT REGISTER
B.8   PRINT FIXED-ASSETS CHANGE REPORT
(9)   EXIT

Figure 11-12   Fixed-assets processing menu

property to be capitalized. If the property was coded and processed correctly, a register of the payables-to-be-capitalized file must be prepared and inspected. This step determines if payables processing was successful in actually transferring information to the file.

Entering new property information is simple enough, provided depreciation and tax methods and tax credits have been determined in advance. In times past, these determinations required considerable judgment. The most difficult figures to supply were the salvage value of the asset and its useful life. For instance, would a chair last for five, ten, or fifteen years, and after this period of time, would it have any residual value? The most difficult decision to be made was what method of depreciation would be most advantageous. The variety of methods meant that each needed to be tested.

Fortunately, recent federal depreciation laws have simplified requirements for reporting new property. A chair is presently classified as a five-year property, for example. Accordingly, 15 percent of the chair can be written off during the first year, and 22 percent can be written off during the second year (see Figure 11-1). Certain complexities remain, however. Some state tax-depreciation regulations differ from the federal requirements, which means that companies must keep different sets of records—those that satisfy federal reporting requirements and those that satisfy state (one or more) reporting requirements. Moreover, additional types of records must be kept for assets acquired before and after the enactment of new depreciating reporting laws—that is, for assets acquired after 1970 and after 1981.

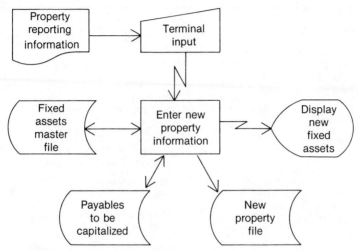

Figure 11-13 Adding new property records

Following the verification of keyed information, including federal and state depreciation and tax values, the completed property record is written to the fixed-assets master file and to the new property file. Next, the file of payables to be capitalized is updated: the property record added to the fixed-assets file must be deleted from the payables-to-be-capitalized file. Third, the terminal operator is asked whether another new property record is to be completed. If so, the process of entering data begins once again. If not, the operator exits to return control to the main program menu.

The Adjust Property Information Program

Several types of adjustments to property records are required after property has been added to the fixed-assets master file. These adjustments follow from decisions to switch from one method of depreciation to another, to change fixed-assets retirement values, to retire fixed assets, to alter maintenance schedules, or to move property from one location to another. Each of these decisions leads to different computer processing requirements. For example, the decision to switch from one method of depreciation to another typically requires the capability to compare different methods of depreciation.

To illustrate such a comparison, we will imagine a situation in which a company acquires a piece of property at a cost of $80,000. The property has an expected life of eight years; after this time, it will have a salvage value of $40,000. Because of higher than expected profits, the company wants a large tax write-off during the first year of the investment, followed by a more gradual tax write-off. By comparing straight-line and double-declining-balance methods of depreciation for our hypothetical transaction (see Figure 11-14), we can see that whereas the straight-line method provides a small but level write-off for all

		METHOD OF DEPRECIATION	
YEAR	STRAIGHT LINE	DECLINING BALANCE	DIFFERENCE
1	5000	20000	15000
2	5000	15000	10000
3	5000	5000	0
4	5000	0	−5000
5	5000	0	−5000
6	5000	0	−5000
7	5000	0	−5000
8	5000	0	−5000

Figure 11-14 Tax depreciation display

years, the double-declining-balance method provides very large write-offs during the initial years but no additional depreciation after the third year. At that time the remaining value of the asset would be equal to the salvage value.

The kind of tax depreciation display shown in Figure 11-14 helps financial officers of a company to decide how best to depreciate property. In our example, the company's officers might very well choose a third alternative to either straight-line or double-declining-balance methods: they might use a combination of double declining balance for the first year only and straight line for the following years. This solution would provide a tax write-off of $20,000 for the first year and $8,571.50 for the second through the eighth years. Such a switch from one method of depreciation to another would be accomplished through the file-adjustment process shown by the flowchart in Figure 11-15. As illustrated, inputs to processing consist of property change reports. For instance, the decision to change methods of depreciation would be placed on a depreciation change report. The same adjustment process is used for all changes to fixed-asset records, not just for changes in depreciation method. A decision to show how property was moved from one location to another, for example, would be placed on a transfer-of-property report.

Outputs to processing consist of updated files and visual displays. That is, after property change information is keyed and verified, the fixed-assets master file and the property change file are updated. The change file in this instance is usually the same file as the new property file illustrated earlier (see Figure

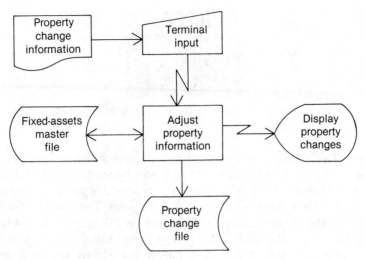

Figure 11-15   Adjusting fixed-assets records

11-13). A single file works well provided the various types of transactions are properly coded. A transaction code of NP indicates "new property," for example, whereas a transaction code of RP means "retired property."

Property Identification and Reporting

Property identification labels are prepared after new property has been added to the fixed-assets master file and after any change reports have been processed. Before identification labels are printed, a *new property register* and a *property change report* must be printed. The new property register lists all new additions and where the property is to be located. Property-control officers are responsible for checking this list and for matching it against new property reports prepared by the traffic division of a company. The property change report, produced from the property change file, lists all intra- and inter-division moves of property. This second list is also matched against property reports prepared by the traffic division.

Printing identification labels follows successful verification of both property registers. The labels themselves are either ordinary gummed labels or special-purpose metallic labels. Figure 11-16 illustrates a bar-coded label. The value of such labels is that they are easy to prepare and to read. Once printed, they are delivered to the property-control department, the staff of which is responsible for affixing all labels to company property.

Various reports are required by property-control personnel to control the movement of property in a firm. These documents include the new property report, the fixed-assets retirement report, the fixed-assets change report, showing the transfer of property from one location to another, and a special type of register called the *property-control report* (see Figure 11-17). This last report is

T10L250306

Figure 11-16 Property identification label

a register of all fixed assets arranged by asset number and location, usually by department. Other than this feature, the report by location is similar to other fixed-assets registers. Each item listed, for example, is briefly described, and the values used in calculating depreciation are given. These values include the useful life of the property, the capitalized and the salvage values, and the date of acquisition. Last, the book and tax depreciation values are compared. Current, year-to-date, and total-to-date figures are shown for book and tax depreciation.

Property-control reports, such as the report shown in Figure 11-17, are necessary for conducting physical audits and inspections of capitalized properties. Most companies schedule continual audits, so that all property is inspected, at a minimum, more than twice a year. The purpose of these audits is twofold: to determine the condition of the property and to verify its location. The condition of the property often determines whether it should be replaced or returned to the vendor for repairs. If the property is deteriorating at a faster than expected rate, it is often possible to write-off any remaining depreciation; likewise, if the property is holding up better than expected, it is advisable to slow the rate of book depreciation. The location of the property should be the same as the location specified by the property-control report; however, an audit is required to verify this assumption. If property cannot be located, an investigation should be undertaken to determine whether property has been transferred to another department (without authorization), was improperly labeled, or is missing.

If a firm is using inadequate controls, theft of company property can become a serious problem. Items such as calculators, typewriters, and even office furniture can disappear if the movement of property from one location to another goes unchecked. In some instances, locks and permanent mountings must be installed to keep certain types of equipment safe from theft. Physical audits of property help to determine whether these special safeguards are required.

Depreciation Projections and Reporting

Besides reporting on where property is located, the fixed-assets computer application must project and report on book and tax depreciation write-offs. Both types of depreciation are computed monthly. At a prescribed time, the program to update end-of-month depreciation totals is activated (see Figure 11-18). This

RUN DATE: APR 08, 19?2 - 16:36:52   M.C.B.A. DEMONSTRATION FURNITURE COMPANY   PAGE 0001

F I X E D   A S S E T   R E G I S T E R

*** BESIDE DEPR METHOD MEANS ITEM HAS BEEN SWITCHED TO STRAIGHT LINE

DEPRECIATED AS OF   1/31/

```
A ACTIVITY CODE  1=ACTIVE
C ASSET CATGORY  1=GROUP ONE    2=FULLY DEPREC   3=NON DEPRECIABLE  4=EXPENSED   5=RETIRED        6=OTHER
                                2=GROUP TWO      3=GROUP THREE                   5=DISTRIBUTION   6=SALES
T ASSET TYPE     1=NEW          2=USED           3=GROUPED          7=OTHER: PFC 100  8=OTHER: PFC 200  5=NOT DEPRECIATED
D DEPR. METHOD   1=STRAIGHT LINE  2=1.25 DECLIN BAL  3=1.5 DECLIN BAL   9=LEVEL   6=LEASED
                 7=UNIT OF PRODUC  6=ACC CST RFC SYS  9=SL WITH HALF YR  5=DBLE DECL TO SL  6=SUM OF YRS DIGS
```

ASSET-# DV LOC A C T G/L C-TX DATE-CAP UNIT-DEP EX-AMT-TX CAP-VALUE TOT-TX-DP NET-BK-VAL(TX) YTD-TX-DP						
------DESCRIPTION------ COD D-BK LF-TX LF-BK LIFE-UNT FX-AMT-BK SAL-VALUE TOT-BK-DP NET-BK-VAL(BK) YTD-BK-DP						
0197A-00006 6 7564 1 3 1 22	5 6	1/01/ 5		2,600.00 / 2,000.00	8,000.00 / 2,000.00	200.00 / 111.11	7,800.00 / 7,806.89 200.00 / 111.11
AUTOMOBILE (VEHICLE # 1)						
01978-00001 6 7564 1 3 1 22	5 6	1/13/ 5		.00 / .00	8,600.00 / 2,000.00	6,345.92 / 4,866.67	1,654.08 / 3,133.33 71.92 / 66.67
AUTOMOBILE (VEHICLE #1)						
01979-00001 5 91020 5 4 1 13	4 1	2/13/ 5		.00 / .00	30,300.00 / 5,000.00	18,600.00 / 9,583.00	11,400.00 / 20,417.00 .00 / .00
EXPERIMENTAL WIDGET BURNISHER						
01979-00002 10 91020 1 2 1 21	4 1	3/12/ 7		.00 / .00	300.00 / .00	173.08 / 82.57	126.92 / 217.43 4.08 / 3.57
STORAGE CABINET						
01979-00003 13 91020 1 1 3 11	4 1	4/05/ 6		.00 / .00	1,500.00 / 420.00	922.22 / 336.00	577.78 / 1,170.00 22.22 / 15.00
2 TYPEWRITERS						
01980-00001 10 422 1 6 1 12	4 7	10/13/ 4	15,250 / 100,010	.00 / .00	9,000.00 / 3,000.00	1,500.00 / 912.00	7,500.00 / 8,088.00 375.00 / 12.00
AUTOMOBILE (VEHICLE #3)						
01981-00001 10 91020 1 1 1 21	1 3	1/22/ 3	500,000	.00 / .00	850.27 / 160.00	20.84 / 21.26	829.43 / 829.01 20.84 / 21.26
OAK PEDESTAL DESK						
01981-00003 11 91020 4 2 1 11	3 4	1/15/ 3		2,125.14 / 2,125.14	8,500.54 / 500.00	.00 / .00	8,500.54 / 8,500.54 .00 / .00
COPYALL PHOTOCOPY MACHINE W/COLLATOR						
01981-00014 15 91204 2 3 1 13	1 4	1/25/ 5 10		.00 / .00	25,400.50 / 2,000.00	.00 / .00	25,400.50 / 25,400.50 .00 / .00
HYRISE SUPER LIFT FORK LIFT - HYDRAULIC						

Figure 11-17 Property-control report

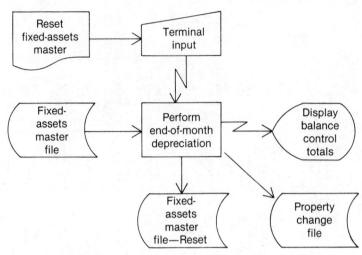

Figure 11-18 Updating end-of-month depreciation totals

program calculates current depreciation totals and updates (resets) quarter-to-date, year-to-date, and total-to-date depreciation totals. It also writes the revised totals to a new fixed-assets master file.

Once new depreciation totals are available, tax depreciation schedules can be printed. Since most business firms must pay taxes quarterly, a quarterly report showing depreciation by asset class is generally prepared. This report should be put together with care, on custom forms, and should be saved for several years to provide evidence in case of federal, state, or local tax audits. In addition to quarterly reports, most firms prepare monthly book and tax depreciation schedules that serve as supporting documents to the month-end financial statements prepared by a business. When the company books are audited by an external accounting group, the listings of depreciated assets must show where each asset can be located, so that individual assets can be visually inspected if necessary. Likewise, month-end reporting of depreciation details must be available to verify the correctness of processing. One method of verification is to calculate depreciation totals by hand and to compare these results with computer-based calculations. A small sample in this instance helps to ensure that the logic followed in programming is correct and that assets are being depreciated correctly. Another method is to add depreciation totals by hand and to compare these with processed totals. Routine tests of user-defined level totals or "break points" simplify this auditing procedure (see the Atlanta break point in Figure 11-7).

The projection of depreciation amounts is another important feature of the fixed-assets computer application. For example, the computer can be instructed to process all records stored on the fixed-assets master file in order to total the allowable depreciation (the tax write-off) for the current fiscal year, quarter by quarter. The computer would then display the results for review.

11-4 PROCESSING CONTROLS

It should be evident by now that both financial and physical controls are required in the auditing of fixed assets. Besides keeping a detailed record of all fixed-asset dollar amounts, property-control reports describe the physical location and, at times, condition of fixed-asset properties.

The batch-balance control equations important to fixed-assets processing include equations for both tax and book depreciation. For tax depreciation, the control equation is

Total fixed-assets dollar amount =
+ Last fixed-asset dollar amount
+ New property additions dollar amount
− Tax depreciation dollar amount
± Fixed-asset adjustments dollar amount

For book depreciation, the control equation is the same, except that book value dollar amounts are maintained instead of tax value dollar amounts.

As might be expected, the total fixed-asset dollar amount increases throughout the month or until the program to update end-of-month depreciation totals is activated (see Figure 11-18). At that point the total fixed-asset dollar amount is sharply reduced. More important, the difference between the old and the new fixed-asset amount should equal the "tax-depreciation-taken dollar amount" plus any special depreciation taken that has been coded as an adjustment.

Financial audits are more difficult when different types of adjustments are made. Assume, as an example, that an asset has been completely destroyed and that it is thus possible to write off any remaining fixed-asset tax or book value (including salvage value). Assume next that the program to adjust property information is activated and that action is taken to retire the asset. It is now possible to delete the fixed-asset record from the master file and to record this change on the property change file. A sort of the change file by retirement code would then show the dollar value of this and all other retired assets.

This method of processing is admittedly quite feasible, but it is not recommended. Such procedures greatly confuse the audit trail. Rather than deleting the fixed-asset record from the master file at the same time that the record is written to the property change file, it would be much safer to flag the fixed-asset record stored on the master file to show that it will be retired by the next run of the program to update end-of-month depreciation totals, and to delete the asset from the fixed-assets master file during this end-of-month run. This procedure of flagging the record preserves the audit trail. During end-of-month processing the dollar value of assets retired from the fixed-assets master file is compared with the dollar value of assets retired as shown on property change reports. For processing to be correct, the two dollar totals should be identical.

The adjustments that cause the most confusion result from assets thought to be lost and later recovered. Although several factors account for this circumstance, the most important one is the failure to report the transfer of property from one location to another. If this practice is tolerated, property-control reports will be highly inaccurate; property thought to exist will be reported as destroyed, missing, or stolen.

When property is believed to be missing, the normal business practice is to flag the property record as missing and to record the date, and to continue to depreciate the property following normal end-of-month processing instructions. This procedure continues until a complete physical inventory cycle has been completed. If the missing property has not been found by this time, the asset is retired, and processing control totals are changed as required.

11-5 MANAGEMENT IMPLICATIONS

Financial managers of a business come to rely heavily on the fixed-assets computer application once it is installed. Two immediate uses of the application are in the control of business property and in the preparation of federal and state tax reports. Many companies benefit simply from knowing where property is located and whether it is in service. This information permits equipment not in use in one department to be transferred to another department where it is needed. Expenditures for duplicate equipment are avoided when such transfers are successful.

Keeping accurate fixed-assets records and preparing numerous federal and state tax reports is another major reason for automating fixed-assets processing. Management quickly discovers that an online approach can save hundreds of hours of clerical and managerial time. With direct inquiry and updating capabilities, for example, records can be retrieved and modified instantly; complicated summary reports can be prepared in hours. This application replaces the age-old procedure of manually attempting to locate a record in massive fixed-asset storage files, delivering the record to the financial department, adding new information to the record, recording the details of processing on a summary log, and returning the record to the file. Later on, the summary details would be consolidated for reporting purposes.

Two additional reasons for implementing the fixed-assets application are that it helps financial officers determine depreciation patterns and trends and establish equipment-replacement policies. As Figure 11-19 shows, projections of depreciation are generally arranged by asset class, or by asset class within each division of a company. The value of this type of projection is that it helps the financial officers of a business to pinpoint when and where depreciation totals will turn down sharply. In Figure 11-19, for example, depreciation totals are quite level during the first and second quarters. During the second and third quarters, however, there is a downward drop in the depreciation totals, caused by reduced allowable depreciation for machinery. Further inspection of the situation would reveal that three large pieces of equipment will be fully depreciated by the third quarter of the year.

When combined with projected acquisitions of plant and equipment, fixed-

| ASSET | QUARTER | | | |
CLASS	FIRST	SECOND	THIRD	FOURTH
BUILDING	326,000	320,000	314,000	308,000
FURNITURE	195,600	188,600	185,400	182,614
TRANSPORTATION	118,456	109,214	101,942	93,114
MACHINERY	532,496	512,331	424,431	416,210
OTHER	156,090	151,612	147,314	143,110
TOTAL	1,328,642	1,281,757	1,173,087	1,143,048

Figure 11-19 Tax depreciation projection

assets depreciation projections take on special importance. They help financial officers to determine when funds will be available to acquire new plant and equipment, when depreciation accounts need to be built up, what types of assets are aging faster than others, and what effects new acquisitions will have on depreciation totals. As we will see shortly in Chapter 14, projected depreciation totals are vital to budget and profit planning. It can be shown, for example, that unless carefully planned, the expense known as depreciation can confuse corporate earnings. Highly cyclical earnings may be due in large part to highly variable depreciation dollar totals.

REVIEW OF IMPORTANT IDEAS

Properties with a fixed life of more than one year must be capitalized and depreciated. These properties are called fixed assets.

The fixed-assets computer application is greatly affected by federal and state tax legislation. The Accelerated Cost Recovery System (ACRS), enacted in 1981, simplifies the reporting of depreciation; however, the rules only apply to 1981 or later purchases. Assets acquired before this time are depreciated using straight-line, declining-balance, and sum-of-the-years-digits methods. Also, if assets were purchased after 1970, they can be written off using the CLADR system of depreciation.

Preliminary processing of fixed-assets records must be designed into the accounts payable computer application. Fixed-asset details are extracted from other payables at this time and are written to a file of payables to be capitalized.

The program to enter new property information adds three types of information needed to fully describe fixed assets: property-control, insurance and replacement, and depreciation and tax information. Once keyed, this new information is merged with information extracted from payables processing. The completed fixed-assets record is written to the fixed-assets master file.

Records placed on the master file are used in a variety of ways. Several reports and displays provide comprehensive summaries of current, year-to-date, and cumulative depreciation for each asset stored on file. A complete set of registers and a variety of tax reports are also produced. Depreciation projections, annual summaries, and analyses of insurance value and replacement costs are printed.

From time to time it is necessary to make adjustments to property records. An important adjustment is to switch from one method of depreciation to another in order to improve the cash-flow position of a business.

Property labels and property-control reports are important products of processing. If adequte controls are in place, the theft of company property becomes more difficult. Moreover, property-control reports simplify physical audits and inspections.

End-of-month processing of fixed-assets records must be done with great care. The main processing control equations are designed to account for all tax and book depreciation dollar amounts. Adjustments must be treated differently. Records stored on the master file are flagged as well as written to the property change file. When flagged records are deleted from the master file their dollar totals are cross-checked. The dollar total deleted must match the dollar total written to the change file.

Financial managers rely heavily on the fixed-assets application. It helps them to manage different types of complicated property records and to produce numerous book and tax depreciation reports. Managers use the application to determine depreciation patterns and to establish which types of assets to replace.

KEY WORDS

Depreciation	Tax depreciation method
Tax write-off	Book depreciation method
Fixed asset	Investment tax credit
Accelerated Cost Recovery System	Insurance-value analyses
Straight-line method	Extract slip
Declining-balance method	Property identification label
Sum-of-the-years-digits method	New property register
Class Life Asset Depreciation Range	Property change report
Capitalize	Property-control report
Fixed-assets master file	

REVIEW QUESTIONS

1. Property is depreciable if it meets which four federal requirements?

2. Explain the main difference between the ACRS and the CLADR systems of depreciation.

3. Name the three methods of calculating business depreciation.

4. When can additional first-year depreciation be deducted?

5. What information is stored on the file of payables to be capitalized? On the fixed-assets master file?

6. When depreciating an asset, why do firms sometimes switch from one method of depreciation to another?

7. What three types of information are contained on the new property report?

8. What is the difference between book depreciation and tax depreciation? Between book value and tax value?

9. What is an investment tax credit? Why is such a credit important in fixed-assets processing?

10. What information is contained in the book depreciation expense report?

11. Why are depreciation-projection capabilities built into the fixed-assets design?

12. How is the new property file used in processing?

13. List the main types of adjustments that are made to records stored on the fixed-assets master file.

14. What must be done before property identification labels are printed?

15. List several uses of property-control reports.

16. What processing functions are accomplished by the program to update end-of-month depreciation totals?

17. Explain how adjustments to processing complicate the process of financial auditing.

18. How should fixed-assets records be treated when property is reported as missing?

19. How can the fixed-assets application indirectly reduce duplicate equipment expenditures?

20. Name four reasons for implementing the fixed-assets computer application.

EXERCISES

1. Figure 11-20 illustrates a more direct way of updating the fixed-assets master file. Instead of using the intermediate step of writing records to the file of payables to be capitalized (see Figure 11-10), new fixed-assets records can be added as part of payables processing.

   (a) Explain the advantages of this more direct design.

   (b) Explain the disadvantages of this design.

   (c) Explain which design you prefer and the reasons for your choice.

2. Compute the first, second, and third year's depreciation on a $100,000 piece of equipment using each of the following methods of depreciation. (Assume that the property has a useful life of five years and that after this period will have no salvage value.)

   (a) straight-line method

   (b) 1.5 declining-balance method

   (c) 2.0 declining-balance method

   (d) sum-of-the-years-digits method

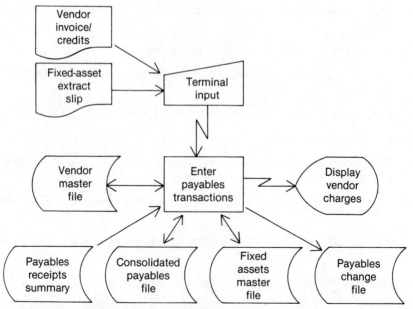

Figure 11-20 Adding fixed-asset records directly

3. Suppose the equipment considered above must be depreciated using ACRS, which specifies a three-year recovery period.

   (a) Compute the first, second, and third year's depreciation using the Accelerated Cost Recovery Table (see Figure 11-1).

   (b) Compare these results with the answers to Exercise 2. What conclusions can you make?

4. Design two or more systems flowcharts to show the batch processing steps required to produce the new property register, the fixed-assets change register, and property identification labels. Remember that identification labels are changed from time to time.

12

Employee Payroll

The employee payroll is often one of the first, if not the first, computer applications developed by a business. Historically, the reasons for automating payroll processing have included the following: faster processing of payroll checks and payroll reports, more accurate processing of payroll records, improved capability to meet governmental reporting requirements, and improved capability to analyze employee payroll data. More often than not, a batch design was used for payroll processing. The advantages of batch processing—at least several years ago—were that the payroll application was relatively easy to install and to maintain, and that it was able consistently to accomplish its purpose, namely, placing employee paychecks in the hands of employees on or before the scheduled date of payment.

Although batch designs of payroll processing continue to be popular, there are special reasons for installing a combined interactive and batch design. As this chapter shows, interactive processing simplifies even further the maintenance of this application. Specifically, interactive steps simplify the adjusting of employee records, the entry and verification of hours-worked information, the retrieval of data stored on computer files, the adding of new employees, and the routine checking of processing controls.

Central to the design of the employee payroll application is the *employee master file*. As with other master files, the employee master file contains a record for every employee. A unique feature of this master file is that it usually contains both personal and payroll data elements. *Personal elements* describe the individual and include such items as the person's name, date of birth, race, and sex. *Payroll elements* describe the terms and condition of payment. This part of the employee's record contains such items as wage or salary, payroll deductions, current earnings, and year-to-date (YTD) earnings.

Placing both personal and payroll information on a single record simplifies the employee payroll processing design; however, it complicates maintenance of the file. Traditionally, the personnel department of a business has been responsible for gathering and feeding personal information into processing, and the payroll department has been responsible for payroll information. With batch processing, this division often meant that two separate runs were required to update the employee master file: one to add personnel-related information to the file and one to add payroll information. The alternative was to use a single form and to pass the form from one department to another. After personnel had added their elements, payroll would add theirs. Next, each completed form would be keypunched; all keypunched cards would be processed.

The problems arose at this point in processing, when the edit report, produced by processing, needed to be reviewed by staff in both the personnel and payroll departments. This dual review created both security and privacy problems, took substantial time, and led to interdepartmental conflicts—especially when one department thought the other was responsible for making the majority of the errors. Today, interactive processing has considerably reduced these problems. A single processing menu, with separate file-updating selections, for example, keeps personnel and payroll data-entry activities quite distinct. People in one department are not allowed to review the information entered into processing by the other, or to notice the errors made by people in another department. Moreover, using the computer to inform data-entry personnel of input errors means that errors are reduced, and there are fewer opportunities for interdepartmental conflicts.

12-1 PRELIMINARY OVERVIEW OF PROCESSING

Figure 12-1 provides a preliminary processing overview of the employee payroll computer application. In many ways, payroll processing is similar to the processing required for the finished-goods application. Several things must be done before the employee master file is set to compute employee pay. All personal and payroll changes must be made *prior to* calculating employee pay, for example. Likewise, the number of hours worked for hourly employees must be entered into processing, since these numbers will be multiplied by employee hourly wages to determine employee gross pay.

The six steps shown in Figure 12-1 can be summarized as follows.

1. *Enter personal changes* adds new employees to the employee master file and makes changes to personal information previously stored on employee records.

2. *Enter payroll changes* adds new payroll information to employee records and makes changes to previously stored payroll information.

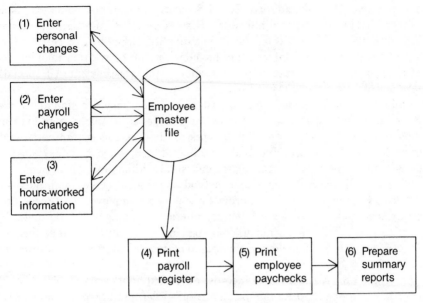

Figure 12-1 Six steps in processing the employee payroll

3. *Enter hours-worked information* verifies and records the number of hours worked by an employee.

4. *Print payroll register* documents employee gross pay, the deductions from gross pay, and employee net pay (take-home pay).

5. *Print employee paychecks* produces employee payroll voucher-checks.

6. *Print summary reports* provides a summary of departmental labor costs and labor cost breakdowns, such as the cost of labor by product, project, line of production, or work order.

Inputs to Processing

The three main inputs to the employee payroll application are new employee forms, employee change forms, and employee time cards. Information from all three forms must be keyed to processing. However, this data-entry work is done to ready the employee master file. The master file serves as the main input to later stages in processing, including the printing of employee paychecks.

The input forms required by this application may differ considerably from one firm to another. If firms place information from personnel and payroll departments on a single form, the keyed inputs to processing usually conform to the following descriptions.

New employee forms are custom-printed data-entry sheets that are used to create an employee record. They are filled in, in part, by the employee. Items such as employee name, address, Social Security number, and home telephone number are supplied by the individual. Besides personal information, job and wage information is placed on the form. Supplied either by the personnel or payroll department, this information includes the job or position number, the department, the hourly rate of pay (or salary), the overtime rate (if special), and the deductions to be taken from gross pay.

Employee change forms are also custom printed. They are similar to new employee forms, except that they show the changes to be made to an existing employee record. The most common types of changes concern an employee's status (active, inactive, terminated), mailing address, wage or salary, marital status, number of dependents, federal and state withholding, deduction withholding (usually several types), and method of payment (take, mail, deposit). This list of changes suggests the order for a possible employee master-file processing menu. As we will see later on, interactive changes can be made by selecting items from such a menu, or by placing a copy of the change form on the terminal screen and keying in changes to match the information recorded on the form.

Employee time cards (or time records) document hours worked, generally by department number, project number, and work-order number or job number (or both). As Figure 12-2 shows, time cards include some preprinted information such as the name of the employee, employee number, shift, and department number. The hours worked are then itemized and totaled. Space is provided on the card for the employee's signature. Last, regular and overtime hours worked are generally recorded and totaled separately.

Once the employee master file is updated, it becomes the main input to processing. Figure 12-3 shows the file segments and the data elements associated with each segment for a single employee record. It also shows the relationship between time-reporting information, which is keyed into processing, and information stored on the master file. As illustrated, the number of stored items is considerable compared with the key-entry requirements.

Keyed time-reporting information begins with the entry of the payroll number, a record code, and the employee number. The *payroll number* is necessary when a company prepares different types of payrolls (weekly, bi-weekly, bi-monthly, and monthly). The *record code* is needed to back out data entered into processing in error. For example, eight hours of sick leave might have been mistakenly entered instead of eight hours of vacation time. The *employee number* is unique (one for each employee) and is required to locate an employee's record stored on the employee master file. With payroll processing, information is not transferred from the payroll master file to a payroll transaction file. Instead, the hours worked are added to the master file. The keying of time-reporting information thus updates the employee master file.

Because of the importance of the employee master file to processing, we need to be aware of how the file is organized. The six record segments illustrated by Figure 12-3 are as follows.

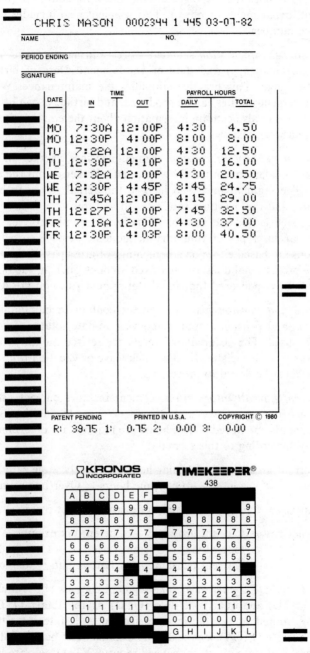

Figure 12-2 Employee time card

- The *employee name and address* segment contains the employee's name and generally both the employee's home and work addresses (for the latter, the plant, department, or office). This segment also includes one or more telephone numbers.

- The *personnel information* segment stores affirmative action information (sex, race, handicaps) and date of employment. Date of birth is stored rather than age. This practice simplifies file maintenance. With date of birth, retirement profiles can be produced, and birthdays can be recognized. This section can also contain information about the employee's educational history and work history.

- The *wage and salary information* segment specifies whether an employee is to be paid a salary or an hourly wage, and whether or not the employee is exempt. The segment may also include the actual salary to be paid, the wage rate, and the overtime rate, as well as three accumulation rates: for vacation, sick leave, and pension. Finally, the number of tax exemptions and the various types of voluntary deductions must be stored. Voluntary deductions are based either on a percentage of gross pay, such as deductions for some professional dues, or on a fixed amount, such as $50.00 per month for a company-sponsored Individual Retirement Account (IRA).

- The *leave and pension history* segment contains accumulated vacation, sick leave, and pension amounts and year-to-date totals for vacation and sick leave used. The accumulated totals are revised monthly, prior to preparing the payroll register. If either sick leave or vacation time is used, the amounts must be keyed to processing.

- The *current payroll information* segment includes current gross pay, all deductions from gross pay, and current net pay. In addition, regular and overtime hours are stored. These hours are required for determining current gross pay, according to this formula:

$$\text{Current gross pay} = \text{Regular hours} \times \text{Hourly wage rate} + \text{Overtime hours} \times \text{Overtime wage rate}$$

By comparison, the equation used in determining net pay is:

$$\text{Current net pay} = \text{Current gross pay} - \text{Current tax exempt} - \text{Current federal tax} - \text{Current state tax} - \text{Current FICA} - \text{Current pension} - \text{Current voluntary deductions}$$

- The *YTD and QTD payroll history* segment consists of accumulated year-to-date (YTD) and quarter-to-date (QTD) payroll totals. QTD totals are generally limited to taxable income, federal and state tax withheld, and Social Security (FICA) withheld. These totals must be reset after producing federal and state quarterly payroll reports. YTD totals are kept for two reasons: for showing employees how dollars have been allocated throughout

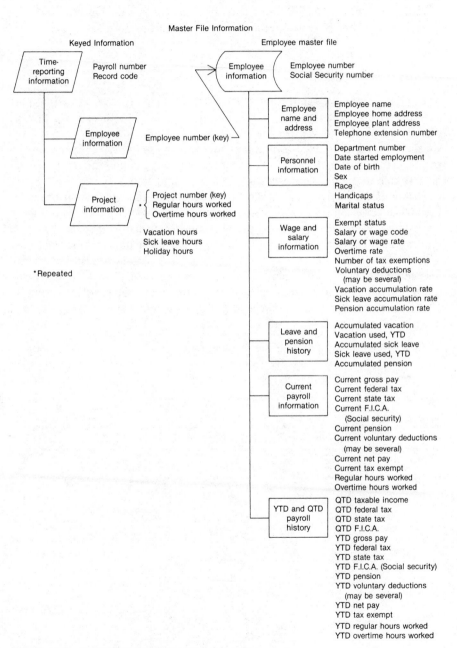

Master File Information

Keyed Information

Employee master file

Time-reporting information | Payroll number
Record code

Employee information | Employee number
Social Security number

Employee information | Employee number (key)

Employee name and address | Employee name
Employee home address
Employee plant address
Telephone extension number

Project information | Project number (key)
Regular hours worked
Overtime hours worked

Vacation hours
Sick leave hours
Holiday hours

Personnel information | Department number
Date started employment
Date of birth
Sex
Race
Handicaps
Marital status

*Repeated

Wage and salary information | Exempt status
Salary or wage code
Salary or wage rate
Overtime rate
Number of tax exemptions
Voluntary deductions
(may be several)
Vacation accumulation rate
Sick leave accumulation rate
Pension accumulation rate

Leave and pension history | Accumulated vacation
Vacation used, YTD
Accumulated sick leave
Sick leave used, YTD
Accumulated pension

Current payroll information | Current gross pay
Current federal tax
Current state tax
Current F.I.C.A.
(Social security)
Current pension
Current voluntary deductions
(may be several)
Current net pay
Current tax exempt
Regular hours worked
Overtime hours worked

YTD and QTD payroll history | QTD taxable income
QTD federal tax
QTD state tax
QTD F.I.C.A.
YTD gross pay
YTD federal tax
YTD state tax
YTD F.I.C.A. (Social security)
YTD pension
YTD voluntary deductions
(may be several)
YTD net pay
YTD tax exempt
YTD regular hours worked
YTD overtime hours worked

Figure 12-3   Relationships between payroll data sets

the calendar year and for reporting required information to federal and state governments. YTD totals must be reset after producing year-end payroll reports and W-2 federal and state tax-reporting forms.

Outputs from Processing

The employee payroll application produces three main types of printed outputs and several different types of online output displays. The three main printed outputs are the employee payroll register, the payroll journal, and employee voucher-checks. Both fixed-format and ad hoc displays are typically used. If an inquiry-and-reporting facility is built into processing, nonprogramming personnel are able to design their own display screens and summary tables.

The *employee payroll register* lists the information to be placed on employee voucher-checks; control totals are also listed. As the register presented in Figure 12-4 shows, three lines per employee are required to list all pertinent payroll information. The first line begins with the department number and continues with the employee number, type, salary, and YTD payroll totals. The second line continues with the employee name, weeks worked, and current payroll totals. Payroll control totals are placed at the bottom of the register. As Figure 12-4 shows, the difference between YTD figures before and after processing must be equal to current payroll totals. That is,

YTD gross amount out = YTD gross amount in + Current gross amount

```
WED, SEP 23, 198-                          M.C.B.A. Demonstration Furniture Company                              PAGE 0001
3:29 PM
                                             P A Y R O L L   R E G I S T E R

FOR DEPARTMENT: 1000
FOR THE PAY PERIOD ENDING 07/14/8-        EMPLOYEE TYPES:  H = HOURLY  S = SALARY        CHECK TYPES:  R = REGULAR   V = VACATION
FREQUENCIES USED ON THIS RUN:  THIS PAY PERIOD: ALL
VACATION CHECK 1: NONE    VACATION CHECK 2: NONE    VACATION CHECK 3: NONE    VACATION CHECK 4: NONE

DEPT# EMP# EMP-TYP CHK-TYP  SALARY  REG-PAY  HOL-PAY     YTD-GROSS  YTD-TX-GRS  YTD-FICA  YTD-FWT   YTD-SWT   YTD-OST   YTD-CWT  OTH-DED
NAME                        WKS-WRK  OVT-PAY  SICK-PAY       GROSS   TXBL-GROSS     FICA      FWT       SWT       OST       CWT   NET-PAY
      SOC-SEC-#             SUP-PAY  VAC-PAY  SPEC-PAY

1000  100000  S        R   450.00     .00      .00    10,236.85   9,712.00    811.67  1,781.02   520.00    16.96     .00     27.50
Whittenhaus, Robert W.        1.00     .00      .00       475.00     475.00     29.69     76.54      .00     2.38     .00    338.89
      324-58-4201             .00      .00      .00

                    OTHER EARNINGS    25.00 PRFTSHR TXBL

      300000  H        R      .00   300.00      .00     8,946.00   8,540.00    327.49    929.45   130.00    12.21     .00     73.52
Jones, Phillip                1.00   51.25      .00       351.25     351.25     21.95     65.50      .00     1.76     .00    188.52
      654-63-5464             .00      .00      .00

      500000  S        R  1,500.00     .00      .00    50,700.00  44,000.00  2,400.00 11,569.04  4,250.00     .00     .00 1,071.42
Hall, Fredrick J.             1.00     .00      .00     1,500.00   1,500.00      .00    428.58      .00      .00     .00       .00
      346-41-6354             .00      .00      .00

ONE OR MORE DEDUCTIONS COULD NOT BE TAKEN ON THE ABOVE CHECK BECAUSE THE NET PAY WAS ZERO

      600000  H        R      .00 7,540.00      .00     8,375.00   8,375.00    523.44  2,236.03      .00    30.00     .00 1,017.49
Marianias, Markos            13.00     .00      .00     7,685.00   7,685.00    490.31  2,032.45      .00    26.55     .00  4,128.20
      654-75-6558             .00      .00    145.00

THE ABOVE CHECK HAD ONE OR MORE CALCULATIONS WHICH EXCEEDED THE ALLOWABLE MAXIMUM

      4 CHECKS TO BE PRINTED        4 REGULAR        0 VACATION

DEPARTMENT TOTALS:                                  YTD-IN      THIS PERIOD      YTD-OUT
            SAL-PAY:    1,950.00     GROSS:      68,246.60     10,011.25      78,257.85
            REG-PAY:    7,840.00     TX-GRS:     60,615.75     10,011.25      70,627.00
            OVT-PAY:       51.25     FICA:        3,530.65        531.95       4,062.60
            VAC-PAY:         .00     FWT:        13,912.47      2,603.07      16,515.54
            HOL-PAY:         .00     EIC:              .00                          .00
            SICK-PAY:        .00     SWT:         4,900.00           .00       4,900.00
            SPEC-PAY:     145.00     OST:            28.48         30.69          59.17
            SUPP-PAY:        .00     CWT:              .00           .00            .00
                                     NET:                       4,655.61
            PRFTSHR        25.00

DEPARTMENT TOTAL: EMPLOYER FICA LIABILITY                          531.95
```

Figure 12-4 Payroll register

Or, as shown for department 1000,

$$\$78,257.85 = \$68,246.60 + \$10,011.25$$

Control totals thus help to verify the correctness of accumulated totals, including the federal withholding total (FWT) and the state withholding total (SWT).

Employee voucher-checks are printed following the review and approval of the payroll register. As Figure 12-5 shows, an employee voucher-check is a two-part form. The voucher portion provides the employee with an earnings record showing the dollar amounts leading to gross pay and the dollar amounts subtracted from gross pay to arrive at net pay. The check portion of the form is negotiable. The printed face amount of the check is equal to the net pay amount printed on the check-voucher.

Payroll journals represent another important type of computer-printed output. A *payroll journal* is prepared to summarize payroll costs, by department, job class, budget number, general ledger number, project number, or some other classification important to a company. These journals feature a summary page and detail pages. As Figure 12-6 shows, the summary page of a labor-cost-

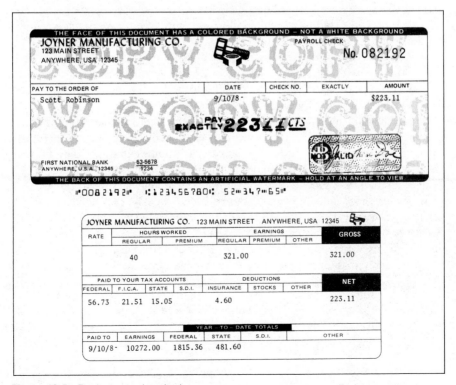

Figure 12-5 Employee voucher-check

Payroll Journal-Budget Number Breakdowns
Pay Period 42   Payroll Period 11/6/

Budget Number	Dollar Amount	Description
501-006	$24,713.60	Direct Labor
502-011	19,726.54	Indirect Labor
503-141	8,911.14	Overtime Premium
506-008	19,600.18	Salaries-Direct
507-057	24,101.14	Salaries-Indirect
724-211	7,278.95	FICA Withheld
724-215	15,043.15	Federal Tax Withheld
724-221	5,823.12	State Tax Withheld
724-225	1,941.05	Federal Unemployment
724-231	680.42	State Unemployment
724-542	6,793.60	ERISA

Figure 12-6   Payroll journal summary totals

by-budget-number payroll journal provides a breakdown of payroll costs by major expense category. The detail supporting this summary page is then attached. A typical detail page prints individual employee totals by budget number, by department. These subtotals, in turn, are carried forward and printed on the summary. If the summary figures look unusual (if they are either too high or too low), individual employee payments are inspected to determine whether the figures appearing on the journal differ from the employee-hours-worked figures initially sent to payroll for processing.

One of the real values of an interactive approach to processing is that individual payroll records can be displayed and examined rather than printed. As Figure 12-7 shows, some employee displays are quite extensive: they provide personal, wage and salary, and payroll history facts and totals. The display of Michael Johnannes's employee record, for example, tells us several things: that he wants his check mailed, is married, and is paid weekly; that he is paid $5.75 per hour; and that his taxable wages for the fourth quarter were $2,101.05.

Ad hoc displays are also extremely useful. As Figure 12-8 shows, an ad hoc display requires the user to specify the type of information required, using worded (rather than number-coded) inquiry commands, such as

FIND PERSONNEL WITH NAME = DAVENPORT OR ALEXANDER

Following the entry of an inquiry command, reporting requirements are specified. In the display in Figure 12-8, the user instructs the computer to

DISPLAY FIRST-NAME NAME AGE SEX SALARY.

If this instruction is acceptable, the computer responds with the word "Ac-

```
DATE    8/15/--                   PAYROLL                   INQUIRY      AMPTI2 W2
                    EMPLOYEE NUMBER              140
COMPANY 01      NAME        MICHAEL JOHNANNES              HIRE DATE  1/01/75
                ADDRESS     28 APPLE ROAD                  TERM DATE  0/00/00
                CITY ST ZIP MENLO PARK, CA      94025      MAIL CHK   N
                                                           PENSION    N
SHIFT 1  DEPT DP20                OCCUPATION PACKER        WRKMNS COMP CD 00002

MARITAL    M     FIT APPLY   Y     STATE  100    REG HRS WORKED           .00
MINORITY         FICA APPLY  Y     COUNTY 000    OVT HRS WORKED           .00
PAY TYPE   H     FED EXEMP  03     LOCAL  000    HOL HRS PAID             .00
PAY FREQ   WK    EXTRA %    .0     UNION  001    VAC HRS PAID           72.00
PROTECT          EXTRA $  20.00                  SICK HR PAID           40.00

SALARY       .00  REG RATE  5.750  OVT RATE  8.625  PREM RATE 11.500

QTR       FIT         FICA      GROSS WAGES    TAXABLE WAGES  SICK PAY   WKS WRK
 1      637.05      117.58      3,054.35        3,034.85         .00       13
 2      588.60      163.92      3,054.35        2,801.40      234.95       12
 3      756.36      149.64      3,605.98        3,582.96         .00       14
 4      441.45      122.94      2,114.55        2,101.05         .00        9
TOTAL 2,423.46      554.08     11,829.23       11,520.26      234.95       48

                                       CK24 END OF INQUIRY
```

Figure 12-7 Employee payroll display

cepted." Last, the computer displays the number of records that satisfy the conditions specified by the inquiry command. As shown, the computer reports "7 records found"; the computer lists these records and prints "end of report" to tell the user that processing has been completed.

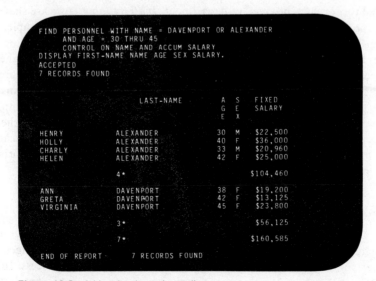

Figure 12-8 Ad hoc inquiry and reporting

12-2 PAYROLL PROCESSING

Figure 12-9 shows the systems organization chart for the employee payroll computer application; Figure 12-10 illustrates the corresponding program-processing menu. Of the five interactive programs, three are required to update the employee master file. The first of these, *ready employee master,* is designed to add, change, or delete employee name-and-address and other personnel information. The second, *ready payroll master,* is designed to add, change, or delete the following master file segments: wage and salary, leave and pension, current payroll, and YTD and QTD payroll history information. The third, *reset payroll master,* is designed to reset current payroll totals to zero, thus making the master file ready for the next payroll-processing period. As we discussed earlier in the chapter, two ready-master-file programs, instead of one, are used so that the personnel and payroll departments of a company can maintain different sections of the single employee master file.

The single display program illustrated in Figures 12-9 and 12-10 generally leads to a secondary menu showing various types of display options. One display might be restricted to personnel information for an employee; another might be restricted to the employee's name and payroll information. Then, in addition, a series of summary displays is generally available. An operator might, for example, instruct the computer to "display departmental payroll costs." In this instance, the name, hours worked, and gross pay for each employee assigned to a department would be listed. Other summary displays show payroll costs by plant (where there are several plants), payroll costs by labor class, and payroll costs by work order. Most companies also display direct costs in order to compare them with indirect costs. *Direct labor costs* are costs that can be directly assigned to a project, product, or department. *Indirect labor costs* are shared by several projects, products, or departments. Janitorial service, for example, is an indirect labor cost if the work done is for several departments.

The batch portion of payroll processing includes programs designed to produce and summarize the current payroll and programs designed to prepare quarterly and year-end statements and listings. Current payroll programs lead to the printing of the payroll register, the hours-worked register, employee paychecks, and payroll journals. Current backup programs produce the employee master register and the employee change report. Quarterly and year-end programs for this design are limited to two: one to print quarterly reports and one to print year-end reports.

Update Employee Master File Programs

Before time cards are processed by a company, the personnel and payroll departments must collect and enter into processing all employee changes. The flowcharts in Figures 12-11 and 12-12 show this file-updating process. In Figure 12-11, processing begins upon completion of the *employee change form,*

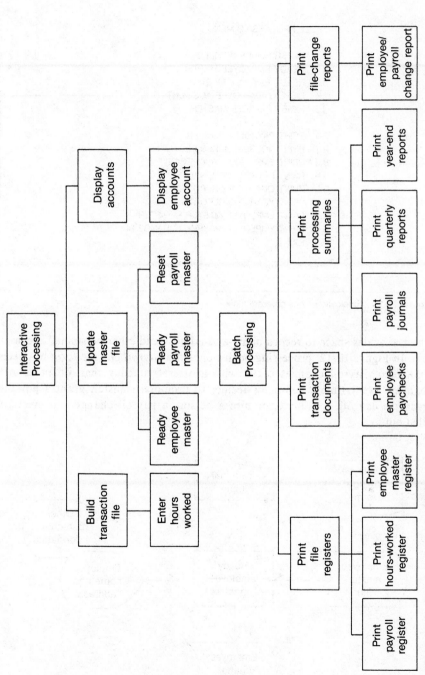

Figure 12-9 Payroll systems organization chart

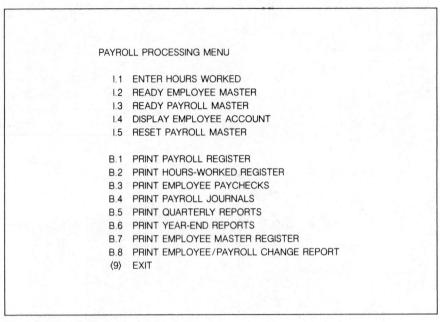

PAYROLL PROCESSING MENU

I.1 ENTER HOURS WORKED
I.2 READY EMPLOYEE MASTER
I.3 READY PAYROLL MASTER
I.4 DISPLAY EMPLOYEE ACCOUNT
I.5 RESET PAYROLL MASTER

B.1 PRINT PAYROLL REGISTER
B.2 PRINT HOURS-WORKED REGISTER
B.3 PRINT EMPLOYEE PAYCHECKS
B.4 PRINT PAYROLL JOURNALS
B.5 PRINT QUARTERLY REPORTS
B.6 PRINT YEAR-END REPORTS
B.7 PRINT EMPLOYEE MASTER REGISTER
B.8 PRINT EMPLOYEE/PAYROLL CHANGE REPORT
(9) EXIT

Figure 12-10 Employee payroll program menu

which provides space to record name-and-address and other personnel information. In Figure 12-12, processing begins once the *payroll change form* has been completed. Payroll changes occur with greater frequency than do personnel changes. Every time a company decides to promote, transfer, grant a pay increase to, lay off, terminate, or hire a person, a payroll change slip must be filled out.

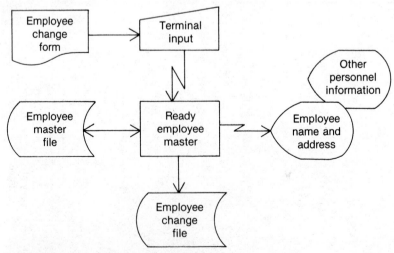

Figure 12-11 Entering personnel changes

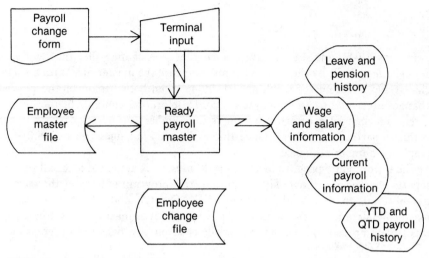

Figure 12-12 Entering payroll changes

Computer processing of either payroll or personnel change forms is greatly simplified with interactive programs. After selecting the option to alter personnel information, for example, the user might be presented with a file-change menu such as that shown in the top section of Figure 12-13. Following the display of the employee number and name, the computer asks:

DO YOU WISH TO CHANGE:
    1. EMPLOYEE NUMBER?
    2. SOCIAL SECURITY NUMBER?
    3. EMPLOYEE NAME?

and so on. The user responds by entering the number of the appropriate question—a "3," for example, if a name change is required—in the designated "enter changes" area of the display. After all changes have been indicated by number, a "12" (exit) is entered. This tells the computer to begin processing the file changes indicated and to exit once the last change has been made.

Suppose for the moment that this menu is presented and that only a name change is required. The user simply enters, "3" and then "12." Next, a name-change display screen is presented, like that shown in the bottom section of Figure 12-13. After the name change is made, the employee name currently stored on file and the revised name are both displayed. Before the employee record is updated, the user must verify the newly keyed information. The computer asks:

IS THIS NAME CORRECT?

If the user indicates "no" instead of "yes," the computer responds with one or more questions such as:

DO YOU WISH TO ENTER A DIFFERENT NAME?

or,

DO YOU WISH TO EXIT?

Figures 12-11 and 12-12 have shown that one change file, the *employee change file,* is built by the two programs to update the master file. With a single change file it becomes possible to determine when both personnel and payroll changes are made to an employee's record. Before the contents of the file are listed, all changes are sorted by employee number (or by employee number within department number). Once this is done the changes can be printed in employee-number sequence.

The third update program, *reset payroll master,* is activated after all payroll reports have been printed. The purpose of this program is to reset the current payroll totals to zero, while retaining all YTD totals and all other employee-master-file detail. As a general rule, a new employee master file is created by this step in processing; the old master file is saved as a backup to processing.

The Enter Hours Worked Program

This program is designed to accomplish several things: it edits hours-worked information entered into processing, computes gross and net pay, updates the employee master file, and writes all time-keeping and payroll information to the hours-worked (and to be paid) file. The flowchart in Figure 12-14 illustrates the steps important to this interactive program. As shown, the employee master file and the project master file are updated by processing. The actual steps in processing are as follows.

1. The employee number, project number, and hours-worked totals are entered into processing and verified.

2. If all numbers are correct, current payroll information is calculated.

3. Following pay calculations, the record segments of the employee master file for current payroll, leave and pension, and YTD and QTD payroll history are updated.

4. Hours worked and labor costs are transferred to update the project master file.

There are good reasons for updating both the employee master and the project master files at the same time. This design step blocks data-in-error from being posted incorrectly to work activities, such as projects, work orders, or work centers. In processing, two keys must be initially verified: the employee number and the project number. If either is incorrect—the right employee working on the incorrect project, or the wrong employee working on a correct project—it becomes impossible to add labor hours into processing.

EMPLOYEE NUMBER: 52314   NAME: JOHNSON, SILVIA ANN

DO YOU WISH TO CHANGE:

1. EMPLOYEE NUMBER?   7.   DATE STARTED EMPLOYMENT?
2. SOCIAL SECURITY NUMBER?   8.   SEX?
3. EMPLOYEE NAME?   9.   RACE?
4. EMPLOYEE HOME ADDRESS?   10.   HANDICAPS?
5. EMPLOYEE PLANT ADDRESS?   11.   MARITAL STATUS?
6. TELEPHONE EXTENSION NUMBER?   (12)   EXIT

ENTER CHANGES: FIRST: _____
                 NEXT: _____
                 NEXT: _____

EMPLOYEE NAME CHANGE

THE EMPLOYEE NAME STORED ON FILE IS:

LAST NAME   JOHNSON
FIRST NAME   SILVIA
MIDDLE NAME   ANN

THE NAME SHOULD BE CHANGED TO (IF NO CHANGE PRESS RETURN):

LAST NAME   PORTER
FIRST NAME
MIDDLE NAME

THE REVISED EMPLOYEE NAME IS: PORTER, SILVIA ANN
IS THIS CORRECT?

Figure 12-13   Entering a name change

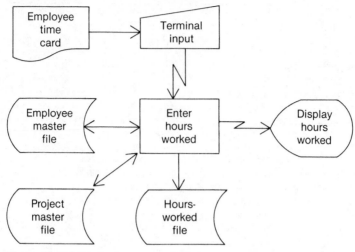

Figure 12-14 Entering hours-worked details

Some firms have found it desirable to replace time-reporting cards with employee identification badges and to enter employee times directly into processing using one-way data collection terminals. To record the start time of work in this processing design, the employee inserts the badge into the terminal, and the employee number printed on the badge is read and transmitted to processing. The computer adds the employee number to the department number and enters the time of day (the start time). These three pieces of information are stored on an employee time-keeping file. Similarly, when the employee leaves the work area, he or she once again inserts the badge into the data collection terminal, and the employee number is logged, together with the department number and time of day. By matching these two sets of data, the computer determines the difference between the start and stop times and stores the information on the employee time-keeping file. Then, at the end of a designated period, such as a work day or a work week, these time-keeping files are sorted by employee number and batch processed to produce an hours-worked register, which lists both the total hours worked by each employee, by work area, and the combined total of the hours worked for all employees, by work area. The employee time-keeping file is also input to the employee payroll computer application to produce voucher-checks. First, however, the file must be adjusted to enter into processing any sick leave or vacation time. If an employee is to be paid for work done while away from a work area, this too must be entered into processing.

Employee Payroll Registers

After hours-worked information has been successfully entered into processing, the employee master file is closed from further modification, and the *payroll register* is printed. As shown earlier, this register provides a breakdown of employee earnings and deductions from earnings (see Figure 12-4). It also provides control totals to help verify the correctness of processing and serves as a legal document suitable for longer-term storage. It fully documents the voucher portion of employee paychecks. These vouchers and actual paychecks are printed after the register is reviewed and approved.

Two additional registers, besides the payroll register, document the results of payroll processing. The first of these, the *hours-worked register,* is printed following a sort of the hours-worked file (see Figure 12-15), which is a combined transaction and change file: it stores all information keyed to processing and all corresponding changes to the employee and project master files. The hours-worked register contains considerably more detail than is shown on the payroll register. It shows what data were keyed to processing and how these data were converted to dollars-paid totals. It shows if any adjusting entries were keyed and processed, and it shows dollar control totals. The dollars posted both to the employee master file and to the project master file are listed separately. These totals must equal the control totals printed on the payroll register.

The *employee master register* also contains considerably more detail than does the payroll register. This register lists the entire contents of the employee master file. Besides current and YTD payroll totals, the register prints all personnel information contained within employee records. This final register is produced for two reasons: to provide a backup listing to processing and to cross-check the accuracy of payroll processing. As with other master-file backup

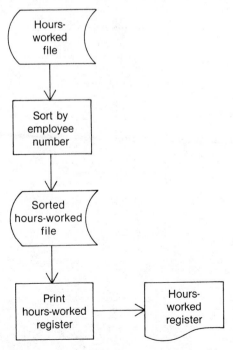

Figure 12-15 Printing the hours-worked register

procedures, a tape copy of the master file is made at the same time as the listing. These materials serve as insurance should the employee master file somehow be lost or destroyed.

The Print Employee Paychecks Program

Employee paychecks can be printed immediately after the payroll register has been approved. Since the employee master file is sequenced by employee number, employee voucher-checks are printed in this sequence. If a different order is desired, such as alphabetical order, a sort of the employee master file is required. This sort, however, should not take place immediately prior to printing paychecks; it should, instead, be scheduled just prior to the printing of the payroll register. In addition, the employee master file should not be sorted by employee name and later resorted to its initial order—employee number. A better alternative is to create a copy of the master file and to sort the copy before printing the register (see Figure 12-16).

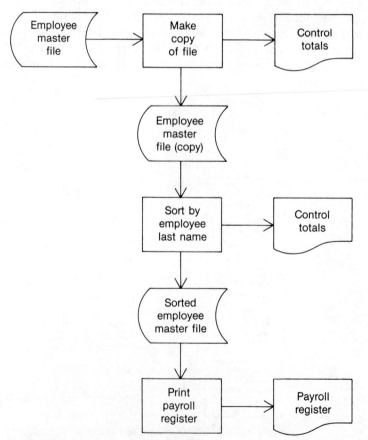

Figure 12-16 Steps prior to printing paychecks in alphabetic sequence

Keeping checks properly aligned is the biggest problem associated with running the employee paychecks program. *Check alignment* refers to printing information in the spaces provided, or "in registration." One way around this problem is to process several voided checks initially, examining each and adjusting printer alignment as necessary. Once the alignment is correct, the total batch of checks can be printed.

As with the checks processed by the accounts payable application, printed checks should not be presigned by the computer. This practice is far too dangerous. As a safety measure, all checks should be endorsed after they are printed. An off-line signature die, controlled by a top-level manager, is used to sign all employee checks.

Payroll Reports

Besides payroll registers, several types of reports must be prepared to fully document payroll-processing activities and to comply with external audit and governmental guidelines and regulations. Reports produced following each run of employee paychecks include several types of payroll journals. As illustrated earlier (see Figure 12-6), the summary page of a payroll journal shows payroll totals by major account, such as direct labor costs, indirect labor costs, FICA withheld, and federal tax withheld. In addition to major summaries, payroll journals are designed to show the details of processing, should summary totals be questioned. Figure 12-17, for example, illustrates a tax-withholding control proof page. The employee accounts appearing on this page are sequenced first by home department and second by employee number. The control proof provides a detailed listing of federal and state taxes and FICA withheld.

Control proofs, such as the tax-withheld control proof, are used in two ways. First, the company totals shown at the bottom of the proof are compared with the totals shown on the summary page of the payroll journal. The two sets of totals must be the same. Second, individual employee accounts are selected by company auditors and subjected to manual testing. If, for example, the H. T. Andrews account is selected (see line-item 1 of Figure 12-17), the checkers will note that since Andrews is single (S) and has no dependents, the single-person federal and state tax tables should be used to determine if the income tax dollars deducted from gross pay are correct. Likewise, the FICA deduction is checked by multiplying gross pay times the FICA withholding rate percentage.

A report produced quarterly is the *Employer's Quarterly Federal Tax Return.* As Figure 12-18 shows, this report is formated to fit federal form 941. The summary totals printed include total wages subject to withholding, income tax withheld, taxable FICA wages, federal unemployment wages, and state unemployment wages. Besides a summary page, detailed supporting pages must be supplied. Federal form 941a, for example, lists taxable FICA wages by employee. The employee's Social Security number and name are both shown on this supporting page together with the employee's taxable FICA wages.

Besides fulfilling quarterly-report requirements, companies must schedule year-end payroll-processing runs. At year-end, federal and state governments

HOME DEPT NUMBER	EMPLOYEE NUMBER		EMPLOYEE NAME	TOTAL HOURS	GROSS PAY	M S	DEP	FEDERAL W/TAX	FICA	DEP	AL	STATE W/TAX	SDI	FIRST NET
308	042150	H T	ANDREWS	.000	850.00	S		195.50	61.66			21.25	.00	571.59
308	362150	A N	HILL	.000	450.00			89.96	47.16	2		14.17	.00	498.71
308	487553	J E	KUPECK	.000	450.00		2	47.88	32.16	2		14.21	.00	525.25
308	535153	P P	LUCAS	.000	650.00		2	83.48	47.16	2		14.17	.00	355.25
308	644056		MAHONEY	.000	900.00	M	3	147.83	65.31	3		19.38	.00	505.21
308	649350	M	OLIVER	.000	900.00	M		138.83	65.31				.00	666.69
308	759350	M	RJOT	15.000	567.50	M		63.22	11.72			11.87	.00	676.48
310	821159		STEWART	12.000	558.00	M	2	70.37	42.40	2		14.75	.00	5.13
310	191026	G	DOUGLAS	58.000	528.00	M		13.50	42.66	3			.00	440.51
310	285957	T T	FLETCHER	48.000	315.00	M	3		28.66	3		12.16	.00	400.97
310	229953	G	FLETCHER	80.000	58.00	M		63.49	43.46	3			.00	268.09
310	302752	K	FREEMAN	20.000	528.00	M	2	63.49	13.46	2		12.16	.00	180.02
310	353057		GALLOW	.000	900.00	M		147.00	65.85			20.42	1.00	408.89
310	379057		HUDSON	88.000	543.40	M		96.92	44.13	1		13.48	.00	71.15
310	400857	A	JENKINS	88.000	528.00	M	3	147.54	44.40	3		12.54	.00	666.69
310	502252	V	LYONS	80.000	528.00	M		147.54	43.46	1		12.16	.00	38.47
310	651750	C	OLSON	10.000	312.00	S		.00	16.51	2		.46	.00	419.58
310	636150	J	OSGOOD	88.000	395.00	M		39.16	32.60	1		8.86	.00	66.26
316	958352	J	PENDELL	12.000	272.00	M		39.00	15.88	1		7.97	.00	408.89
316	151852	L	ROSS	74.000	259.00	M		14.57	22.39	1		5.43	.00	44.39
316	288951	G	COLLINS	98.000	360.50	M	1	32.77	26.39	1		6.00	.00	31.38
316	357657	G	FORDE	90.000	332.50	M	2	22.10	26.84	2		6.23	.00	54.32
316	539858	P	HENRY	10.000	35.20	M		43.83	37.02	2		9.25	.00	291.23
316	605154	A	LYNCH	88.000	455.20	M	2	19.58	25.99	2		5.88	.00	277.33
316	612457	E	NEWTON	90.000	318.50	M		23.32	25.35	1		20.42	.00	26.16
316	689257	D	NORTON	88.000	308.00	M	2	147.58	65.31	2		19.47	.00	363.10
316	710152		PALMER	.000	900.00	M	2	147.58	65.31	2		20.42	.00	262.05
324	852053	M	PLATT	.000	850.00	M	2	133.58	65.31	2		20.42	.00	666.69
324	124255	A	TRACY	.000	900.00	M	2	147.58	65.31	2		20.42	.00	635.59
324	155556	E	CALDWELL	.000	900.00	M	2	147.58	65.31	2		35.83	.00	660.69
324	278853	J	COOPER	.000	1,600.00	M	2	241.04	107.03	2		19.38	.00	1,216.10
324	290957	M T	ELLIS	.000	850.00	M	3	138.58	65.31	3		19.38	.00	676.48
324	319459	T	FERGUSON	.000	900.00	M		138.58	61.06			19.17	.00	635.59
324	342352	H C	FOWLER	.000	900.00	M		138.58	65.31	3		19.38	.00	676.48
324	346056	G	GOLDSMITH	.000	850.00	M	3	213.58	65.06	3		21.17	.00	635.59
324	494054		HAMMOND	.000	900.00	S	1	202.25	65.31	1		21.46	.00	598.69
324	895979	J M	VANDER											610.98

    VCHR

C O M P A N Y T O T A L   1,413.000   24,713.60   3,661.43   1,879.40   548.05   1.00   18,623.72

Figure 12-17 Withholding control proof

```
FORM 941,        EMPLOYERS QUARTERLY FEDERAL TAX RETURN        198-


                       QUARTER ENDED 02/04/8-
                            41-1234567

     2. TOTAL WAGES & TIPS SUBJECT TO WITHHOLDING              23325.54
     3. AMOUNT OF INCOME TAX WITHHELD                           4435.21
     4. ADJUSTMENT FOR PRECEEDING QUARTERS OF CALENDAR YEAR
     5. ADJUSTED TOTAL OF INCOME TAX WITHHELD                   4435.21
     6. TAXABLE FICA WAGES     23325.54 TIMES 13.30% = TAX OF   3102.30
     7. TAXABLE TIPS               0.00 TIMES  6.65% = TAX OF      0.00
     8. TOTAL FICA TAXES                                        3102.30
     9. ADJUSTMENT
    10. ADJUSTED TOTAL                                          3102.30
    11. TOTAL TAXES                                             7537.51
        ADVANCE EARNED INCOME CREDIT PAYMENTS                      0.00
    12. TOTAL DEPOSITS FOR QUARTER AND OVERPAYMENT
        FROM PREVIOUS QUARTER

    13. UNDEPOSITED TAXES DUE. PAY TO IRS

    FEDERAL TAXABLE UNEMPLOYMENT WAGES      23325.54
    TIMES    0.70% =    163.28

    MN STATE TAXABLE UNEMPLOYMENT WAGES     23325.54
    TIMES    1.90% =    443.19
    TOTAL STATE INCOME TAX WITHHELD          1620.04
```

Figure 12-18 Quarterly 941 summary

require business firms to print W-2 reporting statements, which are delivered to all employees who were active, at one time or another, during the calendar year. Figure 12-19 shows the different types of information placed on the W-2 form. The employer identification number and the employee's Social Security number are shown together with year-end totals of gross income and federal and state taxes withheld. The dollar amount of FICA withheld is also printed on the statement.

1 Control number 22222			
2 Employer's name, address, and ZIP code ABC MANUFACTURING COMPANY 906 NE 6TH ST MINNEAPOLIS, MN 55414 L	3 Employer's identification number 41-6666666		4 Employer's State number 4567890
	5 Stat. employee ☐ Deceased ☐ Pension plan ☐ Legal rep. ☐ 942 emp. ☐ Sub. total ☐ Correction ☐ Void ☐		
	6*		7 Advance EIC payment 0.00
8 Employee's social security number 444-55-6666	9 Federal income tax withheld 427.95	10 Wages, tips, other compensation 2250.00	11 FICA tax withheld 149.60
12 Employee's name (first, middle, last) EDWARD PETERSON		13 FICA wages 2250.00	14 FICA tips 0.00
RT 5 BOX 764 ANYTOWN, MN 55333	16 Employer's use		
	17 State income tax 155.85	18 State Wages, tips, etc. 2250.00	19 Name of State MN
15 Employee's address and ZIP code	20 Local income tax	21 Local wages, tips, etc.	22 Name of locality

Form **W-2 Wage and Tax Statement** 198-- Copy A For Social Security Administration * See Instructions for Forms W-2 and W-2P   Dept. of the Treasury I.R.S.
Do NOT Cut or Separate Forms on This Page 16—lb. Paper   IRS App. 6/80 13-2678063

Figure 12-19 W-2 statement

Printing W-2 statements for all employees who were and are active during the calendar year poses special data processing problems. Instead of deleting employees from the employee master file following their terminations, a year-end record must be maintained of the total dollars paid to employees—regardless of whether they are still employed. One solution to this situation is to "delete and save" records when processing employee terminations. In this instance, all inactive employees are deleted from the employee master file and placed on a special year-end payroll reporting file. Another solution is to flag employees as inactive and to continue to store all inactive records on the employee master file. The flag blocks future payments to the employee. After year-end reports are printed, all records containing these special flags are removed. A batch program reads each employee record stored on file, checks to determine if the employee is active or inactive, and, if inactive, deletes the record from the file.

12-3 LABOR DISTRIBUTION

An important product of payroll processing is the analysis of payroll costs. One type of analysis is commonly known as *labor distribution:* the breakdown of labor costs by department, project, product, work center, or some other measurable type of company work activity. Input to labor-distribution reporting is a work-activity master file, such as the project master file shown in Figure 12-14. This file is updated as hours-worked information is keyed and added to the employee master file. For example, the update procedure for adding new project information to the project master file is as follows.

1. A project number is keyed into processing and matched with the same project number stored on file.

2. Once matched, a new trailing record is added to the project record. This trailing record contains the employee number, regular hours worked, overtime hours worked, and payroll costs (the cost of regular hours worked and of overtime hours worked).

3. After the new trailing portion is added, a second project number is keyed into processing and matched, which leads to the creation of another project trailing record. It may be for the same employee (if the employee worked on more than one project) or for another employee. In only the latter case must a new employee number be keyed into processing.

This cycle of matching project numbers and of adding project time and cost information to the project master file continues until all project information for each employee has been successfully transferred.

Following the transfer of work-activity information, the analysis of labor times and costs can begin. This analysis can take place in several ways. Most labor-distribution reports can be printed directly, using the times and costs now stored on file. These reports are designed to compare current hours worked and costs with those for the previous month, with YTD hours worked and costs, or with hours worked and costs for the previous month, a year ago. Some labor-distribution reports show percentage differences between one period and another. Still other reports show whether differences between periods are significant. Because of the many reporting possibilities, labor-distribution results are often displayed rather than printed. As the ad hoc display illustrated in Figure 12-20 makes clear, a substantial amount of detail can be shown on a single display screen. In this example, the computer was initially instructed to find the departments where sorting took place. Second, the computer was told to compare this month's hours-worked total with last month's hours-worked total, to show the difference in hours and as a percentage, and to indicate, by department, where the percentage difference was significant. As illustrated, departments 18 and 62 show much higher levels of activity measured on a percentage basis.

Labor-distribution displays and reports are prepared by companies for several reasons. They are helpful in preparing departmental staffing tables: month-by-month comparisons of hours worked by department, by type of work activity performed, help managers to determine how many employees, by department, will be needed to complete the work at hand. Second, labor distribution breakdowns are helpful in projecting costs for various work activities and in controlling areas of high cost. If, for instance, the cost of operations is increasing while

LABOR-DISTRIBUTION ANALYSIS: SORTING

		TOTAL HOURS WORKED		
DEPARTMENT	THIS MONTH	LAST MONTH	DIFFERENCE	PERCENT
18	635	512	123	24 ˙˙
24	1400	1262	138	11
62	419	312	107	34 ˙˙
79	672	592	80	14
TOTAL	3216	2678	448	17

Figure 12-20 Labor-distribution reporting

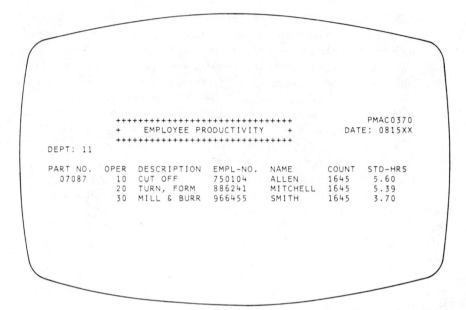

```
            ++++++++++++++++++++++++++++++++          PMAC0370
            +    EMPLOYEE  PRODUCTIVITY     +          DATE: 0815XX
            ++++++++++++++++++++++++++++++++
  DEPT: 11

  PART NO.  OPER  DESCRIPTION   EMPL-NO.   NAME       COUNT   STD-HRS
   07087     10   CUT OFF       750104     ALLEN      1645     5.60
             20   TURN, FORM    886241     MITCHELL   1645     5.39
             30   MILL & BURR   966455     SMITH      1645     3.70
```

Figure 12-21 Labor productivity

production is holding constant, the question of whether labor costs are responsible for this increase can be addressed. Third, labor distribution is useful in identifying areas of high and low worker productivity and in production planning. Figure 12-21 shows the standard hours necessary to produce 1,645 units of part number 07087. The standard-hour rates are determined by multiplying the standard time for pieces per minute by the pieces to be produced (the count). The standard time for pieces per minute is set by industrial engineers and is based on the speed of the machinery required by an operation and on the speed of an average worker assigned to that operation.

12-4 PROCESSING CONTROLS

As with other online business computer applications, both transaction and batch controls are required in processing employee payroll records. A transaction-based control procedure might work as follows. Employees fill out weekly time cards, showing regular and overtime hours worked each day, vacation and sick leave taken, and total hours worked during the week. In processing these cards, data-entry personnel key the weekly total of hours worked, followed by the number of hours worked per day and the vacation and sick leave taken. After the last daily entry, the computer sums the daily hours to arrive at the weekly total and compares this summed total with the keyed weekly total. The two figures must be the same.

Another way to ensure correct entry of hours-worked information is to automate the keeping of employee time. As shown earlier in Figure 12-2, modern electronic time-keeping equipment eliminates the hand calculation of employee hours worked per day and per week. Some time-keeping equipment keeps both employee totals and balances and departmental totals and balances. This practice permits the total hours worked by department also to be carried forward in data processing.

A strict set of batch-balance controls is required following the posting of hours-worked information to the employee master file. The control equations are

Total hours worked = Regular hours + Overtime hours
Total hours paid = Total hours worked + Approved leave hours

These two hourly totals are changed each time new hours-worked information is accepted by the computer. They are critical in the control of the employee payroll.

Since the computer converts total hours paid to total dollars paid, it is rather difficult to plan controls that ensure the accuracy of all paychecks. Control procedures used to guard against higher (or lower) than normal paychecks include subjecting hours-worked and dollars-paid totals to a series of range and comparison tests, and checking payroll figures by hand to determine if they are correct. A typical range test is to flag any paycheck that falls above an upper-control dollar limit and to print this information on the employee payroll register. The upper limit for an hourly employee, for example, might be $3,000. Any monthly check for an amount greater than $3,000 would be flagged for inspection. Another range test is to flag all hours-worked totals that seem unusual—overtime hours that total more than an established upper limit, for example, or a combination of overtime hours to be paid and regular hours that falls below an established lower limit.

Payroll comparison tests are also useful for pointing out unusual or incorrect situations. One comparison is to divide the dollars paid by the hours worked for a pay period, do the same for the last pay period, and match the two resulting figures (which should normally be identical). If this comparison reveals instead that dollars paid per hour worked for the first period are significantly different than those for the last period (say, plus or minus 5 percent), the reasons for the difference must be explained. Another test pits departmental pay averages, this period, against departmental pay averages, last period. Here again, any significant difference must be explained.

With interactive methods of processing it is possible to decentralize the visual review of payroll records and totals. Following the computation of departmental payroll costs, departmental supervisors can be required to display, review, and either approve or disapprove all hours-worked, hours-paid, and dollars-paid totals. If any of these totals looks unusual, it is possible to question an employee directly. In so doing it can be determined whether the hours-worked totals stored on file agree with the totals that were initially submitted by the employee.

Last, manual sets of calculations must be made to verify the correctness of payroll processing. A workable procedure is to select a small random sample, such as 1 percent of all employees, each payroll period and to determine by hand the payments to be made to each employee included in the sample. In each case the hours worked, the hours paid, the gross dollars paid, and the net dollars paid must agree with the figures determined by the computer. Only through hand testing can it be determined if computer-processed payroll totals are correct.

12-5 MANAGEMENT IMPLICATIONS

Companies must exercise special caution in designing employee payroll computer systems. This is the one application in which mistakes in processing cannot be tolerated and the reliability of processing cannot be questioned. Moreover, timeliness in processing is critical. It is not acceptable to distribute checks late or as soon as computer programs are fixed. Nor is it acceptable to print all but a few paychecks. In these instances, word will spread that there are problems with the computer. When this occurs, people begin to question the company's ability not only to process their pay but also to conduct business generally.

In the design of this application, special attention must be given to the appearance of employee paychecks. The paycheck and voucher reflect a company's professionalism and responsibility to its employees. The voucher, in particular, should be easy to read and to understand; employees should not have to question how deductions were made. If some items appearing on the voucher need to be abbreviated, such as Earned Income Credit (EIC), the meaning of the abbreviation should be defined, perhaps on the reverse side of the voucher.

Besides appearance, special attention should be given to the distribution of signed paychecks. Many companies require that supervisors distribute paychecks at a designated time and place each week. This practice gives recognition to the importance of the paycheck. It provides the supervisor with an opportunity to say thanks to his or her people for a job well done. It also provides employees the opportunity to examine their paychecks. If problems are discovered, they can be reported immediately.

After payroll processing is running smoothly, there may be some pressure to expand the application into a much larger, integrated personnel-planning, payroll-processing design. These larger designs entail certain dangers, however: they tend to be more difficult to control and maintain and, unless costed properly, they can make payroll processing overly expensive. And finally, a larger design means that more people are typically allowed online access to employee records stored on the employee master file. When this occurs, there is increased danger that some records will be incorrectly modified and that, as a consequence, some employees will fail to get paid.

With minor modifications to the design, several valuable by-products can be produced from employee payroll application. Besides paychecks and payroll reports, several types of special summaries can be prepared. These summaries include several types of labor-distribution breakdowns—labor costs by department, by plant, by type of position, by project, and so forth. Other summaries include a variety of wage and salary analyses—analyses of regular pay, overtime pay, sick leave, and vacation leave. Affirmative action reports can also be produced from this application, as can seniority profiles. Collectively, these special summaries help to explain several things: whether the wages and salaries paid by a company are fair, whether the hiring practices of a company select new employees fairly, whether the average age of the work force is shifting, whether employee leave patterns are changing, and whether employee productivity patterns are improving, are remaining the same, or are starting to decline.

REVIEW OF IMPORTANT IDEAS

There are special reasons for developing an online employee payroll computer application. Interactive steps simplify the adjustment of employee records, the entry and verification of hours-worked information, the retrieval of data stored on the employee master file, the addition of new employees to the master file, and the routine checking of processing controls. Interactive processing also reduces interdepartmental conflicts—staff groups are responsible for entering and verifying of personnel or payroll data related to their operations.

The employee master file must be fully updated prior to the entry of hours-worked information and the printing of employee paychecks. For new employees, personnel and payroll information must be added to the file. For existing employees, all personal, job, and pay changes must be made to employee records currently stored on file. This preliminary processing of the master file typically requires two interactive programs: one to ready the personnel portion of the employee master file and another to ready the payroll portion of the file.

Hours-worked information must be entered into processing for each payroll run. The number of hours worked is either printed on time cards or entered directly into processing with badge-reading equipment. After hours-worked totals are verified, computer processing determines current employee gross pay, deductions from gross pay, net (take-home) pay, and YTD employee earnings, and adds this information to an employee's record. The results of processing are printed on the payroll register, which shows net pay and how it was determined, as well as the YTD totals updated by processing.

Employee paychecks, payroll journals, and periodic payroll reports are important products of this application. Employee paychecks are two-part forms, showing net pay and how net pay was calculated. Payroll journals summarize payroll costs by department, job class, budget number, general ledger number, project number, or some other classification important to a company. Periodic reports include quarterly and year-end federal and state tax reports.

Labor distribution entails the analysis of hours-worked and payroll-cost information. A labor-distribution file, such as a project labor-distribution file, is updated each time hours-worked and dollars-paid totals are approved. This secondary update provides a company with an accurate measurement of the hours required for different types of work activities. It helps to determine if the costs of operations are increasing or decreasing relative to constant units of production.

Control of payroll processing is complicated because hours-worked totals must be transformed into dollars paid. Range and comparison testing as well as checking payroll totals by hand is required to successfully verify the correctness of payroll processing.

KEY WORDS

Employee master file	Indirect labor cost
Employee time cards	Employee change form
Payroll number	Payroll change form
Employee number	Hours-worked register
Payroll register	Employee master register
Payroll journal	Control proofs
Direct labor cost	Labor distribution

REVIEW QUESTIONS

1. What are the special reasons for installing an online employee payroll design?

2. Name the six steps required in processing the employee payroll.

3. What are the three main inputs to the employee payroll application? How do they differ?

4. What is the difference between the payroll number and the employee number? Between the project number and the employee number?

5. Name the six segments of an employee master file record.

6. What are the three main printed outputs produced in processing? How do they differ from ad hoc displays?

7. How does the payroll register differ from a payroll journal?

8. Why are three interactive programs used in this application to ready the employee master file?

9. List the several processing steps that the program to "enter hours worked" is designed to accomplish.

10. Why must adjustments be made when badge readers are used to enter employee times into processing?

11. What is the difference between the payroll register and the hours-worked register? Between the payroll register and the employee master register?

12. What is the biggest problem associated with running the employee paychecks program?

13. Why are control proofs important to processing?

14. Explain why printing W-2 statements poses special data-retention problems.

15. What is labor-distribution reporting? Why are labor-distribution displays and reports prepared by a company?

16. Describe one range test that is built into the program to enter hours worked. Describe one comparison test.

17. What advantages are associated with decentralized payroll processing?

18. Why must companies exercise special caution when designing the employee payroll computer application?

EXERCISES

1. Prepare a flowchart showing the steps associated with entering employee times directly into processing using one-way data collection terminals. Show all inputs and outputs to processing, including all reference files and files updated directly. Then explain how a processing design would handle the following situations:

    (a) An employee enters a start time of work but fails to enter a stop time.

    (b) An employee works in an area lacking a data collection terminal.

    (c) A data collection terminal breaks down after several start times have been recorded.

    (d) A badge is too dirty to be read.

2. Prepare systems flowcharts to show the steps needed to produce the employee-productivity display shown in Figure 12-21. You are to chart, first, the steps needed to create a productivity master file and, second, the steps required to display the contents of this master file. After you have completed both flowcharts, answer the following questions.

    (a) What data must be keyed to processing when adding new employee-productivity information to the productivity master file?

(b) What data do not have to be keyed when adding new information, but, instead, can be transferred from other files to the productivity master file?

(c) How could productivity master-file data be changed if an incorrect production count had been keyed to processing?

3. Prepare a flowchart showing the steps needed to reset the employee master file. Three different flowcharts are to be prepared. These should show

(a) how the current portion of the payroll master file is reset to zero;

(b) how the quarter-to-date portion of the payroll master file is reset to zero; and

(c) how the year-to-date portion of the payroll master file is reset to zero.

CASE

C

Job Costing

Some companies integrate job costing with the employee payroll application by entering into processing three types of data:

- Regular and overtime hours worked, by employee, by job number.
- Equipment hours used, by machine, by employee, by job number.
- Material consumed, by item number, by employee, by job number.

By entering data concerning equipment and material usage into processing at the same time as hours-worked information, and by using the computer to transform these usage and hours-worked figures into dollars, the ongoing and actual costs of a job can be summarized.

A variety of reports can be prepared as products of the job-costing application.

- *Job ledgers* show the charges for an individual job, including labor, material, equipment costs, and in some instances estimated overhead charges.

- *Material usage reports* show the cost of materials required by different jobs. Each entry on this report typically contains the material number, material description, date used, unit cost of the material, quantity consumed, and extended cost (unit cost × quantity consumed). The extended cost can be shown by material number; however, it is generally listed by job number, employee number, or machine number.

- *Equipment usage reports* show the cost of equipment required by different jobs. Each entry on this report typically contains the machine number, machine description, date used, hourly cost of the machine, hours used, and extended cost (hourly cost × hours used). The extended cost can be shown by machine number, or, as stated above, by job or employee number.

• *Labor-hour usage reports* show the cost of labor required by different jobs. Each entry on this report typically contains the employee number, employee name, date of work, regular pay rate, overtime pay rate, regular hours worked, overtime hours worked, and extended cost (pay rate × hours worked). The extended cost can be shown by employee number, or by job or machine number.

Figure C-1 shows the interactive program required to enter job-costing information into processing and to update the various job-costing files. Seven files are affected by processing; one of these, the employee master file, is used by the employee payroll application.

REQUIREMENTS

1. Outline the processing steps to be designed into the online program shown in Figure C-1 as the "enter time and cost program." Your outline should explain what the computer will be instructed to do first, then second, and so forth. You can assume that hours worked will be entered into processing first, followed by equipment hours used, followed by materials consumed. This information will be entered job by job for each employee.

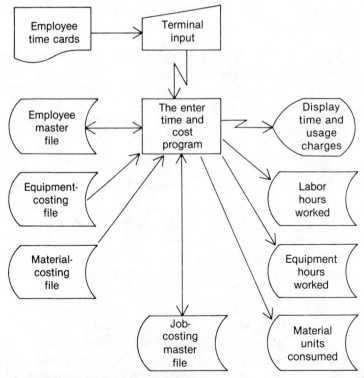

Figure C-1   Entering time and usage detail

2. Show how the computer files are organized for this application. List the names of the record segments and the data elements that make up the records of the following files:

(a)   Equipment-costing file

(b)   Material-costing file

(c)   Labor-hours-worked file

(d)   Equipment-hours-worked file

(e)   Material-units-consumed file

(f)   Job-costing master file.

3. Prepare a flowchart and explain how the charges associated with a specific job (for example, the job ledger) would be displayed for review.

4. Design a job-ledger display screen.

5. (Optional) Explain how data base processing would simplify the file-updating and file-maintenance requirements of this application.

PART

FINANCIAL AND
MARKETING APPLICATIONS

As we have observed throughout the earlier chapters, the products of one application are often passed on to another application. In this final section, we observe this passage of information, but on a much larger scale. The general ledger application, for example, is designed to process financial details passed to it from all financial applications. Such a transfer is necessary to prepare month- and year-end companywide financial reports. For the sales-analysis application, too, sales details saved from customer invoicing or customer order entry are transferred into processing. This transfer is necessary to calculate, summarize, and provide different views of sales performance—by customer, product, or salesperson.

In these last three chapters our attention will shift away from transaction-based applications. As we discuss processing that uses information provided by other applications, we come to appreciate the need to store summary information at different points; we begin to see differences between higher- and lower-order business computer applications. Lower-order applications focus largely on processing specific types of business transactions. With higher-order applications, this interest disappears. The new focus is one of providing timely, reliable, and complete information to management.

CHAPTER

13

General Ledger

A very important, yet poorly understood business computer application is the comprehensive financial application known as the general ledger. This application consolidates all financial transactions of a business in order to summarize, by account number, changes to assets and liabilities. It is the application from which financial statements are prepared. One of these, the *balance sheet,* compares business assets (what is owned) with business liabilities (what is owed). Another important statement, the *profit and loss statement,* shows the revenues, expenses, and profits (or losses) of a business for an accounting period (such as a period of one month). A third statement, the *cash-flow statement,* shows the net increase or decrease in cash for an accounting period; cash gained from net income, depreciation, and other sources; and uses of cash during the period.

The design of the general ledger computer application initially requires the preparing of a master *chart of accounts.* This master chart is needed to properly code different types of assets, liabilities, revenues, and expenses (different types of business accounts). Figure 13-1 illustrates a simplified, personal chart of accounts, which has been designed to summarize a person's wealth and financial health. As shown, two sets of account numbers define major types of current assets (1XX-XX) and other longer-term assets (2XX-XX); two sets of numbers define personal liabilities (3XX-XX) and (4XX-XX). The subheadings attached to each account number further define account categories. Expense account 740-XX, for instance, might subdivide as follows:

740-10   Home insurance
740-20   Life insurance
740-30   Automobile insurance
740-40   Health insurance
740-50   Dental insurance

CURRENT ASSETS	INCOME
100-XX Cash	600-XX Salary
110-XX Marketable securities	610-XX Interest and dividends
120-XX Inventory	620-XX Other income
OTHER ASSETS	EXPENSES
200-XX Real estate	700-XX Housing
210-XX Automobile	710-XX Food
220-XX Furniture and fixtures	720-XX Medical
	730-XX Automobile
CURRENT LIABILITIES	740-XX Insurance
	750-XX Taxes
300-XX Accounts payable	760-XX Contributions
310-XX Taxes payable	770-XX Education
	780-XX Repairs
LONG-TERM LIABILITIES	790-XX Clothing
400-XX Bank loans	800-XX Entertainment
410-XX Finance company loans	810-XX Other expenses
PERSONAL EQUITY	PROFIT (OR LOSS)
500-XX Equity	900-XX Current earnings

Figure 13-1 Personal chart of accounts

The relationships between the master chart of accounts and the financial statements produced by a business are as follows.

1. The company balance sheet consists of the accounts labeled assets, liabilities, and owner's equity. It is called a balance sheet because business assets must equal, or balance, business liabilities plus owner's equity.

$$\text{Assets} = \text{Liabilities} + \text{Owner's equity}$$

In accounting for certain pieces of property, it is common to find multiple entries for one piece of property on different parts of the balance sheet. For example, if a business buys a building for $75,000 but owes the bank $65,000, the business would record assets of $75,000, an outstanding liability of $65,000, and equity of $10,000—the difference between assets and liabilities.

2. The company profit and loss statement consists of accounts labeled income (or revenues), expenses, and current earnings (net income). In this instance, current earnings equals income minus expenses.

$$\text{Earnings} = \text{Income} - \text{Expenses}$$

3. In accounting for business expenses, charges posted to the profit and loss statement must be reflected on the balance sheet. Suppose a $1,000 check is written to pay a single building mortgage payment. Suppose further

that $950 of the $1,000 will pay the outstanding interest on the mortgage and $50 will be applied to reduce the amount of the loan. In recording this payment, several entries must be made. First, the $1,000 must be entered as an expense. Second, the $1,000 would be subdivided. Expense account 700-10 might show interest expense of $950, whereas expense account 700-20 might show principal expense of $50 (see Figure 13-1). Third, long-term liability must be reduced by $50. Fourth, owner's equity must be increased by $50.

Figure 13-2 shows a more complicated chart of account, which uses a twelve-digit classification scheme.

- Digits 1 and 2 separate the different divisions, plants, or parts of a company, such as Division 1, Foods, and Division 2, Feed and Seed.

- Digits 3, 4, and 5 indicate major account groupings, such as gross sales, accounts receivable, accounts payable, and gross salaries.

- Digits 6, 7, and 8 identify *subsidiary accounts* within each major account, such as subsidiary checking accounts within the major account, cash in bank.

- Digits 9, 10, 11, and 12 define the department or the cost center responsible for the account, such as the controller's office or the data processing department.

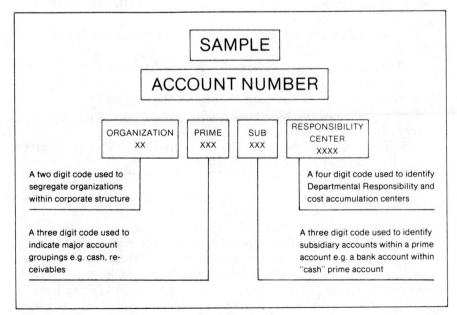

Figure 13-2 Corporate chart-of-accounts classification scheme

Such a chart of accounts is often necessary to define fully the financial activities of a business and to specify which managers are responsible for the control of various expenses and revenues. This is especially true in very large corporations that must constantly evaluate the financial soundness of various corporate divisions.

13-1 PRELIMINARY OVERVIEW OF PROCESSING

General ledger processing is similar to payroll processing, in some ways, and to accounts receivable processing, in other ways. As Figure 13-3 shows, the first two steps in processing update the *consolidated general ledger (G/L) master file,* which stores both current and year-to-date financial account totals. All accounts, in turn, are defined by the master chart of accounts. As shown, the file can be updated in one of two ways: current G/L account totals can be either keyed to processing or posted to the G/L file following the transfer of summary totals from G/L summary files. Only after the general ledger master file is made ready are reports prepared. As a test of readiness, a *trial balance* is performed. If, in testing, assets do not equal liabilities plus owner's equity, or earnings are not equal to incomes less expenses, adjustments must be made. Following this, a second trial, and where necessary a third, a fourth, and so on, must be performed until the general ledger file is finally in balance. Last, reports are prepared from this balanced file. The *consolidated general ledger* is printed together with different types of financial statements.

The five steps shown in Figure 13-3 can thus be summarized as follows:

1. *Enter journal details* to update account totals and to make adjustments to out-of-balance accounts.
2. *Post G/L summaries* to transfer G/L summary details from summary files to the consolidated G/L master file.
3. *Print trial balance* to determine whether all accounts are in balance.
4. *Print consolidated G/L report* to document the contents of the G/L master file.
5. *Print financial statements* to produce the corporate balance sheet, profit and loss statement, and cash-flow statement.

Inputs to Processing

The main inputs to the consolidated G/L master file are summary totals created by the processing of various types of business transactions, using the various applications we have discussed in previous chapters. These totals are placed in summary files for later transfer and posting to the general ledger. As we will see from the following review of applications, a wide variety of input totals is required. (To better understand these different types of input, it may be necessary also to reread earlier parts of the book.)

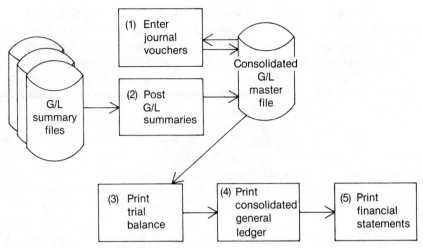

Figure 13-3 Five steps in processing the general ledger

The *customer invoice application* provides summary totals. In processing customer invoice transactions, an invoice A/R summary file is created (see Figure 4-15). If this file is designed only for the accounts receivable computer application, it is not in a suitable form for direct use in general ledger processing. When the summary file is modified by adding general ledger codes, however, direct use is possible. For example, customer invoice dollar totals can be posted to gross sales G/L account numbers; sales tax, freight, insurance, and cash discount totals can be posted to other G/L account numbers.

The *customer cash-receipts application* creates another summary file (see Figure 5-14). As with invoicing, if this file is designed for accounts receivable processing, it must be sequenced differently for general ledger processing. For receipts, all cash payments and cash discounts must be totaled and balanced. These totals are the primary inputs to general ledger processing.

The *accounts receivable application* is modified by the customer invoice computer application and by the customer cash-receipts computer application. The total sales dollars associated with each customer invoice serve to *debit* a customer's account. Likewise, a cash payment received from a customer becomes an offsetting accounts receivable *credit*. With accounts receivable processing, debits and credits must be reconciled as follows:

Beginning A/R balance + Debits − Credits = Ending A/R balance

The A/R register is designed to document this reconciliation (see Figure 6-8). This register shows how *double-entry bookkeeping* works in practice. With double entry, both debits and offsetting credits must be entered into processing. In addition, debits (entries on the left-hand side) must equal credits (entries on the right-hand side).

In the *customer order-entry application,* the dollar value of items removed from inventory must be recorded and posted to the general ledger. Moreover, customer order-entry totals must equal product charges recorded on customer invoices. The best place to capture order-entry information is following the adjustment of customer orders and after or during the printing of customer packing slips (see Figure 7-17). At this point in processing, only the charges for goods picked and shipped will be reported.

The *finished-goods inventory application* is similar to accounts receivable in that all debits (goods leaving inventory) and credits (goods entering inventory) must be accounted for. The best place to reconcile "goods out" with "goods in" information is on the stock-status report (see Figure 8-15). As part of general ledger processing, in and out totals must be compared against the dollar value recorded by the customer order-entry application and by the purchasing and receiving application.

A purchase order encumbrance summary was prepared in the processing of purchase orders with the *purchasing and receiving application* (Figure 9-14 shows a variation of this summary). The summary shows what funds need to be set aside to cover outstanding purchases. When sequenced by general ledger code, the encumbered-fund totals must be entered into general ledger processing. Debits and credits to these totals result when goods are received. The payables receipts summary provides a refined estimate of funds to be encumbered. This second summary, arranged by general ledger code, is also entered into processing.

The *accounts payable application* is a major source of general ledger input. It provides a listing of vendor invoices received and held over for payment and a listing of invoices paid this period. As Figure 10-6 shows, a general ledger summary is prepared for all paid invoices. This summary provides a valuable cross-reference, showing the vendor invoice number, the payables voucher number, and the amount paid. As illustrated, all vouchers are posted against one (or more) G/L expense accounts.

The *fixed-assets application* provides important summary information, and all changes to fixed assets must be reflected by general ledger accounting. Besides showing the dollars associated with all fixed-asset additions and deletions, book and tax depreciation totals must be carried across to the general ledger. As Figure 11-7 shows, current, YTD, and cumulative depreciation totals must be maintained; the remaining value of all fixed assets must be closely monitored.

Besides accounts payable, the other application designed to process business expenses is the *employee payroll application.* In processing, a payroll journal is printed to show all subtotals to be posted to the general ledger (see Figure 12-6). General ledger subtotals include such items as gross pay, federal tax withheld, state tax withheld, and FICA withheld.

Reviewing these inputs to general ledger processing should help to underscore some of the complexities of this application. Added to this complexity is the new requirement of entering financial totals by hand. As an example, suppose the finished-goods inventory equation will not balance. In particular,

JOURNAL VOUCHER				PERIOD OCT	DATE 10/03/	J.V. No. 309/23	Page 1/ of /1
ACCOUNT DESCRIPTION	DIV	PRI	SUB CC	Number	YR PER	L A O C B	DEBIT / CREDIT

ACCOUNT DESCRIPTION	DV	PRI	SUB	CC	ADJUST YR/PER	LA	DEBIT	CREDIT
ACCOUNTS RECEIVABLE	C,2	1,2,1	0,0,1	6,9,0,0	1,0	A	602 197 78	
INTER COMPANY CONTROL	C,2	1,95	1,4,0	6,9,0,0	1,0	A	3106 41	
A/R OFFICERS + Employees	C,2	1,2,1	0,0,2	6,9,0,0	1,0	A	162 00	
TRADE DISCOUNTS	C,2	3,1	0,0,2	6,9,0,0	1,0	A	6182 00	
PRICE ALLOWANCES	C,2	3,1,1	5,1,4	6,9,0,0	1,0	A	1477 92	
TRADE SALES	C,2	3,0	0,0,1	6,9,0,0	1,0	A		61 0019 70
INTRA-DIVISION SALES	C,2	3,03	4,3,2	6,9,0,0	1,0	A		3106 41

SOURCE	JOURNAL VOUCHER DESCRIPTION	TOTAL DEBIT	TOTAL CREDIT
J Doe	Gourmet-Alpha Sales	613126 11	613126 11

Journal Voucher Explanation TO RECORD SEPT

PREPARED BY JD | APPROVED BY RK | BUDGET EFFECT | PROFIT EFFECT

Figure 13-4 Journal voucher

> Beginning inventory + Moves in − Moves out > Ending inventory

In this example an adjustment is required to force the inventory equation to balance. The modified equation becomes

> Beginning inventory + Moves in − Moves out − Inventory write-off = Ending inventory

Regardless of why inventory had to be written off (for example, lost, stolen, destroyed, obsolete items), the only practical way to enter this information into processing is by keying it directly.

As Figure 13-4 shows, manual general ledger entries are initially recorded on a *journal voucher,* which contains space for a description of the account, the account number, the year and the month, and the debit or credit amount. As shown, trade and intra-division sales (credits) are offset by increases to accounts receivable and other more specialized accounts (debits).

Instead of transferring and posting totals from summary files or of keying entries into general ledger processing directly, it is possible to add general ledger file-update procedures to other business computer applications. Figures 13-5 and 13-6 illustrate two such processing designs. Figure 13-5 examines once again the split of the consolidated payables file into two smaller files—the payables held-over file and the payables pending-check file (see Figure 10-6). The general ledger master file is also added to this design, however. During the split, the general ledger update takes place. Dollars transferred to the payables pending-check file are posted to the general ledger file. This action reduces current liability G/L totals and revises current business expense G/L totals.

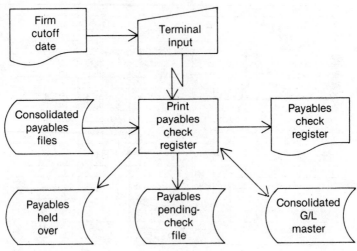

Figure 13-5 Modified check-register flowchart

Figure 13-6 illustrates a second modified flowchart. As shown, the G/L master file is revised following the updating of employee payroll totals (gross pay, deductions from gross pay, and net pay). As with payables processing, debits and credits must be equal for general ledger processing to remain in balance. Net pay, for example, reduces cash-on-hand totals; withholding for federal and state taxes increases short-term liability totals. In addition to changing assets and liabilities, the different types of labor costs are usually separated and reported.

There are advantages and disadvantages related to adding on general ledger file-update procedures to other business computer applications. The advantages include spreading the work of general ledger processing more evenly over an accounting period, editing all general ledger account codes and totals and trapping all errors early, at their source, and reducing the number of summary files to be carried forward in processing. Improved speed in the update of the general ledger master file and the ability to visually verify smaller general ledger trial balances are further benefits. Likewise, there are also some important disadvantages, such as the creation of more complex interactive computer programs, because additional file-processing instructions are added to selected programs; greater difficulty in tracing the audit trail, especially when a large number of adjustments is required; and greater file-storage requirements, because the general ledger file must be online to processing. Despite these disadvantages, increased use of data base management software leads to the direct update of the general ledger file, as opposed to end-of-period updates or follow-on summary file postings. As improved data base management systems are designed, they will undoubtedly include improvements in auditing. Continuous monitoring of control totals by the computer during processing is expected to eliminate many of today's concerns regarding the direct update of several files concurrently.

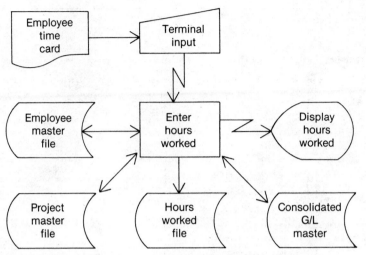

Figure 13-6   Modified enter hours worked flowchart

Outputs from Processing

The main outputs from general ledger processing are the general ledger trial balance, the consolidated general ledger, and different types of financial statements. Figure 13-7 illustrates a *general ledger trial balance report*. As shown, current financial totals are added to opening balance totals to provide the consolidated closing balance. Both prime account and sub account totals are shown on this report. Cash in bank and on hand is a prime account, for example, whereas petty cash is a sub account. Last, balance-control totals are placed at the bottom of the trial balance as checks to make sure that assets equal liabilities plus net worth and that earnings equal income less expenses. These equations must be in balance for the opening balance, the current period, and the closing (YTD) balance.

With an online design it is not always necessary to print one set of trial balance reports after another to prove that all accounts are in balance. Instead, it is possible to enter adjustments into processing directly and to inquire whether the general ledger is in balance. Then, after balance is achieved, the final in-balance general ledger is printed. This final version, the *consolidated general ledger,* is a complete register of the consolidated general ledger master file, showing all records by prime and by sub account, within each organizational entity.

Further consolidation of the general ledger file is required in the printing of financial statements. The balance sheet, for instance, is printed directly from consolidated general ledger accounts. As Figures 13-8 and 13-9 show, the balance sheet summarizes the detailed information contained in the general ledger accounts. The format of the balance sheet often varies; this particular sheet shows only ending balance figures.

```
THE ALPHABET SOUP COMPANY           A C C O U N T I N G   I V                        PAGE 1

                           G E N E R A L   L E D G E R   T R I A L   B A L A N C E         REPORT # RE-254
                                                OCT 19                               PROCESSED 11/4/

  LOC.   PRIME   SUB        DESCRIPTION        OPENING BALANCE      CURRENT MONTH     CLOSING BALANCE

   01     101    CASH IN BANK AND ON HAND
                 001  DEPOSIT - CHASE MANHATTAN    1,727,413.91        509,462.94CR      1,217,950.97
                 002  GWF-MANUFACTR HANOVER        2,429,504.74CR    1,105,932.58        1,323,572.16CR
                 005  IMPREST - ONEIDA NAT BANK      294,298.06         16,660.12CR        277,637.94
                 006  DISABILITY FUND                    568.99            134.38             703.37
                 007  PETTY CASH                      25,320.00                            25,320.00
                 008  CASH-RESEARCH BUILDING           2,025.00                             2,025.00
                 009  P/R FUNDS- ONEIDA NAT          124,621.63            438.97CR        124,182.66
                 010  CASH IN TRANSIT
                 PRIME ACCOUNT 101 TOTAL           255,257.15CR        579,504.93          324,247.78

   01     121    NOTES RECEIVABLE
                 026  NOTES RECEIVABLE                 2,349.00             13.00CR           2,336.00
                 PRIME ACCOUNT 121 TOTAL              2,349.00             13.00CR           2,336.00

   01     122    ACCOUNTS RECEIVABLE - CUSTOM
                 025  A/R CONSUMER PRODUCTS          403,385.11        165,745.57          569,130.68
                 027  ACCOUNTS RECEIVABLE-CUST.   28,819,642.54        375,701.06       29,195,343.60
                 030  ACCT RECEIVABLE-OTHER           10,302.14          3,925.00CR           6,377.14
                 PRIME ACCOUNT 122 TOTAL         29,233,329.79        537,521.63       29,770,851.42

   01     123    ACCOUNTS RECEIVABLE - FACTOR
                 028  ACCOUNTS RECEIVABLE-FACTORED 7,460,578.13        784,022.01        8,244,600.14
                 PRIME ACCOUNT 123 TOTAL          7,460,578.13        784,022.01        8,244,600.14

   01     124    ACCOUNTS RECEIVABLE - OFFICE
                 030  LOANS TO EMPLOYEES               6,241.96            899.00CR           5,342.96
                 032  PAYROLL ADJUSTMENTS             23,994.78          7,632.93CR          16,361.85
                 033  A/R - SALES OF RESIDENTS         1,319.92             50.00CR           1,269.92
                 034  ACCTS REC-PERMANENT ADV.         9,050.00            100.00CR           8,950.00
                 PRIME ACCOUNT 124 TOTAL             40,606.66          8,681.93CR          31,924.73

   01     129    RESERVES ON ACCOUNTS RECEIVABLE
                 042  RESERVE FOR DISPUTED INVO      275,000.00CR                           275,000.00CR
                 043  RESERVE FOR DOUBTFUL ACCT       75,117.30CR         3,400.90CR          78,518.20CR
                 045  RESERVE FOR ALLOWANCES         131,593.05CR         8,323.90CR         139,916.95CR
                 047  RESERVE FOR DEDUCTIONS         397,000.00CR                           397,000.00CR
                 194  CUSTOMER DEPOSITS-RETURNED          19.80                                  19.80
 ---------------------------------------------------------------------------------------------------------

                        FINAL TOTAL                    * * *

                            INCOME/EXPENSE     7,090,169.62CR         45,434.31CR        7,135,512.93CR

                        ASSETS/LIABILITIES     7,090,169.62           45,343.31          7,135,512.93
```

Figure 13-7   General ledger trial balance

The balance sheet is used to determine the financial health of a business. The organization presented in the balance sheet shown in Figures 13-8 and 13-9, for example, is representative of a business facing financial difficulties. Applying financial tests to these company-wide data leads to several conclusions. First, current assets are lower than current liabilities ($7,463.05 to $8,155.02). A financially healthy firm would show current assets to be approximately twice as large as current liabilities. Second, total debt to equity is approximately 250 percent ($13,826 divided by $5,579). This disparity is dangerous—total debt should be approximately equal to owner's equity. Last, current liabilities are approximately 150 percent of total equity ($8,155 divided by $5,579). Once again there is a problem: a financially healthy firm would show a ratio of less than 50 percent.

Figure 13-10, the profit and loss statement for the same firm, is more positive than the company balance sheet. As shown, net income, after taxes, is close to 17 percent of total income (sales). This percentage is quite high. Likewise, if net income continues to average better than $425 ($858.58 divided by 2) per month, the yearly return on net worth will approximate 90 percent ($425 times 12 divided by $5,579). This return is spectacular.

Service Type
An Oregon Corporation

See Accountant's Compilation Report

Balance Sheet
As of 02/28/8X

Assets

Current Assets:		
Cash on Hand	$ 883.85	
Returned Checks	135.78	
Cash in Bank—Bank of the N.W.	670.86	
Cash in Bank—Valley State Bank	631.34	
Money Market Certificates	1,000.00	
Accounts Receivable	3,773.63	
Prepaid Insurance	367.59	
Total Current Assets		$ 7,463.05
Fixed Assets:		
Leasehold Improvements	$ 4,764.92	
Accum. Depr.—Leasehold Impr.	(153.02)	
Net Value Leasehold Impr.	$ 4,611.90	
Fixtures & Equipment	$ 1,618.74	
Accum. Depr.—Fixtures & Equip.	(584.20)	
Net Value Fixtures & Equip.	$ 1,034.54	
Vehicles	$ 6,987.50	
Accum. Depr.—Vehicles	(1,001.23)	
Net Value Vehicles	$ 5,986.27	
Net Value Depreciable Assets		$11,632.71
Other Assets:		
Deposits	$ 310.00	
Total Other Assets		$ 310.00
Total Assets		$19,405.76

Figure 13-8 Balance sheet—assets

Some business firms have a tendency to consider only the bottom line on the profit and loss statement. By now it should be clear that profit alone does not necessarily mean financial well-being. For example, if sales lead to ever-increasing current liabilities, which cannot be adequately offset by current assets, a company is in financial trouble. The high interest expense associated with short-term loans becomes increasingly difficult to offset. And, if short-term requirements become too large, further credit extensions must be refused.

Service Type

An Oregon Corporation

See Accountant's Compilation Report

Balance Sheet

As of 02/28/8X

Liabilities

Current Liabilities:

Accounts Payable—Trade	$ 2,618.22	
Accounts Payable—Other	1,017.66	
Note Payable—Bank of the N.W.	1,611.03	
Accrued Wages Payable	572.28	
Accrued State Withholding	68.63	
Accrued Federal Withholding	55.38	
Accrued FICA Tax	209.01	
Accrued State Unemployment	548.24	
Accrued Federal Unemployment	318.72	
Estimated Federal Income Tax	175.85	
Curr Portion Long Term Liab.	960.00	
Total Current Liabilities		$ 8,155.02
Long Term Liabilities:		
Contract Payable—Bank of the N.W.	3,631.00	
Loan Payable—Bank of the N.W.	3,000.00	
Curr Portion Long Term Liab.	(960.00)	
Total Long Term Liabilities		$ 5,671.00
Total Liabilities		$13,826.02
Equity:		
Common Stock	$ 1,000.00	
Paid In Capital/Excess of Par	2,705.50	
Retained Earnings	1,015.66	
Net Profit (or Loss)	858.58	
Total Equity		$ 5,579.74
Total Liabilities & Equity		$19,405.76

Figure 13-9 Balance sheet—liabilities

Thus, instead of reviewing only the profit and loss statement, business firms must study changes to assets and liabilities *in relation to* changes in profits and losses. This conclusion explains in large part why the general ledger application is so valuable: it produces both balance sheets and profit and loss statements, and, more important, it requires that both statements be in balance relative to each other.

Service Type

An Oregon Corporation

See Accountant's Compilation Report

Income Statement

For the Period 01/01/8X to 02/28/8X

	Current-Period		Year-To-Date	
	Amount	Ratio	Ratio	Amount
Income:				
Sales—Class A	$1,232.87	36.36	35.48	$2,258.45
Sales—Class B	2,158.19	63.64	64.52	4,106.20
Total Income	$3,391.06	100.00	100.00	$6,364.65
Expenses:				
Advertising	$ 62.58	1.85	2.13	$ 135.80
Auto Expense	102.98	3.04	4.45	283.33
Bank Charges	5.12	.15	.15	9.24
Depreciation	135.73	4.00	4.26	270.84
General Expense	42.12	1.24	1.03	65.59
Insurance	27.00	.80	.85	54.00
Legal & Accounting	231.72	6.83	5.50	350.14
Office Expense	57.66	1.70	1.58	100.31
Rent	320.72	9.46	10.08	641.44
Repairs & Maintenance	61.14	1.80	1.81	114.93
Telephone	60.17	1.77	1.78	113.04
Utilities	72.09	2.13	1.96	124.93
Wages—Sales	1,138.87	33.58	32.92	2,095.16
Payroll Taxes	389.98	11.50	15.26	971.47
Total Expenses	$2,707.88	79.85	83.76	$5,330.22
Taxable Income	$ 683.18	20.15	16.24	$1,034.43
Estimated Income Tax	116.14	3.42	2.76	175.85
Total Estimated Income Tax	$ 116.14	3.42	2.76	$ 175.85
Net Income (or Loss)	$ 567.04	16.73	13.48	$ 858.58

Figure 13-10 Profit and loss statement

13-2 GENERAL LEDGER PROCESSING

Figure 13-11 shows the systems organization chart for the general ledger computer application. It is similar to several other charts discussed in earlier chapters, with some important differences. First, no transaction file is created by processing. Instead, the interactive portion of processing consists of updating the consolidated general ledger master file and of displaying records stored on this file. Second, account totals can be keyed to processing by the user of an interactive program called "enter journal vouchers" or posted to the master file

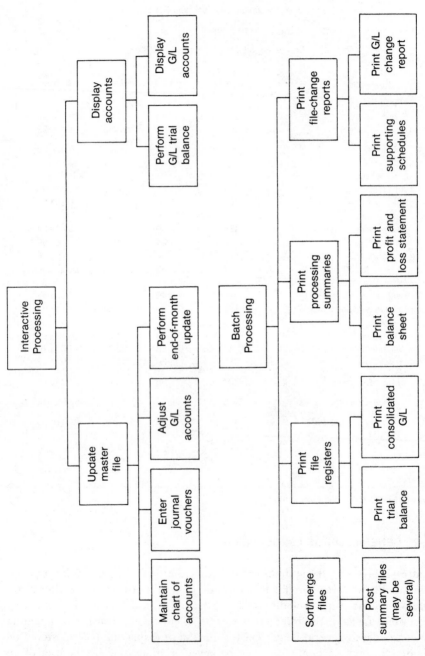

Figure 13-11 General ledger systems organization chart

I.1 MAINTAIN CHART OF ACCOUNTS
I.2 ENTER JOURNAL VOUCHERS
I.3 ADJUST G/L ACCOUNTS
I.4 PERFORM END-OF-MONTH UPDATE
I.5 PERFORM G/L TRIAL BALANCE
I.6 DISPLAY G/L ACCOUNTS

B.1 POST SUMMARY FILES
B.2 PRINT TRIAL BALANCE
B.3 PRINT CONSOLIDATED G/L
B.4 PRINT BALANCE SHEET
B.5 PRINT PROFIT AND LOSS STATEMENT
B.6 PRINT SUPPORTING SCHEDULES
B.7 PRINT G/L CHANGE REPORT
⟨8⟩ EXIT

Figure 13-12   General ledger processing menu

by a batch program called "post summary files." Third, the trial balance can be either displayed by the interactive program called "perform G/L trial balance" or printed by the batch program entitled "print trial balance." Fourth, the main products of processing are financial summaries, namely, the balance sheet and the profit and loss statement. No transaction document, similar to an employee paycheck or a customer invoice, is produced by processing.

Figure 13-12 illustrates the main processing menu that follows from the systems organization chart. Of the thirteen programs, the interactive program entitled "perform end-of-month update" is used to reset the G/L master file. This program sets all current balance totals to zero; the closing balance becomes the opening balance for the next accounting period.

A number of interactive display programs and batch reporting programs can be added to the program-processing menu in order to perform the several types of financial analyses that are often desired by managers. These include the analysis of cash sources and uses (cash flow), of items contributing to profits and losses, of selected assets and liabilities, of income seasonality, and of historical income averages.

Updating the General Ledger Master File

As Figure 13-11 shows, four interactive programs and one batch program are required to update the consolidated G/L master file. Because each of these programs serves a unique purpose, we will briefly review them.

The *maintain chart of accounts program* adds or deletes accounts from the master chart of accounts, changes existing account numbers, and displays portions of the chart for review. If a company designs a comprehensive chart of accounts to begin with, there should be little need to make major account changes from one accounting period to another. Generally most alterations occur when a company that breaks down its sales by product line later decides to make changes to the line. For example, in the detailed breakdown of sales and cost of sales of an automotive dealership, as shown in Figure 13-13, over 60 codes are required to classify sales information. The actual breakdown depends on how the company decides to show sources of income, such as by new passenger vehicles, used passenger vehicles, general service, paint and body service, parts and accessories, and so on. If the company later decides to add new truck and used truck vehicles to its product line, chart-of-account codes must be added to capture and track the income produced by both types of truck sales.

The *enter journal vouchers program* allows direct entry and editing of general ledger transactions. These transaction totals are initially recorded on journal vouchers (see Figure 13-4), after which they are keyed to processing. As Figure 13-14 shows, the amount of information to be keyed is quite minimal. Initially, the journal voucher number, the date, and the control total (the total debit or credit amount) are keyed. Next the first line item on the voucher is entered into processing by keying its account number and, when necessary, its description. The account number serves as the primary key to processing. It must be matched against the corresponding key stored on the master chart of accounts. After the match, the debit or credit amount, the source, and, where necessary, the detailed reference are keyed. The source specifies the number of the supporting journal (the document showing individual entries). The number "CR0021," for example, indicates that the details can be traced to cash receipts, journal number 21. The detailed reference might be used to clarify the reason for an entry, such as "replenish petty cash."

The *adjust G/L accounts program* allows direct entry and editing of general ledger adjustments. Adjusting entries serve two basic purposes: they back out financial totals entered in error and they permit new balancing entries to be entered into processing. In theory, neither type of adjustment should have to be made, since financial accounts should be properly accounted for and in balance prior to their initial entry to the general ledger. Unfortunately, this theory seldom holds in practice, and adjustments to inventory, receivables, fixed assets, and other types of records must be made to correct minor mistakes and to balance general ledger totals, when for some reason they are off by a few cents.

Many companies require all adjusting entries to be inspected and signed by company managers. If especially large adjustments are made, such as reducing the value of inventory by $1,000 or more, several managers may be required to initiate a change. Likewise, any adjustment that affects employee, customer, or vendor financial totals must be subjected to close inspection. These practices are advisable to avoid possible coverups. If general ledger adjustments are poorly supervised, for example, it is possible to juggle financial accounts in order to make a sick business look well or to cover up employee negligence and sometimes fraud.

```
                              SALES
                          COST OF SALES

    Acct. Number
    Sales  Cost

    5100   6100                          NEW VEHICLES

    5101   6101      Passenger - Sedan - Type 1409
    5102             Passenger - Sedan - Type 1409 Discount
    5104   6104      Passenger - Sports Coupe
    5105             Passenger - Sports Coupe Discount
    5111   6111      Passenger - Fastback
    5112             Passenger - Fastback Discount
    5114   6114      Passenger - Hatchback - Type XC14
    5115             Passenger - Hatchback - Type XC14 Discount
    5121   6121      Passenger - Wagon
    5122             Passenger - Wagon Discount
    5141   6141      Truck - Shortbed - Type 2
    5142             Truck - Shortbed - Type 2 Discount
    5144   6144      Passenger - Sedan - Type 1500Y
    5145             Passenger - Sedan - Type 1500Y Discount
    5147   6147      Passenger - Coupe - Type 1505Z
    5148             Passenger - Coupe - Type 1505Z Discount
    5161   6161      Passenger - Fleet and Employee
    5162             Passenger - Fleet and Employee Discount
    5171   6171      Demonstrator
    5172             Demonstrator Discount
    5181   6181      Other Makes
    5182             Other Makes Discount
    5191   6191      Dealer Installed Accessories
           6192      Dealer Installed Accessories - Cost
           6193      Dealer Installed Accessories - Labor


    5200   6200                         USED VEHICLES
    5201   6201      Dealer Makes - Retail
           6203      Dealer Makes - Reconditioning
    5251   6251      Other Makes - Retail
           6253      Other Makes - Reconditioning
    5281   6281      Wholesale
           6283      Inventory Adjustments


    5400   6400                       SERVICE - GENERAL
    5401             Shop Labor Mechanical - Customer Sales
    5402             Shop Labor Mechanical - Factory Warranty Sales
    5404             Shop Labor Mechanical - Internal Sales
           6405      Cost of Labor - General Shop
    5411             Other Shop Labor and Material - Customer Sales
    5412             Other Shop Labor and Material - Internal Sales
           6415      Cost of Labor and Material - Other Shop
    5421   6421      Gas, Oil, and Grease
    5441   6441      Sales Repairs - General


    5500   6500                    SERVICE - PAINT AND BODY
    5501             Shop Labor - Customer Sales
    5502             Shop Labor - Factory Warranty Sales
    5504             Shop Labor - Internal Sales
           6505      Cost of Labor - Paint and Body
    5511   6511      Paint and Supplies
    5531   6531      Contract Paint and Body


    5700   6700                    PARTS AND ACCESSORIES
    5701   6701      General Repair Order - Customer Sales
    5702   6702      General Repair Order - Factory Warranty Sales
    5704   6704      General Repair Order - Internal Sales
    5711   6711      Other Makes General Repair Order
    5721   6721      Paint and Body Repair Order - Customer Sales
    5722   6722      Paint and Body Repair Order - Factory Warranty
    5724   6724      Paint and Body Repair Order - Internal Sales
    5741   6741      Over the Counter - Retail
    5742   6742      Over the Counter - Wholesale
    5744   6744      Over the Counter - Paint and Body Shops
    5771   6771      Other Parts and Accessories
           6772      Inventory Adjustments - Parts
           6774      Inventory Adjustments - Accessories
           6776      Inventory Adjustments - Other
```

Figure 13-13 Detailed sales and cost of sales account breakdown

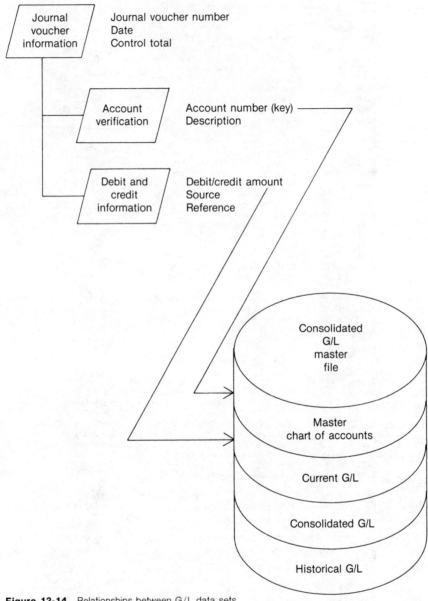

Figure 13-14 Relationships between G/L data sets

The *perform end-of-month update program* moves the current month's financial totals to last month's financial totals and sets current-month totals to zero. As Figure 13-15 shows, this interactive update program creates a new consolidated G/L master file with reset (set to zero) totals. After the new file is ready for processing, the old file is written to magnetic tape and saved. This file-backup procedure makes it possible to recreate the G/L master file if the reset copy is lost or destroyed.

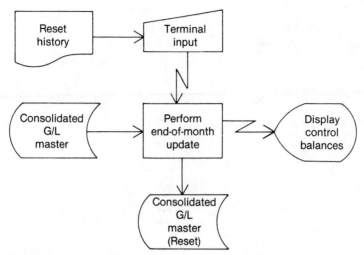

Figure 13-15 End-of-month update

The *post summary files program* transfers general ledger summary records from summary files created earlier by other computer applications. As Figure 13-16 shows, several different types of summary data are usually posted to the general ledger master file. When summary data are improperly sequenced, a sort of the summary file is required to order the file in general-ledger-number sequence.

Instead of printing all changes to the general ledger master file during the posting run, it is usually adequate to display account balances before and after the update and to write all update changes to the general ledger change file (see Figure 13-16). Since summary file totals must be verified prior to posting, an additional print of the file is usually not warranted. Finally, Figure 13-16 shows that it may be necessary to enter financial totals from journal vouchers into processing as part of posting run. Specifically, a debit or credit dollar amount may have to be entered to balance the financial amount entered from the summary file. As an example, suppose all cash-receipt totals are contained in receipts summary files, but accounts receivable totals are entered into processing by hand. In order to balance debits with credits, a journal voucher must be prepared. This voucher records the decrease in accounts receivable brought about by the increase in cash receipts.

Balancing the General Ledger Master File

Once all financial totals have been entered or posted, the trial balance program can be run. As Figure 13-11 shows, either an interactive or a batch program can be used to perform the trial balance. In practice, the interactive program is used first; the batch program is held in reserve and used later on to print *general ledger worksheets,* for use when attempting to determine what must be done to balance the file, or the final vault copy of the general ledger trial balance report.

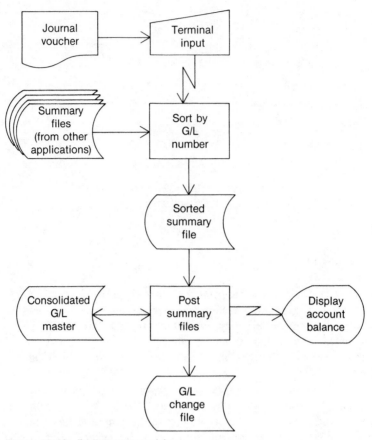

Figure 13-16 Posting summary data

Two popular processing strategies are followed to balance general ledger files. The first is to balance only the current portion of the file, holding off the update of the consolidated, YTD portion until the current portion is in balance. The second is to balance portions of the current portion of the file before attempting to achieve a final balance. Using this latter strategy, for example, one can double-check the debits and credits associated with payroll processing before moving to check the debits and credits associated with receivables processing. In each case, increases or decreases in assets must be offset by increases or decreases in liabilities. Likewise, increases in expenses must be offset by a reduction in profits.

Printing Financial Summaries

Once the current portion of the general ledger is in balance and the consolidated YTD portion is updated, financial summaries can be printed. This is one of the easiest steps in processing. As Figure 13-17 shows, printing the profit and

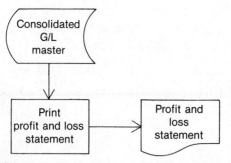

Figure 13-17   Printing the profit and loss statement

loss statement follows directly from the balanced consolidated general ledger master file. Prior to processing, print parameters must be specified (for example, "print current profit and loss only" or "print and compare current and YTD profit and loss totals"). Moreover, if historical month-by-month general ledger totals are kept on file (see Figure 13-14), it is possible to specify such comparisons as current profit this year, to profit same month last year; or profit this YTD, to profit last YTD.

Besides printing common types of financial summaries, newer online general ledger applications are designed to produce various types of financial performance summaries and comparisons. Figure 13-18, for instance, graphs current assets to current liabilities to show differences in their respective trends. Figure

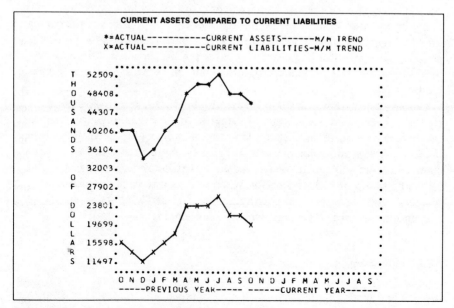

Figure 13-18   Comparing current assets with current liabilities

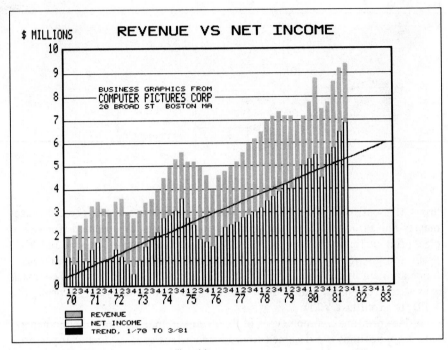

Figure 13-19 Comparing revenue with net income

13-19 compares revenues to net income and presents the corresponding trend. This graph might be prepared for the company as a whole, or several graphs might be prepared to show the performance of various divisions of the company. Finally, Figure 13-20 shows expenditures by department over a twenty-six-week period. This composite bar chart illustrates the proportional differences in expenditures; the attached table shows the columns of figures used in preparing the bar chart.

Graphs such as those shown in Figures 13-18, 13-19, and 13-20 should not be viewed as rare examples of general ledger outputs or of things to come. With the dynamic increase in the development of online graphic display devices, black and white and color pictures of financial performance are already quite common. More important, recent technological innovations suggest that pictures and tables of financial performance will soon replace detailed listings of financial results—at least for portraying financial-performance summary information for purposes of management decision making.

13-3 PROCESSING CONTROLS

The general ledger application clarifies why processing controls are vital to all business computer applications. Companies have discovered that the key to balancing the general ledger lies not within the general ledger application itself,

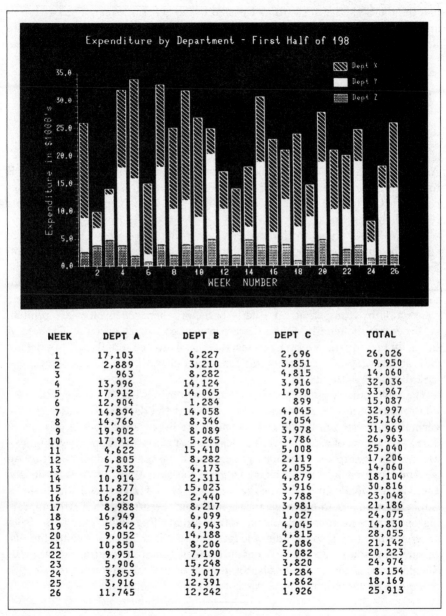

Figure 13-20 Comparing departmental expenses

WEEK	DEPT A	DEPT B	DEPT C	TOTAL
1	17,103	6,227	2,696	26,026
2	2,889	3,210	3,851	9,950
3	963	8,282	4,815	14,060
4	13,996	14,124	3,916	32,036
5	17,912	14,065	1,990	33,967
6	12,904	1,284	899	15,087
7	14,894	14,058	4,045	32,997
8	14,766	8,346	2,054	25,166
9	19,902	8,089	3,978	31,969
10	17,912	5,265	3,786	26,963
11	4,622	15,410	5,008	25,040
12	6,805	8,282	2,119	17,206
13	7,832	4,173	2,055	14,060
14	10,914	2,311	4,879	18,104
15	11,877	15,023	3,916	30,816
16	16,820	2,440	3,788	23,048
17	8,988	8,217	3,981	21,186
18	16,949	6,099	1,027	24,075
19	5,842	4,943	4,045	14,830
20	9,052	14,188	4,815	28,055
21	10,850	8,206	2,086	21,142
22	9,951	7,190	3,082	20,223
23	5,906	15,248	3,820	24,974
24	3,853	3,017	1,284	8,154
25	3,916	12,391	1,862	18,169
26	11,745	12,242	1,926	25,913

but, rather, within transaction-based applications such as customer invoicing and fixed assets. If summary information processed by these applications is in balance prior to posting, the balancing adjustments required by the general ledger application will be minimal.

A brief review of the processing controls required by the customer invoicing application shows the relationship between transaction-based financial balances and the totals carried forward and posted to the general ledger. The batch balances required for invoice dollar totals were expressed by two equations (see Section 4-4):

Total invoice charge =
Product dollars + Tax dollars + Freight dollars + Insurance dollars

and

Total invoice receipts (net dollar amount) =
Total invoice charge (gross dollar amount) − Cash discount

As stated in Chapter 4, these dollar amounts must be in balance if processing is to continue; they are carried forward in processing and serve as the balance-control totals for the invoice A/R summary file—the input file to accounts receivable processing.

What was not stated in this earlier chapter, but can be now, is that invoice control balances and their various subtotals are carried forward to the general ledger. For example, the total invoice charge is posted to one G/L account, the product dollars subtotal is posted to a second G/L account, the tax dollars subtotal is posted to a third G/L account, and so forth. This posting is done transaction by transaction, on a daily basis, or whenever invoices are printed. At the end of the month, summaries are prepared for each account. The sum of the daily tax dollars subtotal, for instance, leads to the month-end tax dollars G/L account total. The same is true for freight charges, insurance charges, and cash discounts allowed.

The importance of this procedure should be obvious: the month-end summation should always be in balance, provided that the daily totals posted to the general ledger were in balance. A second, more important aspect of this procedure—one not as obvious—is that a clear audit trail is always preserved in processing. For example, an auditor can begin with the general ledger and trace an account entry back to a subsidiary ledger, such as the invoice A/R summary. Likewise, the totals appearing on the summary can be traced. Individual entries can be traced back to batch balance figures and, eventually, to figures appearing on shipping documents and customer order-filling slips. This path, from general ledger totals, to subsidiary ledger totals, to batch balance-control totals, to individual source documents constitutes the audit trail required by business. Should financial totals appear suspect, it must be possible to retrace the steps in processing to determine whether or not each step is accurate.

13-4 MANAGEMENT IMPLICATIONS

The general ledger application, more than any other, shows that business data processing must consist of an interrelated data structure. This application finally clarifies why summary data must be collected at various points in processing; it shows the relationships that must exist between the general ledger and subsidiary ledgers, such as summary reports and detailed registers. The general ledger application also helps to better clarify two other concepts important to online systems design: it specifies how the complete company audit trail is constructed; it begins to explain how company audits of computer-based processing are conducted.

Because of the importance of the general ledger application in relation to other applications, some companies believe that a simplified version of the application should be implemented prior to the development of any other transaction-based application, such as accounts payable or employee payroll. There is some merit to this *top-down approach* to design. Clearly, a well-conceived and complete company chart of accounts must be defined in advance. Designers must know when and where account codes will be required; the entries that are to appear on the consolidated general ledger must be specified. Otherwise, it will be difficult to expect summary data to be in the correct format; it will be especially difficult to tie together different types of business information.

Besides consolidating business information, another major implication of the general ledger application is that it provides managers with timely and meaningful financial-summary information. Without automation, the general ledger is often a historical document, arriving three to six months after an accounting period. With the computer, however, the general ledger should be in final form within one to two weeks following the end of an accounting period. If, for example, the books are closed on the fifteenth of each month, upper management should be able to review general ledger summaries within ten days and thus determine before the end of the month whether company performance is acceptable. Moreover, the general ledger makes possible a far-reaching and complete analysis, addressing not only questions of profit or loss but also financial conditions and trends. Provided with a number of special reporting options, managers are able to come up with a clearer, more comprehensive picture of the financial well-being of the organization.

REVIEW OF IMPORTANT IDEAS

The general ledger application consolidates the financial transactions of a business in order to summarize, by account, changes to assets and liabilities. The integration of the various types of incomes, expenses, assets, and liabilities is accomplished by the use of a master chart of accounts that defines the major financial activities of a business and how they are tied together.

The preliminary processing of the general ledger application consists of updating and balancing the consolidated G/L master file. The updating of the file can occur in one of two ways: financial summary totals can be recorded on journal vouchers, from which they must be keyed to processing; or summary totals can be transferred from summary files created earlier by other online applications. The balancing of the file can also take place in one of two ways: either an interactive or a batch program can be used to determine whether the various financial totals are in balance. In practice, the batch program is chosen when a printed copy of the entire master file is desired, or when worksheets are needed to fix out-of-balance conditions.

The summary outputs from transaction-based computer applications, such as accounts receivable and accounts payable, serve as inputs to general ledger processing. In addition, the age-old practice of double-entry bookkeeping is built into the general ledger design. In all instances, inputs to the general ledger must be in balance. Debits must be offset by credits in order to properly post summary totals.

Instead of updating the G/L master file as part of the general ledger application, updates can be incorporated into the design of other computer applications. This practice avoids the need to post data from summary files or to enter data into processing directly. This approach has certain disadvantages, however. Besides expense and program complexity, there is greater difficulty in auditing processing.

The main outputs from general ledger processing are the general ledger trial balance report, the consolidated general ledger, and a variety of financial statements. Most online applications feature various types of financial performance summaries and comparisons.

The general ledger application clarifies why processing controls are vital to all business computer applications. The key to balancing the general ledger (and thus the books of a business) can be traced to transaction-based processing systems. If the summary totals produced by these lower-level systems are in balance prior to their posting, the balancing of the G/L master file is greatly simplified.

The general ledger application begins to show the value of a top-down design. Systems designers must specify early on in the design process what types of summary data are to be prepared. This must be done to successfully tie together the many different types of business information produced by the various paperwork-processing activities of a business.

KEY WORDS

Balance sheet	Debit
Profit and loss statement	Credit
Cash-flow statement	Double-entry bookkeeping
Chart of accounts	Journal voucher
Consolidated G/L master file	Subsidiary ledger
Trial balance	General ledger trial balance report
Consolidated general ledger	

REVIEW QUESTIONS

1. What information is printed on the company balance sheet? On the profit and loss statement?

2. What is a master chart of accounts?

3. Two equations, one for the balance sheet and the other for the profit and loss statement, must be in balance. Show these two equations.

4. What is a trial balance? Of what importance is a trial balance to general ledger processing?

5. What are the main sources of input to the consolidated G/L master file?

6. What is double-entry bookkeeping? How does double-entry bookkeeping apply in general ledger processing?

7. What types of information are recorded on a journal voucher?

8. What are the advantages of updating the general ledger directly (as part of other business computer applications, such as customer invoicing or accounts payable)? What are the disadvantages?

9. Name the main types of reports produced by general ledger processing.

10. What information is printed on the consolidated general ledger?

11. How does the maintain chart of accounts program differ from the enter journal vouchers program?

12. Why are general ledger adjustments important to processing?

13. Name the two popular processing strategies followed in balancing the general ledger file.

14. How does the general ledger application help to clarify why processing controls are vital to all business computer applications?

15. What is the difference between the general ledger and a subsidiary ledger? Between a subsidiary ledger and a batch balance-control total?

16. Why must the master chart of accounts be defined in advance? What occurs if it is not properly defined in advance?

EXERCISES

1. Suppose that the direct update of the consolidated G/L master file is to be designed into the customer cash-receipts computer application.

   (a) Using a systems flowchart, show where and when the update would take place.

   (b) Explain how general ledger debits and credits would be balanced in processing.

   (c) Explain how control would be maintained in processing.

   (d) Discuss the advantages and disadvantages of such a direct update.

2. You have decided to design a personal general ledger system to help you track your personal assets, liabilities, income, and expenses. The entry of data to processing will consist of using a limited number of source documents. These are the voucher portion of your paycheck, your personal checkbook check register, bank statements mailed quarterly to your home, monthly bills, and cash-register receipts for such items as entertainment expenses, lunches, transportation, and educational supplies. Using Figure 13-1 as a guide, explain how data entered from each source document will change general ledger account totals.

3. Company A, the takeover company, merges with Company B. Both firms are very large and use their own unique chart of accounts; both firms have developed online general ledger computer applications. What action must Company A now take to produce a single balance sheet and profit and loss statement for the two merged companies? Discuss several possible design strategies. Consider the strengths and weaknesses of each strategy.

14

Budget and Profit Planning

Two financial-planning computer applications can be implemented in conjunction with the development of the general ledger application. The first of these, the *budget-planning application,* is designed to compare estimated and actual business expenses. This application requires departments and divisions of a company to estimate the amount of money they will need to cover their expenses over a specified period. Once these estimates are approved by upper management, funds can be allocated to various divisions and departments. This process of estimating the need for funds and deciding on what level to approve is known as *budgeting.* Funds allocated to departments signify the dollars included in a *budget:* a formal business planning document showing what amount of money is available to pay for departmental expenses. As this chapter illustrates, budgeting combines both planning and control. Planning deals with the decisions leading to the determination of the amount of money to be included in a budget; control monitors the actual expenditure of funds to determine if the budgeted amount was realistic.

Besides the budget-planning application, this chapter also reviews the *profit-planning application.* Profit planning compares planned business profits with actual profits. Like budgeting, profit planning requires departments and divisions to estimate their expenses over a specified period. Once these estimates are set, however, they are compared against value-added estimates. The difference between the two—value-added estimates less budgeted expenses—leads to a determination of the contributions to profit to be realized by the various stages of a business.

14-1 BUDGET PLANNING OVERVIEW

There are several reasons for developing an online budget-planning computer application. This application can enhance a business's ability to understand and plan for anticipated business expenses; it can also improve budget allocation procedures, tracking of planned to actual business expenditures, and financial reporting. In addition, an online budget-planning computer application enables management to ask a variety of "what if" questions about company finances, such as "What if personnel costs were increased by 10 percent?" In this instance, management would like to know the financial implications, by budgeted area, of a 10 percent increase in labor costs.

The online budget-planning application is usually designed to deal with fixed or variable budgeting. A *fixed budget* does not change as production or sales volumes increase or decrease. Instead each department or cost center is allocated a fixed dollar amount to cover its expenses. If this amount proves to be inadequate—due to higher than expected company activities—the budgeted amount must be adjusted upwards to provide for additional funding for operations. Likewise, lower than expected company activities require that budgeted amounts be adjusted downwards. Typically, these adjustments are made either quarterly or yearly, rather than month by month. With a fixed budget, departments must learn to live with the level of funding made available.

A *variable budget* does change as production or sales volumes vary. For example, the cost of running a machine for 2,000 hours would be budgeted using one set of numbers, whereas the cost of running the same machine for 5,000 hours would be budgeted using another set of numbers. To account for differences in volume, a standard rate, such as the cost per hour or the cost per unit, is established for different work centers. This rate is multiplied by estimated production forecast or *activity figures* expressed as either the total number of machine hours required, the number of labor hours required, or the number of units to be produced. Budget totals are thus based on formulas, such as the following:

Budget total = Machine-hour rate (standard) ×
            Number of machine hours (estimated)

Budget total = Labor-hour rate (standard) ×
            Number of labor hours (estimated)

Budget total = Cost per unit (standard) ×
            Number of units produced (estimated)

Regardless of which type of budgeting is adopted—fixed, variable, or some combination thereof—budgeted expenses must be compared with actual expenses. As discussed in the last chapter, actual expenses are summarized by the current and the consolidated portions of the G/L master file. Thus, the budget-

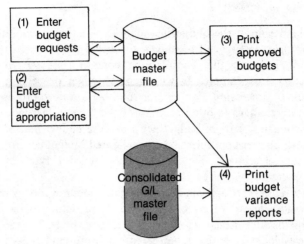

Figure 14-1 Budget-planning preliminary overview

planning application is divided into two phases (see Figure 14-1), the first of which consists of preparing the budget master file and of printing approved budgets. After this is done, the budgeted figures stored on the budget master file are compared against the actual expenses stored on the G/L master file. The purpose of this comparison is the production of a number of budget control reports known as *budget variance reports*. These reports show such things as the difference between budgeted expense and actual expense for the current period, and the amount of money remaining to cover actual expenses for the remainder of a budgeted period.

The four steps shown in Figure 14-1 can be summarized as follows:

1. *Enter budget requests* consists of entering into processing the total dollars estimated as being needed by various company divisions and departments.
2. *Enter budget appropriations* consists of entering into processing the total dollars budgeted to various divisions and departments.
3. *Print approved budgets* produces the documents showing how funds have been budgeted.
4. *Print budget variance reports* produces the reports and displays showing the differences between budgeted and actual company expenses.

Typically, *budget requests* (the requests for dollars to be placed in the budget) are always larger than *budget appropriations* (the actual dollars placed in the budget). Since the different divisions and departments of a company almost always have financial needs greater than what can be supported, budget cuts must be made. These cuts entail reducing requested departmental budget dollars until they reach a level that can be supported.

The Budget Master File

Central to the design of the budget-planning application is the building of the *budget master file*. As Figure 14-2 shows, this file is similar in some ways to the consolidated G/L master file. The file must contain a *master chart of budget accounts* section, for example. As with general ledger processing, this section controls access to processing. Each budget number keyed to processing must be approved before changes to other sections of the file can be made.

Besides the master chart of budget accounts, the budget master file contains budget request, budget appropriation, consolidated budget control, and historical budget control sections. Figure 14-3 illustrates the types of information found in each area of the file.

The *budget request* section contains the total amount of money requested and the date of the request. Many companies require dollar totals to be spread across several fiscal periods. As shown, quarterly, first-, second-, and third-period requests indicate dollar requirements at different points in each fiscal year.

The *budget appropriation* section stores the total amount of money set aside for each budget account number, as well as the total allocation to date, the period-by-period breakdown of the allocation, and the date of appropriation. It is common to appropriate (budget for a department) one dollar amount and to allocate a smaller amount. The dollar difference is held in reserve. For example, $50,000 might be appropriated to cover interest expenses, but $45,000 might be allocated. The remaining $5,000 would be held in reserve to cover higher-than-expected interest costs. This money is allocated once the actual need for funds is better known.

The *consolidated budget control* section holds both expended and encumbered expense totals. As Figure 14-3 shows, two encumbered expense totals are stored: the total open purchase requisition and the total open purchase order. These dollar amounts are transferred from the general ledger during the update of the budget control section. In addition, the total of actual dollars expended is stored in this section of the file. This total, also broken down by period, is compared against the budget allocation total to determine the budget variance.

The *historical budget control* section contains one or more years of budget planning totals and one or more years of actual expense and budget variance totals. Historical budget information is useful for making valuable comparisons such as examining the difference between previous budget requests and budget appropriations, or the difference between the current budget appropriation (or budget request) and last year's budget appropriation (or budget request).

Inputs to Processing

Several types of input are important in the budget-planning application. Of these, four types are required to ready the budget master file: budget account change slips, budget request worksheets, budget appropriation worksheets, and budget change slips.

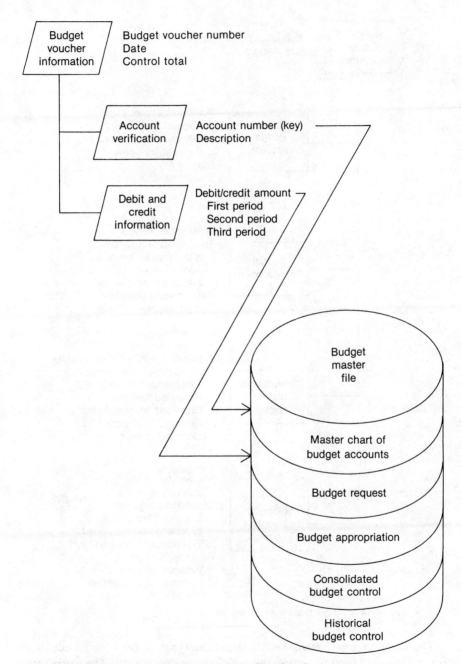

Figure 14-2 Relationships between budget master-file data sets

The *budget account change slip* is needed to add new budget accounts to the budget master file, to change an existing budget account number, or to delete an old number from the chart of budget accounts.

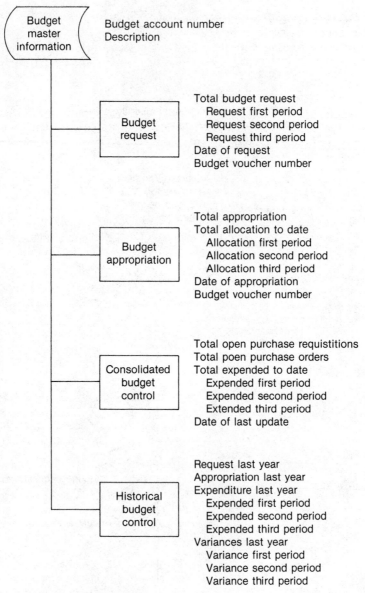

Figure 14-3 Budget master-file record segments

The *budget request worksheet* itemizes the types of funds required, by account number, period by period, for a division or department. The worksheet is a planning document. In some cases it shows how fixed budget requests were determined; in other cases it indicates how estimated activity units were determined. Once completed, the worksheet shows the total and itemized funds needed to cover the expenses of a division or department.

The *budget appropriation worksheet* itemizes the funds to be allocated, by account number, period by period, for a division or department. Appropriated totals must be keyed to processing much like budget request totals. Once keyed, the difference between the total dollars requested and the total dollars appropriated can be reconciled.

The *budget change slip* modifies previously set appropriation totals, when there is a need to adjust these totals during a fiscal year. Suppose Department A loses an employee, for example, and management decides not to fill the position (replace the person). Suppose further that management decides to add another staff position to Department B, with the understanding that a budget change will be processed to transfer salary funds. In this instance, funds will be transferred from the salary account for Department A to the salary account for Department B.

In making up budget request and appropriation worksheets, budget planners find it helpful if they can review their previous worksheets online and make changes to these sheets as required. This practice avoids the need to hand copy all budget entries; it avoids the totaling of budget rows and columns. Such online capabilities are often referred to as *electronic worksheets:* they feature online entry of data into rows and columns, followed by the summation of worksheet entries, as specified by the data-entry operator.

A final input to the budget-planning application is the *flow-of-funds forecast*. This forecast is based on sales estimates and production requirements for the company as a whole. It shows how many dollars can be appropriated, period by period. As an example, suppose the sales forecast indicates that 100,000 units of four-inch liners for potted plants will be sold during the next fiscal period. From cost-accounting data, unit cost data for these liners show that production costs will be approximately $.30 per unit, with selling costs approximately $.08 per unit and administrative and all other costs approximately $.08 per unit. From these per-unit figures and the sales estimate, it can be determined that the production budget should be $30,000, the sales budget, $8,000, and the administrative budget, also $8,000. Such individual-item sales and budget figures are combined with the sales and budget figures for all other products to compose the flow-of-funds forecast. Collectively, they determine the approximate amount of money that can be appropriated during a fiscal period.

Outputs from Processing

Two main products follow from the budget-planning application: annual budget materials and budget control comparisons. Figure 14-4 illustrates the annual budget for a single cost center in Plant A. As shown, two variable cost rates are set for direct labor; one variable cost rate and one fixed cost rate are set for indirect labor. The two variable rates represent the cost per machine hour and the cost per labor hour, respectively. They are applied against the estimated machine and man hours printed in the right-hand corner of the budget sheet. The dollar amount placed in the budget for direct labor is calculated by multiplying the variable rates times the estimated number of required hours. Thus, the total direct labor cost of $47,300 is determined as follows:

Direct labor costs (based on required machine hours) = $23,400 ($5.85000 per machine hour × 4,000 hours)

Direct labor costs (based on required man hours) = $23,900 ($2.39000 per labor hour × 10,000 hours)

The fixed cost rate does not vary with the number of hours required. Instead, it represents the cost per day regardless of the number of hours worked, machine hours used, or units produced. This can be seen by observing how the dollar total for indirect labor is computed (see Figure 14-4).

				ANNUAL BUDGET					
RE-SB4							Annual Activity Units		
Processed: 12/16/							Machine Hours	4,000	
Plant A	Cost Center	98-2035					Man Hours	10,000	
		Finishing					Days	250	

Acct. #	Account Description	Rates			Amounts			
		Var. #1	Var. #2	Fixed	Var. #1	Var. #2	Fixed	Total
501-006	Direct Labor	5.85000	2.39000		23,400	23,900		47,300
502-017	Indirect Labor	1.67500		38.40	6,700		9,600	16,300
503-141	Overtime Premium	.40000	.12000		1,600	1,200		2,800
724-211	Payroll Taxes & Fringe	1.58500	.50200	6.68	6,340	5,020	1,920	13,280
	TOTAL PAYROLL EXPENSE	9.51000	3.01200	46.08	38,040	30,120	11,520	79,680
579-018	Solvent S46B		.06000			600		600
579-040	Other Operating Supplies	.70000	.03000	2.00	2,800	300	500	3,600
581-007	Maintenance Parts	3.00000		1.00	12,000		250	12,250
637-001	Travel Expense			4.00			1,000	1,000
	TOTAL OTHER EXPENSE	3.70000	.09000	7.00	14,800	900	1,750	17,450
711-107	Maint. Labor & Overhead	1.87500		9.00	7,500		2,250	9,750
575-018	Electricity	1.20000		2.80	4,800		700	5,500
580-016	Depreciation			86.00			21,500	21,500
	TOTAL DIST. EXPENSE	3.07500		97.80	12,300		24,450	36,750
714-700	General Plant Expense			88.00			22,000	22,000
716-711	Taxes & Insurance			12.80			3,200	3,200
	TOTAL ALLOCATED EXPENSE			100.80			25,200	25,200
	COST CENTER TOTALS	16.28500	3.10200	251.68	65,140	31,020	62,920	159,080

Figure 14-4 Annual budget

Indirect labor costs (based on required machine hours) =
$6,700 ($1.67500 × 4,000 hours)

Indirect labor costs (based on fixed cost per day) =
$9,600 ($38.40 × 250 days per year)

An interesting feature of a combined variable-fixed cost budget is that cost center rates are also set for cost-center totals. As Figure 14-4 shows, the variable rates are $16.285 per machine hour and $3.102 per labor hour; the fixed cost rate is $251.68 per day. Figure 14-5, the monthly budget, shows how these cost-center rates are applied on a month-to-month basis. Here too the variable rates for the cost-center totals are $16.285 and $3.102; the fixed rate remains at $251.68. Instead of the rates changing, the information subject to change is the

MONTHLY SPENDING BUDGET

RE-SB4
Processed: 4/04/
Plant A   Cost Center   98-2035
                Finishing

Monthly Activity Units
Machine Hours 368
Man Hours   381
Days   23

Acct. #	Account Description	Rates			Amounts			
		Var. #1	Var. #2	Fixed	Var. #1	Var. #2	Fixed	Total
501-006	Direct Labor	5.85000	2.39000		2,153	911		3,064
502-017	Indirect Labor	1.67500		38.40	616		883	1,499
503-141	Overtime Premium	.40000	.12000		147	46		193
724-211	Payroll Taxes & Fringe	1.58500	.50200	7.68	583	191	177	951
	TOTAL PAYROLL EXPENSE	9.51000	3.01200	46.08	3,499	1,148	1,060	5,707
579-018	Solvent S46B		.06000			23		23
579-040	Other Operating Supplies	.70000	.03000	2.00	258	11	46	315
581-007	Maintenance Parts	3.00000		1.00	1,104		23	1,127
637-001	Travel Expense			4.00			92	92
	TOTAL OTHER EXPENSE	3.70000	.09000	7.00	1,362	34	161	1,557
711-107	Maintenance Labor & Overhead	1.87500		9.00	690		207	897
575-018	Electricity	1.20000		2.80	442		64	506
580-016	Depreciation			86.00			1,978	1,978
	TOTAL DIST. EXPENSE	3.07500		97.80	1,132		2,249	3,381
714-700	General Plant Expense			88.00			2,024	2,024
716-711	Taxes & Insurance			12.80			294	294
	TOTAL ALLOCATED EXPENSE			100.80			2,318	2,318
	COST CENTER TOTALS	16.28500	3.10200	251.68	5,993	1,182	5,788	12,963

Figure 14-5 Monthly budget

activity units—the machine hours required, the labor hours required, and the number of days worked.

Annual and monthly budgets are important products of processing—they specify how many dollars are available to be spent and, if based on standard rates, show how the dollars were arrived at. Even so, the reason for developing the online budget-planning application can most often be traced to the preparation of *budget variance* or *budget control reports*. Figure 14-6 illustrates one type of budget control report. This particular report compares actual monthly expenses against a monthly budget and YTD expenses against last year's YTD expenses. For each comparison, the variance is shown. Thus, Account G, "Grand Total All Expenses," shows an actual expenditure of $2,467 versus a budgeted amount of $3,174. The budget variance of $707 is simply the difference between the two cost figures ($3,174 − $2,467 = $707). Likewise, YTD expenses for the same account are $4,942. These are much lower than the expenses for a year ago, which are shown as $9,775. The difference between the two of $4,833 is recorded as the YTD variance.

Most budget control systems feature several budget-reporting options. For example, six reports concerning fixed budgets compare (1) the fixed monthly budget against current monthly expenses, (2) the fixed YTD monthly budget against YTD monthly expenses, (3) the fixed twelve-month budget (last twelve months) against the last twelve months' expenses, (4) the fixed averaged annual budget (annual budget ÷ 12) against current monthly expenses, (5) the averaged YTD monthly budget (YTD budget ÷ months YTD) against current monthly expenses, and (6) the fixed annual budget against the YTD budget. Besides fixed-budget comparisons, a number of reporting options must also be provided for variable budgets.

Somewhat more complicated budget comparisons determine budget-to-expenses percentages. One such comparison is based on the following ratio:

$$\text{Budget variance percentage} = \frac{\text{YTD expenses} - \text{YTD monthly budget}}{\text{Annual budget}}$$

This ratio is best explained by an example. Suppose the annual fixed budget for a department is $50,000, that expenses thus far (YTD) are $38,500, and that the YTD monthly budget (the sum of the monthly budget totals from the first month of the budget to the current month) is $35,000. Use of these figures yields a budget variance of 7 percent:

Budget variance = $38,500 − $35,000 ÷ $50,000 = .07 × 100 = 7 percent

Budget variance percentages, such as the 7 percent figure above, become especially useful when they are plotted to permit month-by-month comparisons. Figure 14-7 illustrates one type of variance graph based on percentages. As shown, actual variance percentages are compared against upper and lower control limits, set at plus 15 and minus 15 percent, respectively. Whenever the budget variance is shown as above the upper control limit, or below the lower control limit, the budget is said to be out of control. An out-of-control situation

ACCT DESCRIPTION	**** THIS MONTH ****			**** YEAR-TO-DATE ****			**** BUDGET ****		** LAST YEAR **	
	TRANS	$AMOUNT	PERCENT	TRANS	$AMOUNT	PERCENT	MONTHLY	VARIANCE	Y-T-D	VARIANCE
010 SALARY	2	1200.00	48.6	2	2400.00	48.6	1300.00	100.00	2800.00	400.00
012 OTHER PAYROLL EXPENSE	2	200.00	8.1	2	375.00	7.5	175.00	25.00-	450.00	75.00
-A-- PAYROLL	4	1400.00	56.7	4	2775.00	56.1	1475.00	75.00	3250.00	475.00
020 ELECTRICITY	1	50.00	2.0	2	120.00	2.4	75.00	25.00	110.00	10.00-
022 GAS	1	46.00	1.9	1	46.00	.9	50.00	4.00	65.00	19.00
024 TELEPHONE	1	38.00	1.5	2	85.00	1.7	60.00	22.00	75.00	10.00-
025 WATER	1	32.00	1.4	2	64.00	1.3	60.00	8.00	59.00	5.00-
026 GARBAGE				1	48.00	1.0	25.00	25.00	38.00	10.00-
027 OTHER	1	58.00	2.3	1	58.00	1.2	24.00	34.00-	22.00	36.00-
-B-- UTILITIES	5	224.00	9.1	9	421.00	8.5	274.00	50.00	369.00	52.00-
030 OFFICE SUPPLIES	2	80.00	3.2	3	130.00	2.6	100.00	20.00	110.00	20.00-
032 CLEANING	1	40.00	1.6	1	40.00	.8	50.00	10.00	40.00	.00
034 LAUNDRY	2	30.00	1.3	2	30.00	.7	30.00	0.00	25.00	5.00-
-C-- SUPPLIES	5	150.00	6.1	6	200.00	4.1	180.00	30.00	175.00	25.00-
040 ADVERTISING				1	80.00	1.6	100.00	100.00	200.00	120.00
042 PRINTING	1	58.00	2.4	1	58.00	1.2	120.00	62.00	250.00	192.00
044 PHOTOGRAPHY				1	135.00	2.7	100.00	100.00	250.00	192.00
046 GRAPHICS	1	200.00	8.1	2	295.00	6.0	150.00	50.00-	300.00	5.00
048 MISC. EXPENSE				1	35.00	.7	25.00	25.00	50.00	15.00
-D-- GENERAL EXPENSES	2	258.00	10.5	6	603.00	12.2	495.00	237.00	1050.00	447.00-
050 MORTGAGE	1	350.00	14.2	2	700.00	14.2	350.00	0.00	700.00	0.00
052 TAXES				0	0.00	.0	100.00	100.00	200.00	200.00
053 INSURANCE				0	0.00	.0	25.00	25.00	50.00	50.00-
-E-- REAL ESTATE EXP	1	350.00	14.2	2	700.00	14.2	475.00	125.00	950.00	250.00
060 REPAIRS - BUILDING				0	0.00	.0	75.00	75.00	3331.00	3331.00
062 EQUIPMENT	1	85.00	3.4	1	85.00	1.7	100.00	15.00	50.00	35.00-
063 FURN. AND FIXTURES				0	0.00	.0	50.00	50.00	300.00	300.00
065 SPECIAL EXPENSES				2	110.00	2.2	30.00	30.00	300.00	300.00
065 UNCLASSIFIED				1	48.00	1.0	20.00	20.00	0.00	48.00-
-F-- BUILDING EXPENSE	1	85.00	3.4	4	243.00	4.9	275.00	190.00	3981.00	3738.00
-G-- TOTAL-ALL EXPENSES	18	2467.00	100.0	35	4942.00	100.0	3174.00	707.00	9775.00	4833.00

Figure 14-6   Budget control report

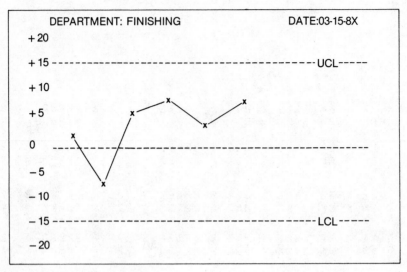

DEPARTMENT: FINISHING   DATE:03-15-8X

Figure 14-7 Control chart

calls for corrective action. If expenses are too high, cost reductions are required to bring expenses back in line with the YTD monthly budget. Likewise, if expenses are too low, a study must begin to determine how or why a department is able to hold off on its anticipated expenditures.

14-2 BUDGET-PLANNING PROCESSING

Figure 14-8 illustrates the budget-planning systems organization chart; Figure 14-9 shows the corresponding program-processing menu. These two figures show that the budget-planning application is similar to the general ledger application in many ways. For instance, several interactive programs are required to update the budget master file. Likewise, budget totals and comparisons can be either printed or displayed. Typically, interactive processing menu selections permit budget requests and appropriations to be both displayed and reviewed. Some selections may include a variety of budget-variance display options, such as department-by-department comparisons and expense-to-budget account comparisons.

The batch portion of processing produces budget worksheets, a variety of processing summaries, and the budget change report. The *budget request worksheet* is a dual-purpose document. Besides listing information stored on the budget master file, it is used in preparing new budget requests. Current budget figures are often very helpful in determining new budget request figures. The *annual budget* and *departmental budget summaries* are also dual-purpose documents. These documents provide a register of the contents of the budget

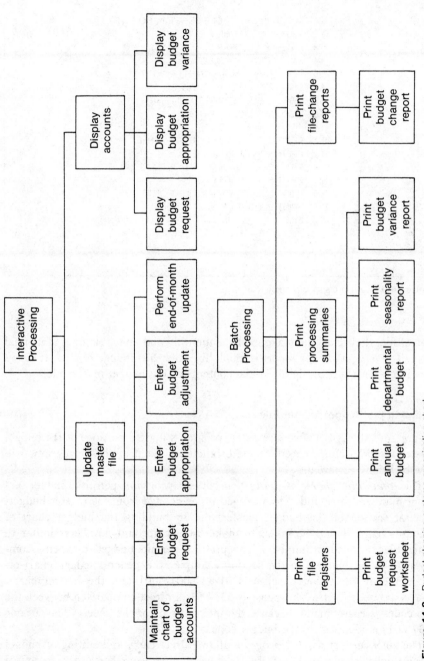

Figure 14-8 Budget-planning systems organization chart

```
        I.1   MAINTAIN CHART OF BUDGET ACCOUNTS
        I.2   ENTER BUDGET REQUEST
        I.3   ENTER BUDGET APPROPRIATION
        I.4   ENTER BUDGET ADJUSTMENT
        I.5   PERFORM END-OF-MONTH UPDATE
        I.6   DISPLAY BUDGET REQUEST
        I.7   DISPLAY BUDGET APPROPRIATION
        I.8   DISPLAY BUDGET VARIANCE


        B.1   PRINT BUDGET REQUEST WORKSHEET
        B.2   PRINT ANNUAL BUDGET
        B.3   PRINT DEPARTMENTAL BUDGET
        B.4   PRINT SEASONALITY REPORT
        B.5   PRINT BUDGET VARIANCE REPORT
        B.6   PRINT BUDGET CHANGE REPORT
        ⟨7⟩   EXIT
```

Figure 14-9   Budget-planning program menu

master file; they show the makeup of the monthly and annual budget in its final form. The *budget change report* is much like other file-change reports. It shows how interactive processing alters the contents of the budget master file.

Updating the Budget Master File

Figure 14-8 shows that five interactive programs update portions of the budget master file or perform specific update functions. Each of these programs will now be briefly reviewed.

The *maintain chart of budget accounts program* permits budget account numbers to be added to, changed in, or deleted from the master budget-account section of the budget master file. In building the budget chart of accounts, care should be taken to make budget account numbers similar to general ledger account numbers. This practice permits budget-to-expense comparisons to be made directly. If, for example, the general ledger chart-of-account code for travel expense is 01-637-001-5001 and the budget chart-of-account code for travel expense is 637-001, a direct comparison between the two codes is easily made, because the internal part of the general ledger code (637-001) is identical to the budget code.

The *enter budget request program* allows direct entry and editing of budget request dollar totals. As Figure 14-10 shows, budget worksheets serve as source documents to processing. The value of a worksheet is that it permits budget

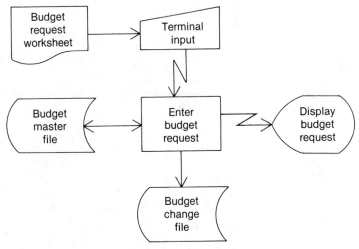

Figure 14-10 Entering budget request information

information to be entered into processing using a predetermined data-entry sequence, such as budget account by budget account, period by period.

Unfortunately, the budget request program is not as simple as it appears. For each budget amount requested, two or more postings to the budget master file must be made, and all changes must be written to the budget change file. The reason for double posting (updating more than one account) is to permit business expense budget totals to be isolated from departmental and cost-center budget totals. An example will help to clarify the difference between these two types of totals.

Suppose department 09, the personnel department, entered into processing a travel budget request for $10,000. The request is entered as follows:

```
DEPARTMENT:        09        PERSONNEL
BUDGET ITEM:       637-001   TRAVEL EXPENSE
TOTAL REQUEST:     $10,000
FIRST PERIOD:      $ 2,000
SECOND PERIOD:     $ 2,500
THIRD PERIOD:      $ 1,500
FOURTH PERIOD:     $ 4,000
```

After the fourth-period dollar amount was entered, the computer would sum periods one through four and match the total against the total request. Following this, the total request and the funds requested for the first, second, and third period would be posted to two accounts: the personnel department budget account and the travel expense budget account. The *departmental budget account,* as its name implies, stores budget information for a single department or cost center. As shown earlier (see Figure 14-5), each departmental budget account contains a number of business expense accounts, such as direct labor,

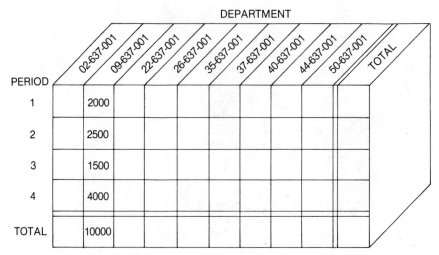

Figure 14-11 Budget-planning matrix

overtime premium, and travel expense. The *travel expense budget account,* in contrast to the departmental account, stores only travel expense information, but for all departments. As Figure 14-11 shows, this second posting serves to complete an entry in a *budget-planning matrix.* Each department within a company makes up a single column of the matrix. When the matrix is completed, the total request for travel funds can be analyzed in two ways: period by period, for the company as a whole, and period by period, for each department within a company.

The *enter budget appropriation program* features direct entry and editing of budget appropriation totals. Input to the program follows from two types of source documents: the *budget appropriation worksheet,* a master planning document that specifies the dollar amount to be appropriated and allocated, and the *activity* (or production) *forecast,* which indicates by cost center the number of machine hours required, labor hours required, and work days for each period. The budget appropriation worksheet itemizes the fixed portion of a departmental budget. Under the heading "direct advertising," for example, the number of dollars to be allocated for different types of advertising would be listed. The production forecast itemizes the variable portion of the budget. Within the forecast, units to be produced must be translated by the computer into machine and labor hours. For instance, if 10,000 units are to be produced over a 30-day period, and each unit requires .035 hours of machine time and .16 hours of a person's time, this production estimate (10,000 units) and standard hourly rates (time required per unit) would be translated by the computer as 350 machine hours and 1,600 labor hours during the next 30-day period.

Like the enter budget request program, the enter budget appropriation program posts appropriated dollars to both departmental and business expense accounts. Figure 14-12, continuing our earlier example, displays the appropri-

```
DEPARTMENT:  09            PERSONNEL
BUDGET ITEM:  637-001       TRAVEL EXPENSE
DATE OF REQUEST:  11-15-8X  OF APPROPRIATION:  12-14-8X


                 REQUEST   APPROPRIATION  /  ALLOCATION


  TOTAL          $10,000      $8,000           $7,000

  1ST PERIOD      2,000        1,500            1,500
  2ND PERIOD      2,500        2,000            2,000
  3RD PERIOD      1,500        1,500            1,500
  4TH PERIOD      4,000        3,000            2,000



  LEVEL         APPROPRIATED:  80%     ALLOCATED:   88%
```

Figure 14-12 Budget appropriation display

ation and allocation of travel expense funds for department 09, the personnel department. As indicated, 80 percent of the budget request was funded; 88 percent of the total appropriated was allocated. These appropriation and allocation figures are posted to the personnel department budget account (an 09 account) and to the travel expense budget account (a 637 account). Once this budget-planning decision is posted, it is also possible to display and review the figures and to revise them, if necessary. Later in the year, when more is known about the financing required for the fourth period, the dollars appropriated, but not allocated, will be either released to the personnel department or transferred to another department to meet an emergency funding situation.

A great deal of work takes place before budget-appropriation decisions are entered into processing. Budget officers must work with several managerial groups to arrive at the final production forecast and to establish company-wide budget funding limits. Once this is done, the difficult task of balancing budget requests with available funds begins. Suppose, for example, that $90,000 is available for travel expense for an entire fiscal year and that requests for travel total $160,000. The computer could be used to make a direct percentage travel allocation of 56.3 percent ($90,000 ÷ $160,000) to each department; however, budgeting is not as easy as this. In fact, most budgetary decisions follow from top-level management committee meetings. Managers at the top of an organization must decide on how many dollars to allocate for specific business activities and then decide on how to divide the total allocation among departments.

The *enter budget adjustment program* is similar in many ways to the enter budget appropriation program. Each time an adjustment in a departmental budget is to be made, a change slip must be prepared and processed. The several types of budget adjustments include releasing previously appropriated but never allocated budget funds; transferring funds from one department to another, while holding constant the total dollars contained in the budget; and increasing or decreasing the total budget. This last adjustment might follow from a revised production forecast—thus changing activity units such as machine and labor hours required—or from an administrative decision to reduce business overhead expenses, such as administrative and selling expenses, if sales have been lower than expected. Other factors such as new wage and salary settlements, sharp increases in selected raw material prices, or major increases in the cost of energy also lead to changes in budgeted totals.

The *perform end-of-month update program* is one of the more important budget-planning update programs. As in general ledger processing, the end-of-month program must ready the master file for next month's processing. With budgeting, this entails shifting the current month's budget totals to last month's totals, resetting the current budget variance totals to zero, and shifting next month's budget totals to this month's budget totals. After the shifts are performed, the old file is generally written to magnetic tape and stored. As with general ledger processing, this procedure makes it possible to restore the budget master file.

The budget perform end-of-month update program also differs from the end-of-month general ledger update program. As Figure 14-13 shows, the interactive program merges and transfers information from the old budget master and the consolidated G/L master file to a new budget master file. By updating, actual expense information is combined with budgeted expense information.

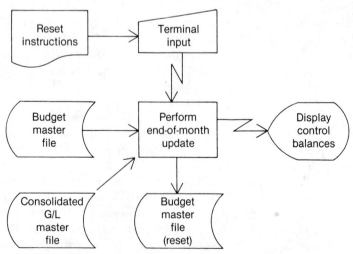

Figure 14-13 End-of-period update

Through updating, the budget-control sections of the file are revised (see Figure 14-3), in one of two ways. Either the consolidated budget-control portion of the file is altered at the end of a period, by adding current expense totals and revising total purchase requisition encumbrances, total purchase order encumbrances, and total expenses to date, or the historical budget-control section of the file is changed at the end of the year, by shifting the total expended to date and period by period for the last year from the current to the historical part of the file. In the second option, the budget variance per period is also calculated and shifted, and the totals requested and allocated are preserved for future budget-planning sessions.

Comparing Budgeted Expenses Against Actual Expenses

Once the budget master file and the consolidated G/L master file are adjusted and balanced, the accounts on each file can be compared. As Figure 14-14 shows, this comparison does not require that the two files be merged—even though totals are transferred from the consolidated G/L master file during month-end processing. Instead, the entry of a single account number leads to the extraction of budgeted dollar amounts and actual dollars encumbered or expended.

Figure 14-15 shows a budget-variance display resulting from comparing budgeted against actual dollar totals. As illustrated, the allocated total is compared with the expended and the encumbered dollar totals. The running balance shown on the right-hand side indicates that the department was under budget by $500 for the first period and that the department remained at this level during the second period. It also shows that expenditures in the third period were much higher than expected. Currently, the department is over budget by

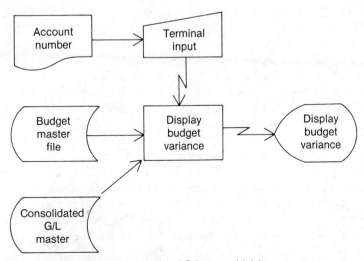

Figure 14-14 Comparing budget and G/L account totals

```
DEPARTMENT:  09                    PERSONNEL
BUDGET ITEM:  637-001              TRAVEL EXPENSE
DATE OF UPDATE:  8-15-8X           OF APPROPRIATION:  12-14-8X


               ALLOCATION   EXPENDED   ENCUMBERED   BALANCE

TOTAL          $7,000       $3,500     $3,000       $  500

1ST PERIOD      1,500        1,000                     500
2ND PERIOD      2,000        2,000                     500
3RD PERIOD      1,500          500      3,000        (1,500)
4TH PERIOD      2,000


LEVEL   APPROPRIATED: 80%    ALLOCATED: 88%   EXPENDED: 93%/81%
```

Figure 14-15 Budget variance display

$1,500. To the trained eye, this display shows an out-of-control budget situation. Unless the budgeted amount is increased to the appropriated level, the department will have problems remaining under budget. As indicated, 93 percent of the yearly allocation has been either expended or encumbered. Even if the additional $1,000 is released (from appropriated to allocated status, as shown in Figure 14-12), 81 percent of the yearly appropriation will have been expended or encumbered.

Because different people like to see budget-variance information presented and interpreted in different ways, it is common to find a number of display options built into the interactive portion of the budget-planning application. One option features a series of budget request, appropriation, and variance tables, such as the tables shown in Figures 14-12 and 14-15. Another option provides planning and control charts for selected budget accounts, such as the chart shown in Figure 14-7, or budget-planning matrices for business expense accounts (see Figure 14-11). There are still other options. Bar charts and other types of computer graphics, for example, are especially helpful in comparing budgeted against actual expenses. The composite bar chart in Figure 14-16 provides one example of how computer graphics can be used. The chart compares liabilities and damages for all drivers to drivers under twenty-five. As indicated, expenses exceed budgeted amounts (premiums).

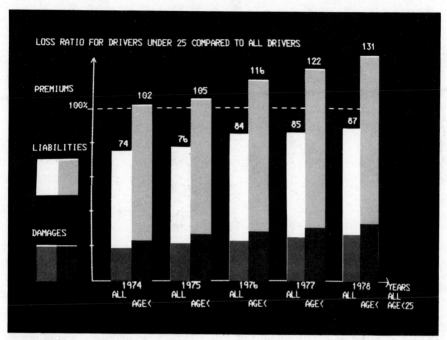

Figure 14-16 Composite bar chart

14-3 PROFIT PLANNING

Figure 14-17 provides a preliminary overview of the profit-planning application. A comparison of this overview with the budget-planning overview (see Figure 14-1) indicates that with profit planning, revenue projections must be determined in advance; profit-center forecasts must be calculated prior to printing cost-center variance reports. *Revenue projections,* in this instance, signify estimates of sales volumes, expressed in dollars rather than units. These projections or forecasts are generally made for each product or for each major product line carried in inventory. *Profit-center forecasts* combine revenue with budget projections. These forecasts yield projected income for each major stage of manufacturing in a business.

Figure 14-18 illustrates one type of profit-center forecast. This seasonality report shows year-to-date (YTD) revenue, expense, and earnings projections on the far right-hand side. The percentage breakdown of these totals, month by month, provides the data needed to perform one type of *income analysis.* The value of a seasonality report is that percent-by-month totals are often easier to estimate than are totals of unit or dollar volumes per month. For example, this

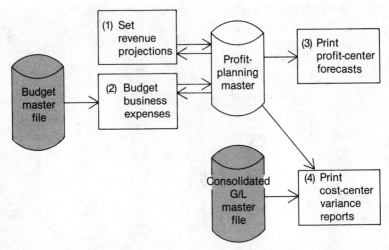

Figure 14-17 Profit-planning preliminary overview

report shows very little sales variation during the year. Sales reach their peak in December (9.2 percent) and their low point in March (7.7 percent). Even then, this small variation of 1.5 percent (9.2 − 7.7) leads to important variations in net earnings. As shown, earnings are much higher at the end of the year than at the first of the year. The last three months account for 30.2 percent of net earnings, whereas the first three months account for but 21.3 percent.

Profit planning is especially useful in appraising company performance. When properly designed, profit planning serves to evaluate company-wide performance and departmental or product profit performance, in comparison with the company's plans, programs, and profit objectives. Unfortunately, in many companies it is practically impossible to obtain contribution-to-profit information at any level other than the top, company-wide level. Most accounting and financial systems were not designed to obtain information about the profit contribution of departments or product lines.

Despite the many problems of compatibility, the profit-planning application does become easier to design and implement once the budget-planning application becomes automated. In budget planning, for example, standard rates are required to "cost out" the charges associated with different volumes of production. In the profit-planning application, these standard rates take on additional meaning. Here, too, different volumes mean different things. With low volumes and high fixed cost rates, the profitability of a department or profit center will be low. At higher volumes, however, which reduce fixed costs significantly, profits will be higher.

Figure 14-19 illustrates a comparison of cost per unit to price per unit. The *break-even point* (BEP) shown indicates the point at which the volume (in units) times the price per unit (P) equals the volume times the cost per unit (C).

MASON ELECTRIC SUPPLY
SEASONALITY REPORT: STORE 14
FOR THE YEAR 195X
(000'S OMITTED)

	JAN	FEB	MAR	APR	MAY	JUN	JUL	AUG	SEP	OCT	NOV	DEC	YTD$
NET SALES:													
RESIDENTIAL	8.4%	8.1%	7.9%	8.0%	8.1%	8.3%	8.4%	8.5%	8.2%	8.6%	8.8%	8.9%	4,768
COMMERCIAL AND INDUSTRIAL	6.2	6.2	6.2	8.3	8.3	8.3	8.3	8.3	8.3	10.4	10.4	10.4	480
RETAIL STORE SALES	8.1	7.5	7.1	7.1	7.5	7.9	8.1	8.1	8.7	9.1	10.0	10.6	492
TOTAL SALES	8.2%	7.9%	7.7%	7.9%	8.0%	8.3%	8.4%	8.4%	8.2%	8.8%	9.0%	9.2%	5,740
COST OF SALES:													
RESIDENTIAL	8.4%	8.1%	7.9%	8.0%	8.1%	8.3%	8.4%	8.5%	8.2%	8.6%	8.8%	8.9%	2,861
COMMERCIAL AND INDUSTRIAL	6.0	6.0	6.0	8.5	8.5	8.5	8.5	8.5	8.5	10.3	10.3	10.3	117
RETAIL STORE SALES	8.1	7.5	7.1	7.1	7.5	7.9	8.1	8.1	8.7	9.1	10.0	10.6	492
DISTRIBUTION EXPENSE	8.3	8.3	8.3	8.3	8.3	8.3	8.3	8.3	8.3	8.3	8.3	8.3	120
TOTAL COST OF SALES	8.3%	7.9%	7.7%	7.9%	8.0%	8.2%	8.4%	8.4%	8.3%	8.7%	9.0%	9.2%	3,590
OPERATING INCOME	8.0%	7.8%	7.6%	8.0%	8.1%	8.3%	8.4%	8.4%	8.2%	9.0%	9.1%	9.2%	2,150
OPERATING EXPENSES:													
CONTRACTS OFFICE	8.3%	8.3%	8.3%	8.3%	8.3%	8.3%	8.3%	8.3%	8.3%	8.3%	8.3%	8.3%	240
MARKETING	8.4	8.1	7.9	8.1	8.1	8.2	8.4	8.4	8.2	8.6	8.8	8.9	571
PURCHASING	8.3	8.3	8.3	8.3	8.3	8.3	8.3	8.3	8.3	8.3	8.3	8.3	300
ADMINISTRATION	8.3	8.3	8.3	8.3	8.3	8.3	8.3	8.3	8.3	8.3	8.3	8.3	108
TOTAL OPERATING EXPENSES	8.4%	8.2%	8.1%	8.2%	8.2%	8.3%	8.4%	8.4%	8.3%	8.4%	8.5%	8.6%	1,219
INCOME BEFORE INTEREST DEDUCTION:													
SHORT-TERM INTEREST	8.3%	8.3%	8.3%	8.3%	8.3%	8.3%	8.3%	8.3%	8.3%	8.3%	8.3%	8.3%	(144)
OTHER INTEREST	0.0	0.0	0.0	0.0	0.0	0.0	0.0	0.0	0.0	0.0	0.0	0.0	0
INCOME BEFORE TAXES	7.5%	7.0%	6.6%	7.6%	7.9%	8.3%	8.3%	8.5%	8.0%	9.9%	10.0%	10.3%	787
INCOME TAX PROVISION	7.4	6.9	6.6	7.7	8.0	8.2	8.5	8.5	8.0	9.8	10.1	10.3	377
NET INCOME	7.6%	7.1%	6.6%	7.6%	7.8%	8.3%	8.3%	8.5%	8.0%	10.0%	10.0%	10.2%	410

Figure 14-18 Seasonality report

Dollars/unit

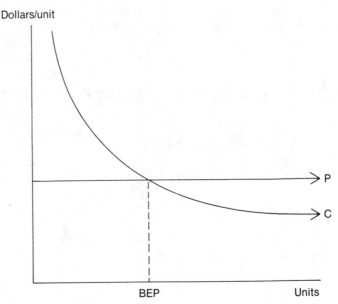

Figure 14-19 Break-even chart

Before this point is reached, costs exceed revenues. Profits begin to be realized after the BEP is reached.

Prices such as the price P shown in Figure 14-19 are typically not the figures quoted to customers. Instead, they represent *value-added* or *transfer prices*. The concept of value added results from the addition of value to a product by the manufacturing process. When, for example, a product is finished by a manufacturing process, it is said to be worth more (to have a higher value) than before it was finished. Likewise, the profit resulting from the profit-planning application does not mean the profit obtained from the sale of a product to a customer. Once again, profit is associated with the value added to the product. Suppose a product enters manufacturing and has a value of $8.98, incurs a manufacturing cost of $3.24, and has a value-added price of $12.61. Thus, the profit per unit resulting from this operation is $0.39 per unit ($12.61 − $8.98 − $3.24). Once computed, this revised value of the product is transferred to the next department, that is, to the next stage of manufacture. At this point, the $12.61 price becomes the new "value of (the) product before manufacturing."

Setting the value-added rates at each stage of manufacturing is the most difficult part of the profit-planning application. It involves determining and entering into processing *profitability standards,* much like the cost standards required for budgeting. In the example above, the profitability standard rate entered into processing would be $3.63 ($12.61 − $8.98). This rate is stored with all other rates in the profit-planning master file.

Once value-added rates are keyed, the profit-planning application closely resembles the budget-planning application. Besides displaying profit-center rates and plans, the application must be designed to compare actual profit-center totals against projected totals and to display profit-center variance. In addition, actual profit for each product line carried by a business must be broken down by profit center and compared against projected contribution to profit totals. If the comparison is not favorable, the assumptions leading to setting the value-added standard rates for the various stages of manufacturing must be questioned. Finally, a variety of *profit control reports* must be built into this application. These permit managers to review projected to actual profit in several ways.

14-4   MANAGEMENT IMPLICATIONS

Most business organizations are faced with the same crucial financial problems: rapid inflation of the dollar, high interest costs, high labor costs, and ever-increasing national and international competition. Taken in combination, these problems are severely challenging the profit-making capabilities of both large and small business firms.

In times past, there were three ways of improving overall profitability: raising product prices, increasing employee productivity (thereby lowering the costs of operation), and improving the management of existing financial resources. Today, these three alternatives are not all necessarily feasible. It is highly impractical, for example, to set prices higher when competitors fail to do the same. Moreover, improvements in employee productivity are never automatic and cannot be improved by making simple business decisions. Thus, of the three, improving the management of existing financial resources may be the only avenue open for improving profitability. This reasoning helps to explain why many firms are beginning to rely so heavily on budget- and profit-planning computer applications.

Several important managerial advantages result from well-designed financial-planning systems. Managers are able to determine the total commitments and actual expenditures for a single department, a division, or the company as a whole, and to compare these totals against planned commitments. They are also able to determine the points at which departmental, divisional, or company-wide expenses *begin* to exceed budgeted amounts, as well as the points at which profit centers *begin* to return lower-than-expected profits; and they can identify the profit centers that are able to hold to desired profit-making levels. Financial-planning systems enable managers to gain a better appreciation of financial conditions and problems by using current rather than dated financial information and by examining this information in several ways, using different display formats, to highlight particular features.

Viewed in combination, the implementation and proper use of financial-planning systems can lead to major savings for a company. For example, one large industrial firm discovered that they could improve their overall profit margins by more than 2 percent following the installation of an integrated online budget-planning application. By tracking and evaluating budget plans in relation to actual and encumbered expenditures, they were able to make selected budget cuts, where necessary, to stay within tightly set company-wide budget plans. More important, they were able to make the cuts that had minimum effect on the operations of their business.

Other companies have realized that there are initial disadvantages associated with budget- or profit-planning applications. These systems cannot be simply dropped into place but, instead, must be finely tuned before they become fully operational. Hundreds of rate changes may be required, for instance, before rates begin to represent standard conditions. However, once this phase is past, the full advantages of automated financial-planning systems begin to become apparent. Managers soon realize that they can react to changes in the marketplace much faster than before. While other firms are trying to find out what types of expenditures are eroding their profit margins, those firms with automated financial-planning systems have already taken the necessary steps to allow them to control these types of expenditures.

REVIEW OF IMPORTANT IDEAS

The budget-planning application is designed to compare estimated against actual business expenses. The profit-planning application is an extension of budget planning. With profit planning, value-added profits are compared against actual profits.

The budget-planning application must be designed to handle both fixed and variable budgeting. A fixed budget does not vary with changes in production or sales; a variable budget does vary with these types of changes.

Budget requests provide an estimate of the dollars needed by a department. Budget appropriations are the actual dollars placed in a budget. Whereas both requests and appropriations are stored on the budget master file, only appropriations are compared against actual expenses. The transfer of actual expense data to the file is performed after the update of the consolidated G/L master file.

The budget master file stores the master chart of budget accounts and consolidated and historical budget-control items, in addition to budget requests and appropriations. Budget variances are determined by comparing actual and encumbered expenses, stored in the consolidated budget-control section, against budget appropriations.

Annual and departmental budgets are important products of the budget-planning application. Even so, a major reason for developing the application is the preparing of budget control reports. Because individuals like to see information presented in different ways, most budget control systems feature a variety of reporting options.

Five interactive programs are necessary to update the budget master file. Three of these maintain the master chart of budget accounts, enter budget request information into processing, and enter budget appropriation information into processing. The fourth update program is designed to process budget adjustments, and the fifth performs an end-of-month update. This final program transfers actual expense information from the consolidated G/L master file to the budget master file.

Substantial work is necessary to prepare budget requests and budget appropriations. Company-wide budget funding limitations must be established before attempts are made to balance requests with available funds. To simplify this time-consuming task as much as possible, flow-of-funds forecasts and budget-planning matrices are computed. Budget matrices match departmental requests and business expense accounts.

The profit-planning application is designed to handle variable revenues and expenditures. As with budget planning, the profit-planning application requires forecasts to specify the levels of activity in upcoming periods. The two forecasts required are the revenue and profit-center forecasts.

Profit planning is especially useful in appraising company performance. By comparing estimated against actual profits, a company can determine if performance is consistent with plans, programs, and profit objectives.

The concept of value added is essential to profit planning. For profit planning to be successful, value-added profitability rates, expressed in dollars, must be set for each stage of manufacturing. Determining these rates is the most difficult aspect of this computer application.

The profit-planning application closely resembles the budget-planning application, once profitability rates are entered into processing. The major reason for developing this application is to compare projected profit totals against actual totals. Profit control reports must be designed to show these comparisons.

KEY WORDS

Budget planning	Flow-of-funds forecast
Budgeting	Budget control report
Budget	Departmental budget account
Profit planning	Budget-planning matrix
Fixed budget	Activity forecast
Variable budget	Revenue projections
Budget variance report	Profit-center forecast
Budget request	Income analysis
Budget appropriation	Break-even point
Budget master file	Value-added prices
Master chart of budget accounts	Profit control report
Electronic worksheet	

REVIEW QUESTIONS

1. Explain how the budget-planning application combines both planning and control.

2. Explain why companies develop the online budget-planning application. Give several reasons.

3. What is the difference between a fixed budget and a variable budget?

4. What is a budget variance report? How does it differ from a budget control report?

5. How does a budget request differ from a budget appropriation?

6. Name the five sections of the budget master file.

7. How is the flow-of-funds forecast used in the budget-planning application?

8. What is a fixed cost rate? A variable cost rate? What are cost-center rates?

9. Explain why budget control reporting options are important.

10. Show how a budget variance percentage is calculated.

11. Why should budget and general ledger account numbers be similar?

12. Explain the purpose of double-posting budget totals.

13. What is a budget-planning matrix? Why is it important in processing budget request information? In processing budget appropriation information?

14. What is the difference between appropriated and allocated budget dollars?

15. What are budget adjustments? Explain several types of adjustments required by the budget-planning application.

16. Why are computer graphics important in budget planning?

17. What is the difference between income and budget analysis?

18. What is a break-even point?

19. What are value-added prices?

20. Explain how financial-planning systems, such as the budget- and profit-planning applications, can lead to major savings for a company.

EXERCISES

1. The perform end-of-month update program does three things: it resets current totals to zero; it revises the consolidated budget-control portion of the file; and it updates the historical budget-control section of the file. Using Figure 4-13 as a guide, explain

   (a) how the reset instruction source document would be designed to separate the three types of updates;

   (b) what types of control balances would be displayed for the three types of updates;

   (c) why control balances are important to processing;

   (d) what steps would be taken if the control totals show an accounting imbalance; and

   (e) what types of printed reports are necessary as backups to processing.

2. Since the profit-planning application is similar to the budget-planning application in many ways, it can be designed with these similarities in mind. Using Figures 14-8 and 14-9 as guides,

   (a) design the profit-planning program menu;

   (b) describe the functions to be performed by each program shown on the menu; and

   (c) explain how your design differs from the budget-planning menu.

3. Suppose you were assigned the task of developing budget- and profit-planning reporting display options for management.

   (a) Explain how you would determine which options would be needed.

   (b) List and explain several types of variable-budget reporting options.

   (c) List and explain several types of profit-planning reporting options.

   (d) Explain how you would determine whether or not the options selected were used by managers.

CHAPTER

15

Sales Analysis
and Market Planning

Implementing the customer-invoice, order-entry, and finished-goods computer applications does more than permit rapid processing of customer and product transactions. These applications create and maintain valuable master and summary computer files. As this chapter will show, information placed in these files permits the design of two management-reporting applications: sales analysis and market planning. The sales-analysis application evaluates past sales performance in order to provide managers with a better understanding of factors important for improving the sales volume and profitability of sales. The market-planning application compares internal company sales with external economic and corresponding market conditions in order to identify factors important for improving the market share of a business. In this chapter, we will begin with the sales-analysis application, because it is the easier of the two to understand. We will then build upon this design in describing the market-planning application.

15-1 SALES-ANALYSIS OVERVIEW

Sales analysis is a loosely defined term with different meanings for different companies. To some, it means an *analysis of net sales volume,* that is, the study of sales transactions leading to the net sales total of the profit and loss statement. To others, it concerns *distribution cost analysis,* the study of profitability of market territories, products, customer groups, or other sales control units. Of the two, profitability analysis is the wiser choice, because studies of sales volume often contribute to misleading findings. Large-volume, old-line product groups, for example, might contribute very little to company profits compared with lower-volume, new-line product groups. Finally, to some, sales analysis means an analysis of *sales-force performance*. This type of study examines the activities of members of the sales force to determine which types or patterns of behaviors contribute to high sales performance.

Before sales-analysis information can be processed, the customer-invoicing computer application must be modified so that it can ready the computer files for four different types of sales analysis: daily sales analysis, customer sales analysis, product sales analysis, and sales-force sales analysis. The invoicing application is actually a logical starting point, because, as you will remember, it captures both net sales volume (sales less returns) and net sales profits. In addition, it can be modified to update a sales-force master file as sales details are entered into processing.

Figure 15-1 provides an overview of the sales-analysis application. Prior to producing sales-analysis reports, four files must be readied: the daily sales file, the customer master file, the product master file, and the sales force master file.

The *daily sales file* stores the sales receipts (and customer returns) for a business day (see Figure 15-2). Once completed, this file is used to produce a daily record of sales activities, by invoice, for each salesperson, store location, or product line. The contents of the daily sales file are similar to the contents of the invoice A/R summary file (see Figure 4-15); differences include the addition of the salesperson number and name and the product cost. The salesperson number permits records to be grouped on the file according to that number. Knowing the product cost, in addition to the total invoice charge, permits the gross profit to be calculated for each customer order filled and shipped by a business.

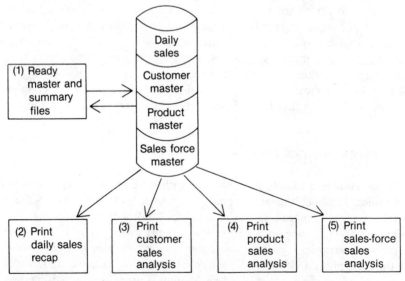

Figure 15-1   Sales-analysis preliminary overview

Salesperson number
Salesperson name

Customer account number
Customer sold-to name

Invoice number
Record code
Date of invoice
Total invoice charge
Cash discount

Product cost
Gross profit

Figure 15-2 Daily sales file

The *customer master file* stores facts to describe each customer of a business. For the sales-analysis application two new segments, concerning sales history and the customer profitability, must be added to each customer record (see Figure 15-3). The sales-history segment stores historical sales-volume totals. This information permits customer sales trends to be displayed. The customer profitability segment stores historical customer profit totals. This information allows current and year-to-date totals to be displayed and customer profit trends to be plotted.

The *product master file* stores facts to describe each product carried in inventory by a business. Unlike the customer master file, no new record segments need to be added to perform a product sales analysis, that is, if a product sales history and product profitability record segments have already been added to the file as part of the finished goods inventory application (see Figure 15-4). With these two segments, the records can be used to plot and compare product sales volumes and profitability totals.

The *sales-force master file* stores facts to describe each member of the sales force. As Figure 15-5 shows, each record contains five or more record segments: *descriptive information,* which includes each salesperson's name and how they can be located; *sales expectations,* which stores the sales volume each salesperson is expected to attain (his or her sales quota), both this month and over the coming months; *current performance,* which holds totals of orders taken and quantity sold for the current period and for the year to date (YTD); *historical performance,* which shows quantity-sold totals for the fiscal or calendar year; and *other performance measures,* which holds sales-performance indicators such as the number of customer calls made and the number of days worked.

Figure 15-1 shows that after the daily sales files and the customer, product, and sales force master files are readied, a variety of reports can be produced. The four reports illustrated and the purpose of each can be described as follows.

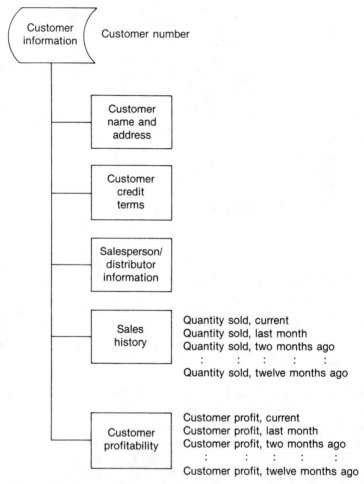

Figure 15-3 Expanded customer master file

The *daily sales recap* provides a daily accounting of sales activity by invoice, for each member of the sales force. Sales managers use this report to identify areas of marginal sales productivity and profitability.

The *customer sales-analysis report* provides a monthly and YTD summary of sales activity, by customer. Sales managers depend on this report to identify customers whose sales volumes show an increasing or a decreasing sales trend. The sales-trend line can be inspected more closely when displayed. Interactive displays permit sales managers to study the buying behavior of individual customers.

The *product sales-analysis report* provides a current and YTD summary of sales activity by product, within each product line. Sales, merchandising, and product managers use this report to identify product-line and individual product sales and profitability trends. Like customer analysis, interactive displays sup-

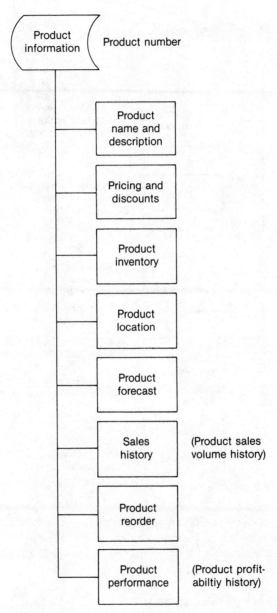

Figure 15-4 Product master file segments

plement the report. They permit product-line and product comparisons and trends to be examined in detail.

The *sales-force sales-analysis report* provides a current and YTD summary of sales activity by salesperson. Sales managers need this report to evaluate the sales coverage provided to customers and the performance of the salesperson.

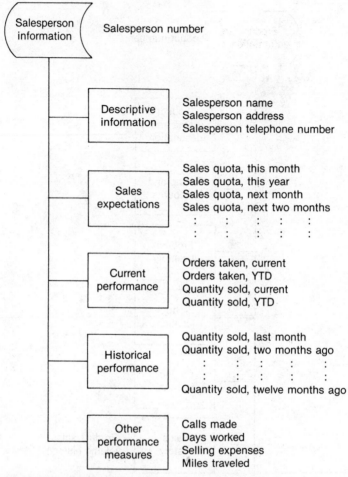

Figure 15-5 Sales-force master file

Special performance measures can be displayed as well as printed. For example, the ratio of the number of customer orders to the number of customer calls helps to isolate the most and least productive members of the sales force.

15-2 SALES-ANALYSIS PROCESSING

Before sales-analysis information can be printed or displayed, computer files required in processing must either be prepared or updated. Fortunately, all processing requirements can be accomplished during the entry of customer invoice transactions. As Figure 15-6 shows, sales-analysis files are updated directly by the program to enter invoice transactions. These updates include adding current sales and profit totals to the customer master file, for each new

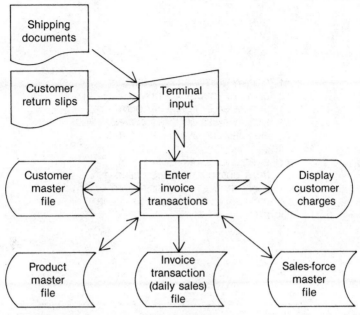

Figure 15-6   Sales-analysis systems flowchart

customer order; adding current sales and profit totals to the product master file, for each new line item of a customer order; and adding current sales and profit totals to the sales-force master file, for each new customer order. Each of these updates also includes changing current and YTD sales and profit totals. All of these updates are automatic. No new information needs to be keyed into processing. The initial keying of the customer number leads to the update of the customer master file; the keying of the product number leads to the update of the product master file. The entry of the salesperson number is avoided by storing the number in each customer record. This provision means, however, that only one member of the sales force is permitted to contact a customer. If several members of the sales force contact the same customer, the number of the appropriate salesperson must also be keyed and transmitted for each entry.

Records stored on these three master files can be retrieved and displayed both before and following their update. As Figure 15-7 shows, the sales-analysis processing menu features five interactive programs, three of which allow for direct examination of records stored on the customer, product, and sales-force master files. The fourth program permits information stored on these files to be compared, and sales histories to be plotted. *Sales-comparison displays* are typically designed to compare current sales against last month's sales, or against last year's sales. One such sales comparison is shown in Figure 15-8. As illustrated, May sales are compared with April sales for items in Class 15, Lab Supplies. *Sales-trend displays* are designed to plot or chart yearly sales (see Figure 15-9). These displays help sales managers to visualize increasing and

I.1   DISPLAY CUSTOMER ACCOUNT
I.2   DISPLAY PRODUCT ACCOUNT
I.3   DISPLAY SALES-FORCE ACCOUNT
I.4   DISPLAY SALES COMPARISONS AND TRENDS
I.5   PERFORM END-OF-MONTH UPDATES

B.1   PRINT DAILY SALES RECAP
B.2   PRINT CUSTOMER ANALYSIS REPORT
B.3   PRINT PRODUCT ANALYSIS REPORT
B.4   PRINT SALES-FORCE ANALYSIS REPORT
(5)   EXIT

Figure 15-7   Sales-analysis processing menu

decreasing sales-volume trends, seasonality associated with a customer's purchases, and unusual customer buying characteristics, such as large purchases every other month. Finally, the fifth interactive program is designed to reset end-of-month sales figures for customer, product, and sales-force accounts. End-of-month performance reporting is scheduled just prior to activating this program.

The Print Daily Sales Recap Program

A valued sales management report is the *daily sales recap*. Prior to the printing of this report, the daily sales file is sorted by customer number, within salesperson number. Once sequenced, the report is printed directly. Figure 15-10 illustrates one version of the daily sales recap. As shown, each invoice processed is listed in customer number sequence, within salesperson number. The details printed for each invoice include the invoice number, amount, cash discount, net sales amount (invoice amount less cash discount), invoice cost, gross profit (net sales less invoice cost), and profit percentage (gross profit divided by net sales amount).

Designers of this print program generally specify that exceptions to profitability norms be flagged for management review. A special flag would be placed alongside invoices for which the percentage of gross profit is either too

Active command
key (reverse image)

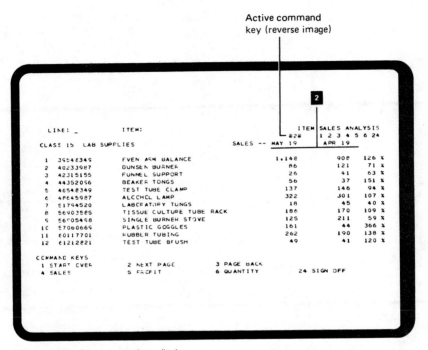

Figure 15-8   Sales-comparison display

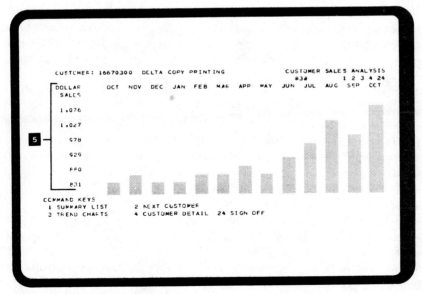

Figure 15-9   Sales-trend display

```
5/C3/                           CAILY SALES RECAP                          PAGE   1
                                   CMAS CORP.

          SALESMAN / CUSTOMER    INVOICE  INVOICE  INVCICE   CASH   NET SALES  INVOICE   GROSS    PROFIT
             NC / NAME             NO      CATE    AMCUNT  CISCCUNT  AMOUNT    COST    PROFIT  PERCENT

   01    ARCHER
 1010000C  ABBCTT BEAUTY CORP.     776003  5/03/    67.01     .63     66.55    43.95     22.60     34
 11100CCC  BAINTREE APPLIANCE CENTER 776001 5/03/ 1,886.89          1,965.51 1,380.55   584.96     30

          TOTAL-ARCHER                           1,953.90     .63   2,032.06 1,424.50   607.56     30
```

```
5/03/                           DAILY SALES RECAP                          PAGE   2
                                   CMAS CORP.

          SALESMAN / CUSTOMER    INVOICE  INVOICE  INVCICE   CASH   NET SALES  INVOICE   GROSS    PROFIT
             NC / NAME             NO      CATE    AMCUNT  DISCCUNT  AMOUNT    COST    PROFIT  PERCENT

   C2    BALLARD
 2100CCCC  QUINN & ASSOCIATES      775079  5/03/   73E.59-  12.89-   767.28-  546.7C-   220.58-    29
 25000020  UNIVERSITY CONTRACTORS - APTOS 776000 5/03/ 642.67  11.07  638.64  487.57   151.07     24

          TOTAL-BALLARD                             93.92-   1.82-   128.64-   59.13-    69.51-    54
```

```
5/03/                           CAILY SALES RECAP                          PAGE   3
                                   CMAS CORP.

          SALESMAN / CUSTOMER    INVOICE  INVOICE  INVCICE   CASH   NET SALES  INVOICE   GROSS    PROFIT
             NC    NAME            NO      CATE    AMCUNT  CISCCUNT  AMOUNT    COST    PROFIT  PERCENT

   C4    JACKSCN
 2C000C4C  PCWER PLUMBING - SUNNYVALE 776002 5/03/ 479.81    8.40    499.80   394.90    104.90     21

          TOTAL-JACKSCN                            479.81    8.40    499.80   394.90    104.90     21
```

```
5/C3/                           CAILY SALES RECAP                          PAGE   4
                                   CMAS CORP.

          SALESMAN / CUSTOMER    INVOICE  INVOICE  INVCICE   CASH   NET SALES  INVOICE   GROSS    PROFIT
             NC    NAME            NO      DATE    AMCUNT  CISCOUNT  AMOUNT    COST    PROFIT  PERCENT

          FINAL TOTALS                           2,339.79    7.21   2,403.22 1,760.27   642.95     27
```

Figure 15-10   Daily sales recap

high (say above 40 percent) or too low (say below 10 percent). Lower than acceptable profit percentages may occur, for example, if salespersons are imprudent in offering price concessions, overriding product prices stored on file. Sales managers need to know where and when this occurs. Likewise, if a salesperson sets a price too high—to make a hit-and-run sale—this must also be brought to the attention of the sales manager.

Besides sales managers, members of the sales force like to review their portions of the daily sales recap. Through review, salespersons are able to verify that customer orders were filled. Moreover, since members of the sales force often have sales quotas and are paid direct commissions, daily sales have special meaning. These sales totals help salespersons to track their actual performance and to compare it with planned performance totals.

Finally, financial managers depend on the daily sales recap to make sure that cash discounts have been computed properly. If company policy is not to allow discounts for slow-paying accounts and up to 3 percent for fast-paying accounts, for example, the computer can be programmed to flag situations thought to be abnormal. For instance, a customer with a very high credit rating, such as AAA, should receive a 3 percent discount. If no discount is allowed, this situation should be flagged for management review.

```
  4/29/                              CUSTOMER SALES ANALYSIS                                    PAGE   1
  AS CF  4/29/                             DMAS CORP

                                                                        PROFIT      DRCP-SHIP       DRCP-SHIP
                                                                        PERCENT     SALES AMOUNT    PROFIT
            CUSTOMER NAME          SALES AMOUNT        GROSS PROFIT    *CUR**YTC*      *YTC*          *YTO*
                                  *CUR*      *YTD      *CUR*   *YTC*

  10100000 ABBOTT BEAUTY CORP.      143.06    1,075.85   48.01    419.56   34   39     .00             .00
  10300000 ALEXANDERS' HCSPITAL SUPPLIES  171.34  1,435.77  58.84  552.78  34   39     .00             .00
  10800010 A & S RESTAURANT         388.73    2,650.68  134.86    945.29   35   36     .00             .00
  10800020 DEW-CRCP-INN             422.78    2,733.24  147.63    992.04   35   36     .00             .00
  11100000 BAINTREE APPLIANCE CENTER  4,051.89  10,303.30  1,193.67  3,125.76  29  30  .00             .00
  11300CC0 CALDWELL INDUSTRIAL SUPPLY CC.  206.05  9,760.52  45.90  1,972.18  22  20   .00             .00
  11380010 ROWE ELECTRONICS         178.29    5,145.97   47.96  1,467.12   27   29     .00             .00


  27C000C0 WADELL & SIMPSON         565.72    3,846.75  202.64  1,471.55   36   38     .00             .00
  27300000 WENTZEL BROS.           1,299.14   11,959.71  395.55  3,578.49   30   30     .00             .00
  28C00CC0 XAVIER HARDWARE & PAINT   341.60    9,865.65  101.70  3,523.10   30   36     .00             .00
  290C0CC0 YCUNG & STRICKLAND SUPPLY  208.53   8,839.37   65.07  2,395.43   31   27     .00             .00


  FINAL TCTALS-                   26,167.05              7,666.45             29
  NC. RECORCS-   32                         202,852.91             62,518.55        31   1,702.89      495.02
```

Figure 15-11   Customer sales-analysis report

Customer Sales Analysis

At the end of the month, the customer master file is readied to print the *customer sales-analysis report*. Since the customer master file contains all the information needed, arranged by customer number, processing of the file requires no intermediate steps. Figure 15-11 shows one version of a customer sales-analysis report. The current and YTD sales volume, gross profit, and profit percentage are shown for each customer of a firm. In addition, special columns such as average order size (sales amount divided by the number of orders), customer returns volume, drop-shipment volume, and split-shipment volume can be placed on the report.

Interactive displays, rather than the sales-analysis report, are generally recommended for showing special types of customer-analysis detail. For example, if the sales manager wants to know the names of the ten most profitable customers in the Eastern sales region, the customer master file would be searched by customer number within region. Following this, a smaller search is conducted to identify the ten most profitable customers. Once this secondary search is completed, the results of processing are displayed.

Although the special types of customer analysis are numerous, the most commonplace include the identification of accounts that are the most profitable and the least profitable, and accounts showing the greatest profit improvement, the poorest profit improvement, and the greatest customer return volume. Studies of this type are performed interactively, using especially designed file-processing menus, such as the menu shown in Figure 15-12. Each menu selection leads to a different type of customer sales comparison.

Product Sales Analysis

As with customer sales analysis, the program to print product analysis can be scheduled as soon as possible after month-end closing. Since this file is arranged by product number, no preliminary processing should be required, except when products need to be arranged by product number within product class. In this

1. SALES VOLUME ANALYSIS
2. GROSS PROFIT ANALYSIS
3. PROFIT PERCENTAGE ANALYSIS
4. DROP SHIPMENT ANALYSIS
5. DISTRIBUTOR SALES ANALYSIS
6. CUSTOMER RETURNS ANALYSIS
(7) RETURN TO MAIN MENU

Figure 15-12 Customer sales-analysis processing menu

instance a computer sort is required to achieve the desired report-writing sequence.

Figure 15-13 illustrates a typical product sales-analysis report. This report with subtotals summarizes the current and YTD sales history for each product within each major product class. The history includes totals for quantity sold, sales volume, gross profit, profit percent, and number of orders.

Interactive displays are suitable substitutes for computer-printed reports. With displays, it is possible to "page through" different product classes, select-

```
4/29/                                      ITEM CLASS SALES ANALYSIS
AS OF  4/29/                                     OMAS CORP.
                                                                                                        PAGE   3

                                                                                          PROFIT
          ITEM NC          ITEM DESCRIPTION      QTY SOLD        SALES AMOUNT       GROSS PROFIT       PERCENT   NO. ORDERS
                                                *CUR*   *YTD*    *CUR*     *YTD*    *CUR*     *YTD*  *CUR**YTD*  *CUR**YTD*
9391000000000-1 PINBALL MACHINE                   5     137    112.89   3,903.19   38.94   1,066.96   30    30   1     6
9502000000000-1 ROBOT - 3FT                      32     382    411.30   4,909.87  122.02   1,456.59   34    31   2    11
9581000000000-1 TALKING PHONE                     5      95     26.70     483.67    9.20     151.17   31    32   1     5

10 * TOYS *                      CLASS TOTAL-                  851.56             266.33             31           7
                                                                     12,554.10             4,019.39        32          38


CLASS-11          * SPORTING/RECREATIONAL *

9701000000000-1 CAMPER TIRE 7.00-15 *TUBE        10      86    303.85   2,638.41   93.85     832.41   31    32   2     8
9710000000000-1 OUTBOARD MOTOR                    4      27    507.00   3,416.84  175.00   1,175.84   35    34   1     6
9737000000000-1 BICYCLE - 26IN                    6      28    625.80   3,322.70  212.10   1,392.10   34    42   2    10
9742000000000-1 POOL TABLE                        0      22       .00   5,127.82     .00   1,294.32    0    25   0     4
9773000000000-1 BASKETBALL - R/W/B               12     226    546.00  11,087.05  186.00   4,307.05   34    39   2    11
9796000000000-1 SKIS - 180 CM                     8      52  1,229.20   8,099.55  349.20   2,379.55   28    29   1     5

11 * SPORTING/RECREATIONAL *CLASS TOTAL-                3,211.85            1,016.15             32           8
                                                                     33,692.37            11,381.27        34          44


FINAL TOTAL-                                                26,167.05            7,666.45             29
                                                                    202,852.91            62,518.           31

NO. RECORDS-    70
```

Figure 15-13 Product sales-analysis report

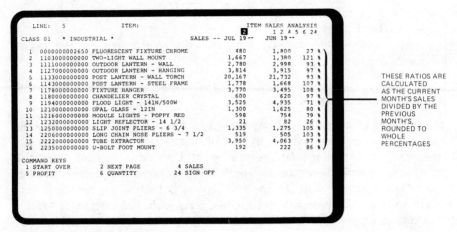

```
   LINE:   5            ITEM:                           ITEM SALES ANALYSIS
                                                         2  1 2 4 5 6 24
   CLASS 01   * INDUSTRIAL *                SALES -- JUL 19 --   JUN 19 --
   1  0000000002650  FLUORESCENT FIXTURE CHROME           480     1,800    27 %
   2  1103000000000  TWO-LIGHT WALL MOUNT               1,667     1,380   121 %
   3  1111000000000  OUTDOOR LANTERN - WALL             2,780     2,998    93 %
   4  1127000000000  OUTDOOR LANTERN - HANGING          3,814     3,915    97 %
   5  1133000000000  POST LANTERN - WALL TORCH         20,167    21,732    93 %
   6  1143000000000  POST LANTERN - STEEL FRAME         1,778     1,668   107 %
   7  1178000000000  FIXTURE HANGER                     3,770     3,495   108 %
   8  1180000000000  CHANDELIER CRYSTAL                   600       620    97 %
   9  1194000000000  FLOOD LIGHT - 141N/500W            3,525     4,935    71 %
  10  1210000000000  OPAL GLASS - 12IN                  1,300     1,625    80 %
  11  1216000000000  MODULE LIGHTS - POPPY RED            598       754    79 %
  12  1232000000000  LIGHT REFLECTOR - 14 1/2              21        82    26 %
  13  1250000000000  SLIP JOINT PLIERS - 6 3/4          1,335     1,275   105 %
  14  2206000000000  LONG CHAIN NOSE PLIERS - 7 1/2       519       505   103 %
  15  2222000000000  TUBE EXTRACTOR                     3,950     4,063    97 %
  16  2235000000000  U-BOLT FOOT MOUNT                    192       222    86 %

   COMMAND KEYS
   1 START OVER       2 NEXT PAGE       4 SALES
   5 PROFIT           6 QUANTITY       24 SIGN OFF
```

THESE RATIOS ARE CALCULATED AS THE CURRENT MONTH'S SALES DIVIDED BY THE PREVIOUS MONTH'S, ROUNDED TO WHOLE PERCENTAGES

Figure 15-14   Item sales-analysis display

ing different reporting formats, in order to quickly spot weaknesses in product sales. As Figure 15-14 shows, interactive displays make it relatively easy to spot low and high product performance. For example, in a July-to-June sales comparison, sales of "Fluorescent Fixture, Chrome" decreased to 27 percent of June sales; however, sales of "Two-Light Wall Mounts" increased to 121 percent of June sales.

In addition to showing such month-to-last-month sales comparisons, interactive-display menus generally allow individuals to review several types of sales-volume totals. These include comparing this month's sales with current YTD sales, with sales for the same month last year, with average sales for the previous twelve months, and with current quarter-to-date (QTD) sales. Besides sales-volume displays, individuals are also permitted to review several types of profitability and quantity-sold totals, for example, to compare this month's profit with that for the same month last year and this month's quantity sold with the current YTD total. Interactive display formats thus provide a variety of ways to examine product sales performance. More important, displays enable an individual to tailor the process of analysis to suit his or her particular needs.

Finally, as discussed earlier in Chapter 8, interactive displays permit single-item finished-goods performance to be examined in detail. Besides showing product inventory status, single-item displays can be designed to show inventory turnover and return-on-investment statistics, inventory shrinkage averages, and gross profit comparisons and trends. Collectively, these displays help business managers get quick, accurate answers to questions such as:

- How many items were sold this month? Sold this year?
- How much profit was made on this product so far this month? So far this year?

• What is the return-on-investment associated with this product during the last twelve months?
• What trend has developed for the quantity sold during the last twelve months?

Sales-Force Sales Analysis

The last type of sales analysis important to sales managers is the month-end summary of sales-force activity. By way of illustration, Figure 15-15 shows a comparative *salesperson sales-analysis report*. Like the daily sales recap, this month-end report includes current and YTD gross profit and profit percentage totals. The difference between the two reports is that no supporting invoice detail is placed on the month-end summary. As such, the analysis provides a consolidated summary of the information shown earlier on the daily sales recap.

With the advent of interactive displays, the analysis of salesperson performance becomes easier to interpret. If information about sales expectations and historical sales performance is stored in the sales-force master file (see Figure 15-5), it becomes possible to plot and compare expected sales trends with actual trends. Likewise, if other performance measures such as calls made, orders taken, and miles traveled are stored on file, different types of salesperson performance ratios can be calculated, compared with sales-force averages, and displayed (see Figure 15-16). Ratios of particular interest include orders per call, average order size, calls per day, selling expense to total sales dollars, miles traveled between calls, and percentage of sales quota realized. As illustrated, the salesperson named Archer records high sales performance compared with sales-force averages. On inspection, the only ratio that might give cause for

```
   4/29/                      SALESMAN SALES ANALYSIS                    PAGE   1
   MONTH-END                          DMAS CORP.


      SALESMAN                    SALES          COST         GROSS    PROFIT   NUMBER
      NO / NAME                  AMOUNT         AMOUNT        PROFIT   PERCENT   ORDERS

   01  ARCHER        *CUR*     10,475.57      7,366.57      3,109.00     30       12
                     *YTD*     64,316.91     45,226.94     19,089.97     30       56

   02  BALLARD       *CUR*     10,107.97      7,224.22      2,883.75     29       15
                     *YTD*     87,678.73     59,879.60     27,799.13     32       73

   03  BROWN         *CUR*      2,166.40      1,488.92        677.48     31        8
                     *YTD*     28,935.02     20,508.83      8,426.19     29       45

   04  JACKSON       *CUR*      2,651.16      1,873.12        788.04     29        6
                     *YTD*     15,228.32     10,049.24      5,179.08     34       30

   05  LEVITRE       *CUR*        765.95        547.77        218.18     28        4
                     *YTD*      6,693.93      4,669.75      2,024.18     30       22


   DELETED TOTALS    *CUR*           .00           .00           .00      0        0
                     *YTD*           .00           .00           .00      0        0

   FINAL TOTALS      *CUR*     26,167.05     18,500.60      7,666.45     29       45
                     *YTD*    202,852.91    140,334.36     62,518.55     31      226
```

Figure 15-15 Salesperson sales-analysis report

```
MONTH-END   JULY, 19XX

SALESPERSON          PERFORMANCE        SALESPERSON        SALES FORCE
NO/NAME              RATIO              AVERAGE            AVERAGE

0001   ARCHER                           CUR    YTD         CUR    YTD

                    ORDERS PER CALL     .844   .667        .352   .344
                    AVERAGE ORDER       582    612         418    396
                    CALLS PER DAY       3.5    3.4         4.2    4.8
            EXPENSES PER SALES DOLLAR   .041   .045        .067   .065
                    MILES PER CALL      35.4   36.8        12.2   12.5
                    PERCENT OF QUOTA    108    122         96     98

MARKET POTENTIAL   $1,500,000
```

Figure 15-16   Salesperson performance ratios

some concern is Archer's calls per day (3.4 YTD versus the sales-force average of 4.8). Even then, this lower ratio can be explained by Archer's higher than average ratio of miles per call. It is considerably higher than the average for all members of the sales force.

15-3 MARKET-PLANNING OVERVIEW

Market planning begins with a consideration of market and sales potentials. Once these are established, management can make a sales forecast, determine its sales territories, set sales budgets, and assign sales quotas. Besides determining potentials, market planning involves collecting actual sales information and comparing it with projected forecasts, budgets, and quotas. These comparisons determine the quality of overall market plans. They acknowledge whether market plans are based on sound analyses of potential markets and competition, and of economic and social trends.

Market planning involves the use of a number of special terms, including *market potential,* the expected sales of a product, good, or service for an entire industry; *sales potential,* the share of market potential that a company might expect to achieve; *sales forecast,* the estimated sales of a company showing the difference, if any, between sales potential and expected (actual) company sales; and *sales quotas,* the expected sales performance of each member of the sales force. The differences between these four terms are several. Sales potential, for instance, is a percentage of market potential. If the market potential is a million dollars and the sales potential is a hundred thousand dollars, the company can be expected to capture 10 percent of the entire market. Likewise, the sales forecast is often less than the sales potential. Inadequate production, lack of trained employees, or insufficient numbers of retail outlets, and so forth, can prohibit a company from realizing its full sales potential. Finally, sales quotas are treated much like the sales forecast, except they are related to both the sales potential and the sales forecast. For example, if the sales potential in the Southwest territory is 5 percent of the total company sales potential, then 5 percent of the sales forecast would be set as the salesperson's sales (volume) quota.

Figure 15-17 illustrates the market-planning overview. Since market planning involves establishing forecasts and quotas followed by comparing these totals against actual sales totals, two types of computer files are required: files containing planning information and files containing actual information. Later on in processing, when planning and actual information are consolidated, a variety of reports can be prepared. A brief summary of four consolidated reports is as follows.

The *market performance report* compares projected sales totals against actual totals and shows percentage differences. This general report examines the extent to which a company is able to achieve its sales potential.

The *customer performance report* compares projected sales totals against actual totals by customer class. Sales managers use this report to determine the accuracy of customer surveys. With surveys, customers indicate what they intend to buy over future periods. The customer performance report compares these results with what customers actually buy.

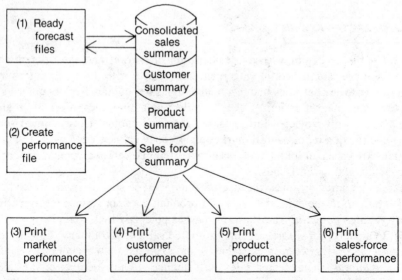

Figure 15-17 Market-planning preliminary overview

The *product performance report* compares projected sales totals against actual totals by product class. Sales managers use this report to verify the accuracy of product inventory forecasts. Product forecast information, itself, consists of two main types: that which follows from the finished-goods computer application and is stored on the product master file, and that which follows from sales predictions for new products. Of the two, forecasts for new products are generally given the most attention. Since there is limited historical sales information (less than one year), sales managers must use considerable judgment in projecting sales figures for new products.

The *sales-force performance report* compares sales quotas against actual sales totals for each member of the sales force. As discussed above, sales quotas follow from the estimate of sales potential for a sales territory. The difference between the actual sales and the sales quota represents the degree to which a salesperson is able to achieve his or her sales quota.

15-4 MARKET-PLANNING PROCESSING

Figure 15-18 illustrates the market-planning processing menu. Compared with the sales-analysis menu (see Figure 15-7), the choice of processing options is similar; however, the market-planning application contains an important new interactive program entitled "enter market forecast." Another difference is that

```
    I.1   ENTER MARKET FORECAST
    I.2   DISPLAY CUSTOMER ACCOUNT
    I.3   DISPLAY PRODUCT ACCOUNT
    I.4   DISPLAY SALES-FORCE ACCOUNT
    I.5   DISPLAY MARKET COMPARISONS AND TRENDS
    I.6   PERFORM END-OF-MONTH UPDATES

    B.1   PRINT MARKET PERFORMANCE REPORT
    B.2   PRINT CUSTOMER PERFORMANCE REPORT
    B.3   PRINT PRODUCT PERFORMANCE REPORT
    B.4   PRINT SALES-FORCE PERFORMANCE REPORT
    B.5   PRINT FORECAST CHANGE REPORT
    ⟨6⟩   EXIT
```

Figure 15-18 Market-planning processing menu

the market-planning application compares projected sales performance against actual performance; the sales-analysis application is limited to the breakdown of actual sales totals.

The most difficult part of the market-planning application is determining the market potential and sales potential for a product or line of products. Setting the market potential calls for an analysis of product demand. Most market-demand studies make use of broad-based market factors, such as population, housing, and income statistics. By comparing the trends of external market factors against industry sales (the product sales for the entire industry), a company is able to determine the correlation between the two trend lines. For example, a very high correlation such as +.898 indicates that by knowing one trend line, a planner can predict with accuracy the shape of the other trend line.

Attempting to correlate sales data is not as easy as it may appear. The following example may help to clarify some of the difficulty. Suppose a business sells kitchen and bathroom fixtures. Suppose further that the marketing manager of the company believes that there is a high correlation between new housing starts and the sale of fixtures. After limited study, the manager rejects this idea, however: a plot of housing starts against the sale of fixtures shows little correlation.

Suppose next that the decision is made to lag housing-starts statistics and to compare this trend line with the sale of fixtures. This comparison leads to a very high correlation. Moreover, once the discovery is made, the reason for this relationship becomes clear: general contractors place orders for fixtures approximately six months after they have received the approval to begin work on a new home.

The Enter Market Forecast Program

The first processing step in the market-planning application is to enter sales forecast totals into processing. As Figure 15-19 shows, the entry of product and customer forecasts leads to the updating of several files. These updates include adding sales forecast or sales quota totals to the customer master file, to record estimated sales within customer class; to the product master file, to record estimated sales by product or by product line; and to the sales-force master file, to revise the sales expectation segment of salesperson records. In addition to these three updates, a record of all forecast changes must be maintained. These are stored on a forecast change file.

Unlike the sales-analysis application, the file updates called for by the market-planning application are seldom automatic. Instead, new sales-forecast information must be carefully matched against previously stored sales forecasts. For example, in order to determine if sales-forecast information is reasonable, forecasted totals are initially compared with product inventory forecasts. As you will remember, product inventory forecasts—one for each product—are set and maintained by the finished-goods inventory application (see Chapter 8).

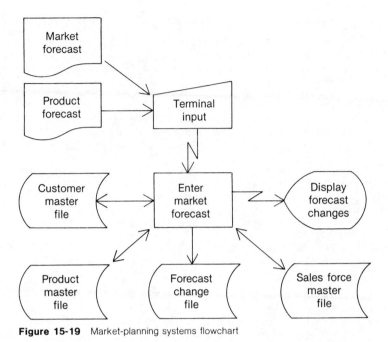

Figure 15-19   Market-planning systems flowchart

Figure 15-20 illustrates what might occur when sales forecasts are compared with product inventory forecasts. In this example, the sales forecast is higher than the inventory forecast for four of the five product lines. It is especially high for cassettes and ribbons. The difference between the two forecasts for these two lines is 27 and 21 percent, respectively.

Differences in forecast totals suggest that either the sales forecast is too optimistic, sales managers are predicting heretofore unanticipated changes in the market, or product-inventory forecasts are incorrect. In any case, forecasted data must be revised so that both the sales and the product inventory forecasts are similar. Figure 15-21 shows the effect of modifying the sales forecast by making it more pessimistic. As shown, the forecast for the sale of binders is brought into line with the inventory forecast; however, because of improved market conditions, sales managers also show that the product-inventory forecast requires some adjustment. Specifically, the inventory forecasts for cassettes, ribbons, and tapes are adjusted upwards. Last, the inventory forecast for labels is shown as being too high. Sales managers indicate this by not adjusting upwards the sales forecast for labels.

Product-line sales forecasts are added to the product master file once sales and product inventory forecasts have been reconciled. The actual update occurs in either of two ways: both individual product and product-line forecasts are revised or only product-line forecasts are revised. The more common method is

```
SUMMARY PAGE
PRODUCT SALES FORECAST


PRODUCT       SALES      INVENTORY          VARIANCE
  LINE       FORECAST     FORECAST     DOLLARS    PERCENT

BINDERS       55000        50000        5000       1.10
CASSETTES     38000        30000        8000       1.27
LABELS        15000        18000       (3000)       .83
RIBBONS       46000        38000        8000       1.21
TAPES        340000       300000       40000       1.13


TOTAL        494000       436000       58000       1.13
```

Figure 15-20   Comparing the sales and inventory forecasts

```
PAGE 1:  REVISED SALES FORECAST
PRODUCT SALES FORECAST


PRODUCT       SALES      INVENTORY          VARIANCE
  LINE       FORECAST     FORECAST     DOLLARS    PERCENT

BINDERS       50000        50000          0         .00
CASSETTES     33000        30000        3000       1.10
LABELS        15000        18000       (3000)       .83
RIBBONS       42000        38000        4000       1.11
TAPES        310000       300000       10000       1.03


TOTAL        450000       436000       14000       1.13
```

Figure 15-21   Revising the sales forecast

to update only product-line forecasts. When this option is selected, forecast totals are placed in a *market-planning table,* located at the beginning of the product master file. This table is designed to store actual as well as sales-forecast totals. In processing, the market-planning application initially loads the table; the customer-invoice application updates it by adding actual sales totals. The market-planning table rather than individual product records is used in preparing month-end performance reports. If the table is kept small, month-end performance can be displayed as well as printed.

Revising the sales forecast to fit product-inventory forecasts leads to changes in customer and sales-force forecasts as well. Figure 15-22 illustrates a revised customer forecast. The summary display of customer sales forecasted for the next period is reduced by $44,000. Instead of store sales of $16,000, the forecast is lowered to $15,000. Likewise, sales to wholesalers (W/SALE) have been reduced by $15,000 (from $135,000 to $120,000).

Figure 15-23 shows where but not why store sales were reduced by $1,000. These facts could also be shown, however. For example, store sales for labels were reduced by $500 to indicate increased local competition. In addition, a decrease in demand for ribbons is expected. Thus, these sales are reduced by $500.

Once the customer forecast has been adjusted, the revised forecasts totals are added to the customer master file. Like product-line forecasts, customer sales-

SUMMARY PAGE
CUSTOMER SALES FORECAST

CUSTOMER CLASS	SALES FORECAST INITIAL	REVISED	REDUCTION DOLLARS	PERCENT
STORE	16000	15000	1000	.06
W/SALE	135000	120000	15000	.11
MANF	33000	29000	4000	.12
DIRECT	185000	175000	10000	.05
DIST	125000	111000	14000	.11
TOTAL	494000	450000	44000	.09

Figure 15-22 Revising the customer forecast

```
PAGE 1:   REVISED STORE SALES
CUSTOMER SALES FORECAST


    PRODUCT        STORE SALES            REDUCTION
      LINE      INITIAL    REVISED    DOLLARS    PERCENT

    BINDERS       1500       1500         0         .00
    CASSETTES     3500       3500         0         .00
    LABELS        2500       2000       500         .20
    RIBBONS       5500       5000       500         .09
    TAPES         3000       3000         0         .00


    TOTAL        16000      15000      1000         .06
```

Figure 15-23 Revised store sales

forecast information is summarized by class of customers, rather than by individual customer. Accordingly, forecast totals are stored at the front of the file (or in a separate file) in a market-planning table. Later these forecasts totals are compared with actual customer sales. Actual sales figures, as before, are supplied by the customer-invoice application.

Figure 15-24 shows the final step in entering market-planning forecasts into processing. As illustrated, sales-force quotas must be the same as product and customer sales-forecast totals. An alternative to this is to set a profit quota for each member of the sales force. Since a sales-volume quota is based on units sold times the average price per unit, it is rather easy to compute a profit quota based on units sold times the average profit per unit.

The market-planning application must be designed to update the sales-force master file differently than the update of the product and customer master files. In this instance, revised sales quotas are added to each salesperson record. This addition sets the level of sales expectations for the coming sales period. Later these sales quota expectations are compared with actual sales totals supplied by the customer-invoice application.

Market Performance Analysis

The addition of market-planning information to the product, customer, and sales-force master files means that sales information can be analyzed in managerial terms. That is, the sales-analysis application showed us that historical

```
SUMMARY PAGE
SALES-FORCE QUOTAS
```

PERSON/	SALES QUOTA		REDUCTION	
TYPE OF SALE	INITIAL	REVISED	DOLLARS	PERCENT
STORE	16000	15000	1000	.06
DIRECT	185000	175000	10000	.05
ARCHER	65000	58000	7000	.11
BALLARD	70000	62000	8000	.11
BROWN	42000	38000	4000	.10
JACKSON	68000	62000	6000	.09
LEVITRE	48000	40000	8000	.17
TOTAL	494000	450000	44000	.09

Figure 15-24 Revising sales quotas

sales information can be analyzed to reveal sales volume and profitability trends by customer, product, or member or the sales force. These studies, however, are limited to summarizing what did occur as opposed to what might have occurred. Market-planning studies show the latter: they show the extent to which market plans were accurate; they show the degree to which a company is able to achieve its sales potential.

The performance reports displayed or printed as products of the market-planning application compare the expected and actual performance data for four areas: the sales supported by a particular market, the sales of a particular product or product line, the sales made to individual customers—what they were expected to buy versus what they actually bought—and the sales produced by salespersons, both individually and as a group. Market-performance analysis permits each of these situations to be examined in detail. It is not enough to know that forecasted sales were $450,000 and actual sales were $430,000. Differences such as these must be studied to discover why and where sales totals were lower than anticipated.

Figures 15-25 and 15-26 illustrate how sales differences are displayed. In Figure 15-25, actual sales were lower than forecasted sales for more than one reason: direct mail sales combined with Jackson's and Levitre's disappointing performance led to most of the poor showing. This display does little else than point the finger at weakly performing parties, however. Figure 15-26 provides more insight. As shown, weakness in three product lines—labels, ribbons, and tapes—indicates that a softening in demand is broad-based. Such market condi-

```
SUMMARY PAGE
SALES-FORCE PERFORMANCE

PERSON/               SALES              VARIANCE
TYPE OF SALE    QUOTA     ACTUAL    DOLLARS    PERCENT

STORE           15000     17000      2000       1.13
DIRECT         175000    162000    (13000)       .93 **

ARCHER          58000     60000      2000       1.03
BALLARD         62000     61500      (500)       .99
BROWN           38000     41000      3000       1.08
JACKSON         62000     52500     (9500)       .85 **
LEVITRE         40000     36000     (4000)       .90 **

TOTAL          450000    430000    (20000)       .96
```

Figure 15-25 Sales-force performance summary

tions suggest the presence of much stronger competition or of a dramatic shift in the consumer's willingness to buy. In either case, the interactive displays help to define the nature of the problem. Even then, displays rarely show how to solve a market problem. The reason for the downturn in demand must be determined by sales managers and product managers.

15-5 MANAGEMENT IMPLICATIONS

Providing management with an organized series of interactive displays illustrates once again why online computer applications are so important to business. With a series of pictures, sales managers are able to review and analyze the market's reaction to overall market plans as well as to individual selling plans. Moreover, pictures permit managers to investigate factors contributing to better (or poorer) than expected sales showings. Without computers, comprehensive studies such as sales and market analysis are seldom done. It simply takes too long to consolidate and prepare the sales summaries needed by managers. With computers, however, information stored on easy-to-access market-planning tables can be channeled into online displays in seconds. Special studies also take much less time. Since detailed sales information is stored on three or more files, special studies based on file contents can usually be prepared within a few hours.

PAGE 2: CUSTOMER CLASS: DIRECT MAIL SALES

·············· PRODUCT PERFORMANCE ··············

PRODUCT	SALES		VARIANCE	
LINE	QUOTA	ACTUAL	DOLLARS	PERCENT
BINDERS	20000	21500	1500	1.08
CASSETTES	18000	17500	(500)	.97
LABELS	5000	3000	(2000)	.60 ··
RIBBONS	12000	8000	(4000)	.67 ··
TAPES	120000	112000	(8000)	.93 ··
TOTAL	175000	162000	(13000)	.93

Figure 15-26 Direct-mail performance summary

There are associated dangers with fingertip access to sales information. Managers can be subjected to too much information: page after page of sales figures begin to look alike if a person is bombarded with all details at once. Likewise, fingertip access to information can lead some managers to overreact. They tend to forget that markets are often cyclical and show both highs and lows. Suppose that 50,000 units of product 34-684 are forecasted to be sold during the month of August and that as of August 15, only 15,000 units have been sold. Suppose next that a sales manager takes this information and begins to lash out at members of the sales force, blaming them for poor performance. Later the manager may well discover that although product sales per day are always low during the first half of the month, they normally become extremely heavy toward month-end, reaching levels as high as 5,000 units per day.

Once an interactive approach to sales analysis and market planning is properly understood, situations such as overreacting to changes in the marketplace become less common. With understanding, the true value of the sales-analysis and market-planning applications become clear. The next two examples show the impact of these two applications on organizations.

Example 1. An extensive sales analysis was recently undertaken by a large gasoline conglomerate. By careful tracking of sales volumes and profitability, the company was able to identify and eliminate 2,000 of its least profitable service stations. The investigation also led to improved control over product inventory and coordination of complex supply and distribution channels.

Example 2. A medium-sized publisher was able to develop more efficient market-analysis procedures for targeting its sales efforts. By collecting, storing, and displaying a variety of school-district market factors (size, socioeconomic conditions, ethnic variability, median I.Q., and so forth), managers were able to predict what magazines would sell well in different school districts.

Examples such as these show that marketing and sales organizations are relying more and more on computers to assist them in organizing sales information. With interactive capabilities, computers are being used to compare and plot sales totals as well as to predict where goods will be sold, by whom, and for what purpose. Sales managers report that the ability to display sales information in different forms is critical to sales and market planning. Other managers state that displays help them to organize their thoughts and improve the clarity of their thinking.

REVIEW OF IMPORTANT IDEAS

The sales-analysis computer application evaluates past sales performance in order to provide sales managers with a better understanding of factors important to sales volume and profitability. Market planning, in contrast, compares internal company sales with external economic conditions. This second application provides sales managers with a better understanding of factors important to achieving a desired market share.

The sales-analysis application is relatively easy to design provided the customer-invoice computer application can be modified to ready the files required in processing. Besides a daily sales file, the customer, product, and sales-force master files must be updated by the invoice application. The design calls for the retrieval of records from these three master files for display purposes.

A variety of sales-management displays and reports are produced by the sales-analysis application. The daily sales recap provides an accounting of sales activity by invoice, for each member of the sales force. The customer, product, and sales-force analysis reports provide a current and YTD summary of sales activity by customer, product, and salesperson, respectively.

The market-planning application is an extension of the sales-analysis application. It compares actual sales totals to projected sales forecasts, budgets, and quotas. Unlike the sales-analysis application, preliminary processing is required to add sales-forecast information to the customer, product, and sales-force master files. These forecasts show the estimated sales of a company, indicating the differences, if any, between sales potential and expected company sales.

Estimating future sales is the most difficult part of the market-planning application. An analysis of product demand often involves attempting to correlate external market factors with internal sales trends.

Following the entry of forecasts into processing, the market-planning application compares estimated sales with actual sales. As in the sales-analysis application, actual sales totals are supplied by the customer-invoice application. By comparing estimated and actual sales, sales managers are able to determine if market plans were accurate and the degree to which a company is able to achieve its sales potential.

A series of interactive displays is critical to the design of both the sales-analysis and market-planning applications. These displays permit managers to discover the strengths and weaknesses of product lines, customer classes, market territories, and individual members of the sales force. A major benefit of interactive displays is that they help managers to organize their thinking.

KEY WORDS

Sales analysis	Product sales-analysis report
Distribution cost analysis	Salesperson sales-analysis report
Sales-force performance analysis	Market planning
Sales-force master file	Market potential
Daily sales file	Sales potential
Sales-comparison display	Sales forecast
Sales-trend display	Sales quota
Daily sales recap	Market-planning table
Customer sales-analysis report	

REVIEW QUESTIONS

1. What is sales analysis and how does it differ from market planning?

2. How is the customer-invoice application used in the design of the sales-analysis application? In the market-planning application?

3. What three master files are required in the design of the systems-analysis computer application? In the market-planning computer application?

4. How does the customer sales-analysis report differ from the product sales-analysis report? How does it differ from the sales-force report?

5. What information must be keyed into processing to update the master files required by the sales-analysis application?

6. What is the difference between a sales-comparison display and a sales-trend display?

7. When printing the daily sales recap, why should exceptions to profitability norms be flagged?

8. What types of interactive displays are designed for customer sales analysis? For product sales analysis?

9. What is a salesperson performance ratio? How are performance ratios used in the sales-force sales analysis?

10. What is the difference between market potential and sales potential?

11. Name the four types of performance reports produced by the market-planning computer application.

12. What is the most difficult part of the market-planning application? Explain why it is difficult.

13. Name the three types of sales forecasts prepared for the market-planning application.

14. What is a market-planning table? How is it used?

15. Sales-analysis displays show "what did occur," whereas market planning displays show "what might have occurred." Explain this statement.

16. What dangers can be associated with fingertip access to sales and market information?

17. Why are interactive displays important to the design of the sales-analysis and market-planning applications?

EXERCISES

1. Using Figure 15-15 as a guide, design a summary report for sales-force performance. The report should compare sales quotas with actual sales for the current period and YTD for each member of the sales force. In addition, it should show the gross profit and the profit percentage on actual sales and compare this with the total estimated gross profit and profit percentage to be realized once the sales quota totals are achieved.

   Fill in your report for the salesperson named Archer, using some of the data shown in Figure 15-15. Besides these actual sales totals, you have been provided the following estimated totals: April sales quota of $11,000, YTD sales quota (January through April) of $65,000, April estimate of profit of $3,190 and YTD estimate of profit (January through April) of $18,200.

   What can be said about Archer's sales performance for the first four months of the year?

2. A sales manager asks you to design secondary menus to simplify the process of telling the computer how to perform a specific type of sales or market comparison. The manager likes the idea of placing a "display sales comparisons and trends" selection on the sales processing menu and a "display market comparisons and trends" on the market-planning processing menu. However, he wants to see what happens after either selection is made.

Prepare two menus to show the types of information to be displayed, following the decision to select the program designed to display sales comparisons and trends and the program designed to display market comparisons and trends.

3. Suppose a company wants to calculate and display the salesperson performance ratios shown in Figure 15-16. Suppose further that you are the systems designer handed this project. Your manager gives you the following two-part assignment.

   (a) Provide answers to these questions: What types of information must be keyed into processing? Who would prepare this information? When would the information be prepared? What information would be entered as a batch, for the entire sales force, and what information would be entered interactively, for one salesperson at a time?

   (b) Show how the systems-analysis application would be modified to handle this additional processing requirement.
      - Prepare the revised sales-analysis processing menu (see Figure 15-7).
      - Develop the systems flowchart to show the steps required by this new program.
      - List the revised contents of the sales-force master file (see Figure 15-5). Expand the other performance measures record segment, as needed.

Intradivision Sales

Most business firms must set up special record-keeping procedures to account for the transfer of merchandise within different units of the same division of a company. Special problems result when separate general ledgers are maintained for each unit. Because each unit is treated as a profit center, any transfer of goods between units must be recorded as a special type of sale. In processing intradivision sales, personnel are instructed to do two things: to cooperate with other units of the company and to protect the unit's profit margins.

SITUATION 1

Different car and truck tire retail sales stores often find it necessary to transfer merchandise from one store to another. For example, suppose a customer wants four 165×13 radial tires. Suppose further that Store 1 has only two 165×13 tires in stock. In attempting to satisfy the customer, Store 1 discovers that a nearby store, Store 2, has two 165×13 tires in stock and that they are willing to send them over immediately. The customer is told that his car will be ready soon after the transfer of stock is completed.

REQUIREMENT

Explain, by answering the following questions, how the paperwork and computer processing documenting the sale and transfer of merchandise from one store to another would be handled by store personnel.

1. What type or types of transfer forms would need to be completed? Which documents would be filled out by personnel in Store 2? In Store 1?

2. What details of the transfer would be keyed to general ledger processing? List the specific types of data to be keyed.

3. How would the transfer affect Store 1's balance sheet? Store 2's balance sheet? How would the transfer affect Store 1's profit and loss statement? Store 2's profit and loss statement?

4. How would the transfer be reported by sales-analysis processing for Store 1? For Store 2?

SITUATION 2

Suppose Store 2 discovers that the replacement costs for 165 × 13 radial tires have increased. That is, the tires to be transferred were acquired at a dealer cost of $25.00 per tire; however, the dealer cost for the same size tire is now $27.50 per tire.

REQUIREMENT

1. Explain what if any changes are to be made to data that are to be keyed to processing.

2. How would the transfer now affect Store 1's balance sheet? Store 2's balance sheet? How would the transfer affect Store 1's profit and loss statement? Store 2's profit and loss statement?

3. How would this type of transfer be reported by sales-analysis processing for Store 1? For Store 2?

INDEX